STARVING THE DREAM

STARVING THE DREAM

Student Hunger and the Hidden Costs of Campus Affluence

NATHAN F. ALLEMAN,
CARA CLIBURN ALLEN,
and SARAH E. MADSEN

JOHNS HOPKINS UNIVERSITY PRESS | *Baltimore*

© 2025 Johns Hopkins University Press
All rights reserved. Published 2025
Printed in the United States of America on acid-free paper
9 8 7 6 5 4 3 2 1

Johns Hopkins University Press
2715 North Charles Street
Baltimore, Maryland 21218
www.press.jhu.edu

Library of Congress Cataloging-in-Publication Data is available.
A catalog record for this book is available from the British Library.

ISBN 978-1-4214-5090-2 (hardcover)
ISBN 978-1-4214-5091-9 (ebook)

Special discounts are available for bulk purchases of this book. For more information, please contact Special Sales at specialsales@jh.edu.

NATHAN:
To Dot, for modeling high standards, careful conceptualization, and fierce advocacy for those on the margins

CARA:
To my best friend and partner, Joel, whose encouragement and coffee sustained the research and writing journey

SARAH:
To my parents, who always made sure that we had food on the table—even and especially when times got tough

CONTENTS

Acknowledgments ix

INTRODUCTION TO THE DREAM: Foundational Contexts and Central Issues 1

PART I. THE DREAM

1. Selling the Dream: The Official Campus Tour 25
2. Establishing the Ideal/Normal: Campus Tour as Hidden Curriculum 59
3. Starving the Dream I: The Library, the Rec Center, and the Residence Hall 76
4. Starving the Dream II: The Student Union, the Dining Hall, and the Convenience Store 99
5. Starving the Dream III: The Academic Buildings and the Administrative Buildings 117

PART II. ADMINISTRATING THE DREAM

6. Dreaming of More: The Historical Convergence of Food and Prestige 139
7. The Logics of Administrating Hunger 148
8. Administrating Hungry Students 166

PART III. NAVIGATING THE DREAM

9. Navigating Pathways through College 199
10. Navigating the Dream I: Adapting 209

11. Navigating the Dream II: Sacrificing   230
12. Navigating the Dream III: Prioritizing   241
13. Navigating the Dream IV: Maximizing   258
14. Navigating the Dream V: Surviving   279

THE DREAM REVISITED: Opportunity, Confluence, and Contradiction   306

Appendix   337
Notes   341
Index   371

ACKNOWLEDGMENTS

We are deeply grateful for the gift of time and story by our participants, who shared their triumphs and struggles—their dreams and their hunger—with us so vulnerably and humanly.

Writing this text was a communal endeavor, and we are indebted to the rich community of scholars and colleagues who served as thought partners, early readers, editors, and co-dreamers alongside us: Dan Chambliss (Hamilton College), Mitchell Stevens (Stanford University), Elizabeth Lee (Saint Joseph's University), Ted Cockle (Baylor University), Dot Finnegan (The College of William & Mary), and the doctoral students of the Higher Education Studies program at Baylor University.

We are especially thankful for the labor, support, and efforts of Pacey Ham Mitchell, who diligently edited, formatted, and organized this manuscript (and its many footnotes—or is it endnotes?) and who daily cheered us and this project on.

Baylor University provided seed funds through the BAY-SIC grant to support our data collection efforts—institutional backing that made this work possible and for which we are immensely appreciative.

We also extend gratitude to the institutions that we studied—Flagship U, Lib Arts U, and PRU—for allowing us access to their campuses and communities.

A final posthumous "thank you" to Peter Magolda, a scholar who deeply influenced this book through his research on the campus tour as well as through his generous gift of advice and friendship as this project was taking form. Your legacy of deeply human concern and systemic critique lives on in this text.

STARVING THE DREAM

INTRODUCTION TO THE DREAM

Foundational Contexts and Central Issues

As we neared the completion of this book, we spent an hour catching up with Ariel, a remarkable young woman of Middle Eastern descent whose journey through higher education looked nothing like she expected. When we first met her two years ago, Ariel was a senior at a selective, affluent liberal arts university. Despite her intent to graduate that spring, when we followed up with her, Ariel had only just received her diploma. Right before graduation, Ariel learned that she had not passed a class due to a low grade on a heavily weighted group project. By the time she found out that she was not going to graduate, her extended family had already booked flights from Western Asia to attend her ceremony. Not wanting to disappoint her family, who had made exceptional financial sacrifices for her to attend college, Ariel elected to walk across the stage and keep secret that she was not receiving a diploma. After COVID lockdowns and months of work, Ariel finally completed her degree.

At her university, Ariel experienced tremendous opportunity—serving as a residence hall student worker, interning with a local nonprofit, leading the campus Pride Alliance, working alongside administrators who fostered her social justice activism, and shaping her institution's student food aid initiatives. Amid this opportunity, Ariel's struggle to afford food regularly and pay bills intensified, even as she expended a great deal of time and energy managing significant mental health issues. As a result, she became more pointed in her critiques of the university, despite close relationships with several administrators she had come to trust.

Though Ariel was openly critical of her institution, her credentials had already begun to pay off. After officially graduating, Ariel landed a job in her field that came with the instant security of a $70,000 salary. An unlikely exemplar for the power of opportunity, Ariel's postcollege outcomes nevertheless reflect many of the reasons students and their families pursue admission to a prestigious university. Yet Ariel's story is also reflective of another subset of college experiences: students who struggle to afford food at selective, affluent institutions like hers are often caught between the opportunity cost of getting enough to eat and fully participating in the benefits that well-resourced campuses have to offer.

This is a book about exceptional college students who struggle to afford food at exceptional universities, not merely because students' financial resources are limited, but also as a *consequence* of pursuing the ideal student experience in a prestige-oriented university environment. In this text we pursue a simple question: *what are the effects and implications of student hunger in a campus environment of affluence and opportunity?* Before launching into the stories of our three campuses and the administrators, faculty, and students who navigate and manage them, this introduction provides orientation to the key issues and concepts that give this book focus.

College Student Food Insecurity

We set out to study the experiences of students struggling to access food at affluent, selective institutions. However, what became clear through our conversations and time spent on campus is that food is an unexpectedly essential component of the college campus environment and experience. Food at competitive universities is not only a material good but also a symbolic good as well—transmitting assumptions about socioeconomic class positions on campus, communicating lifestyle norms, and facilitating inclusive and exclusive social connections. Full, unimpeded access to food facilitates full, unimpeded participation in campus life. Students who struggle to afford food are confronted with the negotiation of food as a source of exclusion *and* belonging.

Students who are unable to get enough to eat have always been a part of the college environment.[1] Beginning with the first modern universities in Europe, the opportunities of higher education have drawn both the well-heeled and the least-resourced students. However, a convergence of economic, social, and political factors over the last several decades have increased the cost of college and, with it, the awareness of college student food insecurity as an urgent issue.[2] "Food security" is a technical term used by the US Department of Agriculture (USDA) to define households that have "access to enough food for active, healthy living."[3] *Food insecurity* is language employed by researchers, administrators, and policymakers to describe a lack of consistent access to food or sufficiently nutritious food.[4] More recently, scholars have explored the implications of food insecurity by explaining the psychological strain that comes with uncertain food access and the challenging decisions households make about how to spend limited financial resources. The result is often the choice between eating and paying for a household's other basic needs such as water and electricity.[5]

Several factors have converged that might increase college students' likelihood of experiencing disruptions to food access during college. Throughout the twentieth century, colleges and universities expanded access to populations who were not traditionally able to attend, including women, People of Color, and low-income students.[6] Over the past half century, the price of tuition has escalated, while increases in federal Pell Grant allotments have not kept pace.[7] At selective institutions, financial aid structures have shifted from need-based aid to merit-based aid—a system that primarily rewards households who are already advantaged.[8] A few elite institutions cover the full price of college for families whose incomes fall below a certain threshold, and yet some students still experience disrupted access to food because of the cost of living associated with college and the precarious nature of the college experience.[9]

Who Experiences Food Insecurity in College?

Households that are not "food secure" fall into one of two categories: those with *low food security*, that is, households that report reduced quality and variety in diet, or *very low food security*, which describes households that have disrupted or reduced food intake, such as skipping meals. Nationally 12.8% of US households are food insecure.[10] By contrast, the nation's first and only representative, national-level survey of food insecurity on college campuses found that 22.6% of undergraduate students reported low or very low food security. Estimates placing food insecurity rates at almost double the national average may seem extreme.[11] However, because this percentage represents an aggregation of all food insecurity levels, the degree and extent of disruption experienced by any particular student is easily lost. Food insecurity may be infrequent yet situationally extreme, ongoing but relatively manageable, or some other combination obscured in attempts to represent generalized student population rates.

Thus far, scholarly research about food insecurity on college campuses has largely focused on establishing its prevalence and describing the nature of students' experiences with an emphasis on factors that shape college completion. Studies have shown college students experience food insecurity across all institutional types: two-year, four-year, public, and private.[12] Only a handful of studies have noted the prevalence of food insecurity at selective institutions.[13] What we do know is that students are more likely to experience food insecurity if they come from marginalized backgrounds and social locations, including Students of Color, low-income students, LGBTQIA+ students, international students, student-parents, first-generation students, or former foster youth.[14] Experiencing food insecurity negatively affects college students' academic experiences and outcomes, including an inability to focus in class, a lower GPA, social exclusion, and increased anxiety and depression.[15]

Responding to Student Need

The modern profession of student services is made up of administrators who are sensitive to and ready to respond to the needs of students.[16] Not surprisingly then, practical responses to food insecurity on college campuses have outpaced research related to the topic. Responses to college student food insecurity in the form of food pantries on college campuses have existed since the early 1990s, but research and scholarship in this area did not begin to emerge until around the time of the economic recession in 2008.[17] The #RealCollege movement, largely initiated by the Hope Center on College, Community, and Justice at Temple University, formerly the Hope Lab at the University of Wisconsin, has been a key part of raising the collective awareness of the lived experiences of college students—in particular those experiencing challenges with basic resources access. Campus food pantries also proliferated, in part through the logistics and best practice support of the College and University Food Bank Alliance (CUFBA), an organization begun by a group of committed administrators working at several universities. Organizations like Swipe Out Hunger—which recently acquired CUFBA—have further helped universities capitalize on existing resources to meet immediate student food needs by sharing extra meal plan "swipes" with students who lack access to the dining halls on campus. By 2015, student affairs professionals began regularly giving presentations about campus responses to food insecurity at national conferences, contributing to both an emerging collection of best practices as well as standardizing expectations that campuses across the country respond in kind. The result of this professionalized peer pressure was that administrators responded to student food access needs, sometimes without a full picture of the causes and consequences of experiencing food insecurity.

Because of the nature of the immediate student need, research and practice in this space has largely been crisis-oriented: activists have demonstrated the urgency of the issue, researchers have focused on establishing the prevalence of the problem and its impact on students, and administrators responded quickly to ensure that students are successful. The resulting areas of emphasis in the literature are a natural consequence of the nascent state of the issue. However, a consequence of this triage mentality is that the field is still working toward clarity about the ways that food insecurity shapes the student experience across and within various contexts.[18] Given the urgency of the problem, the field's focus on demonstrating the presence of this crisis nationally and then on developing pragmatic solutions is understandable. However, understanding how the particular challenges of the selective, affluent university context alters the experiences and tasks of administrators and students requires the closer investigation that this book pursues.

What Difference Does Context Make?

In conversations about food insecurity, campus context, though noted by researchers as immensely important, is often functionally ignored.[19] In particular, features of institutional selectivity and relative student body family affluence are often underestimated as factors that shape the broader student experience, of which food access is an integral part. Yet ample evidence demonstrates that the college experience for low-income students differs across campuses based on admissions selectivity.[20] The student bodies and campus environments of selective, affluent universities are often stratified socially and economically in ways that shape both perceptions of fit and belonging, as well as the types of organizational and preprofessional involvement students pursue.[21] Selective, affluent university contexts can produce divisions in the student body based on shared experiences not available to everyone, such as study abroad or spring break trips, and status-signaling through material goods such as clothes and personal technology that reinforce class-based identities.[22] These charged, *classed* environments can create exclusion for low-income students in ways not present at open-admission institutions. And yet, although low-income students are underrepresented at these institutions, for those who do attend, these universities serve as a gateway to opportunity.[23] Selective, affluent environments, in part motivated by public success metrics such as freshman-to-sophomore-year retention, create an administrative scaffolding of student support aimed toward student success. This extensive student support infrastructure includes emergency mental and physical health resources, specialized tutoring, and subgroup-specific student organizations aimed at increasing positive outcomes for historically underrepresented students.[24] Consequently, these environments result in opportunity and challenge for students from marginalized backgrounds.[25] Yet the intersection between these exclusive environments, their students, and the costs and outcomes of limited food access is largely uncharted territory.

Study Sites: Prestige-Oriented Universities

Across American higher education, only a few colleges and universities can truly be described as "elite": a subset of Ivy League and other institutions, that, while commanding disproportionate attention in the popular press, actually educate a small fraction of high-achieving college applicants. Instead, this book focuses on what we call *prestige-oriented universities*. The prestige-oriented university exists in a hotly contested space where institutional notoriety is based on their comparative successes and failures at image-making relative to their similarly ranked competitors. These are universities positioned outside of the top 25 but inside the top 100 of *US News & World Report* rankings. The rankings "neighborhood" occupied by our case universities is one of intense competitiveness and peer awareness, one where institutions pursue similar ends even as they strive to differentiate themselves from similar peers.[26]

The data for this book was collected at three prestige-oriented universities chosen for their similarity of admissions selectivity, cultural campus affluence, market competitiveness, and their differences in size, administrative control, and mission. Institutional type also significantly shapes the student experience based on the variety and scale of resources, facilities, academic options, and the culture of campus life. For this reason, we included a large public flagship university (Flagship), a small private liberal arts university (Lib Arts), and a midsized private research university (PRU)—the typical university types where leaders seek to differentiate their universities from their peers through prestige metrics.[27] None of the authors had any prior affiliation with the three case institutions. As part of our access agreement, institution and individual names and locations were given pseudonyms and are generalized to allow us to preserve as much specific campus detail as possible.

Based on our prior research that revealed the importance of socioeconomic context in shaping how students experience and how institutions respond to food insecurity, we chose institutions that were normatively *affluent*.[28] In the case of this study, the universities we chose had a compelling combination of factors that shaped the campus in ways that benefit the economically secure student, including pricing tuition policies such as merit-based aid prioritized over need-based aid, admissions and academic policies that privilege standardized test scores, student body median income that exceeded market segment peers, clear sensitivity and responsiveness to competitive market forces, and on-campus amenities and services that reflected upper-middle-class lifestyles.[29] Also included in our selection decisions were strong postgraduation outcomes of students attending the institution, such as their social mobility and employment. Thus, we made a holistic determination for each institution that pointed toward the fact that experiencing food insecurity was normatively incongruent with this environment, despite a range of services and resources intended to support students on the margins.

In addition to being normatively affluent, universities chosen for this study were selective in their admissions decisions. Although selectivity has been questioned as a marker of institutional quality, it is a metric that continues to be an important factor related to institutional prestige and competition.[30] Institutions in this study were picked because they fit the categories of selective or highly selective admissions. In addition to federal Integrated Postsecondary Education Data System (IPEDS) data to determine selectivity, we also utilized Barron's selectivity index. Barron's selectivity index is a college ranking system that sorts colleges into tiers of selectivity based on student aggregate SAT scores, high school GPA, class rank, and institutional acceptance rate.[31] Barron's selectivity scores range from 1 (most competitive) to 6 (noncompetitive), described below.[32]

Beyond selectivity and affluence, all three universities had contextual similarities. In mission, all three universities emphasized the importance of creating "leaders" who were equipped for a globally competitive world. At the time of data collection, administrators at all three universities had an awareness of college student food insecurity on their campuses, although the type and extent of institutional response varied. In addition, all three institutions were situated in urban settings, included expansive student organization systems, claimed academic excellence via student and alumni achievements, and heavily promoted university athletics. The majority of students attending all three campuses were between ages 18 and 24.[33]

Lib Arts University

Perched on a ridge above a metropolitan area, Liberal Arts U, in presence and program, projects a desirable convergence of long-standing academic tradition with forward-looking professional preparation. Lib Arts is considered "selective" by IPEDS data metrics and receives a 3 on Barron's selectivity scores, making it a "very competitive" institution.[34] As the smallest of our case institutions, Lib Arts enrolls around 4,000 undergraduate students and around 500 graduate students.

What makes Lib Arts stand out as culturally affluent is the unique makeup of the campus body. The institution is among the lowest compared to in-state peers in accepting students from the bottom 20% based on family income. Lib Arts is one of the highest among private, selective colleges in shares of students from the top 0.1% by family income, ranking in the top 5% of selective institutions nationally, reflecting a reputation the campus has developed for attracting students from extraordinarily wealthy families. Over half of the student body has a median income in the top 10% of earners. The school enrolls about 6% of its students from the top 1%, which includes wages over $630,000 a year.[35] As such, a disproportionate percentage of Lib Arts students come from some of the wealthiest families in the

United States. The disparity between students from high-income and low-income backgrounds at Lib Arts is significant.

In addition, the liberal arts mission and positive student outcomes upon graduation make the institution attractive to wealthy families, as it perpetuates middle- to upper-class values and cultural tastes.[36] In terms of outcomes, over 20% of students who attend the institution move up two income quartiles, experiencing social and economic upward mobility. The institution also scores near the top among selective, private colleges and universities for students who end up in the top 1% of wage earners upon graduation.

The complex intersection of specific institutional features contributes to the value of this university in this study. The institution is religiously affiliated and is recognized by the federal government as a Hispanic Serving Institution, meaning that over 25% of the population identifies as Hispanic. Half of the students are residential, choosing to live on campus. Recently, students have advocated for support for those experiencing food insecurity on campus, and the institution has begun exploring and implementing response options. For several years, the campus has had a student-run food pantry stocked with donations that students fundraise. Lib Arts has also developed a partnership with a local church where students can access emergency food. Additionally, they invested in a social services website where students can use their address to find community and university resources. At the time of data collection, the institution did not have data on what percentage of students on campus experienced food insecurity.

Private Research University

Private Research University (PRU) is located at the edge of a major metropolitan city in a highly affluent urban neighborhood. Though campus is disconnected from the city in terms of the campus "bubble," the university pursues internship and alumni connections across the broader metropolitan area. Adjacent to campus are stores and restaurants that reflect an upper-middle-class student lifestyle, including a boutique running store, coffee shops, and local upscale restaurants. PRU is a "highly selective" institution according to IPEDS, and has a Barron's selectivity score of 2, ranking it as "highly competitive."[37] The university enrolls over 6,000 undergraduates and around 5,000 graduate students. The median family income is over $190,000, making it the most affluent of the three campuses we studied, and near the top amongst peers nationwide. Less than 5% of students come from the bottom 20% of household earners.

Postgraduation, alumni tend to fare very well. Because of the highly affluent nature of the student body, fewer students cross income quartiles as at Lib Arts U. But by their mid-30s a quarter of PRU students rank in the top 5% of median income earners. On average, students from low-income and high-income households fare similarly in terms of income by their mid-30s.[38]

The campus has invested heavily in its residential college-model experience, requiring first- and second-year students to live on campus. Many students continue to live on campus after their second year, with over 50% participating in sororities and fraternities. The institution has developed a makeshift food pantry on campus, created and operated by one employee at the institution but not supported financially by the university. At the time of data collection, the institution did not have data on how many students on campus struggled to afford food.

Flagship University

Embedded in the heart of its metropolitan location, Flagship's campus boundaries bleed over into the surrounding blocks of restaurants, office buildings, and apartment complexes. Flagship University is a large, "highly selective" institution according to IPEDS data. Flagship U's Barron's selectivity score is a 2, making it "highly competitive."[39] The institution enrolls over 40,000 undergraduate students. The student body at Flagship is highly affluent, ranking in the top third among its peers in median income and near the top in terms of share of students from the top 1% of median income.

Adjacent to traditional campus buildings, "North Campus"—a commercially developed area with luxury student housing situated above high-fashion stores, local coffee shops, and an ever-changing food scene—reflects the most desirable living options for the urban-embedded university. Students noted selecting Flagship because of its integration with the city and the opportunities for internships and future employment. Students have the option to live either on or off campus, utilizing the free city bus pass to commute to classes. As a result, many low-income students live on the other side of the city in less expensive housing. The student population includes a large Greek life presence, though its visibility exceeds its numeric representation. But with over 1,000 student organizations, matriculates have many other engagement options to pursue.

As a result of a health survey conducted a few years ago, Flagship administrators believe that just under one in four students on campus struggle to afford food. In response, they created a full staff team focused on basic resource needs that includes one full-time staff member, one graduate assistant, and five paid student workers to operate a food pantry and clothes closet. The institution recently completed remodeling its space for a combined food pantry and clothing closet that is also staffed with a case manager to provide students with access to other campus resources and supports.

Data Collection

Data for this book was collected over two years, concluding in April 2020. Interviews included student-led walking tours of campus and traditional "seated" conversations with both students and administrators as the primary forms of data collection. These interviews were supplemented by observations, focus groups, document analysis, and website analysis. We interviewed 35 students (Lib Arts: 15, PRU: 8, Flagship: 12) who self-identified as food insecure and were confirmed by the USDA six-item food security measure to have very low food security (see the appendix for student demographic details). Nearly all students participated in a series of three interviews: an initial background and college experience interview lasting 60–120 minutes, an alternative campus tour lasting about 60 minutes, and a concluding analytic interview lasting 90–120 minutes. In all, we conducted over 100 student interviews totaling over 175 hours. Students were identified through administrator recommendations and emails directed toward student subpopulations most likely to experience food insecurity, direct social media campaigns, and referrals from participants. Student participants were compensated for their time with a gift card of their choice before each interview.

We also interviewed 59 other individuals, including administrators (45 total; Lib Arts: 12, PRU: 16; Flagship: 17), faculty (9 total; Lib Arts: 5; PRU: 2; Flagship: 2), and cultural informants (5 total; Lib Arts: 1; PRU: 1; Flagship: 3). In some cases, we interviewed key individuals more than once. These 74 interviews each lasted between 45 and 120 minutes, totaling approximately 75 hours in aggregate. Individuals were chosen for their roles related to campus responses to food insecurity, their positions of importance within student life or student support services, or their centrality to and knowledge of the on-campus admissions experience. Additionally, we participated in multiple official campus tour experiences per university, audio recording the events and taking field notes for comparative analysis. At Flagship, we conducted a focus group with the student advisors who work with the campus food pantry, as well as with several former students who played key roles in initiating the campus food pantry.

Three Core Elements of the Prestige-Oriented University

Through our data collection across the three campuses, we initially set out to understand how students experience and how faculty and administrators make sense of food insecurity in selective, affluent university contexts. What we uncovered in our time spent exploring the role of food, or the lack thereof, at prestige-oriented universities is that

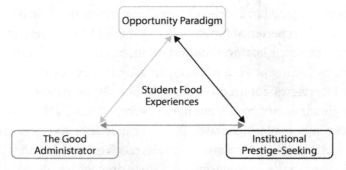

Conceptual Model of the Prestige-Oriented University

food is a symbol through which the mechanisms of these university types and the students and administrators who participate in them can be further understood.

To understand food and food insecurity in the context of the prestige-oriented university, we must grasp the unique aspects of this campus environment. Environmental features play a unique role in student experience, and inversely, studying food and food insecurity in these spaces highlights important features of the institutional context. What emerged from this study are three elements that are core to the prestige-oriented university through which food experiences and food access in these spaces can be better understood: *Institutional Prestige-Seeking, the Good Administrator,* and *the Opportunity Paradigm* (see figure above).

Institutional Prestige-Seeking

The competitive environment of institutional prestige-seeking universities, or prestige-oriented universities, can be better understood through the criteria used to distinguish it. Scholars demarcate prestige-seeking schools from "reputation-based" and "tuition-dependent" institutions.[40] *Institutional Prestige-Seeking* is a university-wide orientation and sensitivity to market forces, rankings, and metrics of competitive superiority that provides an implicit rationale and motivation for institutional structures, policies, behaviors, approaches, programs, and priorities, including the Opportunity Paradigm and the Good Administrator.

For highly competitive colleges, status is created primarily through three specific "prestige generators": *student quality,* in terms of attracting highly qualified applicants; *research,* in terms of nationally recognized doctoral programs, world-class research facilities, and top-quality research faculty; and *athletics,* in terms of the success of sports teams, particularly in high-visibility sports such as football and basketball.[41] All three of these categories are oriented toward an external market or "consumer." As such, all three require extensive investments in terms of time, specialized administrative staff, and dedicated facilities, making them extremely expensive financially. For this reason, every prestige-seeking institution selectively invests in each of these to various levels and breadths. The result is that each competitive institution has a different "prestige profile" that creates for it advantages over competitors as well as areas where others are likely to excel over them.

Although prestige-seeking is a strategic choice in which universities attempt to attract high-quality students and position themselves competitively in the market, institutions can become trapped by their prestige-seeking pursuits.[42] The result is that these universities can make decisions based on their desire to maintain status among peers and their reputation in the eyes of the general public by investing more money into athletics and other highly visible activities.

Prestige-seeking institutions also create an admissions model that carefully cultivates and selects a student body while also emphasizing institutional mission. To attract high-ability students away from other prestige-oriented institutions, colleges and universities create research opportunities, invest in state-of-the-art recreation facilities, tend a buffet of student organizations and internship opportunities, and pass down traditions that initiate students into a deep sense of campus belonging and enthusiasm.

In addition to high-abilities students, these amenities and institutional reputations also attract students from high-income households. Prestige-seeking contributes to an environment of public visibility that attracts motivated students who are looking to leverage their particular academic abilities toward future professional opportunity. The archetypal "normal" student in these classed environments can afford high student fees, the extra expenses associated with expansive student organizations, and the costs of expensive extracurricular programs, such as studying abroad.[43] Consequently, the campus expectation of affluence represents a source of alignment between students' family backgrounds and the institution's history, identity, and culture.[44] Though these campuses primarily enroll students from affluent backgrounds with upper-middle-class interests, students from nonaffluent backgrounds also enroll and attend these selective, culturally affluent institutions.[45]

In recent years, prestige-oriented institutions have been more responsive to calls for increased college access for traditionally marginalized students. Among the factors contributing to this sensitivity to diversity was a change in 2019 to how *US News & World Report* ranked colleges and universities, when a marker for "social mobility" was added to its ranking system. This social mobility measure includes graduation rates for students who receive a Pell Grant—a federal college aid grant based on family income—with scores adjusted to reward schools that enroll a larger share of Pell Grant–eligible students. In addition to *US News & World Report*'s revisions to their calculations, other college ranking systems—e.g., CollegeNet, the *Wall Street Journal*, the Institute for College Access and Success, Niche, and College Scorecard—include factors such as institutional selectivity, social mobility, and the amount of debt students take on to attend a particular college. Consequently, colleges and universities committed to the prestige game are incentivized by rankings and metrics to enroll students from low-income households, ensure that they are successful, and support them financially. What results from this convergence of marginalized student backgrounds and prestige-seeking contexts is a culture of upper-middle-class values and practices that is invisible to students who align with it but a source of constant tension and navigation for those who do not.[46] Administrators across our campuses knew that prestige-seeking was at least an implicit if not an explicit driver of their work, and at times they felt caught in the tension between the demands of peer and market sensitivity and the immediacy of responding to students effectively. Students were frequently drawn to prestige-seeking institutions with the belief that university name recognition would be beneficial for their future goals.

Part I of this book, entitled "The Dream," embeds the reader in our campuses by narrating the official campus admissions tours and the student participant–led "alternative" campus tours. These tours are used to expose the layered institutional self-projection and expectation-setting of prestige-seeking as it takes form in the physical, social, and organizational environment. The official campus tour is contrasted with the alternative campus tour where students who struggled to afford food were the guides narrating their experiences with food and food insecurity, describing their approaches to navigating a campus environment of choice and opportunity.

The Good Administrator

The second element of the prestige-oriented university framework is the concept of the *Good Administrator*. Colleges and universities have built an extensive administrative scaffolding, or structures of interconnected roles, to support varied organizational aims, some articulated, and some not. One such goal is promoting the university's visibility and notoriety by creating student engagement opportunities and support systems that contribute to student persistence and graduation rates, in addition to a rich student experience generally. At prestige-oriented universities, student life outside of the classroom competes for priority with what happens inside the classroom. The "co-curriculum" is where bonds are formed in social and preprofessional interactions, often in the form of student-directed organizations, that can serve the student beyond the university in the future. It is the role of the Good Administrator to create, structure, and support these opportunities, and then respond to student needs, ultimately feeding the prestige markers of the institution.

As campuses have become more demographically diverse, so too have the administrative substrata expanded and specialized. This atomization of roles is reflective of an implicit professional orientation that each particular student population and educational issue is sufficiently unique as to require its own expertise and experts. Whereas in a prior generation a single administrator might be responsible for multiple elements of student life, now a complex organizational chart of directors and assistant directors specialize in areas such as first-generation students, campus traditions, and study abroad opportunities. Even these categories have become their own containers for more particular administrative foci, such as offices that specialize in first-generation Students of Color, or academic advising for athletes.

The obvious "cost" of such expansion is literally that: between 1993 and 2007, the ratio of administrators per 100 students grew by 39% and the funds spent on administrators increased 61% (adjusted for inflation).[47] For a 30-year period starting in 1987, higher-education institutions added over half a million campus administrators.[48] By 2014, for every $1 spent on instruction, $1.82 was spent on noninstructional matters.[49] An entire professional field has emerged over the past century; an invisible administrative behemoth that includes residence life, student activities, identity-specific centers, first-year orientation, and student academic career support. Additional student-serving or student-engaging offices have also become professionalized that are only tangentially part of the student affairs family tree. These include university admissions (including campus visits), financial aid, student success centers, study abroad, mental and physical health services, and student emergency services. More invisible still are the administrators whose offices are seldom seen by students, such as donor relations officers, financial administrators, professionals responsible for institutional research and reporting, Title IX, general counsel, and university grant administrators. Among the benefits of this expansion have been an increased awareness of and resources for students historically marginalized by prestige-oriented universities.

Beyond what might seem like essential academic and support services, this massive administrative infrastructure has also become necessary to staff resort-like recreation centers with outdoor adventure specialists, support quasi-professional athletics with dedicated academic advisors, and plan elaborate annual university homecoming festivities through a multitude of student activities roles, among many other expensive functions of dubious educational value. Together, these offices create a web of resources and engagement forms with the built-in expectancy that students in prestige-oriented universities are highly involved and seek administrative support when needs arise.

Throughout the book, we explore the ways that Good Administrators at our study sites operated with the professional values of *care* and *efficiency*, tending to both student needs and institutional status-striving. Administrators are thus "Good," from the perspective of the prestige-oriented university, when they are attuned to the particular needs of students, like hunger, while also operating effectively within their organizational and peer-oriented environment.

Part II of the book, "Administrating the Dream," details the Good Administrator and their attempts to manage student hunger and administer support to students who regularly struggle with basic needs. Following a brief telling of the history of administrating food in higher education and its gradual connection to university prestige, we investigate the implicit dual professional "logics" of *care* and *efficiency*, and the ways that they coalesce in and with an environment of competitive status. We show how, despite many administrators' own empathy and personal experiences of marginalization, the very elements that make these universities players in the arena of prestige-oriented higher education sometimes constrain administrators' imagination for responses. Consequently, their food aid strategies adopt practices developed in very different college settings, such as regional state universities and community colleges, and those that fit preferred organizational modes shaped by expectations of student affluence.

Opportunity Paradigm

The third core element of the prestige-oriented university is the *Opportunity Paradigm*, or the implicit campus expectation of extensive and intensive student involvement, and the infrastructure to support it. The Opportunity Paradigm is the organizational mechanism for and anticipation of student engagement that converts cultivated precollege student tendencies and preferred types of knowledge into postcollege resources.[50] The Opportunity Paradigm is facilitated by the organizational structures, resources, and supports created and tended by the Good Administrator. This system is, in part, a consequence of institutional prestige efforts, benefiting students and the Good Administrator. The Opportunity Paradigm results in a vast array of engagement forms that draw upon the skills and relational capital of administrators, faculty, and alumni.[51] At the prestige-oriented university student involvement is informed by precollege ways of being that are established and perpetuated by upper-middle-class families that students utilize to navigate and engage in campus in ways that will benefit them beyond their college careers. Middle- to upper-class families expect engagement opportunities for students that will advance them socially and professionally, justifying the outlay of hundreds of thousands of dollars in tuition, living expenses, and the nearly innumerable financial costs of maximizing one's collegiate experience.[52]

Prestige-oriented colleges and universities create a network of opportunities at the convergence of status and future interests for students, including internships, study abroad trips, student organizations, avenues for activism, robust dining halls with a variety of cuisine offerings, fitness centers with climbing walls and lazy rivers, lavish residential environments where students can be leaders, and expansive athletic facilities boasting nationally competitive sports teams. These amenities reflect and perpetuate an expectation of what the college experience is and should look like for the students.[53]

These normatively affluent campus environments create a culture that sustains a particular set of expectations of how college should function that is representative of the middle to upper class, often in ways invisible to them.[54] For upper-middle-class students who have been socialized to engage outside of school to create social networks that beget opportunities, the Opportunity Paradigm of the prestige-oriented environment is familiar and a resource to be maximized.[55] The result of this engagement for universities is a committed and connected alumni, which consequently begets more prestige for the university through associated notoriety and giving to campus projects and priorities.

The challenge of the prestige-oriented university is that the student experience is not monolithic, and the Opportunity Paradigm is not equally accessed or experienced. How students engage the opportunities offered to them on college campuses can create better or worse paths of social connections that pay off in dividends in the future.[56] Students from upper-middle-class backgrounds enter the prestige-oriented context often with more experience and socialization of how to navigate the environment and how to invest in the university in ways that can benefit them beyond graduation.[57]

Simultaneously, because administrators are attuned to the needs of students as well as to prestige outcomes, colleges and universities have invested significantly to support the increasingly diverse student body through initiatives such as first-generation programs, identity centers for women, LGBTQIA+, and Students of Color, summer bridge programs, and emergency services to support students at times of crisis. For students experiencing food insecurity, the convergence of prestige, class, and administrators creates an environment of expectation that may be at odds with economic marginalization and struggles to deliver on tacit promises to support them. As such, students experiencing food insecurity are confronted with a selective college environment that simultaneously promotes and undermines their success.

Part III of the book, "Navigating the Dream," centers student navigation strategies at the intersection of the Opportunity Paradigm and institutional prestige-seeking. Food insecure students at prestige-oriented universities show awareness of what constitutes the ideal/normal experience; expectations that they have, to various degrees, internalized and around which they have tried to orient their own experiences. But the contradictions of daily life, of which food is an important element, are obvious, frustrating, and often painful.[58] This part details how these inconsistencies require adaptive strategies, structured around a typology of five navigational strategies, each with its own internal logic, opportunities, and liabilities.

Thus, this book explores how prestige-seeking, the Good Administrator, and the Opportunity Paradigm are in dynamic relationship with one another in the prestige-oriented university environment. For a subset of the student population who are on the economic margins, the convergent pressure of the three elements appears in an unexpected place: students' experiences with food.

PART I

THE DREAM

CHAPTER 1

Selling the Dream
The Official Campus Tour

College admissions websites and social media are replete with bucolic scenes of smiling, backpack-toting students from diverse backgrounds strolling to class along tree-lined walkways, or listening intently to knowledgeable-looking professors surrounded by high-tech lab equipment, or exploring the winding, picturesque streets of a faraway city on a study abroad trip. Particularly for high-ability students applying to selective universities, these idealistic visions of the campus experience disguise the precollege stress and pressure of the admission process, culminating in a flurry of evaluating, visiting, applying, and waiting ... and waiting.[1]

What results for those fortunate enough to leverage the right combination of abilities and resources is entry into a highly desirable prestige-oriented university, a joining wholly unique in American culture. Particularly for financially secure families, this intensive arranged marriage is the result of a lifetime of grooming. Sociologist Mitchell Stevens argues that the implicit terms of this union have become so deeply engrained in the American upper-middle class that the very definition of good parenting dovetails with the criteria for admissions into selective colleges.[2] Parents self-consciously monitor the cultivation of their child's most modest talents, signing them up for private lessons, academic tutoring, selective travel sports teams, STEM summer camps, and international service opportunities, all of which crescendo in competitiveness, time, and expense through the end of high school. For many well-off families, the matchmaking process is smoothed by pricey college consultants who package a student's talents together and align them with the most ideal and the most realistic options.[3]

The importance of college-going, however, extends far beyond the experience of college. Long after the courses, parties, study abroad trips, and late-night study sessions are over, *alma mater* becomes a fixed point on a person's biography and family history. "Grandpa was a Yale man" or "Your aunt came through Berkeley" are signals of familial achievement as well as expectancy. To attend, and graduate from, a selective university marks a person for life.[4] Jobs can be changed, churches switched, spouses divorced, club memberships rescinded, but alumni status is a permanent affiliation, and one with deep social and economic significance for those fortunate enough to attend institutions with broad marketplace recognition.[5] For young people whose family history is largely missing the symbolic and functional resources that accompany prestige-oriented university access, the importance—and pressure—to gain this advantageous affiliation is hard to overstate; a potential fast-pass to financial security and social mobility. Thus we set out to understand our three case universities through what might be thought of as the first formal date of the matchmaking process, and one intently and intensively designed to impress: the official campus admissions tour.[6] Witnessing the remarkably convergent "pitches," integrated into a single tour narrative, highlights the shared emphasis on opportunity and the *nearly* invisible role of food within it.

Before the Tour

We arrive at Flagship University early to take in the new admissions welcome center before our scheduled tour. The interior is bathed in the university's distinctive colors. This carefully curated holding tank offers to waiting families (and it is nearly always families) a kind of living promotional pamphlet for the resources and accomplishments of Flagship's students, alums, and faculty. One wall lists key statistics, emblazoned on backlit glass: number of Nobel and Pulitzer Prizes won by faculty (more than we expected), student organizations (over 1,300), study abroad programs (over 400), libraries (17), museums (4), and NCAA national championships (50+), among many others. A column in the center of the room, sheathed in shelving, holds dozens of books authored by Flagship faculty. On the far end, beyond the modern minimalist seating festooned with Flagship logos, is a timeline of university events and achievements, including graduation dates of famous politicians, business leaders, and actors, photos from presidential debates held on campus, and images of the construction of notable buildings. Glancing up, we notice the university motto, "From Here, the World Changes," cast in light onto the ceiling. Despite a sales pitch so earnest and unabashed, it is hard not to be impressed at Flagship's legacy of achievement, and at least a little swayed at the implication, if not outright claim, that those admitted here will have a similar effect on the campus and on the world.

The centerpiece of the campus visit center is small auditorium seating perhaps 75–100 people. Ringed in lights in Flagship's signature school color, three large screens flash images of campus and city locations, hinting at the lifestyle that awaits. The sole purpose of this space is to deliver the preamble to the tour, a kind of university pep rally before the main event. Here, in a format very similar across our three institutions, the admissions experience shifts from informal and self-guided to formal and highly prescribed.

A similar "sell" awaits us at Private Research University (PRU), though in a presentation style conveying a very different sort of institutional identity. Descending a grand staircase in the visitor's center, we join a small crowd—about 50 people, all of whom appear to be White—entering a space that could double as an executive board room were it not for the rows of screen-facing chairs. Here, heavy dark wooden double doors open to a room awash in light, the high ceiling ringed by crown molding. Devin, assistant director for campus tours, understands the challenge of his task: to both pitch his university and engage his audience, all in the next 20 minutes.[7] Like an in-person infomercial, Devin talks briskly yet clearly, works in humor and detail, summarizes points frequently, and conveys that he is on your side as an honest broker, despite his clear affiliation:

> So, I'm excited to tell you a lot about PRU today. I will say that, truthfully, I come from the oldest of four siblings and my last brother just graduated high school last year. I legitimately visited 65 college campuses with all my three brothers and myself. So, when I present here today, I have been in your shoes. I'll spare you kind of the cliché overused lingo in terms of the admissions office and really get at the core of what makes PRU unique and different.

Devin and his staff embrace what seems to be a twofold task: relate in a way that conveys human warmth and dignity during a stressful process, and clearly deliver details and distinguishing features of PRU that impress as well as inform.

At Liberal Arts University (hereafter, "Lib Arts") we also join a small collection of prospective students and parents shepherded together for a pretour pitch, though this time in more of a modest setting compared to Flagship and PRU. Lib Arts admissions personnel seem to recognize that attempting to compete with the scale of resources and achievements at places like Flagship or PRU does not play to their advantage. Instead, the Lib Arts tour talk begins in a tiered, semicircle classroom. The simplicity and human scale of this academic setting (though still strategically lined by admissions-related banners) conveys a sense of relatability and scholarly seriousness.

Despite the key differences of space and style, pretour talks at all three schools highlight three general points. First, an emphasis on *place*, both the possibilities provided by the metropolitan context each campus enjoys and the physical beauty and resources of the grounds. "Life's too short to have an ugly campus," says Devin, quoting PRU's president. Even daring to *breathe* the question "What do attractive grounds have to do with educational quality?" seems like heresy in an environment so manicured and pristine. Second, the university is a place of *opportunity*. Opportunity is the entry point for describing, in a remarkable feat of summarization, the basic structure of academic programs (arranged in five "colleges"), bent toward the more essential theme, that PRU is a place of academic customization. Devin intones:

> Probably the most important question I like to ask when visiting any college campus is "What does academic flexibility look like at your college campus?" And what does academic flexibility mean? Academic flexibility for us means that students can very easily double major, not only within the same academic college, but they can do two different majors across any undergraduate college. Students here can do an engineering degree, while also pursuing something in the fine arts. They can be a psychology major, while also going into business. So, a key takeaway for us is that many of our students will double major.

Flexibility is both a feature of these universities and of the type of young people they attract. Devin describes ideal candidates as "interested in many different areas" and "multifaceted," which "tends to be a PRU trait." PRU in this telling is like an academic 3-D printer, able to create from source material whatever shape of program matches the ambitions of the highly capable student: "Those type of people find themselves here because they have that flexibility," Devin asserts.

In addition to academics, *opportunity* describes the student experience: more internship opportunities than students who want them, eleven residential "commons" with associated crests and rituals in the style of Harry Potter's "houses"; intensive, if not somewhat ludicrous traditions relating to the live campus mascot (which is tended by a highly selective student organization in a top-secret location); faculty-in-residence programs merging academics, mentoring, and socialization; 150 study abroad programs; and many others. The video montage that follows is of successful alums reinforcing Devin's assertions, summated by an African American alumna who began her own business after college: "The biggest benefit of PRU is opportunity!" she exclaims.

If *opportunity* is the call, the third theme is the response: *expectation*. In the closing section of the pretour talk, Devin presents a series of infographics to simplify a number of anxiety-producing aspects of the admissions process, including multiple deadlines, financial aid options, and requirements for admission. Many of these facts and dates are available online, but Devin offers some inside information about the sort of student PRU is seeking: "I work with students who are really strong in the classroom, they had standardized testing, but then the rec letters, essays, or extracurriculars do not demonstrate that they're a great community member. At that point I will not admit that student because they're uninvolved, uninterested, or not bringing anything to campus outside of the classroom."

Within this admission ultimatum, Devin uses the term "community member" to frame the idea that PRU wants students who, of course, are academically excellent, but more than that, enter the university expecting to make use of the elaborate opportunity structure constructed for them. This, beyond opportunity, is an implied *responsibility*. He concludes: "Students who find themselves at PRU are bringing a little bit of everything here as far as the application process." A final video, this time featuring students and their parents, illustrates the desired convergence of place, opportunity, and expectation echoed at Flagship and Lib Arts as well: "PRU has helped by giving me a variety of options and plenty of resources," a student gushes. A parent confesses that "it's so nice to have my son in good hands." Another student concludes with the clincher: "The school has made an everlasting mark on my life, and I'll always call PRU my home."

The Tour

One might rightly wonder why a tour is necessary at all after such heavy preaching. Expending the time, money, and bother to travel to a campus in the age of accessible and immersive technology may also seem like something of an antiquated practice, but one that continues to be the centerpiece of the admission process, at least for middle- and upper-income families. We put this question to Jeff Kallay, co-founder of Render Experiences, a business that specializes in campus tour consulting. Render has worked with more than 300 colleges and universities over the past 14 years and was recently acquired by the admissions management consulting firm RNL, previously known as Noel-Levitz (since arranged marriages are not limited to students and universities). In our conversation, Jeff first compared the tour to purchasing a house, then reflected, "If you're choosing to go place-based education, not to get your degree online ... it is an intimate product choice. You sleep there, you live there, you eat there, you get sick there, you get naked there, you might get naked with other people there, and people want to see it for themselves, they want to see it for real."

Jason, Flagship's director of admissions, further emphasized how the tour provides space for moments of connection that communicate fit, beyond what the official tour features:

> I think that when you look at pictures that are online of things you'll see the landmarks, you'll see University Hall, the stadium, and then every institution usually has their obligatory student life selling point, whether it be the pool or some really cool feature on campus. But it's really about all of that, how it all comes together, and do you feel as if that's really a welcoming place for you? Do you feel like you're at a place that really is an exceptional academic and student life community? I think you can only make that decision when you walk onto that campus.... So, as a student, being able to walk on each one of those, you may have seen pictures of it, but when you walk on them and see what that space looks like, you may have a completely different reaction that may help you understand "this is where I actually want to go to school."

Perhaps, then, parents and students invest in walking the grounds for the same reason that many selective institutions still do in-person admissions interviews. In a competitive environment the family, like the college, is looking for additional sources of information that will distinguish one similar candidate from another; for the opportunity to look the person, or campus, in the eye to discern whether they are prepared to honor this potential union, and secondarily, for that spark of connection.

Jeff casts some of this concern as generational. The Gen X parent who has raised their child in the era following Columbine and 9/11 is first of all concerned with safety, which requires a change of direction in terms of tour tactics:

> For 14 years we told clients on campus tours "lead with academics, lead with academics," when what they really want to know is, "Where is parking? How does housing work? How does food work? Where's wellness? Where's the counseling center?" It's the stuff that's lower on [Maslow's hierarchy of needs]. And saying to schools, "You need to reveal that first, earn the family's trust that we have the basics covered, then move them up the hierarchy and into academics more."

The campus tour, then, serves an important function for all parties involved, a dance of what sociologists call "signaling," or symbols, physical, organizational, and relational, that this is a place that can meet concerns for well-being, can match aspirations with resources, and has that final elusive element of "fit" that turns a potential applicant into a future alum.[8]

We cluster and squint toward our guide in the low morning sun of a brisk fall day, just outside the newly renovated welcome center at Flagship University. It is quickly evident why the admissions folks have set us up with this tour of the three departing at our time slot (we requested admissions at each institution schedule us with whoever they felt best represented the university). Our tour guide, Kimmy, is a White female senior double majoring in neuroscience and family sciences with a minor in sociology and a certificate in prehealth professions, which seems like a daunting list of credentials to achieve in four years. Tall, energetic, with layers of curly brown hair, Kimmy simultaneously exudes ability and humility, shifting from accomplishments to self-deprecating stories of personal struggle throughout the tour. Like Devin at PRU, Kimmy effectively uses relatability as a tool for reassurance, a tacit encouragement that if a girl from a small high school who changed concentrations eight times can make it here, so can you.

Our tour is made up of just three students and accompanying adults. This group is far smaller than we might have expected if not tipped off earlier by an admissions administrator who stressed that small groups provide an opportunity to connect with each family and personalize the experience on the fly. The emphasis on being known is clear and in contrast to the scale of the university. Yet the effect of this philosophy is evident on the tour.

If Flagship is at all representative of tours elsewhere, the era of the polo-wearing, loudspeaker-style guide walking backward and spouting campus facts is over. Throughout the 90-minute tour, Kimmy uses the walking time (facing forward) between venues to circulate between the prospective students in one-on-one casual conversations, plying interests, experiences, and backgrounds for clues about campus perceptions or locations that might be of interest. Impressively, she coaxes a reserved student interested in computer science into divulging that he has already invented four smartphone apps, the first at age 12. Kimmy gushes, and the success of that exchange is evident in the student's sheepish grin and increasingly open posture. We note as well that the engineering and computer science building, not part of prior tours we attended, suddenly was a featured stop. Kimmy is on her game: "This tour is just to show you a little bit of the student's perspective. The information session was a lot of the application details and deadlines—I don't really remember those anymore, so this is a lot about the student experience. I remember being in your shoes and going on all of the college tours. For me it was a huge part of whether or not I decided to go to a school." In a fascinating wrinkle, Kimmy's commentary throughout the tour sells the importance of it as the *real* source of meaningful decision-making information, and of her, as a student, representing a trustworthy and relatable confidant.

The series of tour stops as we circulate campus at Flagship are remarkably similar to those we experience on tours at PRU and Lib Arts: the library, the rec center, the student center, a STEM academic area, a historic building of significance, a residence hall, and the food establishments/dining hall. What we will learn on these tours, beyond facts, dates, and building locations, additionally supports the emerging picture of the prestige-oriented university sketched out through the design of the welcome center and pretour information session. Namely, that above all, these universities are opportunity machines, and the students who thrive here come prepared to seize on the intensive intersection of resources available to create a future customized to their own ambitions.

The Library

On all three tours, the main library is a featured stop. Amanda, our tour guide at PRU (African American senior; PRU tee, ripped, high-waisted jeans, double major in economics and marketing) gathers us in a high-ceilinged area flanked by glass walls through which the tour group can observe Actual Students Actually Studying:

> Right now, we're in Franklin Library, and this is definitely known as the main library. It's most central to classes. This is our largest one with four stories, and right now we're cutting across on the second floor. This is also the only library that is open 24/5. So, what that means is during the school year the library is open for 24 hours a day any day that we have school the next day and then during finals it's open 24/7.

Amanda takes a moment to detail each of the specialized libraries on campus, then emphasizes, "So, we say each library kind of has a different vibe, different feel, and we just recommend that students test them out and see what you want and what fits your study style the best. Again, regardless of the name, they're open for all students."

At Lib Arts our tour guide, Liza (Hispanic, senior; double major in environmental science and political science), draws our attention to the massive windows that line the back of the Clinton Library. Her prompting is unnecessary; the entire tour group cannot help but stare as sunlight filters through the trees beyond:

> If you noticed, the entire back wall is glass windows. And we are on a hill, so when you're up on the second floor, you are overlooking the tops of all the trees. It's absolutely beautiful and serene. I always like to point out this area right here. This is my favorite view in all of campus. Lib Arts is really big on getting to know the world around you. And we believe that there's no better way to do that than to be out in that world.

Liza's sly use of this impressive architectural feature as an analogy for the university experience—being part of a college that opens you to the world beyond—is either a brilliant connection in the moment or a carefully crafted admissions talking point. Either way, the chance to position Lib Arts as a portal to opportunity has not been missed.

Back at Flagship, Kimmy informs us that Hamilton Library is one of 17 libraries on campus, and as the generalist of the family, "is a great place for freshman, especially, to start out. Some people end up studying here a lot through their years. But that's because there's a ton of different resources here in this library." Since Kimmy raised the issue of "resources," one might anticipate a quick description of specialized collections or databases of scholarly works. Instead, Kimmy leads us around the ground floor past a menagerie of spaces dedicated to various support services, including a math lab, a computer lab, a public speaking center, and STEM drop-in tutoring center. Not only does Kimmy spend our entire time in the library discussing support services, the topic of books never comes up. We experience a similar recital at Lib Arts, where Liza draws our attention to the writing center, digital media center, and online bookable study rooms that line the second story balcony.

Studying was also a key point of conversation at Flagship and PRU. Specifically, the importance of matching how you like to study with the options provided. Kimmy clues us in:

> So, this floor as well as the fifth floor are collaborative floors, so you can speak, you can get with group members, there's always conversations in the background. Then the other floors are quiet floors, specifically the fourth and the sixth floor. By quiet floors, I mean VERY quiet floors [*laughs*]. I once studied there and brought a bag of chips and opened it as a snack and it was like the loudest thing on the floor. But it's perfect for people who really need that environment to focus. *It's all about learning how you best study as well.* Like I said, I have never really had that environment where I needed to study [in high school], and so I had to learn pretty quickly in college, because that's what you spend a lot of your time doing. If you like to study in this library, one of the other 16 libraries, outside at a coffee shop in the city, in your dorm room—whatever it is, it's just important to kind of figure out what works best for you.

Selling the Dream

Through these conversations about study styles, the underlying themes of choice and customization are ever present. At PRU, Amanda begins a similar recital, though with the unexpected emphasis that the library is the social hub of campus:

> Some fun things about Franklin: as I mentioned, this is the largest library. There's always a lot happening.... The first floor is more of the social scene. A lot of students refer to it as "Club Frankie." It's where we have our full-service Starbucks. You'll notice that all the tables and wipe boards and chairs are all completely mobile. So, it's great if you're meeting up for a group project and you kind of want to pretend like you're studying in between classes or something like that. The first floor is probably the best place to do that.

For those who have not been on a college campus for a while, few spaces have shifted functions and even appearance like the university library, propelled by a simple question: If the world's knowledge is online, what is the purpose of a library?[9] The resulting identity crisis and reimagination has produced a location more like a Barnes & Noble bookstore than the hushed, musty book depository of past generations. The scholarly literature describes the "transformed" library as "outward facing, de-siloed, technology diffused, and collaborative."[10] The shorthand for this jargon is that libraries have repositioned themselves as hubs of student services as part of a posture of engagement with patrons, rather than warehouses of knowledge that students will come asking to access.[11] The question raised by a parent, when Amanda (PRU) mentioned the Starbucks in the library, was not "Why on Earth...?" but "Can we stop there...?" (answer: "Sorry, it's too busy; the one in the Rec Center will be easier"). Perhaps more telling, as we follow Kimmy into the library we pass by a full-service coffee shop, which receives neither mention nor notice. This is the new normal. This services emphasis results in both predictable (technology support) and unpredictable offerings, as Amanda expounds on the opportunities of "Club Frankie":

> Then Franklin is also really, really known for a lot of our fun activities. Especially around finals week. So, during finals Franklin sponsors a lot of

fun events here. This last round of finals that happened in December, we had therapy puppies and therapy pigs. One day they brought out massage therapists so you could sign up, get a massage if you wanted to in between classes. They do a midnight nacho bar since it is open 24/7. So, if you're looking to kind of have a study break you don't necessarily need to go all the way back to your room and decompress and come back, that can all happen in one space if you want it to.

At Lib Arts, the library appears to function a bit more like a traditional library; at least no therapy pigs or nacho bars were mentioned, though a local food truck was stationed on the patio outside. The form and functions of the libraries clearly varied in some ways between our three campuses, based on relative physical location, the function of other campus buildings, and the intentions of administrators. However, the academic library might be thought of as a telling symbol of broader university reorientation from a place where students come to be given knowledge to a place intent on offering students whatever forms of engagement they desire.

The Rec Center

In contrast to the identity crisis and reimagining the academic library has undergone, no such casting about for alternative models has beset the campus rec center. Resorts, high-end hotels, and toney fitness clubs are already exemplars, even if the educational setting might be expected to temper comparisons.[12] Kimmy (Flagship) turns and addresses the group just outside the doors as students stream past on either side, many decked out in the ubiquitous all-purpose undergrad uniform: pony tails and yoga pants for the women, athletic shorts and logoed tees for the men. We're caught in a midmorning class change, and the main drag buzzes with the coordinated chaos of chance meetings, excited conversations, and the constant hazard of electric scooters. "So, in just a sec I'll show you the inside of the gym real quick, and then we're going to briefly go outside to see the pool. There's probably going to be no one out there since it's really cold, but it is my favorite part of the gym."

Kimmy proceeds to catalogue exercise classes and facilities of all imaginable types. Flagship, the largest of the three campuses, naturally is built at a scale to accommodate huge numbers of undergraduates, making the description of available athletic resources almost gaudy. On our walk through she also points out volleyball and basketball courts, an indoor track ("if you don't want to run on the treadmills"), and pool and ping-pong tables as we traverse the central section of the rec center, an open atrium extended upward several stories to a glass ceiling. In addition to fitness and athletic resources of various levels of intensity, the rec center is also a kind of outdoor adventure center, loaning out camping, boating, and climbing gear for weekend excursions.

By the back door, Kimmy adds to the list of resources and opportunities that make the all-inclusive vacation sound like an increasingly apt comparison:

> Like I mentioned earlier also four different pools. So, there's the indoor pool, three outdoor pools, they are heated all year 'round, which is especially important at the moment. But the three outdoors pools—there's a leisure pool, a lap pool, and then there's a competition pool for water volleyball competitions. Then we have an 18-person hot tub as well. So, we are going to step outside to look at all of those, because it's one of my favorite places. I like going there just between classes and laying out and just studying on my laptop. There's palm trees everywhere, so it kind of feels like you're at a resort.

Indeed, as we exit the doors the impression is quite resort-like: palm trees ring a pool, casting leafy shade over the line of deck chairs on two sides. Contrary to predictions, several students lapping the heated pool keep the shivering lifeguard in her chair. Yet Flagship offers something else no resort can offer: big-time college athletics. Kimmy notes the various nationally ranked teams, and games accessible for one all-inclusive price, called The One Pass. This ticket, at $175 annually, gives a student access to all sporting events, including six home football games. A parent inquires about family discounts to football games before we head back inside, passing both an Amazon drop site filled with lockers and a juice bar filled with the rattling drone of smoothie blend-ers, neither of which receive mention. At PRU and Lib Arts, all sporting events can be attended "for free," speaking to opportunities of scale and competitive level.

At the PRU Rec Center, Amanda stands in a hallway flanked with similar vertical layers of sport-specific spaces: basketball and volleyball courts, indoor soccer, studio rooms for power yoga, judo, Pilates, dance, cycling, and whatever trendy self-punishing workout is making its rounds on social media. Beyond the pool on the lower level is a glass wall with doors leading outside to two sand volleyball courts and a tanning pool. Amanda suggests how a student might try and manage such an abundance of athletic opportunities in the face of impending academic responsibilities: "We also have full-sized locker rooms down here, which is really great—for students who work out in between classes and you don't necessarily have to go all the way back to your commons to freshen up. You can do all of that here. The gym is open from 6 a.m. to midnight every day."

Accessibility takes a number of forms. Amanda highlights that, in addition to flexible time to work out and get clean, these resources, and more, are for "ordinary" students:

> All the resources that you see here are free. We do have some resources that you might want to pay for if you're looking for that, if you're looking for a personal trainer or something like that, you can kind of get that set up through the gym but that would come at an extra cost. But again, we do have free fitness classes and we have a nutritionist on campus that does a lot of free consulting and stuff, if you're kind of looking to work through that part of your life here at PRU. We also have a recreational pool. All the facilities that you see here and all the resources offered here are for nonathlete students. So, we have a separate gym for our swimming and diving team. Separate training centers for all of our division one sports teams, so this is just for nonathlete students.

The not-so-subtle message reinforced through this leg of the tour is that student involvement includes the body as well as the mind. All of this dovetails with what tour expert Jeff Kallay asserted to us: whereas millennials cared about amenities, Gen Z has embraced "wellness," including emotional, spiritual, mental, and physical dimensions. When wellness is the unassailable virtue, the difference between necessity (exercise) and stress-reducing relaxation (tanning pool) disappears, so long as it promotes the highest of priorities: student success.

At Lib Arts, the newly remodeled recreational facilities make wellness a central feature. Liza (Lib Arts) pauses for dramatic effect beside an entrance that could be mistaken for that of a day spa: "This is the Recreation and Athletics Center, also just known as the Rec. This facility just turned a year old in January, and it was recently renovated to include a wellness aspect."

Shifting to what seems like a more scripted talking point, Liza launches into a pitch for the importance of wellness to an audience that likely requires little convincing:

> There are a lot of studies done across the United States that point to one of the biggest problems on college campuses is the lack of sleep that students were getting. And Lib Arts thought it was kind of ridiculous to have all this research out there and not do anything about it. So, with the renovation of our Recreation and Athletic Center, they included that wellness aspect. This facility has nap pods. It has a yoga studio. This one right here, which is super nice, because we do sunrise yoga. And so, when you're up super early, you can see the sun rising over all of these trees. It's absolutely serene. . . . And so, it is one of the ways that we practice what we preach. So, we not only want to make sure that you are taken care of physically, but also mentally and emotionally. And this is one of the spaces that we do that.

The vision of a clean open space where rows of spandex-bedecked undergrads greet the day, eyes closed, faces calm, bodies in a relaxed meditative state, is a dramatic departure from the old dimly lit college gymnasium filled with sweaty jocks and poorly maintained exercise machines experienced by prior generations. In these spaces, the laudable concern with student mental health is impossible to disaggregate from the sense that the college campus itself has become a living showroom where the "pitch" of student-as-lifestyle has become commensurate with the college experience.

The Residence Hall

An important feature of the selective university life in America is the on-campus residential experience. Across our three campuses, the requirements for and percentage of students who live on campus predictably varies by size and emphasis: Lib Arts has the highest percentage and requires two years on-campus residency, as does PRU; Flagship does not require first-year students to live on campus but encourages them to live in university-owned housing of some kind.

At PRU, Amanda leads us into one of nearly a dozen residential "communities." From the outside, the building looks much like the residence hall most people would associate with a college campus: a large U-shaped structure with rooms off of long hallways leading to centralized lounges on each floor. The effort to rethink the residential experience at PRU is part of a larger national movement toward a "residential college"–style system that places faculty in the living spaces and more tightly unifies opportunities for learning and belonging.[13] The origin of this structure of learning is the English commons model, but it is easy to imagine that the rampant popularity of Harry Potter's "house" system has added to the attractiveness, which Amanda does not miss the chance to reference: "A lot of people kind of ask, 'Hey, do I get to pick what commons I live in?' The answer to that is, 'No.' We say that in the residential community system, it's also very similar to, like, Hogwarts sorting hat type of thing."

Amanda extolls the advantages of housing that is more than housing: an internal system of government ("community council"), a unique crest, mascot, themed events, and even an intercommunity competition ("Community Cup") with points granted for winning at quiz nights and other events. A faculty-in-residence program is part of the residential community system: "So, here in Morton Hall, Professor Finnegan lives here with the students. She's a film professor. She likes to host the event 'Morton at the Movies' once a semester. So, everybody who lives in Morton goes to a local theater off campus and everyone who lives here gets to enjoy a movie together. She facilitates a conversation after. So, just a couple of weeks ago she took everybody to see *The Joker,* which is really fun." We file down the hall to the surprisingly empty model room, past doors layered with decals for obscure bands and posters for upcoming hall events. Seeing an unadorned room and hearing discussion of suite-style living versus "community-style" (traditional rooms with two beds and hall bath) raises both the nervous energy of the group and questions about basic processes. A parent asks how often the common bathrooms are cleaned (twice daily). We are reminded of tour guru Jeff's admonition that showing how basic needs will be met is paramount and prerequisite to programmatic and academic details.

Quite different from the brick and pillars of PRU, the residence hall on display at Lib Arts is an architectural statement that Lisa describes as "New York Industrial." The geometric colored-glass structure, we're informed, was designed by an award-winning South American architect. "If you wanted to feel like you moved away from home and went to New York. These are the buildings for you." Liza assures the group that more "homey" accommodations are also available, as are furnished and unfurnished apartments for juniors and seniors. Designed with upper-level rooms surrounding a modern courtyard dotted with metal seating and tables shaded by large umbrellas, the residence hall includes a dining hall on the first floor, which adds both convenience and experience: "So, you'd want to know that something to notice is that breakfast, the smell of breakfast rises. My friends who lived in this building freshman year would text me and let me know if it was pancake day, because they could smell it in the morning. And pancake day was my favorite."

At Flagship, Kimmy leads us into what looks like two apartment towers connected by an indoor shopping plaza with (another) Starbucks, a convenience store, and a fast food restaurant purported to be the highest-grossing location in the country. Several students stand behind a folding table with a griddle, beckoning: "Pancakes! $1 for a good cause!" Kimmy greets a pair of young women "friends from camp orientation," she smiles, then introduces the building, again steering our attention to the extent and ubiquity of support services: "So, we're walking into Jefferson. This is actually Jefferson Center, and then we have Jefferson East and Jefferson West resident halls. Jefferson Center is just a ton of different resources. So, right here you can see there's a career counseling center in one of the residence halls. Upstairs has the tutoring center for the whole campus, it's on the third floor."

In contrast to the uniformity of the residential college model at PRU, the selling point at Flagship is variety:

> We do have a ton of different options, like I said, there's 14 different residence halls. This one is the largest. All of the rest is all different sorts of types based on where they are on campus. We have some that are part of the honors quad. We have one that's freshman only. They're all smaller than this one, too, so if it sounds scary to live in one this large, it's okay, they're all smaller than this, so you can pick one that's a good size for you as well.

Kimmy is also quick to point out how residential staff work hard to facilitate relationships between students, and the opportunity that living in a building with lots of potential social connections:

> I personally lived in Jefferson, like I said, and I did it because I kind of wanted to put myself out of my comfort zone. I was like, "Let me make myself as uncomfortable as possible just to get comfortable quickly." So, I moved into the residence hall with 3,000 people and I have a group chat of 65 people from my floor freshman year and we still talk in it all the time, still meet up. We would have potlucks every Tuesday in the study room and it was just kind of a great environment because you were constantly meeting people and the RAs [Resident Assistants; student staff] would put on all sort of events. So, the first few weeks they would have dodge ball or yoga, free food, movie marathon, petting zoo, all different sorts of things so that people in the building could get to know each other.

The importance of creating contexts for relationships to form is a point of emphasis widely advanced. This is particularly so in the opening week of school that scholars note as vital to establishing a social network that will be one's core support hub for the first several years.[14] Apparently though, the once obligatory "ice-breaker" activities and team field games no longer suffice. Setting aside the momentary rush or terror of 3,000 new best friends, the sample room is much like the one at PRU; undecorated, with stackable beds, modest storage, a desk, and the bonus of a microwave/fridge combo that comes with the room. A similar discussion over community bathrooms and suite-style living ensues before we are ushered out as the next tour group fills in behind us. Despite the impressive resources of these universities, there is something underwhelming, and perhaps in that, humanizing, about the actual living quarters for first-year students. This may also be one small symbolic moment where students are reminded that they are entering a world much bigger than themselves and a bit of humility, in terms of similar modest accommodations, might do them some good.

The Student Union

Student unions are often a kind of catchall for various student-centric university functions. However, as services and supports diversify and the divide between academic and nonacademic resources further blurs, what one can predictably expect to find becomes less certain, as the variations among our three case campuses attest. At Flagship, we trail Kimmy single file through the crush of lunchtime activity, snaking our way past offices, lines for food vendors, and clusters of seating (including a lounge in contemporary decor with a burning gas fireplace). To arrange the tour in a way that produces this intense navigation seems like a questionable strategy, but we recalled Flagship admissions officer Jason's words about some of the larger aims of the experience:

> We also would like for them to be able to see the students walking around. You know? So, if you don't see students engaged or seem like they're really committed to the university, then you know, folks might say, "What's the point of coming here? I mean, there's really no student life." But I think depending on the time you take a tour you could very well be amongst hundreds of people walking around, and I think that could be a really positive experience for students and get them excited about this as a great place to be.

Whether his goals were being met in this moment or not, touring students were likely having an evaluative moment of fit. Imagining their future selves in a space with so many others, regardless of reaction, represented useful intel for families to process afterward. We emerge on the other side of the building, where Kimmy huddles us in a shady spot to talk about what we just experienced:

> So, this building that we just walked through is the student activities center. It was built by the students for the students, and the students petitioned for it to be built. The university spent an entire year doing focus groups on what people wanted to see inside this building. So, they included a lot of things that people did not expect. So, for example, there is a black box theater, there's a ballroom, there's an art exhibit on the rooftop, there's napping stairs on the second floor where you can nap in between classes. All of those were because of feedback that they got from students for what they wanted to see in this building.

Emphasizing the mass and variety of resources and opportunities, Kimmy continues:

> There's also, as you saw, some restaurants, Starbucks, tons of different meeting rooms, places where you can study alone or with groups. We have ten different resource centers as well, so it's designed to make students feel like they have a home on campus. So, we have the gender and sexuality center and the multicultural engagement center, the mind and body lab, there's the student government offices, and then we also just have meeting rooms for other organizations as well.

Like Flagship, PRU's student union is a tour de force of diverse amenities and activity options. Amanda takes us in to the ground floor of the student center, a large brick building with a central atrium, several restaurants and seating on the lower level, and a variety of offices on the upper levels undergoing an extensive remodel. Whereas Kimmy mentions restaurants offhand, Amanda (and similarly, Liza, our Lib Arts guide) seize on the moment to expand on the campus dining options, prompted by PRU's newly renovated Chick-fil-A and Taco Stop.

Conversation quickly veers from the structure of the "unlimited" meal plan to student use of it as a kind of competitive activity:

> So, as I'm sure you guys are aware at PRU you are required to live on campus your freshman and sophomore year. With that on-campus living requirement comes our unlimited meal plan. So, what that means is that out of the two dining halls on campus you have an unlimited number of swipes in the dining halls per day. We say "unlimited," there's really a limit of like 99 swipes, I think. The highest number of swipes I've heard has been 80. So, literally what that means is you're free to walk in and out of the dining hall as many times a day as you'd like.
>
> **Parent:** *In one day?*
>
> Yeah. I don't know if people are eating or if they're just bored and trying to set a record [*group laughs*]. People sometimes swipe in, grab an apple, something like that. So, the dining halls are typically open from 7 a.m. to 8 p.m. every day.

The idea of the dining hall as more of a kitchen where your parent is always making food (within posted hours, anyhow) is a mindset shift from the traditional restaurant-style "three squares" previous generations of college-goers often experienced. "Unlimited" dining hall access elicits impressed murmurs from several parents. Amanda details the finer points of "flex" dollars, essentially a slightly discounted debit system, which can be used at any of the campus restaurants and the two Starbucks. Flex dollars can also be used in The Market, an upscale student convenience store replete with a vegan section, a sushi bar made fresh on-site, and "craft" trail mix, among many other niche offerings. Amanda shares insider information for maximizing the flex dollar structure:

> So, what these are, are kind of like dollars that are attached to your meal plan. They range anywhere from $200 to $500 per semester. Just whatever your parents are willing to pay. But the great thing is, whatever you don't use in the fall will roll over into the spring semester. I always recommend finding a friend with $500 of flex, because no one ever uses it all. During the last week before school gets out, people are buying out

all the Chick-fil-A and Starbucks, just to get rid of all that flex because it won't roll over to the next year.

We look around and wonder if the doublespeak of flex dollars is lost on tour families: parents are encouraged to load up cash that students inevitably will not use, and then will try to quickly spend on food and drinks they do not need or perhaps want because the university does not allow those dollars to roll over to a new academic year. At Lib Arts, Liza describes a similar structure and outcome, a kind of last desperate rush to cash out dollars that university vendors will simply pocket once the academic year ends. Liza details retailers' efforts to help students spend down their remaining funds rather than roll over or refund unused money: "What you don't use in the fall will carry over to the spring. But what you don't use in the spring, won't carry over to that next fall. So, the dining halls, the coffee shop, the convenient stores here on campus, they start selling things in bulk, like you would a Sam's Club or a Costco. So, you can finish out your meal plan."

Back at PRU, we work our way up the stairs and past a giant collage of the school's winged mascot made from post-it notes in its distinctive shape. Upon each one a student has written aspirations, ranging from the serious to the goofy, for the coming year, such as "get a summer internship," "sleep more," and "ask Andrea out." At the first-floor landing, Amanda echoes Kimmy's emphasis on opportunity spaces, support services, and resources in the student center, including parking services (Yes, first year students can have a car on campus!), the post office (Students get their own addresses!), Greek Life offices (about 40% of students are in fraternities and sororities), and student involvement organizations. Amanda makes no mention of the multicultural center, LGBT center, or women's center; we're left to wonder if this is intentional or simply a result of the array of topics possible to cover. She does, however, highlight the career center, a resource aimed at helping students with social networking, social media, in addition to polishing up and honing standard employment process details.

A visit to the student union would not be complete without reinforcing the importance of joining or initiating a student-run organization.

The student organization has become a central selling point as a mechanism for encouraging—and regulating—student engagement on campus in areas of interest that the administration could not otherwise anticipate.[15] All three tour guides emphasize the opportunities for engagement and initiative that student organizations represent. Amanda (PRU) provides a personal example, emphasizing the opportunity and value of organizational involvement:

> So, here at PRU we have over 200 clubs. My roommate is a psychology major here and she felt like there wasn't a lot of awareness for women's mental health, especially in underrepresented communities, whether it be women and LGBT, minority students, lower-income students, so she started a club called Check Yourself. I run all the marketing for that. But it's really cool because my roommate is graduating in May, but now this will be a PRU tradition that will hopefully go on forever. So, if you are looking for something that's not here, please bring it to campus. We have lots of money to give students to start these things. We have clubs that send students to amusement parks and study business practices—all that kind of fun stuff. So, don't think small when it comes to getting involved on campus. There are a lot of ways to get involved already.

The question "What organization would you start if time and money were not barriers?" is implicit in Amanda's description. Although we felt confident that this characterization includes a dash of hyperbole, the repeated environmental expectation that *the only barrier is your imagination and initiative* was a clear theme across campus and campuses. Liza (Lib Arts) informs us that to start a student organization "all you need is you, three other students, and an advisor and that is your club!" Kimmy (Flagship) also presses the importance of organizational involvement and the founding of organizations as a thing central to the student experience, but in a way that makes the substance of them far less important than the joining:

> So, we have over 1,300 organizations on campus. We have social organizations, we have academic organizations, general interest clubs. We have lots of different honor societies, ones that are specific to majors or

professions. So, I know a lot of you said you were prehealth of some sort, so we have a lot of different prehealth societies, premed societies. We also have tons of different computer science organizations as well. So, even if you think you don't have a hobby or anything like that, we have some really out-there ones . . . we have like a squirrel watching club. We have a hot wings club where they meet and eat hot wings together every week. So, even if you're like, "Oh, I don't have a hobby or any interests" . . . if you like food or something like that there's an organization that you can find where you feel like you fit in.

The idea that an 18-year-old whose life has been consumed with organized activities might arrive at college without hobbies or interests strikes us as curious. Then again, perhaps Kimmy has hit upon the important difference between activities cultivated for the purposes of college admissions grooming and a student's own personal interests. Similarly emphasizing the informal and perhaps vacuous, Liza (Lib Arts) advises us that "the most popular club is the Disney Club, because you sit around and watch Disney movies all day. It sounds ridiculous, but you go to a meeting, and then you understand why you need a Disney day sometimes." All three tour guides press the student organization as a worthwhile opportunity that somehow unites the measured seriousness of organizational leadership with the expected ridiculousness of student interests.

Student organizations, however, also offer another key element of the university experience: belonging. At Flagship, the scale of a place with a bewildering variety of resources represents a strength (find your place!) and a liability (too many choices!), that Kimmy attempts to navigate for the group with reference to her own experiences:

> For me, organizations were kind of the way that I found my home on campus. It was almost like a domino effect. I joined one my first semester, I met more people, heard about more and joined more. I kind of just kept going and once I felt like I had a home in those organizations it made me realize that Flagship isn't just one really large university, it's thousands of these smaller groups that make up the whole. It's all about finding the

Selling the Dream   49

people that you want to surround yourself with, those opportunities that you have.

The guides of our three tours each worked at navigating the poles of resource-rich environments versus manageable space of belonging in different ways, reflective of the physical and student body size of their respective campuses. At Lib Arts, where campus scale is not overwhelming and the grounds can easily be seen in an hour, descriptions of the variety of opportunities are differently important than at Flagship, where the opposite is the case. Nevertheless, although these student volunteers were unlikely to know the social theory behind emphases on belonging, fit, and social integration, the recognition that a student has the best shot of making it if they find their place socially and academically permeates the campus tour.[16]

The Academic Building

Whether from prospective student interest or their own compulsion, tour guides did find ways to work the details of curricular opportunity and expectation into the tour, despite tour expert Jeff Kallay's assertion that safety and security concerns trump interest in academic details. In transit between building stops, guides pointed out locations of certain areas of focus and wove in mentions of general education requirements. Notably, however, the only places where we specifically lingered were either STEM (science, technology, engineering, and math) or business buildings. These locations make sense on several fronts: in terms of impressive facilities and outputs they are "wow" moments on tour ("We have the world's second largest supercomputer!") and are areas that significantly contribute to institutional prestige through research dollars, high-profile partnerships, and headline-generating inventions. STEM and business also make for visually interesting tour destinations in ways that a humanities building full of classrooms simply cannot. Still, the tacit message of institutional priorities accompanies this focus, implying that the majors housed in the buildings visited are where the *real* action is. Meanwhile those venerable, if not slightly musty academic areas are what make you "well-rounded" but do not represent the cutting-edge professions of the future.

At Flagship, Kimmy leads us into an engineering building, a glass and steel structure with an entry opening onto a multilevel concourse that reminds us of a contemporary airport. At the bottom, circular clusters of informal seating are packed with students lounging, chatting, and studying between classes. Along the far glass wall are group study spaces. On our left we see signs for tutoring help and study abroad experiences specifically for engineering students. Kimmy intones:

> But right now we're in one of our engineering buildings, specifically electrical engineering. There's specific labs for people that need to use it for class and research and stuff like that, but there's also a free 3-D printer vending machine that's available to all Flagship students. So, you can kind of send in a design and they'll let you know when it's going to be printed and come in and watch it be done and then it's printed and it dispenses out to you.

Again picking up the theme of opportunity, Kimmy describes resources and supports specifically for engineering: career advisors (each college has its own), study abroad coordinators ("I believe we are number two among engineering schools for study abroad"), and financial aid advisors. This list of offices and personnel on the wall behind her reminds us how the confluence of academic specialization and student customization results in the proliferation of administrators as well as opportunities.

At PRU, Amanda also tours us through the engineering building, and also highlights the maker space and 3-D printers available to engineers and others after appropriate safety certification has been secured: "So, this 'innovation gym' is really just where students go to bring their ideas to life. Any student is free to use it at any point in the day. We've had people go in there and make 3-D busts of their face, just because they could, and make 3-D flowers for their moms for Mother's Day, just because they could." Amanda emphasizes small class sizes, the high percentage of female engineering students ("twice the national average"), the dedicated career center ("about 85% of students already have a job lined up before it's time to graduate"), and the opportunities to customize majors ("over 90 different specializations").

Weaving our way back across the main drag, Kimmy (Flagship) leads us into a modern-looking minimalist concrete building with a swoopy central seating area shaped like a DNA strand, one of the many natural sciences buildings clustered on this side of campus. Kimmy informs us of the centrality of research across the university: "We're going to walk down this hallway. There will be some labs on the left side. Traditional labs you would expect, where there are chemicals, microscopes, all that stuff. But we do have research in every single college on campus." We file past large windows that open into laboratory classrooms filled not only with complicated-looking glass tubing, electronic devices, and imposing storage units but also with students in white lab coats actually using this equipment, which seems like a serendipitous campus tour coup, or just the product of good planning. Kimmy capitalizes on the moment, describing in detail how freshmen can join a research team:

> Whatever it is that you're interested in, you can kind of choose one, they'll place you, and within the first couple of months here at Flagship you will be doing research in that lab for your full freshman year. After that you have the option to stay on as a lab mentor and you can either get credit for it, just research experience, or you can get paid as you continue up as well.
>
> If you stay in it all four years you're guaranteed to be published by a medical or scientific journal by the time you graduate. So, if research is something that you know that you want to do, that's a really great program, I definitely recommend looking into it. I personally had thought nothing about research before I came here [*laughs*].

The sciences buildings ("wet" and "dry") are also a featured stop at Lib Arts, where Liza describes at length a friend whose research was recently published in a prominent sciences journal. For a small liberal arts college, these are key tour moments to show that despite their size, coming here is not a compromise. Here again, opportunity is the prized commodity of the prestige-oriented university experience:

> At a lot of different universities you have to wait until your junior, senior year, to join a research program. At Lib Arts we think that there's no reason to make you wait if you're here and you're excited. Right off the bat, your freshman year, you're more than welcome to join a research project or pitch your own to a researcher and have them jump on board with you. And if you play your cards correctly you can do anywhere from four to six different research projects while you are here on our campus.

The academic portion of the tours left us with the sense of academics not merely as learning but as meaningful *doing*. The message that students' academic work makes a difference right now was clearly delivered across the three campus tours.

The Historic Building

Status at a selective university campus is conveyed visually in a number of ways, but the presence of sleek, cutting-edge STEM buildings and stately venerable historic structures may be chief among them. As historian John Thelin notes, the colonial colleges, all situated along the eastern seaboard, were founded as bulwarks against the imposing expanse of apparently unsettled territory that seemed to stretch out to the west without end.[17] The educational roots of many of these colleges' founders were in European universities such as Oxford, Cambridge, and Edinburgh, where centuries of slow growth had produced impressive gothic structures, typically in quads surrounding a central lawn, and organizationally structured in a series of semiautonomous "colleges." Thus, the function and symbolism of a new college's first building was not lost on the ambitious college builders as they endeavored to raise a campus in the wilderness from nothing. A college needed to house, feed, teach, and provide office space as basic functions. What better way to meet these ends than in a single visually impressive building? Of course, one of the few constants across time is that buildings are expensive, especially those intended to project educational grandeur. Consequently, many founders settled for constructing a single hall that fronted, rather than surrounded a common quad, around which other buildings would later be added.[18]

Thus, some version of "Old Main" became the standard structure by which a college in America could be recognized. Over the centuries, the relative age and at times, almost cartoonishly dour neogothic architecture of these structures has only served to heighten their projected seriousness and permanence, even if the reality of their origins and history are less grand.[19] Each of our case campuses boasts a building of this sort, and the tours leverage it to great effect as a symbol of institutional significance and tradition.

At Lib Arts, Liza leads us through Main Hall, where renovations have just been completed on a new campus welcome and meeting space. Our route down the winding central staircase and out the front of the building, facing away from campus, proves to be strategic. We emerge from this historic stone structure, described in promotional materials as "iconic," onto a view of the nearby city that justified the bother of building on a hill. A similar hilltop view awaits us at PRU, where we've also entered the back of the building for a similar big reveal:

> All right, so right now we're in Founders Hall, which is definitely the main building on campus. This is one of our biggest buildings, one of our prettiest buildings on campus. Everyone has already noticed the seal [*Amanda directs our attention to the large bronze insignia in the center of the marble floor*]. Not only is it such a beautiful building, but it also holds a lot of history here at PRU. When the university started, this was the only building on campus. This is where students ate, where they slept, we had a barber shop in the basement, this is where they took class. With that we have some fun traditions and myths. So, I asked you guys to not step on the seal as you walked in and that's because it means that if you step on the seal you will not graduate in four years. Some people go for it, some people try to get out in three and a half. Go for it, but don't say I didn't warn you.
>
> So, this is how we walk from the back of Founders Hall, you'll do that with your entire incoming class right at the beginning of freshman year. So, you and about 1,500 of your new best friends will walk through the back without stepping on the seal. Then you'll walk down the stairs of Founders Hall and that symbolizes becoming an "Eagle," starting on this four-year journey. It's really cool because you get to do the same thing

when you graduate, but in reverse. You walk up the front of Founders Hall, jump, hop, cartwheels, whatever you want to do on the seal, and get out the back, becoming "world changers" and starting on your next journey.

As we stand by, passing students respect the tradition, evidently unwilling to test the fates despite the fact that the seal ritual has become something of a trope.[20] Regardless of students' specific compliance, the message is that these buildings are not merely locations of learning but places of deep, almost spiritual significance. By joining, you commit yourself to lifelong membership, complete with initiation rites that solidify both your belonging and your compliance with this self-veneration. Higher education scholar Peter Magolda described these rituals as invoking "a romanticized image of the lost American college campus (which probably never existed), a campus where professors teach, students learn and enjoy life, staff administer, and alumni treasure their years on campus. In total, all members of the community are clearly defined and content with their particular roles."[21]

Of course, campus traditions and rituals come in many forms, varying in seriousness, scale, and participatory expectation, but all rituals communicate belonging, identity, and collective purpose to those on the "inside." At PRU, we heard about an annual birthday carnival celebration for the school's mascot. At Lib Arts, an old oak tree was, by legend, where the university's founder sat and picked the spot for the university that exists today. This hallowed ground is now a gathering place for studying, socializing, and graduation picture-taking. At Flagship, the pageantry of big-time college football facilitated a host of smaller rituals: tailgating before the game, coordinated cheers and chants during, and lighting the tower of Main Hall in school colors after a victory. Magolda's critique is of the false sense of homogeneity university rituals cast over socially and politically contested spaces, observable on our case campuses as well. However, on the tour, we perceive that the lack of bewilderment at these events on the part of tour participants suggests that the societal-level project of higher education as religion, campus as temple, and student life as sacrament has become sufficiently normalized that the costs and expectations of membership require little to no justification.

The Dining Hall

For all the hype about facilities and the opportunities they provide, none of the tours actually took us through a dining hall. Although it was referenced as we passed by, the emphasis of direct visual contact was instead on the restaurant options, even though many students eating on campus get their food in the dining hall through a meal plan. At Lib Arts the small campus size and intensive residential experience means most first- and second-year students eat in one of two campus dining halls on a regular basis. In contrast to PRU, Lib Arts has a debit card system that deducts meal purchases per food item rather than a "swipes" system that provides entry to buffet-style eateries. Flagship includes both a buffet-style "swipes" meal plan as well as cafés that are pay-per-item. Liza (Lib Arts) pitches the logic of the debit a la carte system:

> For freshman, we have two meal plan options. We call them "the big one" and "the bigger one." And how it is, is a debit card system rather than a swipe system. At [other universities] they do a swipe system and that's 16–18 swipes a week. But here, you have a set amount, like you would at a grocery store. That's so you can check your balance and that way you don't feel like you're losing out on a swipe if you eat out that day. Or you just snack that day, you're not wasting any of your money.

Lib Arts' operational disadvantage is that it cannot capitalize on the economy of scale the way large peer universities can. A staff member tipped us off that Lib Arts used to run on a swipes system. However, student complaints about the quality of food of buffet-style eating compelled administrators to make the bargain that most students will care more about eating well than what it costs to do so. As such, Lib Arts shifted the emphasis from *choice* to *wellness*. As Liza elaborates: "Everything is locally sourced. I believe the furthest ingredient we get is—everything comes from a 200-mile radius. And that's really cool, because a lot of people who have allergies will let me know about how things being locally sourced has really helped them." Liza does not mention what impact partnering with a food service provider that offers locally sourced foods has on the cost of the meal plan, but the emphasis on social responsibility and student wellness plays well with our small tour group.

Kimmy's (Flagship) discussion of food options was prompted by a parent's very parental-sounding question: "Do you get three meals a day?" Like Amanda at PRU, Kimmy discusses a dining plan structure that indirectly eliminates the very concept of "meals": the "unlimited" plan. "So, the meal plan, there's one meal plan and it's kind of included with just the living on campus price. And basically, you get unlimited swipes for all the buffets all year long, all day long." As at PRU, the structure then becomes multitiered, with "dine-in dollars" that function on a debit system within the dining halls, and an alternate "campus cash" currency that can be used elsewhere:

> So, we have, like, Wendy's, we have Chick-fil-A, we have Panda Express, all of that stuff. It also works for about 35 other restaurants off campus and north campus which was my favorite part of the meal plan because you can leave campus and you can still use your meal plan basically to go to these other restaurants. So, there's three different ways that you can pay for it, but basically you could just eat the buffet all year long if you want and save that money, or you can go off campus, or a la carte.

Choice and flexibility of food options are important themes echoed by Amanda (PRU) as we pause outside one of two campus dining facilities. Understanding that sometimes students are discontent with the requirements of on-campus housing and dining, she works in a pitch for the meal plan as well:

> I also want to take a moment to point out Grace Hall, which is the building to you all's right. Honestly, since moving off campus the meal plan is one thing I realized I took advantage of the most. I hate being in the kitchen. I hate cooking and I really wish I still had a meal plan. But it's really nice, it's like your traditional buffet style. They have the everyday things like the

omelet bar, salad bar, pizza, burgers, but we also have a lot of other fun stations—so we have Mongolian Grill, a Tex-Mex station, home cooked meal station—we have a gluten-free pantry for dietary needs like that.

Food, Amanda (PRU) informs us, is not just about choice, but the focal point of campus rituals as well:

At G's [Dining Hall] we have cookie bell tradition. So, what that means is every time a fresh batch of chocolate chip cookies is brought out of the oven the workers will ring the cookie bell and you'll just kind of see everybody run up and do a mad dash to the dessert bar to see who can get the most hot cookies at one time. But it happens every 20 minutes, so if you miss it on the first one . . .

As we ponder the image of a mob of students rushing a hapless food service employee like some sort of culinary Black Friday sale, Amanda directs our attention to the grassy quad we just passed, site of a variety of campus traditions both formal and informal:

I just kind of want to highlight Founders Hall Lawn, which is what we just walked through. We have a lot of our really large schoolwide activities on Founders Hall Lawn, so one example is Light Up the Night, which is our winter celebration that we have every December. We have the giant Christmas tree, all of our musical performance groups are singing carols. This year they built an ice-skating rink, we had reindeer, we had a life-sized snow globe, all out here on the lawn. In April, coming up, we'll have Screech-a-palooza. Screech is our mascot here at PRU. We like to throw him a birthday party every spring. So, we have Screech out here, we have carnival rides, character drawings, deep-fried Oreos, corn dogs, all of that kind of fun stuff always happening on the Lawn.

Returning to the admissions welcome center, Amanda gestures toward a nearby parking circle, and mentions that twice a week it is populated by various gourmet food trucks. The places and ways food has been described over the past hour of touring could cause the casual observer to be skeptical that there are students at these universities for whom food is something other than a ritual, amusement, and part of a lifestyle of choice.

CHAPTER 2

Establishing the Ideal/Normal
Campus Tour as Hidden Curriculum

All structured social systems—governments, hospitals, businesses, schools, the military, and certainly universities—have meaning encoded in their policies, behaviors, and even physical locations that those involved are expected to understand and follow. Although scholars describe this baked-in influence with a variety of useful concepts, we find the language of *hidden curriculum* to be particularly insightful.[1] "Curriculum" used in this way is understood not in the traditional sense of formal class plans and organization but rather as the informal knowledge one is to learn inside and outside the classroom about "how we do things around here" to be successful. Social theorists Eric Margolis and colleagues spin out the term "hidden" to potentially include information yet to be discovered, information left purposefully unfound, and information that has been intentionally concealed.[2] Of the latter, the authors outline several types. Some things are purposefully hidden in plain sight through rituals and symbols such as campus monuments to civil rights or Confederate military figures where they are evident but not mentioned. Some things are hidden because of a collective agreement not to see, such as a college's refusal to acknowledge historical racism or founders' participation in enslaving individuals. And, still others are hidden behind the scenes, such as admissions processes that appear meritocratic but preference upper-income or legacy families.[3]

The campus tours explored in chapter 1 can be thought of as an important moment of hidden curriculum transmission—"transmission," not in the sense that much if any of the general information received is new to those who participate. Indeed, the close alignment of our three tours suggests a predictable template. Rather, "transmission" in the reassurance to parents, and later, employers, that these aspirational universities can be trusted to have aligned themselves with the known markers of prestige and in those, to also have staked out distinctive and valued territory that will be conveyed to their graduates. Scholars have noted the irony that within a competitive environment, distinction is achieved not by acting in novel ways that would set an organization apart but by being the best at conforming to largely unspoken ideals.[4] As such, the analytic points that follow represent both a reification of society-wide beliefs about prestige-oriented universities and the elements through which particular institutions attempt to create differentiation within a peer environment of sameness. The product of this intended/unintended sameness is the coalescence of shared knowledge about what a college experience is supposed to look like, and for aspirational parents, what markers of distinctive sameness they should seek. For students, the combined effect once on campus is an unspoken but generally agreed upon understanding of what constitutes the ideal/normal college experience, and within that, how university policies and practices will honor those expectations. Distilled into specifics, the tours reveal three messages about food on campus and seven lessons about the environmental hidden curriculum of the prestige-oriented university.

The Hidden Curriculum of Food

The position of food, a central concern in this book, is meaningfully peripheral but not absent from the official campus tour. The messages of values and expectations embedded in the tour convey important insights about the position of food within the prestige-oriented university experience. These three lessons about food are integral to the elements of the hidden curriculum of the prestige-oriented university that follow, and they provide key explanations of what makes struggling with the cost of food strategically different in this sort of environment than in other collegiate settings.

Food Lesson #1: Food is "free" and "unlimited." Food, in terms of a student's meal plan, is a cost that can be tucked into a long list of college expenses, and often a nonnegotiable one for first-year students in a residential setting. Since high-dollar meal plans are available that require no further accounting for price, tour guides frequently used "free" as proxy for "included in" the costs. Students at PRU and Flagship can simply "swipe in" at their convenience and take whatever they want from the dining hall, be it a full meal or a cup of yogurt. At Lib Arts, even the language of the "big" or "ultimate" meal plan required of first-year students projects a sense of boundless resources, reinforced by cultural practices, such as morning stops at The Grind coffee shop. Kimmy's (Flagship) reassurance to a parent that food is taken care of reinforces the tour theme that the university will handle your child's basic needs, so long as the checks clear. Additionally, the proliferation of free food at campus celebrations and organizational events can extend the sense that food is everywhere and for the taking without additional cost.

Food Lesson #2: Food is an amusement and an inducement. Once food as a basic need has been surpassed by "unlimited" access, food is freed to serve other functions within a campus environment of amenities and opportunity. The trope of student activities planning has long been that if you want students to attend events, offer them free food. On all three tours, campus events leveraging food were integral to descriptions of campus life. At the start of the year, clubs and organizations tempt new students to their tables with free donuts, candy, and other snacks. The finals week "nacho bar" at the PRU library seeks to relieve the pressure of intensive studying. Seasonally, campus-wide carnivals, whether honoring holidays or mascots, advertise occasion-specific foods, such as Christmas cookies, corn dogs, or whatever snack can be further sensationalized by a turn in the deep fryer. In the PRU dining hall the "cookie bell" turns eating dessert into a competitive game. Even testing the limits of the "unlimited" swipes option becomes a source of campus hijinks laughed off by tour guide and participants alike. In this category, food ceases to be a matter of meeting physical needs and shifts to meeting needs of belonging and entertainment, at least for those whose basic needs are already met.

Food Lesson #3: Food is plentiful and part of a lifestyle choice. Perhaps the most consistent food-related message of the tours is that it is not merely widely available but also rich in variety in ways that dovetail with a student's culinary preferences as part of a broader expression of identity and lifestyle. Even the lowly freshman meal plan provides access to an impressive variety of dining hall food "stations," including pizza, burgers, "Mexican," salad, "homestyle," sushi, and stir-fry. Since food options alone will not satisfy the aspirations of undergraduates, food access has expanded in several waves. First, by bringing mini versions of chain retailers on campus. Perhaps not by chance, both PRU and Flagship featured fast food chicken, Tex-Mex, and "Asian" offerings. Few chain vendors manage to also signal lifestyle attainment like the upscale coffee shops, headlined by the ubiquitous campus Starbucks. These branded beverage retailers offer expensive specialty drinks that deliver the daytime drug of choice for well-funded students and those who want to fit in with them.

Second, expanded food service systems provide access to nearby off-campus eateries through student ID–based debit card arrangements, though this option was more typical at Flagship. Suddenly, the nearby "strip" of fast food, hipster dives, and boutique eateries are just a swipe away. Third, the simple campus convenience store is transformed into an upscale food market with sushi chefs, a vegan section, and locally sourced seasonal fruits and vegetables. In promotional materials, PRU describes its campus environment as a "foodie paradise." This shameless self-promotion might smack of hyperbole, but administrators understand what food represents and how to pitch it.

The Hidden Curriculum of the Prestige-Oriented University Experience

These three messages about food embedded in the prestige-oriented university tour are given form and context through seven similar lessons about what prospective students and their families should expect from the ideal/normal college experience. Students require little encouragement to imagine how the above lessons about food integrate into a larger campus culture marked by the tour lessons that follow.

Tour Lesson #1: The purpose of college is to provide you with opportunities. A prestige-oriented university is a system designed to generate multiple points of involvement and contact for undergraduate students. We have identified this way of thinking about higher education with the term *Opportunity Paradigm*. The Opportunity Paradigm prioritizes creating connections that result in experiences and relationships. Those relationships enmesh students with other privileged and knowledgeable persons and signal to future employers and graduate schools that a student is certified for future success, and indeed, is already well practiced, via undergraduate research, internships, and the like, in desirable skills and capacities.[5] As sociologists Dan Chambliss and Chris Takacs highlight, the specific journey through college of any given student is the product of a great deal of environmental serendipity: friends made, classes chosen, mentors developed, and organizations joined.[6] Many of these outcomes are the result of seemingly random encounters and spur of the moment choices that could have gone very differently. As their decade-long study demonstrates, some students' routes through college are more advantageous, in terms of the variety and significance of relationships and experiences, than others. Scholars refer to the best of these as "preferred pathways." Anyone who has been through a four-year college or university has a sense of what these pathways look like. The star student who seems to be on every committee and ends up at a prestigious graduate school; the scholar-athlete on the cover of every publication who receives special recognition from administrators for their service efforts.

Since the limits of logic, resources, and the free will of teenagers eliminate the possibility of engineering an ideal path through college for each student, the best alternative is to create an environment so dense with opportunities and employees so primed for encouraging relationships and involvement that, no matter what a student chooses, someone is there to help them actualize it.[7] All students have to do, is *choose*.

Of course, students from upper-income families with college-educated parents are often already primed to make the "right" choices, such as involvement in exclusive sororities or fraternities, social clubs, and preprofessional organizations. Their college pathways typically fall in line with their classed socialization.[8] As higher-education scholar Julie Park put it, "The inequality that stratifies students' pathways to college does not end once classes start."[9]

Lib Arts University was perhaps the most upfront about designing an environment ready to connect students with informed faculty and administrators as an institutional strategy. In our interviews, university officials noted it is a goal that each student have at least two significant adult relationships before they graduate. A campus publication, strategically stacked in high-traffic areas around campus, used infographics to illustrate the social and involvement networks of several "typical" students. The pictorial linked faculty, internships, organizational leadership, majors, graduate school entry, and other supplemental resources together as a logical outcome of enrollment and campus engagement.

Throughout the admissions talk and tour, university personnel and student tour guides emphasized the expectation of student involvement in student organizations, study abroad, professional associations, undergraduate research, and student government. The gleaming new admissions welcome center at Flagship symbolically repeated the same refrain over and over through its displays of accomplishments: *this is a place of achievement, and you will too.* It was hardly surprising that the mottos of the three schools, touted throughout the tours, were nearly interchangeable (indeed, we struggled to keep them separate in our heads), each emphasizing some minor variation on *you will change the world, beginning now.*

It was a small wonder then that Devin, who led the PRU pretour talk, pressed the point that the students who succeed at this university are those who are already accustomed not simply to academic excellence. Rather, the successful student is one who arrives already engaged in the precollegiate Opportunity Paradigm, the one run by their parents, which has prepared them to maximize the collegiate Opportunity Paradigm, the one run by administrators, faculty, and their peers. College is also a place of convergence with others similarly prepared to maximize this environment of opportunity. In fact, that desirable convergence has long been one of the primary draws and defining characteristics of elite higher education: the good schools are the ones where the good families send their children.[10]

The product of this mutual striving is a community of achievement undergirded by unspoken expectations of its ideal form and purposes. Sociologist Peter Magolda's work on the campus tour as ritual highlights the centrality of a quest for community as a tacit message of the tour.[11] The tour, Magolda argues, reveals implicit messages about "normalized" community expectations. That is, what "normal" students do. The act of normalization by definition places the noncompliant or nonparticipant student on the margins, and it privileges "certain individuals, activities, roles and relationships" that are then sustained by selective rituals that further justify the dominant culture.[12]

By contrast, Mitchell Stevens, a sociologist who studies competitive universities, emphasizes the smooth transition families make into elite higher education. This easy(er) integration happens thanks to college prep high schools and high-priced college advisors who aid families in shaping and delivering the "raw materials" (young people) elite colleges require.[13] Taken together, the hidden curriculum of college expectancy that is represented in the ritual of the college tour is less a matter of socializing those unfamiliar with it and more a matter of demonstrating that the life of status ascendency expectation that upper-income families have constructed over nearly two decades with their child will be continued in college. As campus tour expert Jeff Kallay asserted, the tour is not primarily designed for the small part of the student body that represents the expanding diversity of higher education;

it's for the wealthy and frequently White family for whom college represents a continuation of socioeconomic stability.

Of course, the path of choosing is considerably smoother for those who are able to meet food and housing needs in and through university-prescribed mechanisms, such as the "unlimited" meal plan (with plenty of "flex" cash for snacks or unscheduled meals in between) and on-campus housing. The density of opportunities demands the expedience of fast, convenient food if choice is to be fully maximized. Cross-campus trips to the food pantry between classes, off-campus employment, and long lines at the student union microwave at lunch incrementally stratify full access to choice in the Opportunity Paradigm, even among those motivated and knowledgeable enough to seize upon it.

Tour Lesson #2: College is a customized experience. Based on what we observed on the campus tours, university administrators have decided that the best way to encourage engagement is to maximize opportunities for personalization. The university has become a resource-rich sandbox. Where once students selected a major (and perhaps a minor), now double majors, multiple minors, professional certificates, research opportunities, and career preparation internships are the materials from which a unique mosaic of academic qualifications are constructed. Phrased positively, these options facilitate self-exploration, expression, and marketplace positioning.[14] Phrased less charitably, these options pander to generational narcissism and self-importance.[15] Life outside the classroom is similarly du jour: students are encouraged to pick from the vast array of student organizations or start their own, to study the way they like to: crypt quiet, low buzz, or full-on social hour. To exercise the way they want to, be that on a treadmill in front of a TV or on an indoor track with panoramic views of the city. Once again, the normality of deep involvement is reinforced through an environment of activity expectation, undergirded by assumed financial abundance where the only real choice is how and when to do [fill in the blank], and not *whether*.

For financially stable students, food is an extension of that customized experience. Dining halls are centers constructed of options through food stations available for mixing and matching. The very idea of "flex" dollars encourages students to imagine where else they might spend their food funds, whether on campus or at nearby vendors. At Flagship, multiple dining forms—buffet or a la carte in the traditional halls, grab-and-go convenience, food trucks, and national brand fast food spread strategically around campus—seek to match preferred times, locations, and types with other aspects of students' customized decisions. For students struggling to make ends meet, a secondary layer of strategy becomes necessary where "customization" means identifying the cheapest food options that are also the least inconvenient, or avoiding the temptations to engage in this world of food offerings altogether.

Tour Lesson #3: We will make sure you succeed. Nationally, students of all social, demographic, and economic backgrounds graduate at higher rates from selective institutions than from their nonselective peers. However tempting it is to assign this outcome to a difference in inputs (that is, selective institutions bring in "better" students), this finding still holds even controlling for academic ability.[16] That means, if the same student were admitted to both selective and unselective institutions, the likelihood of graduation is higher from the more selective institutions. Although this outcome is the result of multiple converging factors, among them is the extraordinary variety of academic and social support systems built into the Opportunity Paradigm university. Kimmy's introduction to the library at Flagship with support centers for writing, speaking, and STEM tutoring, among others, is exhibit A, quickly followed by specialized academic advisors, financial aid guidance, and study abroad counseling nested within some (usually STEM or business) academic units. Scholars argue that an important part of what a family pays for financially, and in terms of the effort to gain admission, is the reassurance that very few students from these institutions fail.[17] At Flagship in particular, the sheer scale of the university and vastness of resources makes connecting students who begin to flounder with supports that much more vital. Still, the strange contrast that a gathering of some of the world's most academically prepared students should require so many supports is striking.[13] No doubt, some of the supports reflect the extraordinary pressure students feel to succeed, fed by parental investments of time and money (not to mention anxiety) and by a competitive university environment where most students were at the top of their high school class. Nevertheless, the implication is clear: the stakes for parents, students, and universities are too high to chance failure, even if such a padded room is at cross purposes with larger goals of independence and autonomy at times.

But this social contract of student success assurance implicitly hinges on the degree to which families are also able to pay for food and housing at a level that allows students to access these resources. Often, off-campus employment means missing faculty office hours or tutoring center schedules when they mirror traditional 8–5 working schedules. Long commutes to affordable housing reduces the frequency of time on campus while also pressing students to cram as many classes and activities into those windows of time as possible, leaving little room for pursuing support services. And, not having money to pay for food or eating low-nutrition foods frequently results in an inability to concentrate academically, even for highly capable students. As such, it is students who are seen to have "failed" to take advantage of the services and supports offered by the university.

Tour Lesson #4: Amenities are necessities. This lesson is manifested in two intersecting forms. First, "amenities are necessities" is reflected in the unspoken message that the scale and intensity of serious effort required to succeed in an academically demanding environment should be matched by the scale and intensity of recreation and amusement the university offers. Examples abound. In the rec centers at all three universities, students can borrow camping gear to plan a wilderness adventure or sign up for a university-led trip. Flagship students can attend more than twenty nationally competitive D-1 sporting events, including nationally televised football games. At PRU, where football is also a major cultural if not athletic attraction, the center of campus is transformed into a tailgate mixer called "Lawning" for current and former students, complete with lavish culinary spreads, corporate sponsors, and plenty of alcohol. At PRU and Lib Arts, the university sponsors a bevy of annual amusements, from fall/winter carnivals to a mascot birthday party and fireworks. By highlighting these events on the tour, universities affirm that college will be fun as well as work, but they do more than that.

In an important sense, the hidden curriculum of higher education positions the university experience as a consumer good that parents and students "co-purchase" (to use Jeff Kallay's language) based on a checklist of priorities. Once in college, the work hard / play hard mentality is a primer that inculcates students to anticipate a postcollege adult lifestyle of classed work and recreational consumption.[19] Participation in university-sponsored events for alumni, like Lawning, inducts young people into a consumptive community through which important relationships are built and opportunities exchanged—at least by those who have the social and financial resources to dress, talk, and behave in prescribed ways. In many ways, the typical middle- to upper-income student has already had a lifetime of "training" for this future role through access to affluent private (or high-quality public) schools, expensive vacations, the latest personal technology devices, and nonchain, locally sourced sustainable restaurants, among many others. The tour affirms that the university will provide continuity to the project of socialization that reassures matriculates that they deserve the opportunities of employment and lifestyle that await them postgraduation.[20]

Second, anything that helps students succeed is a necessity, not a luxury. The social expectancy of the selective university as the educational capstone in a life carefully constructed to maintain or exceed the social and economic position of one's family places considerable pressure on universities to deliver on that promise.[21] That burden intersects with the thoroughly integrated work hard / play hard mentality to produce an incredible range of amenities described alternatively as "fun" and "stress relief." At one end of this spectrum is the wide range of tutoring and support services that have a clear academic focus but far exceed what students have access to at less selective universities. At the other end are events such as the various carnivals and seasonal events with no particular academic relevance but that receive loose justification under the previously described ethic that hard work demands similarly "intense" relaxation, and perhaps as well, a sense of belonging. In the center of the spectrum are the most interesting cases, exemplified by the various diversions offered by PRU's library during finals week: "therapy" pigs, "therapy" puppies, and the midnight nacho bar, among others. Tour expert Jeff Kallay clarified the justification for these campus offerings when he described the shift of focus from the lazy rivers and rock walls built for millennials, to the current focus on wellness and support services for Gen Z students. Jeff summed it up: "When you look at our society, wellness is the new luxury. . . . I think with parents we have a saying that *'services are the new amenities.'* They want to see the things that help their son or daughter stay in school, graduate from school, and go to the next level be it professional school, graduate school, or a job. Right? So, career centers, counseling centers, academic support and service centers, services are the new amenity."

Together, the two aspects of "amenities are necessities" produce a complicated but telling confluence. The prestige-oriented university must meet the expectations of the social elite for a campus experience that matches their status image. It must also produce professional outcomes in line with families' aspirations for future education, employment, and lifestyle. The shifting cultural emphasis toward wellness combines with the "services as amenities" expectations of well-heeled families to produce an environment where almost any service or event can be justified in terms of promoting the success of students. And, when lavish services that promote self-care become the new normal, they cease to be luxuries and become necessities, requiring no further justification.[22]

It is easy to picture the odd confluence of amenities and necessities experienced by students struggling to meet their basic needs. Where amenities are redefined as necessities, students may not be able to find or access the campus food pantry, but they can grab a couple slices of pizza from the student organization seeking new members, or take a quick study break for a library-sponsored massage. The lives of these students, so markedly different from their upper-income peers for whom these structures and resources are normal, expose the strange contradictions of university financial decision-making, often to their bewilderment and occasionally, vitriol. "How can my university justify X amenity when it refuses to offer Y basic resource to me?"

Tour Lesson #5: Belonging is a necessary part of the university experience. From the perspective of both scholars and higher-education practitioners, a sense of belonging in college, or a perception of connectedness to place, purpose, and persons, has become a compelling concern over the past half century.[23] Foundational theoretical work by Vincent Tinto in the 1970s focused on the ways that students integrate into a campus socially and academically as a predictor of persistence to graduation. Although scholars since then have critiqued his approach and conceptualization of "integration," the insight that the motivation to continue educationally is linked to factors that promote a sense of ownership in one's studies and membership in one's relationships has only grown in importance as the student body has become more diverse, institutions more complex, and retention and satisfaction measures more tightly tied to prestige.[24]

Belonging is also a central feature of the Opportunity Paradigm, functioning as both input (the more a student feels they belong, the more likely they are to get, and remain, involved) and output (the more a student is involved, the more of a sense of belonging they are likely to generate for themselves and others). The seeds of this circular system are generously sown throughout the tour. First-year students involved in research get connected to other students as they work on a project, to faculty who may become mentors, and to a topic that they might feel passionate enough to pursue as a major, and perhaps, as a career. Students join, or start, student organizations and invest time and energy in a shared interest that increases interpersonal knowing and bonding.[25] In the residence hall, beginning-of-the-year events (e.g., Flagship's petting zoo and movie nights) facilitate social mixing. PRU's complex residential college model capitalizes on "house" pride via symbols (crest, colors, mascot), traditions (faculty-in-residence-hosted events), and various competitions with other units for house glory and free tee-shirts. The entire catalogue of mechanisms designed to draw students into further social and organizational connection need not be listed to make the point that the mythology of a college experience is bound up in an affective sense of affiliation that is not reflected in the outputs of learning and credentialing alone. Ultimately, belonging has become a burden and resource of operating in a competitive, prestige-oriented environment where highly qualified students are a sought-after commodity—students who have been told that when you meet the right college and make that special connection, you will *feel* it.

Feeling it, for any particular student, depends on a host of factors for success. For students of modest means, belonging is particularly complex. Predictably, the inability to participate in social eating practices in the dining hall, to join peers for late-night coffee runs to that new gourmet shop, or hesitations about meeting for a study session in the student union over dinner dim students' sense of connection to persons and place. Further, decisions to splurge for the sake of social connectedness often come with the pangs of guilt and the pains of budget shortfalls for basic necessities. However, the picture is additionally complex, since students on the social and economic margins often manage to find each other, resulting in solidarity, shared resources, and an encouraging sense that they are not, in fact, *completely* alone. As well, their acute needs often motivate them to seek the support of faculty and administrators who then become important sources of affiliation, guidance, and even basic needs resources.

Tour Lesson #6: You will make a difference now. In some vague and historical moment, a college commencement speaker would gaze across the sea of eager faces and exhort the graduating class to go out into the world and "make a difference." That expectation is still present, but at a prestige-oriented university the timeline to begin the job of changing the world has been moved up from graduation to new student orientation. Throughout the tours we were pointed to examples of student involvement with real-world effects in the present tense. At Flagship students all but poured the concrete for the new student center. At Lib Arts and Flagship, students engaged in undergraduate research that contributed to new discoveries and scholarly works. At PRU, students in the business school manage millions of actual dollars in a fund that supports student scholarships. At all three universities students had started nonprofits to address social issues such as the treatment of migrant workers, women's health topics in low-income communities, and food access challenges among college students. We found it hard not to be impressed at the many ways these universities had embraced an apprenticeship model for real-world achievement. The question that persisted for us was of the opportunity cost of this level of engagement, especially for those on the social and financial margins, leading us to our final insight about the campus tour as hidden curriculum: the time required to do it all.

Tour Lesson #7: You have plenty of time to be involved in everything. Perhaps the most hidden of all the hidden lessons is the tacit expectation that students have time to be involved in everything. The tours articulated categories of involvement: of course, academics, but also student clubs and organizations, undergraduate research, fitness and athletics, internships (often unpaid), social clubs/Greek life/residential community events, in addition to a constant stream of programming and events put on by the universities that are also located in or near metropolitan areas with their own endless menu of enticements. As presented, these are categories not to choose *between* but to choose *within*. Which combination of majors? Which student organizations? Which research projects, internships, or study abroad programs? Which sport or facility? Which restaurant to try this weekend? However tempting it is to reject the notion that students are expected to be engaged on all fronts, the tour guides functioned as implicit models of this ideal student life. Kimmy (Flagship) in particular had a personal example to lend to every one of these categories, even as she joked about moments of feeling lost, switching concentrations, and challenging herself in scary ways. The unspoken refrain "I figured it out, and so will you" became the mantra of the tour. Perhaps this message was reassuring to tour participants, but scholars tell us that the pace of life to which many high-ability middle-class young people have been socialized pre-college is only different by intensity, not by structure in college.[26] Perhaps prospective students need this reassurance because they are already familiar with the high cost of the myth of endless time.

Not surprisingly, the false narrative of sufficient time for everything is least convincing for those students who are not able to functionally purchase more of it through convenience foods and near-campus housing. Nevertheless, some high-ability, struggling students managed to engage with campus on many of the fronts named. For a subset, this meant paying the price by simply ignoring eating. Others were either more fortunate or strategic, leveraging the resources of the jobs, internships, organizations, or friends to provide them food to minimize the time penalty that came with life outside the shelter of convenient food.

Summary

Fitting together the elements of the hidden curriculum named thus far, we can see that messages about the ideal/normal student experience is "hidden" only because they so saturate every element of the tour experience that naming them becomes unnecessary. And yet these lessons, in total, are received very differently based on family background and prior life experience. For the well-heeled or well socialized, these lessons are reassuring and align with lifestyles of convenience, comfort, and aspiration already in place. For those of modest means, as we will see in the next few chapters, these lessons are both enticing and alienating.

Food, as well, is deeply integrated into various aspects of the hidden curriculum. Prestige-oriented universities demonstrate the ability to surpass basic food needs with amenities that become necessities for students who are busily involved in changing the world. Students find campus belonging by eating with friends, by being noticed for eating and drinking the right things and at the right places on and off campus, and by observing that the university is sensitive to culinary preferences and dietary needs both de facto and du jour. To students and administrators who are familiar with the logic of higher education, all of these functions of food have become commonplace, exactly the definition of hiding information in plain sight. How they appear to a student who struggles to pay for food on a regular basis is a far more complicated question.

CHAPTER 3

Starving the Dream I
The Library, the Rec Center, and the Residence Hall

On a stifling hot August morning we stand outside the student union, scanning the throngs of passing students for the approach of our tour guide. Even before meeting her, Leah, a junior biochemistry premed major at Flagship, is impressive. A military brat, she grew up with six siblings and was inspired to pursue medicine after watching doctors care for her mother during her battle with cancer. Leah is one of those students who seems to pack more activities into a day than most do in several—in addition to a rigorous academic schedule, she runs training for first-year student researchers, participates in a leadership program for first-generation students, is part of an undergraduate honors program for low-income students, holds a work-study job, is a leader in a campus spirit organization, and volunteers at a hospital NICU. However, these many roles do not typically include "tour guide," and this is not an official university tour. We asked Leah, and more than 30 students like her, to take us on an "alternative" tour of *their* campus, as a student who struggles to pay for food in college.

Soon we spot her, hurrying toward us, reusable coffee cup in one hand, bags slung over both arms. Leah is nearly two hours late, though her delayed arrival was preceded by a flurry of apologetic texts and location updates. Catching her breath, she explains that the city bus app and the actual bus were apparently not in agreement about the morning schedule. Since the next bus on that route would not arrive for another hour, she elected to take an unfamiliar route, missed a transfer, and had to improvise her way to campus. Dropping her bags for a moment of recovery, Leah expresses that she is doubly embarrassed as a person who prides herself on being responsible and who has learned to build extra contingency time into her daily schedule for unexpected situations like this.

As with many in her difficult financial position, Leah's life as a student is frequently confounded by an environment that assumes access to a range of expensive conveniences: living on or near campus, owning a car or using a ride share service, and consuming boutique coffee and grab-and-go food. Particularly in a university environment that is large, highly competitive, and normatively affluent, the normal-ness of expenses is nearly invisible to those who are able to participate fully. However, the consequences of the environmental mismatch Leah experiences are various and considerable, in type and degree. Sometimes, it means foregoing the coffee she did not have time to make or begging out of lunch with a classmate who suggests they stop by a new gourmet food truck. Other times, the three-bus trip from her affordable shared apartment across town becomes a two-hour series of frustrations before her school day has begun:

> I have an 8 a.m. class this semester. So I will most likely try to leave 6:45 a.m. just so I can get there on time. I try to give myself ... for the first week, an hour and thirty minutes just so I can get used to the walk and, like, get used to the bus route.
>
> —*How long should the bus ride take? Like on a good day?*
>
> 20 minutes.
>
> —*How often do you have good days?*
>
> Never.

The inconvenience of the bus and housing far from campus are necessary compromises that, on a very minimal level, are working: despite the extra time required, the bus *usually* satisfies Leah's needs for transportation (it is free with her student ID) and her apartment *mostly* meets her basic needs for shelter (though safety, walkable access to groceries, and travel at odd hours are ongoing concerns for her). A third compromise, and one invisible that morning save for her travel mug of instant coffee, is food. In the following tour narratives that span the eight locations we also visited on the official campus tour, we explore how students experience the opportunities and barriers of physical, social, and organizational spaces as they attempt to maximize their university experience and also meet their basic food needs.

The Library

Of all the virtues of a large campus, a major challenge for most students is sorting through the overwhelming variety of possibilities to find spaces that are their own. We weave our way through the steady stream of students and follow Leah (Flagship) up the hill toward the center of campus. As we walk, Leah describes her dislike of Flagship's central library ("the lights are a weird shade of yellow which makes me feel anxious") and her fondness for a sciences library hidden away in the rabbit warren of rooms and levels of Main Hall. One of the 17 campus libraries Kimmy mentioned on the official tour, Leah is drawn to this one for its combination of aesthetics and college life "hacks." "It's an underappreciated spot," Leah enthuses. "They left a lot of the old ceiling art and architecture in it, so it's really nice." The structure is indeed impressive, part New York City public library, part Hogwarts Great Hall; the soaring ceiling, ornately painted timbers, large windows, and glowing chandeliers seem to instill the activities of huddled students with a sense of gravity. Aesthetics are not Leah's only motivation, however:

> They have a textbook scanner, which comes in handy, so you don't have to buy your textbooks. You can rent it for, like, an hour here and then scan the pages you need.
>
> —*Do you do that a lot?*
>
> I do. It's how I didn't have to buy a textbook my freshman year.
>
> —*Okay. So you've done that? Like every chapter?*
>
> Yeah. Scanned them, make a PDF, and then good to go.

Leah's misappropriation of the textbook scanner not only illustrates her creative mindset but also highlights the intersection of spaces and learning resources that make libraries so important to many of our alternative tour guides.

Despite Leah's dismissal of the central library as "prison-like," at Flagship University and Private Research University (PRU), the geographic centrality of these structures makes them a prominent part of campus life and the starting place for many student tours; at Lib Arts University, it was a frequent stop as well. Based on our conversations with students, campus efforts at rebranding the library as something other than books, nerds, and "shushing" have succeeded in transforming it into a space of eclectic if not contradictory uses. Within the Opportunity Paradigm, university spaces and resources like the library are part of a tacit campus-wide commitment to student success that obscures to irrelevance the line between preference and necessity. Janis, a library administrator at PRU, described this intentional shift, and the spaces, activities, and mindset that have resulted:

> So, we had a major renovation that totally revamped this whole space. Essentially, our library has kind of become the student center, student union.... We want students to create the spaces and activities that they want. We want this to be what they want it to be. We see ourselves as kind of facilitators of that. When the students have needs of any kind, we want to be a part of that. For example, finals week—all the stress of that, we have a series of things we have going on that try to support students' psychological health as well—their wellness. We'll have therapy dogs and we'll have meditation going on, and we'll have ways for them to play games or stop working for a while to let go.

Under the banner of "wellness," the seemingly superfluous becomes a justifiable service in an environment of wealth and academic expectations. As our unofficial tour guides direct us around the library, they identify many of its more typical roles: a social hub for chance meetings and purposeful group study sessions, a place to relax away from others, a location where serious studying gets done, and a collecting point for resources that include technology, academic support, and even food. William (Lib Arts) introduces us to how he perceives library use and purpose, explaining: "This over here is the library. It's one of the most popular spots on campus. Your friends are going to be in here. This is where everyone would be doing homework, procrastinating homework, and stuff."

Expanding on the centrality and multifunctionality of the library, Corbett (PRU) lends the credibility of student perspective to Janis's assertions: "This is Franklin Library. This is kind of a central hub for most students, whether it's for studying or hanging out. . . . So, this is kind of where I come to meet for group projects. I come here to go study." William and Corbett hint at the often-challenging intersection of social and academic imperatives for which the library offers both resources and temptations. Phillip (Flagship) fills us in on his shift away from regular library use: "A reason I avoid this place is because there's different levels to the space. The 5th floor is like a party. It's social hour. It's really fun. So, that's why I can't come here, 'cause I only come here when I don't have anything to do."

As Phillip's account illustrates, the theme of customizing the college experience Kimmy described in the official tour is present in the library use decisions of our unofficial tour guides as well. Whether preferring complete silence for studying ("I don't like it quiet, but to study I need it quiet"—Lucas, PRU) or a little noisy ("I can't study in complete silence, I don't know why, it just freaks me out"—Jill, PRU), preferring to study with friends ("So usually I just go with people to study and talk"—Gina, Flagship) or alone ("I get easily distracted"—DeShauna, Flagship), students developed a strategy for study spaces, each with their own internal logic.

Many students who are at the financial margins quickly learn that in a campus of abundance there are free or low-cost workarounds to many of the requirements of academic life. The library is an important gathering point for these resources, as Leah's example of the document scanner illustrates. Printers (though only Lib Arts had printing included in campus fees) and computers for in-house use or for loan can bridge gaps of technology access invisible to most students. For DeShauna (Flagship), this was a draw, in addition to a study space: "I did most of my studying here last year because it's the central area for students to study. I did some printing in here last year because I didn't always have a printer, and they have printing attached to your Campus Cash that you get your freshman year." Similarly, access to computers and technology support drew Camila (Lib Arts): "This is one of my favorite places to go on campus just because it's a great place to study, it's quiet. There's a lot of computers and electronics and a lot of help." Some students, like Kelsy (Lib Arts), who own a computer but cannot afford the latest and slimmest model, find the difficulty of lugging an aging cinder block of a laptop ("It is ridiculously huge . . . I hate taking it around") makes the convenience of library computers important to her daily routine.

The library is in some ways one of the most class-neutral spaces on campus because of its multifunctionality, broad appeal, and few cost-incurring services. Libraries have been designed and redesigned to offer resources that range from traditional stacks and study carrels to computers and tech-imbued "smart" learning spaces available to anyone with a student ID. Further, the library is not only a space intended to meet a wide range of student needs but also learning preferences. These ends are pursued through "learning labs" with moveable tables, white boards, and group collaboration spaces designed to be molded into the shape of the needs of students, as Janis, the library administrator, explained:

> [Students] are pretty proactive in telling us if our spaces are not working for them, or what we also do is we take pictures. We don't reset any of the furniture or the spaces. If they pull the equipment somewhere and stick it in a corner, we go take a picture of that and try to figure out, "Okay, they're not liking how this is set up, maybe they don't need the equipment or maybe they don't . . ." They'll drag furniture all over the place. So, we take pictures of that. We're not trying to correct anything. *There's nothing to correct.* We're trying to learn what kind of spaces they're building for themselves with what we have. Then provide more of that.

The mindset that the student determines what constitutes proper use of the library is miles away from traditional expectations of how library resources should be used, but one that centers student agency and control endemic to the Opportunity Paradigm. For those students who feel estranged by the economic and cultural expectations of the ideal/typical student experience, the library offers them the potential to find or make their own comfortable niche. Camila (Lib Arts) reflects: "They have a study area way in the back, so it's kind of secluded.... I just work better when I study by myself and things like that, or when I'm just wanting to read. It's a good place to kind of isolate all the class stuff. So, *when I'm here, I don't feel like I'm in school, really.*" For some students like Camila, relief from the pressures of student life is afforded by the aesthetics and human-scale spaces a student can, temporarily at least, claim as their own.

The Library and Food

Despite these virtues, the presence of food in a space once so vigorously protected from it both reinforces and undermines the library as a broadly welcoming space. Some libraries promote welcoming through the emerging policy shift that makes bringing food into the building and consuming it acceptable, a radical departure from traditional expectations focused on book preservation still maintained in many other libraries. Students living off campus and those who cannot afford nearby convenience options find that packing meals and eating while working increases both flexibility and expedience. Anali (Flagship) brings lunch to campus and eats while she prepares for her afternoon classes. Gavin (Flagship) finds that working and eating harnesses both time and energy: "So after class I'll go to the [nearby campus stores], pick something up, come here, and then I'll eat it, do my work, I'm still energized, still have 'brain juice,' and I'm like ... 'I have brain juice, I'm going to maximize the time.'" The library is often an ideal space for students to capitalize on the resources of time and energy.

The shift toward food as an acceptable feature of the library experience means that libraries increasingly not only welcome food but also offer it. Some students, like Miranda (Flagship), use the vending machines as a meal replacement during long study sessions. At Lib Arts, Camila connects librarians' practice of setting out a bowl of candy or grab-and-go snacks to her positive feelings about the place: "They do put free snacks out sometimes, which is really helpful. But, yeah, it's a good space." Librarians may not realize how some students functionally rely on the caloric boost of these snacks to get through an afternoon study session while symbolically internalizing it as a sign of welcoming.

At PRU, the confluence of a posture of student engagement and an openness to food in the library resulted in library administrators creating a campus food pantry in a space previously used as a staff break room. The geographic centrality of Franklin Library (PRU) to campus made the pantry more convenient to most students compared to the larger and more elaborate food pantry space located in an administrative building on the edge of campus at Flagship. PRU's pantry location had the additional benefit of projecting the library as a place sensitive and responsive to the needs of marginalized students. Following their campus tour, Alec[1] (PRU), a first-year student, commented about their shifting view of the library because of their awareness of the food pantry:

> Yeah, I mean, the only thing that's really happened is just, like, the library has become a lot more important to me.
>
> —*What do you mean, the library's become a lot more important?*
>
> Well, I mean, I guess for, in terms of food, . . . it's not some place where I have direct access to meals and stuff, but I do understand that now the food pantry is located in the library. And so that was kind of like, "Oh, cool! When I need help, I know where to go." So, it was just kind of nice to know that.

The sense of comfort and belonging resulting from the flexibility and resources (including food) at the library is also part of Chelsea's (PRU) experience. Chelsea, a single mother, found that the microwave located near the food pantry offers her the flexibility to heat up her packed lunch and continue working in a nearby study room in the gaps between classes while her son stays with a relative.

Despite these positive messages and perceptions, the location of the food pantry and the policies related to access frustrate some students.

Vera (PRU) meets up with us for the tour carrying a bag of food she just picked up at the campus food pantry. Despite her appreciation of it, she is critical of the difficulty she and her friends had in finding it, as well as the consistency of stocking.

> Well first of all, nobody knows about the food pantry and then the location of it really doesn't help it. But I'll show you where it is. [*We turn a corner and head down a narrow hallway.*] So honestly, it's really hidden. I had a hard time finding it [*laughs*] even though the librarian navigated me to get there.
>
> —*She told you how? They didn't walk you over?*
>
> Oh, they walked me over. But again, I usually don't come in since most of the food runs out, but I was fortunate to go today, but yeah. When my friends go, they usually have a hard time finding it too.

Lucas (PRU), tried and failed to locate the food pantry on his own, with great frustration:

> I'd never heard of it until I was looking for—I even googled "food assistance at PRU," all this stuff, and I could find nothing. . . . And I googled "PRU food pantry," and I could never find anything about it. Yeah, and then I saw we were doing fundraisers for it, and I'm like, "Where the fuck is the food pantry?" And I don't want to walk up to the front desk and be like, "Hey, where's the food pantry?" in front of everyone. So, I just gave up on it.

Ironically, the motivations of student privacy that informed the administrator's decision to keep signage to a minimum had the unintended effect of inhibiting some students from getting the help intended for them.

Another effect of the shift toward student engagement is one that also carries the mark of university prestige and aspiration: the integration of a coffee shop into the library. Both Flagship and PRU had upscale chain coffee shops embedded within them. The Flagship coffee shop, lacking the visual impact and name recognition of the vender at PRU, received no mention among students, likely in part because of the mini-mall of food and beverage options directly across the street that *also* included a Starbucks. The Starbucks in the PRU library, however, had become a social hub and cultural fixture in the routines of many students. Alternative tour guides struggled with the ever-present temptation of taking a budget hit to fulfill caffeine needs or join friends in the excitement of buying a "special" drink. Our tour meeting with Carli began near PRU's Starbucks, and an explanation for the impressive-looking beverage in her hand:

> I actually—it's been a while since I've had Starbucks. And my friend Kate, she was like, "You *really* need to try this." And she was like, "You *got* to get the big one." And it's kind of difficult because you know, I don't really spend money on this. But I was like, "Oh, I'll give it a shot." You know, kind of treat myself. . . . Oh, my gosh, this thing is sweet. It's good. It's like that vanilla mocha thing.

Where lifestyle food consumption meets high-status higher education, the effect is constant pressure to *want* to join in, as Carli's splurge illustrates. Chelsea (PRU), who previously enthused about the library food pantry, pays the high price of exclusion for her inability to participate in this melding of social and academic life around food: "I miss out on a lot of studying opportunities with my friends. I've struggled, a lot of meetings, like, 'Hey, let's meet up at Starbucks,' and I can't afford it. . . . I can't afford any food, everyone is eating, and I can't afford food. So, I struggled feeling like I don't belong here."

The push and pull between knowing and honoring one's food budget and wanting to participate in the thrill of social rituals based on food was a common refrain and an emotional drain, regardless of which way students choose. As the authors of *Scarcity: Why Having Too Little Means So Much* emphasize, the psychological act of going without necessities—real or socially constructed—creates obsessive thinking about whatever thing is unattainable.[2] The process of libraries redefining their missions to align with students' preferences for work and social interaction comes with potential costs that are often hidden. The introduction of lifestyle food and beverages in these spaces can presume a standard of affluence that excludes students from low-income families. Further, these changes risk alienating some students from spaces that might otherwise facilitate belonging.

The Rec Center

Far more than the library, the rec center was a polarizing space for our alternative student guides. As a first-year student, Leah (Flagship) lived across the walk from the gym, "So I went to Arnold Gym a lot." Now that she lives off campus, her routine is different: "For the gym, I have one at my apartment, so I don't usually use the one here, even it though it is nice. . . . But it's just inconvenient because I don't want to be sweaty when I get on the bus." "Nice," as Leah phrased it, may be an understatement. The rec center's scale and variety of accoutrements make an immediate impression, favorable or not. Carli (PRU) recalls her initial impression of her rec center: "So, okay, so think of 24-Hour Fitness, but on steroids. And I'm like, wow, is this real?" Chelsea (PRU) offers a more critical view of the same space:

> Now you're going to see our tanning beds. So, this is it. A lot of people like to come out, lay back, get tanned. That's not a swimming pool, it's just a place where you can wet your skin if you're getting a little too hot. This is literally a tanning place. So, it was a lot of money just to get that done. If they can get that done I'm pretty sure they can get other things done to the campus.

Campus rec facilities play an important role in reinforcing expectations of the ideal/normal, including that students will customize their experience through recreational activities, that health and wellness (not to mention the cultivation and display of an attractive physique) will be priorities, and that physical fitness activities are pursued seriously as well as socially. This integration of social and physical activity imbues the rec center with energy and anxiety. Cadence (Lib Arts) articulates this cultural tension as we approach Memorial Gym: "You kind of feel the need to keep up, you know? Because everybody is so athletic and everything."

For other students the motivation to exercise comes from those in their social circle, as Paloma (Lib Arts) notes that her joining stemmed from her sister, also a student: "My sister's kind of forcing me now to go, because she does the cycling class, and she's like, 'Come join me.'

I'm like, 'Okay.' . . . I think it's, like, 30 dollars each semester, but if you don't have the pass, you could just pay like three dollars or something."

Yet despite access to some impressive facilities and baked-in campus expectations of physical fitness, about one-third of our alternative student guides reported that they do not use the rec center on campus, and for at least one of three reasons: the busyness of the facility, the busyness of their life, and a sense that they do not belong there. Camila's recital of reasons not to use the fitness facilities (small/crowded/time) summarizes the responses of others who pointed to a lack of space in their schedule ("That's the gym. I've actually never been to it. I've never had time"—Beth, Lib Arts), and capacity ("But it's just always so busy. There's just so many people and if you have to use something you have to wait pretty long"—Miranda, Flagship).

An additional element not widely shared but importantly telling, is the sense a few students have that they do not belong in this space, even if it holds some interest to them. When we ask DeShauna (Flagship) if there are spots on campus that do not feel comfortable to her, she reflects: "Hmm. I guess the gym. I've never been in the gym. Yeah. I think there are people that go to the gym every day, it's their life. I think I would just feel like an outsider in there." Standing outside the rec center at PRU, Lucas explains why he has never used the rec center:

> I've been told that one of them has a rock-climbing wall and all sorts of stuff. But honestly, it feels weird, and it's probably in my head, but I do feel out of place at times in here. So, it's just really weird walking into a new place on my own just to see what it is. And everybody's looking at me, like, "Who is this kid? Why is he disheveled?" And fucking I don't even know. I don't fit the part. So, I honestly just try to lay really low here. I'm not shy by any means, I still talk to people in my classes, and I'm usually the one that starts conversations and stuff. But campus wise I try to lay pretty low, which is counterproductive with my van and how I look, I guess.

The core of Lucas's discomfort is his general unease with how the persona he's cultivated—long hair, retro van, punk rocker meets vagabond clothing style—meshes with what he perceives to be the dominant mode of student self-presentation. He senses how his reluctance to even *enter* a space where he feels out of place is his own doing, part of his personal negotiation with the ideal/normal student experience, but that his choices also mean he may be missing out on something desirable. Alec (PRU), too, feels the rub of their identity and the impressive facilities, describing it in terms of their low-income background as the child of east Asian immigrants: "I mean, being here makes me just feel so weird. I'm so privileged and it's so different from what I'm used to." Yet unlike Lucas, Alec embraces the opportunity to engage in athletic activities for enjoyment and relaxation: "So, this is where I work out a lot. I love to do those things where you do with the abs. And then I also like to row. Rowing is really fun. . . . Obviously, we have our rock climbing, and all that type of stuff. So, quite fun, quite fun. I love coming here. It's like my escape." The comparison of experiences between Lucas and Alec highlights how differently two students who are both apparently outsiders to campus culture and normative economics respond, reflecting the complications that come with assuming how economically struggling students will experience and navigate the same environment.

Many of our alternative tour guides, like Alec, live with the ongoing tension between the draw of attractive amenities, the demands of hectic schedules made more hectic by outside employment, and the time and physical cost of getting enough to eat. Alejandra (Lib Arts), views exercise as part of an attainable "healthy lifestyle," particularly when the quantity and quality of food is lacking: "I guess regarding the healthy lifestyle, you know, it's hard to eat healthy sometimes because of the food options [I have]. . . . But if you're here to stay active and healthy when you have a facility that's been [newly renovated], you can't eat healthy, but you can still stay healthy with an active lifestyle."

Carli (PRU) finds that exercise, even though inconvenient, helps her to appreciate her college experience and reduce the stresses related to food and time that are with her constantly:

—*So, do you work out in the gym?*

I try to. I've been making a new regimen for myself. I focus at like six o'clock in the morning, because that's all the time I really have. Or sometimes I go running out here during the afternoons, because now that I have one job, I can do that. And it's so nice actually having time. You know, we're constantly worried about when our next meal is happening or this issue or that, and yet we never take the time to actually appreciate the little things. So, I found that, and I love it.

—So, you feel like you have space to make that part of your life?

Yes. Because all work and no play makes Carli a dull girl.

In contrast to Alejandra and Carli, whose rec center experiences helped them cope with food insecurity, Phillip's (Flagship) love of basketball and its role in managing the stress of a rigorous premed program came into conflict with his struggle to get enough to eat. His frequent pick-up games with friends, combined with a high metabolism and infrequent meals led him to drop weight dangerously quickly.

> I got the smallest I have ever been. So, I came into college at 185 pounds, I got down to 170, so, I was very concerned. I was like, "Yeah, that's not okay." I started to just make efforts to try and plan for food. And I told myself, "I have to spend more money on food just to be able to live the lifestyle I live." Which means, you know, I have to eat a certain amount of calories a day or I will just get very skinny. That's my stress relief, playing basketball. That's how I get through the tough course load, being super busy. Playing basketball allows me to calm down, but when I'm not eating well, I literally can't play as much because I'll be burning too many calories.

Phillip's realization that the student "lifestyle" he felt he needed was an impossible reality if he could not consume enough calories to sustain himself, a consideration foreign to most of his peers. Ironically, the activity that was his stress relief from the rigors of the premed track became its own source of stress. His efforts to embrace the exercise aspect of the Good Student led to unexpected consequences due to the implicit expectation that students will have plenty to eat. For our student participants, the physical and psychological roles of exercise as a habit of life and a campus lifestyle relate to food in complicated ways that reveal the contradictions and compromises that come with the struggle to afford food.

The Rec Center and Food

In some sense, universities do understand that constructing buildings that encourage intense physical activity also require of students the fuel to maintain this active lifestyle. Of course, the same press of peer awareness and market sensitivity that made climbing walls and lazy rivers into symbols of collegiate prestige have made sports drink vending machines passé, in favor of more elaborate—and expensive—offerings. At PRU, a smoothie shop installed when the new rec center initially opened was recently replaced by the ever-popular Starbucks, which received little mention (besides occasional use) from our alternative tour guides. At Flagship, Miranda is a willing commentator as she leads us into Albert Gymnasium. Rather than heading back through the atrium to the pools, elevated track, or climbing wall, she directs our attention to the food available just inside:

> So, this is Albert. They have a place in there ... I think it's open. We can actually probably go inside. But there's a place in there, that they sell healthy food. Like it's really ... almond butter, protein shakes, everything like that. It's just really expensive. It's not worth the money. My first time at Flagship, I tried it. And it was good, and it's definitely something that I'd want more for myself. But it's just really overpriced.
>
> *—So, when you're in some place like that and you're like, "Hey, what a great option if you have the money," how does that influence the way you think about campus or the opportunities that are here?*
>
> It just reminds me that it's a wealthy place, an elite place and that my version of expensive is their version of affordable. So, it's not a really big place for me. So, yeah, right here. So, you order right there, the menu is just ...
>
> *—You know you're in trouble in any place that doesn't have the prices written down.*
>
> Yeah, I hate that. If I go somewhere and there's no price tag, I'm like, "This is already too much." But it's great. I came here like twice, it was really good. They have things that I probably wouldn't buy for myself.

Like, I wouldn't buy an Ahi bowl for myself, or, like, a protein powder, just because I don't think I would that often. But, like, to be able to come here, it would be nice but it's definitely not in my price range. And their sizing you can see is a regular looks like a small some place, and a large probably looks like, not that large.

Embedded in Miranda's commentary, beyond her compelling reasons why she should not indulge in these options, is a desire to participate in the full "Good Student" experience, which on this campus includes expensive smoothies in the rec center. She recalls, with some relish, her first experience at Flagship, trying out and trying on what students here do by participating in their rituals of upper-middle-class consumption. The self-rebuttal to each of Miranda's declarations that such amenities are not for her is her equally emphatic, if not begrudging acknowledgement "... and it was good." Many food-insecure students are high achievers who come to a competitive university because they want to be part of an institution with the resources to facilitate their pursuit of personal and professional aspirations. What they find is that the unspoken ideal of the Good Student experience assumes a level of affluence that excludes them, or worse still, that is attractive but forbidden fruit, financially speaking: pleasing to the eye and good for a sense of inclusion. The burden of choices—belonging versus financial sustainability—is an invisible cost that food-insecure students must decide how to navigate over and over again. It is particularly difficult when it shows up in unexpected places, such as the campus rec center.

The Residence Hall

Leah is among the many students at Flagship who chose to live on campus for their first year. She and several thousand others were housed in Jefferson Center, the massive residence hall that includes, among its services, two dining halls (one buffet, one a la carte), a fast-food restaurant, a Starbucks, a convenience store, a tutoring center, and a lounge specifically for Black students. Of her experience, Leah reflects: "Dorm living was cute for my first year, but now that I've had my own room and my own bathroom, I can't go back." Although "cute" may be dismissive, it hints at the cloistered campus experience epitomized by the residence hall. Scholars have applied the sociological concept of the "total institution" originally developed to describe mental health facilities to the college dormitory as a place of constant care and, in particular, monitoring.[3] Although "monitoring" may sound nefarious, first- to second-year student retention is an issue of intensive focus and organizational investment, as well as a mark of institutional prestige and a rankings metric.[4] As such, universities make considerable investments in keeping tabs on first-year students, from the constant positive energy of student residence assistants (RAs) to far less visible student success predictive analytics software employed on an increasing number of campuses. The residence hall is a key component in the needed flow of information about students' adaptation to the ideal/normal campus experience.

Within American higher education the residential experience also represents a kind of gold standard of collegiate idealism and the starting point for life as a college student preferred by parents and administrators alike. The residence hall, in combination with the dining hall (discussed in chapter 4), offers first-year students a full measure of *total support*—the security and convenience of constant campus presence, perpetual student activities programming, and immersion in the student social scene. That students who live on campus are more likely to remain at college past their first year is not lost on administrators as well.[5] Carli (PRU), a first-generation college student, notes the importance of easing her parents' worries with the advantages of location. Recreating the scene, she recalls,

> And I have, I actually took a video of me finding the dorm, climbing up the stairs, and then finding the actual room. I was on live with my friends. And I was like, "Guys, I can't believe it. I have my own place!" Initially, I thought I was going to share it with someone, but it was like my own little sanctuary. And when my parents found out, they were like, "This is going to be great for you because you don't have to worry about making it home. You can save on gas. You can be in the area. Everything's going to be fine."

Many of our food-insecure tour guides had elected to (those at Flagship), or were required to (at Lib Arts and PRU), stay on campus as first-year students, with exceptions for those who lived with a parent or guardian nearby. The undeniable utility of combined *room and board* represents a time of relative abundance even as our students learn how to manage high academic expectations, a new social system, a new city, and rooming with a nonfamily member. In sum, Carli's emphasis that the accumulation of services and amenities results in a worry-free experience was a theme widely echoed, particularly in comparison to the struggle that followed once first-year-only funding dried up.[6] Alejandra (Lib Arts) recalls with fondness her first-year residential experience as she shows us the living space where her collegiate experience began. Over the drone of leaf blowers, she explains,

> Wingert Hall was my dorm room freshman year. I loved it. It kind of brings back memories of like, I didn't have a worry in the world and my scholarship was a full-ride scholarship. And like I told you about it, the meal plan was, like, a thousand something [dollars]. And I didn't worry about food. It didn't even cross your mind. You buy something and . . . you'd have friends who'd forget their ID and you'd get them something too. . . . So it was like things like that. And then now you're like, it's a whole different story from freshman year.

Immersion in the collegiate "total institution" of room and board often had a kind of anesthetic effect on students' sense of price, as the actual spending happened in large chunks when the tuition bill was due but was otherwise invisible on a day-to-day basis. Additional advantages of living on campus as a first-year student included the ready-made opportunities for social engagement with hordes of similarly eager-to-connect peers propelled into interaction by a residence life staff made up of both students and professionals. As we stroll with Brooke (Lib Arts) down the hall toward her advisor's office, talk of her experience shifts to how her life has changed now that she lives off campus. Brooke likes having her own space—an apartment not too far from campus—and the advantages of affordability are undeniable. However, she says,

> Living off campus definitely makes me feel disconnected. Because... it's just when you live on campus you're just *inherently present,* you know, you live here. And you kind of, I feel, are more connected with what's going on. Because usually, typically, living on campus means you're living in a dorm setting, or even if you're living in the apartments, you're very close to other people. And there's a lot of postings about what's going on, emails from your RA, things like that, versus living off campus, you don't really have the same level of connection to campus events.

Brooke identifies, with her phrase "inherently present," the unavoidable virtue of proximity. Easier access to classes, to friends, to activities, and to a sense of being part of campus. However, given the dramatically higher cost of living on campus, only a few of our alternative tour guides elected to remain in a residence hall past their first year without an RA position. Those who stayed on engaged in a challenging cost-benefit calculation, weighing increased housing cost against the "costs" of time and inconvenience of living in an off-campus apartment.

Despite manifold conveniences, living on campus the first year of college included the unexpected lesson of economic stratification, in the form of different accommodations for different income brackets. Campus housing, as most parents of a prospective student can attest, is its own complicated menagerie of options and tiered costs: single rooms, suite-style rooms, and traditional rooms; hallway bathrooms or shared suite bathrooms; themed housing, apartment-style housing, and residential colleges with live-in faculty are among the most obvious derivations. These "options," not all available to everyone, are compounded by different price levels sometimes attached to newer or more conveniently located buildings which unintentionally can result in campus housing that is separated by race and social class.[7] Alfredo (Lib Arts), a senior who claimed that he "lived in every community space, except one" in his four years in on-campus housing, including two as an RA, gives us the lowdown on this phenomenon as we tour what was his first-year hall:

> So, Wingert is the cheapest, cheapest building you can have as a freshman. All freshman rooms look like prison cells. They're cold. They got

bricks. . . . So, you're either poor, or you're the last person to register for housing at orientation. That's who lives in Wingert. Harlow Hall . . . those are for students that can actually afford the price. And that's actually right across the street from the student center. And it's like two person, two people per room. The room is bigger, and you have a bathroom, which is also bigger. In Wingert, four people share a bathroom. So, I call, it's like with the "bougie kids," I call them the rich kids kind of like live in Harlow, all at the top of the hill. So, its location is more convenient, costs more money. Generally, just has the stereotypical class difference.

When we ask what he makes of that separation, Alfredo reflects, "At freshman year you just kind of notice it. Everyone notices it. It doesn't go unnoticed, I guess. Yeah, everyone just kind of doesn't talk about it. It's kind of like a joke and then no one really looks deeper into it. But it's just funny. Because poor kids are literally at the bottom of the hill, away from most of campus. Whereas the rich kids are conveniently centered."

Although Alfredo jokes that despite this unintended segregation "everyone comes to Wingert to have a fun time . . . with the poor kids," the daily effects of inconveniently placed housing and lesser-quality rooms as the collecting point for many low-income students seems at odds with the social justice mission and messaging of the university. Despite this, Ariel (Lib Arts), who had been an RA, advocated for the university not to bulldoze the aging residence halls that Alfredo described as "stratified" and the rooms as "prison cells":

I went and asked the Dean of Residence Life, I said, "I really appreciate the fact that The Lofts are going to add a new type of living for upperclassmen, but what I want to ask you is what happens to North and Wingert?" She was like, "What do you mean?" I said, "Well, if there is no North and there is no Wingert you're removing the most affordable housing on campus." The same way that that hurts public property, you don't have affordable housing you don't end up having Black and Brown people living there because they're systematically marginalized, if you remove that affordable housing from campus the freshmen that you get [on campus] are predominantly White. The freshmen that you get are predominantly well-off. So, if you're a

Starving the Dream I   95

university focused on diversity and inclusion and you're focused on social justice and teaching people how to fight for a more just world, then how can you marginalize your students by not having affordable housing?

Alfredo's and Ariel's perspectives highlight the power of housing functionally and symbolically. Simultaneously, lower-cost campus housing can be a source of marginalization *and* a source of solidarity; a challenging reality for campus planners, administrators, and students.[8]

Among those who chose to remain in on-campus housing after their first year, cost continued to be a driver in housing selection. Many students opted for the least expensive of the on-campus options, swallowing several thousand extra dollars in housing cost for the opportunity of continued immersion in campus life, or at least to avoid the inconvenience of a daily commute. Walking along the cut stone residence hall where Valeria (Lib Arts) lives, we ask whether she likes living on campus, and why. "I do. I think it outweighs ... I mean, considering that I did live 45 minutes to an hour away beforehand, it obviously beats it. But I think living on campus makes it a lot easier for me emotionally, mentally, like, if an emergency happens, then I have immediate resources that I otherwise wouldn't have had if I lived off campus, even if it was in an apartment. And I hate commuting [*laughs*]." The advantages of staying within the campus services "bubble," or the collection of elective expenses—chiefly a full meal plan and on-campus housing—that provide for basic student needs on campus, was an attractive investment for some students, but few could stomach the extra debt. Although none of the math we saw bore this out, several participants who lived on campus past their first year asserted that it was actually less expensive, or that because of the aid and scholarships they receive, this choice smoothed the logistics of campus life and financial navigation.

Whether intended or not, financial aid and housing function in an integrated system that subtly works to encourage students to stay on campus, even for students who may be struggling financially. Vera (PRU), who lives in a themed hall, links her decision to live on campus to advantages of price and convenience, adding considerations of food access to the equation:

Well, it was many things. One, it's cheaper to live here and it's more convenient. I was able to save myself $10,000 because, one, I don't have to have a meal plan because I have the kitchen. Two, it's $2,000 . . . about $2,000 cheaper than . . . to live here than the residential complex on campus. The other thing, too, is that I knew a few people that were living here, and they told me that they had a great experience living here and that since everybody living here is very involved in campus that they usually bring food here, so it's like . . . it was kind of a good thing for me because it helped me in two ways. One, with tuition, and with my food situation.

The ability to make her own food and take advantage of found food that residents gathered from on-campus events and brought back to Vera's building was a nontypical strategic advantage. Universities' expectation that room and board go hand in hand, outside of those living in more expensive on-campus apartment-style housing, meant that students either took on the additional financial burden of a meal plan or were forced to navigate a housing system not designed for students providing their own meals. Camila (Lib Arts) recalls how minimal kitchen facilities her sophomore year made it difficult for her to feed herself, when she had only a mini-fridge in her room and a shared fridge in the student lounge. On our tour with Valeria (Lib Arts), she leads us along the 10-minute walk between her low-price residence hall and the on-campus apartment where a close friend generously shares her kitchen, an arrangement of opportunity and inconvenience:

My dorm doesn't have a kitchen. It is so stupid. It's ridiculous. I pay so much for that dorm and they don't have a kitchen. My friend has an apartment and she has a kitchen, and so we both manage to pool $50 every two to three weeks and we'll cook together. . . . So the biggest downside I think is that I can pack my food for the day before, sure, but I can't get breakfast because I try to eat, like, yogurt or, like, some fruits, but I don't have a fridge in my dorm. And so my friend can't meet me in the morning so, like, if I'm going to eat my groceries, which I should be, I'd usually be skipping breakfast because we don't have time during the day to go and get it. So it's a lot of, like, missed conflicting schedules.

The lack of facilities in some buildings was further complicated by residence hall policies and practices that assumed both a low-level of student responsibility and that residents' in-building food was a luxury, not a necessity. Tia (PRU) expressed her frustration that even though there is a kitchen in her residence hall, the student staff told her residents are not allowed to use it because of sanitation concerns. Instead, the student staff use it for storage. "Everything in there works, we just don't have access to it, which doesn't make sense."

Unlike spaces such as the library and the rec center, which are ostensibly for all students, the residence hall can be one of the least egalitarian spaces on campus. Not surprisingly, it is one that most portrays, or perhaps betrays, assumptions about the ideal student experience of *total support*, and the high cost associated with it. Scholars have found—and administrators are happy to repeat—that residential housing increases students' experiences of belonging, academic success, and persistence to graduation, at least in aggregate.[9] Access to food is an unspoken part of this equation, as residential living structures assume that students either remain in the culinary care of the institution, pay the extra money for apartment-style facilities with full kitchens, or simply eat out frequently. Students on the financial margins are forced to decide which parts of the ideal/normal they can afford, often without understanding the full extent of impending inconveniences, such as a lack of food preparation facilities, or kitchen facilities that are closed to them.

CHAPTER 4

Starving the Dream II

The Student Union, the Dining Hall, and the Convenience Store

The Student Union

The student union, otherwise known as the student center, is the physical manifestation of the Opportunity Paradigm campus. Student services offices, flexible meeting rooms, student government chambers, open seating areas, convenience stores, the post office, and a variety of food vendors are among the many features that make up these hubs of student life. A few such structures still shelter movie theaters, barber shops, and bowling alleys; the campus "lazy rivers" of earlier times.[1] More contemporary innovations include sleeping stairs, hammock stands, and charging stations aplenty. Flagship has two such buildings. One, a sprawling complex in a traditional architectural style that, despite being well cared-for, gives the impression of a space stretched to accommodate uses for which it was not designed. The second is a study in visual contrast: high ceilings, modern lines, and natural materials; light and aluminum everywhere. A gas-fed fireplace adds more ambiance than heat to a cozy corner bedecked in university colors. Nevertheless, the essential ingredients—offices, meeting rooms, amenities, food—are present in both locations.

Leah (Flagship) notes that the surplus of seating, "better AC," food selection, and relative noise level as advantages of the elder union building. For our alternative tour guides, the attraction of the student union is as varied as the uses and spaces of the building, but food, directly or indirectly, connects to many of them. Phillip's (Flagship) experience in the student center, and indeed on campus generally, finds its epicenter in the Multicultural Affairs Office, or MAO. Double glass doors open to a high-ceilinged room illuminated by large windows at the far end. Tables down the center adapted for work or socializing purposes are flanked on the left by administrative offices and on the right by cubicles, storage, and a kitchenette. Phillip jokes about the reputation he's developed as the MAO's unofficial representative: "because that's like where I work, that's my home basically. People will associate that with me big. Like everyone will say, 'If you walk into the MAO, you'll probably see Phillip. If he's not here, oh, he was here 30 minutes ago.'" Phillip recognizes that his comfort in the MAO leads to an expanded social circle as well as to opportunities to satisfy a range of needs: "I just feel very comfortable. All my people are in there. I meet a lot of people every day even. I talk to people I don't . . . even like yesterday I talked to two girls that I don't even know that well. Now we're a little more cool, just because I've seen them and we're sitting at the same table, in the same conversation, and that's nice. So, meet a lot of people, get to learn about a lot of people." In the same stream of thought, Phillip connects the MAO as a social space to the MAO as a place where his needs more generally are met. He continues: "Plus, I have everything I need in there for the most part. . . . it's the summer, so they have snacks and stuff from the orientation events in there. It's always . . . it's very solid for me. I have no complaints. That's my home. That's where I can be Phillip."

Vera (PRU) serves on a university programming board that plans campus events out of the student center. Not only does this affiliation offer her a point of connection that she values ("It's very diverse"), it also provides food as part of her organizational duties: "I'm usually here every Wednesday just for a general meeting for the program counsel, and they usually have food during their meetings as well."

The student center is, for some of our guides like Phillip (Flagship) and Ariel (Lib Arts), places where important mentors work, making their offices a kind of second home as a result of the empathy and care they experience in those spaces. Ariel, joking, asserts: "Student Life, if you're part of that 'cult' there's free food there," then describes an administrator who has been central to her persistence at Lib Arts:

> I was struggling this last semester, especially with buying food, getting food. Sometimes it was time management and a lot of the time it was money, why I wouldn't have eaten breakfast that day or lunch that day or whatever. Dr. Williams would buy me food. Outright. And they don't get meal plan dollars, the professors and adjuncts and stuff, they don't get that. They have to spend their real money and they don't get a lot anyway. There are some few really caring, really involved people on campus that make sure that the students have what they need.

As with to Phillip, the emotional and financial support Ariel finds in the student center increases her sense that these are spaces "for" her. Asked to reflect on the campus spaces where she can be herself, Camila (Lib Arts) describes the third-floor student center as

> a comfortable space 'cause I know it. Even the people who come there I kind of recognize them, even though I don't talk to them. So it's just a place where I can just really hang out. And it's usually a quiet space as well where everybody's just there either to study . . . so everybody's just on their own and doing their own thing. So I kind of appreciate that 'cause throughout the day it can be kind of hectic and you're always around people.

Such experiences of belonging in the student center are not the case in all times and places. When we ask Camila if there are places where she feels excluded, she contrasts the social neutrality and vague sense of known-ness on the third floor to another part of the student center:

> Oh my gosh. The Grind Coffee Shop. Yeah so, The Grind. I think "excluded" is probably a strong word, but I just don't feel . . . I don't know. I just don't have a need or, like, a want to go just because, well first of all, the food is kind of overpriced and sometimes I don't know . . . but, like, the baristas there can sometimes, I don't know . . . I just feel judged sometimes when I have to change an order because I'm like, "Oh, okay. That's a little too

much." So, yeah, I just don't like getting myself into those situations, and I just try to stay away from there just because, I don't know, it's money that I shouldn't really be spending. So The Grind is definitely a place. But I still go to it every once in a while.

The Grind is an unflinchingly hipster coffee shop occupying a high-traffic corner of the student center at Lib Arts. The low lights, mellow music, and industrial textures are a siren's song calling students to consume a *lifestyle* with their lattes.[2] Camila's repeated equivocating "I don't know..." belies her experiences of "humiliation" for having to pay attention to the cost of food in a space where affluence means that many items bear no price information. That Camila nevertheless returns to The Grind underscores the reality that fiscal responsibility and campus belonging are frequently at an inverse relationship when the focal point is food. Many participants reflected on their freshman year indulgence at The Grind and the painful lesson of quickly depleted meal plan totals and bank accounts that taught them to live more frugally. Paloma (Lib Arts), who confesses to her own affinity for a morning stop at The Grind, describes buying food there as "a trap":

> Yeah. My friend was way worse than me, getting food at The Grind. That's a trap right there because their prices are super high, and so you just . . . you're going to get a coffee, just a coffee, but in the line there's breads and, like, cookies and a bunch of food, but you don't realize how expensive it is until you pay for it. And a bread is like $4. I'm like, "Whoa, this is a slice of bread. Like, a pumpkin bread. $4.00—come on!" But we're hungry at that moment so, like, our minds are thinking of food, not the price.

The temptation to indulge in relational- and hunger-motivated impulse purchases is exacerbated by the fits and starts of finances that makes upscale coffee and accompanying accoutrements accessible one day and inadvisable on another. At Lib Arts, students were required to take on one of several meal plan options in part to create financial sustainability for their for-profit food vendor on a small campus. Students could spend their dining dollars at The Grind as well as at the two campus convenience stores. For those students who chose the most expensive meal plans, the constraint of cost for food was as nonexistent as the price tags. For students who chose smaller meal plans, often those of limited means, lessons about budgeting were often hard-won. Selina, who went to Lib Arts on a generous scholarship that covered her meal plan the first year, recalls the mindset that she developed, and the need to change it:

> I never thought about the price of the food, because I did have the big meal plan. I knew I wasn't going to run out of it. And I would use it here, I would use it at The Grind, and I could get coffee every single day and still be fine meal plan–wise by the end of the semester. And it was pretty awesome. But I never really did think about how much I'm actually paying for my meal. Not until my sophomore year, when I had a smaller meal plan. Then I was like, "Oh, if I want to make this last, I can't have The Grind every single day anymore. I have to, like, one day a week."

Following our tour, Camila (Lib Arts) discusses the struggle of fiscal management in a campus food scene developed around the expectations of lifestyle and abundance, further shaped by the lack of nearby alternatives:

> It's so hard. It was so hard. It was a lot of temptation too, just because you are on campus. It's so much easier to just go out to the cafeteria than to take a bus to the grocery store or to a restaurant. So, you . . . like, I found myself really just choosing to spend the $10 at the cafeteria downstairs than the $3 going [off campus]. So, it was a lot of convenience for me, which is kind of a bad thing because I ended up spending a lot more and I ran out a lot faster. Just a . . . I guess it comes to self-control as well. There's just things you shouldn't be buying. Like the coffees at The Grind are like $5 a cup and I think that's what a lot of students struggle with in general. Just buying things throughout their day.

Many of our tour guides described living in the tension between the convenience and availability of on-campus food vendors, frequently located in the student center, and the constraints of their budgets, or of whatever was left in their checking account on a given week. Leah (Flagship) has learned the hard way to keep a close eye on her available funds, even for small food purchases: "So, usually I'll get the small side items. Fries are usually not that expensive. The fruit cups are usually not that expensive. When it gets to a meal, that's when it gets to where I can't really do it, 'cause $8 doesn't feel like a lot until you have $5 in your bank account." After Leah took a $35 overdraft fee from her bank a few times, her hard-earned solution is to use her bank's app and double-check before food purchases: "I usually try to hide when I'm looking at my bank account. So, if I'm in line at Chick-fil-A, usually I try to . . . I check my bank account just to make sure I have enough money."

Resourceful students also soon learn where the microwaves on campus are located, key resources to reduce the temptation to impulse buy food during a busy class schedule. Lacey (Flagship) gives us the scouting report: "So, we'll go to the student center, that's where they have food vendors. There are two microwaves in there. The union also has one in-campus dining. There's two microwaves in there. Then all the other places are kind of like, I think, kind of like more for administration, but they don't care if you use them. There's random kitchens and different hallways for people."

Gina (Flagship) brings leftovers or instant mac and cheese cups to heat up in the microwave tucked around the side of the taco shop. However, Miranda (Flagship) notes the opportunity cost of counting on a microwave meal for lunch: "So, usually there's a long line for the microwave. Yeah, you end up waiting a while. And then it's harder if you need to go between classes and usually this line is out to over there. Just really long."

Between cost, inconvenience, and the weight of environmental expectation, some students simply choose not to go to the student center food areas as a matter of course. Layla (Flagship) prefers to avoid situations where she must exert additional willpower: "It's just very loud. And then it's like, 'Oh, you could go get food' and then you have to do the mental math of, like, 'Can I do it this month?' So when you're near accessible but expensive food, it's always just frustrating." Anali (Flagship) details her general strategy: "I don't ever go to the student center, because there's a lot of food there and people go there to eat and stuff. I don't go. I don't have money to go buy food. But if somebody wants to meet there, then I'll meet them there. But I don't like going there."

Anali's assertion of confident fact ("I don't ever go . . .") is tempered by her acknowledgment that social and academic life on campus sometimes presses her into these uncomfortable spaces. Walking us through the student center, Anali further elaborates on the texture of her response, and experience: "But so this is just the open areas and then . . . there's a Starbucks that always smells really good, which makes me angry. So I don't ever like to sit in front of it. Right. My friends will buy me Starbucks sometimes, which is really nice. And, like, from the 'grab-and-go,' which is just snacks basically. So basically, I just try to sit places where I don't see food, just so I don't tempt myself, I guess."

Although Anali describes the environment as one of personal temptation, the real stumbling block is her attempt to be part of a campus social ecosystem in which buying upscale convenience food is an expected part. As is often the case with an in-demand service, savvy students find ways to work the system or work around the system. The expectation of food access and use of food as an inducement to student participation means that leftovers and off-the-books access are easily exploited, though with the occasional cost of guilt, as Ariel (Lib Arts) relates about her strategies: "I will go to Student Life and I will scavenge because they'll do a lot of events at the end of the year and so there's food in the fridge. So, I think for, like, the past three days, I've eaten lunch in Student Life quietly while no one's watching because they have food. And I'll keep an ear out for whenever they have events 'cause they always have food."

Ariel's "scavenging" weighs the benefits of eating and free food against the possible embarrassment of being seen, real or imagined. Beth (Lib Arts) has figured out that some of those "forbidden fruits" at The Grind are available at a lesser financial cost, though they hardly make for a sustainable food source: "I do go to The Grind . . . because they sell like day-old pastries and stuff. And that's a dollar versus ten dollars. It's filling but it's not good because it's just pastries all the time."

For many of our alternative guides, the student center, as a central collecting point for many offices, organizations, activities, and food, is a space fraught with temptation not merely of budget-breaking decisions but of participating in a student lifestyle that was part of their attraction to the university. These "temptations" to fully engage are not easily avoided. Impromptu study groups, necessary trips to various Student Life offices, or simply an efficient throughway to one's next class pulls students into a location symbolic of the destabilizing unpredictability of life on an affluent university campus. Will there be free pizza left in the fridge? Will my friends offer to buy me lunch? Will the line at the microwave be too long? These students are, in many respects, fortunate to inhabit a campus where so often free food and generosity abound. For those who can easily afford it, these aspects of campus life are simply normal, and an expected part of the prestigious collegiate experience. However, for those on the financial margins, coming to depend upon this largess creates daily cycles of boom and bust that are psychologically destabilizing.[3] Knowing one has barely enough money to eat has the thin virtue of predictability. Being unsure if the office fridge will be empty or the line at the microwave too long leaves students grasping for what control they can muster. Consequently, these spaces draw in some students like Phillip (Flagship) who find not only belonging and food, but food *through* belonging. Some, like Anali (Flagship), are less fortunate and are pushed away, except in those serendipitous moments when a friend offers generosity. Most students experience a confusing combination of these forces, as Camila (Lib Arts) recalled, contrasting the comfort of the third-floor Student Life office with her marginalization at The Grind.

In sum, when the desire to fully engage in the student experience wins out in the form of buying expensive lifestyle convenience food, these students internalize the responsibility, pressure, and "failure" to maintain a budget. These behaviors increase their reliance on avoidance strategies that distance them from the forms of engagement, such as eating with friends, that are a compelling part of the prestige-oriented university experience. In doing so, students make themselves morally culpable, freeing the institution to be an amoral services provider without responsibility for creating a normative environment that excludes access to the "goods" tacitly promised.

The Dining Hall

The dining hall is a central element in the daily rhythms of the residential undergraduate experience, more so at Lib Arts and PRU, but also for many first-year students at Flagship. Sleepy students stumble through the breakfast line, or perhaps pocket a piece of fruit on the way to an 8 a.m. class. At lunch, undergrads hurry from their classes in a vain attempt to beat the noon cafeteria rush. In the evening, a huddle of students in the corner discusses the weekend's plans over dinner. Although a student might evade buying food or coffee while sitting around a table with friends in the student center, there is no club on campus quite as exclusive as the dining hall. On our tour together, DeShauna (Flagship) ushers us up a short ramp and into the foyer of one of her campus's several dining halls. Flagship's scale means that dining halls and their models—some buffet, some pay-per-item, some pay-per-weight—require careful knowledge of local systems, unless one is prepared with a sufficiently generous meal plan. DeShauna rarely eats in the campus dining halls, which makes the chance reunion that ensues that much more serendipitous:

> This is it. It's a buffet. I don't know if we can go in without paying, but maybe we can take a peek. Yeah. That's how it works.
> **[To the cashier]**: We're just on a tour, yeah.
> **[To us, after entering]**: You get your food, and then you . . . well, you pay first . . . sorry, I know her . . . [*laughs*] . . . You pay first, and then you get your food, and then you sit down, and then, yeah . . . Do you mind if I say, "Hi" really quick?
>
> —*That's great. Go ahead.*
>
> **[To a group of students seated with their lunches]**: How are you guys? Oh my gosh, my babies . . . how are you guys doing? I'm on a tour right now. Yeah. But I'll definitely see you guys around. I'm going to text you, okay? We need to meet up this Friday. Bye!
> **[To us]**: They went to the same high school as me. They're a year younger than I am.

—Oh, that's cool. So, that's the first time you've seen them on campus?

Yeah, I knew they were coming here. I'm surprised that I saw them, actually.

As a social hub, the dining hall creates a space of "chance" meetings like this that accumulate over time, enlarging and reinforcing a student's social circle, as DeShauna experienced on our tour. Standing outside the dining hall embedded in the student center, Paloma (Lib Arts) describes the difficult moments that come with being a dining hall "outsider." Times when she sits and watches her friends eat, or maybe they offer to buy her some fries "but it's never a full meal." Paloma concludes, stating the obvious but painful fact: "But yeah, because eating is a huge form of socializing, it kind of sucks when you don't get to do that."

These hard experiences contrast with her brief experience with full "club" access. When we asked what she feels she's missed out on because of the cost of food, Paloma reflects on last summer when, as part of a summer research scholarship, she lived and ate on campus: "And it was the first time I never worried about food. And I would comment to other McNair [Scholarship] friends, like, 'Hey do you want to get lunch?' and I never did that before. So, it was a nice experience. And we would have breakfast together, and lunch together, and dinner together. So, it was nice to bond over food over the summer, which is something I probably missed out on during the school year. Yeah." Paloma draws a direct line between an abundance of food and a rich social experience in her brief season of full access. For many participants this full access is intermittent at best, creating an awareness of an ideal not, or no longer, available to them.

Camila (Lib Arts) walks us past a cluster of academic buildings and toward the second of two dining halls. This one, a bit farther from the center of activity, is part of a residence hall/dining hall/convenience store complex often inhabited by first-year students. Camila reflects on how no longer having a meal plan changed not only her eating but her sense of what spaces are for her: "This place is pretty big. I do like it, in that sense. But if I want to have dinner with friends, I will just go out and buy something to eat with them. But yeah, this isn't a space that I would call 'my space,' where I go a lot. But this was my favorite place my freshman year when I had the meal plan."

The luxury of the dining hall is the ability to "swallow" the price of acceptable, albeit somewhat repetitive, food options as part of the packaged student experience that aligns a student with the life of other students. Student demand for improved food quality and variety can easily overshadow how the invisible expense of the meal plan facilitates convergence with the schedules and spaces of other students. Yet even this opportunity cost can fail to yield the full measure of advantage if the rest of a student's life does not dovetail with the template of the student experience around which services are constructed. As the sizable minority of our participants who elected to pay for a meal plan after their first year found, the logic of the meal plan—what is available and when it is available—is also embedded in a way of thinking about the typical student experience that is often disrupted for students who hold jobs that help them pay for their expensive meal plan.

We stand with Jill (PRU) in the entrance to the subterranean dining hall, spotlights illuminating the rows of featured items as students mill about, trays in hand, searching for that last lunch item or an open seat. Reflecting on the start of her first year when even coming to the dining hall was foreign, Jill expresses her frustration with what she sees as a lack of alignment between dining hall schedules and academic schedules:

> Yeah, I started off not even going to the dining hall, then I did go to the dining hall. It closes very early. I think I remember it closes at 9 p.m. and I had night classes until 9:30. So, if I didn't go before . . . it's so stupid. Why would it close when there's still classes? It doesn't make sense. Then even though it closes at nine they literally close everything down at 8:00 p.m. They start shutting everything down at 8:00, which I understand the workers need to go home, but the only thing open is the sandwich station and so for those nights, like if I didn't go in early to get something to save for later, then I just wasn't going to eat dinner for that night.

Similarly, Selina (Lib Arts) explains how poorly the dining hall schedule fits with her academic and employment schedules. When we ask about a week that was difficult in terms of food choices, she responds:

> I think... I mean, the best example would be kind of like when my classes sort of... like, my exams or assignments just sort of pile up and I have to decide what's more important, I have to prioritize things. And it's more like do I have time to eat, because sometimes the times I would have available that's the time that the lines at the dining hall are super long, so I won't get out of there as fast as I need to. Or also the dining halls close at 8:00 p.m., so if I don't eat by 8:00 I have to figure out another way to eat later on that night.

The typical 8–5 class schedule is built around a traditional three-meal schedule, but neither one represents how students live who are negotiating between the demands of internships, employment, clubs, volunteering, and a rigorous academic plan. Selina's note that she has to "figure out another way to eat later" highlights the cost of not conforming to the tyranny of the dining hall schedule, a cost that is invisible for those who can afford to simply order a pizza or pick up a snack at the campus convenience store.

Tia (PRU), despite her meal plan, experienced misalignment with the baked-in expectations of the academic calendar most acutely during the "breaks" that are highlights for many traditional students. She named breaks as the "hardest period of time" because of the dining hall closures and the minimal warning she received: "So, a lot of the places were closed. The dining halls were not open at all. They were open maybe the night of the first day of fall break. And then the day after fall break. So, fall break is a week, a little less than a week. And my friends and I were like, 'I don't know what we're about to do, y'all, we're starving!'" Recognition by the university that not all students have the means to travel home at every break is often not matched by a recognition that many of the students who stay are dependent upon their expensive meal plan and flex dollars to eat.[4]

Although some institutions have recently amended these policies, students at many universities are forced to make impossible choices between important priorities that seem beyond what is reasonable to expect. Recently, Camila (Lib Arts) struggled between eating and saving for a trip home over spring break. Alone in her dorm room with no on-campus food vendors open, Camila recalls, she was "too embarrassed" to ask her adult siblings for help.

> I literally just survived off the vending machine. [*Pauses.*] I just get so emotional talking about it. [*Long pause.*] It's crazy. For seven days, surviving off of . . . I say "surviving" because it literally felt like . . . I was so hungry and it's not nutritious food at all. It's literally just Pop-Tarts and Snickers and Cheetos. I thought I'd be okay with it, because it's stuff I love to eat, but I think two days in and I was just like, "This sucks, and I don't know who to talk to for help and I feel gross and I'm alone." So, that was a really hard thing to do, but I had to allocate whatever money I had to my bus ticket, which I felt was more important at the time.

Although breaks in the academic calendar are often eagerly anticipated by students who have the means to vacation or simply travel home, for those on the financial margins they represent periods of food uncertainty. Guides such as Alfredo (Lib Arts) and Corbett (PRU), who paid for or received meal plans as part of their work stipends, *only* experienced gaps in their food access because of dining hall closures during the summer. Considering this dilemma, Phillip (Flagship) suggests a simple institutional goal for students: "If you have a meal plan, you should have one fall back place that you can always go." Implicit in Phillip's assertion is the question of student versus institutional responsibility. Converging forces of student consumerism, institutional prestige-seeking, and a student services model predicated on student care would seem to shift universities toward responsiveness, and indeed, as we will explore in part II of this book, responsiveness to student needs is generally valued. Yet the sticky persistence of the traditional model of university life exposes areas where organizational structures reinforce notions of what a Good Student looks like, and who bears responsibility when students fall through the cracks of this implicit system.

Campus Convenience Stores

Sometimes embedded in residence halls, other times in the student center, and occasionally simply located in free-standing structures, the campus convenience store in any form represents the traditional campus response to student food needs that are not met during regular hours through the dining hall. Not surprisingly, campus convenience stores received attention—and ire—from our alternative student guides on all three campuses. Selina (Lib Arts) walks us toward a modern-looking glass and steel rectangle that could be at home on an upscale urban city block, let alone on a college campus beside a new residential complex: "They just opened it. It was opened late this semester as well. It's cute. It's like a little convenience store, but I feel like they made it really 'bougie.' More than what is necessary. Some of the brands that they have, it's all just like organic stuff like that. And I'm like, 'That's cool, but that's really expensive.'"

As we stroll the aisles with our guides, the sorts of items available are striking: in addition to traditional chips and soda snacks we notice fresh produce—and more than just a few bananas and Red Delicious apples in a basket—strawberries, blueberries, and other seasonal fruit, a row dedicated to vegan snacks, and a made-to-order sushi bar, among other unexpected amenities. The campus convenience store has clearly become more than a place to buy note cards or a pack of gum; at these universities it is an integral part of meeting—and perpetuating—the lifestyle expectations of upper-middle-class students.

Scanning the shelves we are taken by the products as well as the prices, which students are quick to point out as well, even when the items are of the more ordinary variety. Entering Flagship's sprawling Jefferson complex, which includes student housing, dining, and retail, we navigate among clusters of students through a mall space lined with shops, eating establishments, and vendors. Terrence is on a mission to show us what expensive convenience looks like:

> This place is very . . . "Hello *we're* doing well!" Yes, this place is *very* expensive. It's like a convenience store. It's, like, everything in here is, like,

significantly more expensive for some reason. Like, this toothbrush, it looks like a very basic toothbrush. It looks like it's worth 30 cents but it's $1.19 here. Like, there's no way I'd pay like, "mm-hmm" [*negative*]. Yeah, the Nyquil's like $11. That would never happen. That's probably, like, five or six at Walmart or less, you know? Or you can get the Walmart brand. But yeah, everything in here is significantly more expensive.

Tia, Selina, Phillip, Miranda, Ariel, and William also engage in this price comparison dialogue with us, pointing out items that they know of or purchase from big box retailers and decrying the campus convenience store markup. Valeria (Lib Arts) reflects: "The prices are doubled if not tripled from what they actually are. So, I try not to go in there at all because I have no point for being in there. It's not cheap [*laughs*]." Phillip's response is a bit more pointed:

> So, it's horrendous, the prices in the market, because they can charge that much and people have to pay it, because you're a freshman and you live in a dorm and you don't know how to get around, you're too scared to go out and figure stuff out and it's too much of a hassle to get out and figure out this stuff. But its right here in the dorm for you. But something that will cost ... you can get a Snickers at the [grocery store] for 98 cents; you go in there, the Snickers is two, two-fifty. Disrespectful. That's blasphemous.

Phillip is not just upset at having to pay a higher cost; he feels *disrespected* by what he perceives is his university taking advantage of students.

Implicitly, our guides contested the market logic embedded in the campus convenience model. Universities appear to assume that, in exchange for the ease of access the campus store offers, students should be willing to pay a higher sticker price, though issues of stocking and shelf volume figure into inflated costs as well. Students, however, critique this system on two fronts: first, as Phillip (Flagship) illustrated above, he and others rejected the "company store" model in which the sheer inconvenience of shopping elsewhere creates a monopoly of services upon which students become dependent.[5] Ariel (Lib Arts) rails against what she perceives is a process that traps students, betraying a lack of care for students who struggle with the cost of food and other basic resources:

> If you cared about food insecurity on campus, your food would not be that expensive. Because it's not necessary for your freaking pizza rolls to be double the price they are at the grocery store. But guess what? I can't walk to the grocery store, nor can I drive to it, so I have to buy this. Like, you're trapping me. I get that it's all a business game, I get it. But if you cared, you would have done something about it.

Second, like the company stores that would simply draw down employees' wages to pay for goods, students are encouraged to spend "flex" dollars attached to their meal plans so that no physical money changes hands. Alfredo (Lib Arts) resists what he calls a tendency to treat flex money as "fake money" when we ask him who shops at the campus convenience store: "I kind of think they just make the assumption that whoever is buying on campus has a meal plan, so they can burn the meal plan money. Because there's also a joke on campus where, like, if you have a meal plan everyone calls it 'fake money.' I remember hearing that freshman year and I was like, 'It's not fake money because you paid for it to be in your card!'" The ease of transactions and apparent inexhaustibility of meal plan and flex money reduces hesitation students might feel about paying the steep price of convenience. Indirectly by doing so, students reinforce a standard of lifestyle and consumption unattainable by some of their classmates.

Second, student guides suggested by their incredulity toward on-campus prices that the aim of the campus store should be to *ease* the campus experience of all students by increasing access to convenience items, rather than financially capitalizing upon students' efforts to maximize their time in an activity-intensive environment. Tia, a performing arts major at PRU, sometimes grabs a snack that stands in for a meal at a small convenience store in her academic building: "So, they have this little place, it's called the Pod. I want to show you that. I get Lunchables there sometimes if they have them. . . . So, sometimes I get those, not often, because they're $5 for no reason." Tia's rejection of what she perceives to be a high price "for no reason" hints at her frustration that easily accessible foods that allow her to stay on task exact a hit on her budget.

Further increasing the "company store" modality is the lack of prices on at least some items, which was particularly evident as we explored the two shops at Lib Arts. Cadence (Lib Arts) points this out as well: "You don't really usually know the price and so you get up there and your total is like $20." The invisibility of cost in the face of convenience and desire serves a subset of the student population who are either able to ignore cost or are not careful enough to monitor it. But the effect is to further isolate from the benefits of convenience those for whom careful tending of their budget is a daily discipline.

One outcome of the campus store model on those struggling financially is forcing choices between access to needed supplies (including food) in a timely manner and maintaining very tight budgets. However, the outcomes of inaccessible convenience foods go beyond simply making difficult financial choices. For example, Ariel (Lib Arts) argues that the expensiveness of fresh healthy foods pits the desire to eat *well* against the need to eat *enough*, when she can buy a small amount of healthy food or a larger, more filling item that is unhealthy: "Because if you're paying $5 for a drink, or $5 for a small box of berries, you can't even choose to be healthy. Because the cheapest thing that satisfies hunger would be, 'Okay, I'm going to buy chicken tenders, tater tots, and whatever,' and that in itself is like $5.50, $6.50, and that makes more sense to me, because that's more food."

Although the welcome presence of fresh fruits and vegetables would seem like a boon to student well-being, their association with upscale sustainable and locally farm-sourced foods tended to result in a pricing approach that reduced access for some students wanting this choice. This intersection of the nutritional and the psychological is also part of Anali's (Flagship) experience of feeling "stuck" on campus, heightening her stress and anxiety:

> Especially during points where I really don't have that much food, I get very, very anxious and I get very irritated also, and because I want to eat and I want to do something but either I don't have that much food at home and

also I'm stuck on campus a lot. And a lot of people just would buy something from the little stores and food places there on campus. But I don't . . . I usually don't have that option.

The combined effect for our student guides was that not only were the resources needed to maximize the university experience tantalizingly unavailable, but the lack of clear prices and presence of high prices sent a message about who the food is for, and by extension, who the campus is for. After touring the new convenience store on her campus, we questioned Selina (Lib Arts) about its implied clientele. "I think sometimes, this might sound weird, but it's the people here without a scholarship, that they can afford to pay for it." Students thus come to perceive that when student affluence is assumed as part of the system, transparency and access are often the cost that they pay.

CHAPTER 5

Starving the Dream III

The Academic Buildings and the Administrative Buildings

Academic Buildings

In contrast to singular student collecting points like the library, rec center, and student center, all campuses include a broad array of academic structures, from highly specialized scientific laboratories to nondescript classroom boxes occupied on an as-needed basis. Leah (Flagship) guides us through an assortment of the specialized variety, traversing the well-funded and dramatically styled business school ("I barely spend any time here; I just pass through because it has great AC") and into the sciences building that houses the very labs Kimmy led us through on the official tour. Leah began working in this lab as a freshman and stayed on as a mentor "so I could continue my research" she reports, as if performing experiments with therapeutic applications to cancer treatment is a typical first-year student activity. Leah concludes her description of something called an "optimer stream" with the casual observation that "this is where I spend most of my time." This offhand comment is a valuable reminder that for all the emphasis on organizational involvement, campus activities, and student services, the heart of the university enterprise is, still, traditional academics. For the many of our alternative tour guides who were in preprofessional programs or career trajectories, the experiential aspects of their academic track were immersive and demanding, requiring lab or practicum time, in addition to more traditional forms of class attendance. Vera (PRU) confirms the immersion required of her academic program as she leads us toward a stately brick structure, describing a sciences building as "where I am 24/7." She then pivots the conversation from academic engagement to food: "Yeah, so they have events for one of the organizations that I'm in, which is a minority association of pre-health student at PRU, and the events that they have there usually involves like, kind of, a lot of food [*laughs*]. Since they know that most of the minorities here are from low-income families and we usually go to the events for the food. So that's why they have a lot of food there."

For students with marginal food access, long hours in the lab, studio, or in a study session require them to proactively plan for or reactively ignore food needs. In those fortunate moments when the demands for academic engagement can be met alongside the demand for food, students temporarily achieve an economy of operation. For some students, environmental food awareness means learning where convenient sources of inexpensive or free food are, the best of them aligned with spaces where students are able to work at all hours, as Camila (Lib Arts) describes: "It's a 24-hour lab for students and you can access it with your student ID, which is really cool. This one, I found out about it my second semester here at Lib Arts, and it's really cool, just because it has the water fountain and the vending machines there. So, you don't have to leave to get food. But it is just vending machines."

Just as scholars emphasize that college is constituted from the serendipity of relationships with faculty and peers, so our students pointed out how their experiences are shaped by occasional free food opportunities that converge with their academic labors.[1] Beth (Lib Arts) also has mapped the vending machine scene, adding mention of less predictable food sources:

> So a lot of my classes actually are in this building, and there's a vending machine, so I usually go to that in between classes and it makes it easy. And I really like this because during exam week and whatnot, either in the building or way outside of it, they'll have like little tables with food or drinks that are like a dollar or free or something.

—Do you know who does that?

No. I think it's different companies or organizations. They never tell us. They're just like, "Hey, it's free!" Yeah, but this is the only place that they do it here and they don't tell you. You just see it if you happen. Yeah. So they need to work on communication for sure.

The "feast or famine" of free food tied to difficult-to-predict circumstances, be they an organizational event, seasonal festivity, or compassionate academic unit, leads students to establish time-consuming scavenging routines and pathways around campus, hoping that *today* is one of those lucky days. A few students, like Jill (PRU), were more fortunate than Beth (Lib Arts) in the predictability and excess they supplied. Her job at the law school serendipitously places her in a space where free food is frequently available to harried law students:

So, they always do these promotions and stuff for them to keep their spirits up. There's always coffee. They would have tacos and always have free lunches, Jimmy Johns and stuff. And they would always send me home with the leftovers and so literally I would just have like cases and cases of food and I would just walk them back to my room and eat them over the course of the week, so that was really helpful. I don't think they knew that I needed it, but I definitely needed it and I definitely was like, "Oh, if this is going to go to waste, I'll just . . ." you know?

Jill and others like her find that the unspoken university modus operandi that matches intensive academic expectations with extensive resources produces an abundance beyond the needs of those for whom it is intended, and opportunities for those with the right connections who do.

For those not as situationally fortunate, in addition to vending machines some locations also house cafés, sandwich carts, or small convenience retailers. Typically, our guides viewed them as financially inaccessible, or for emergencies only. Showing us around the building where she interns, Layla (Flagship) directs our attention to a counter and cluster of chairs off in a corner: "There's a little café. It's like seven dollars for a sandwich. Nobody ever eats here. But it is there if it's like last minute."

For those who cannot afford the convenience foods designed to support students rushing from one task or class to another, making the most of their academic experience means planning ahead and budgeting carefully, so small meals and snacks are available to sustain energy and focus through a rigorous academic schedule. When Leah's food runs out or planning fails, the academic cost is significant, in terms of her ability to focus in class. Leah recites her emotional and physiological downward spiral, set off by not eating:

> I get either sad or I just sit there, and I don't want to participate, and I don't want to be a part of it. I just want to go home and eat. And I'm just like, "I don't even listen when I'm in class if I'm hungry." It's like, "I just kind of want to go home." And I'm like, "Why am I in class if I'm not going to listen?" Which sucks, because I'm like, "I'm trying to learn," but also I have a headache. And the bright lights don't help. It's bright lights and then I'm dehydrated. I'm starving. And I'm just sitting in class trying to take notes on like organic chemistry and I'm like, "I can't." I already don't understand the subject. I'm just not in the best mood to learn right now. And I try to take as many notes and I always end up having to go back on the recording and once I'm in a better mood to, like, get the notes again to, like, understand what I was writing. So I'll just write, and I'll pick up on, like, things she's saying. But I'm like, "Oh, it's recorded. I'm just going to, like, take a nap." Sometimes I nap in the middle, like, for five minutes. I'm like, "Maybe when I wake up, I'll feel better" [*laughing*]. And it helps. It does help sometimes. I'm like "okay." I rest my eyes. Because I'm also tired on top of dehydrated, hot, hungry, sweaty. Being hungry makes me exhausted.

Leah's frustrations with the academic costs of hunger are palpable. Her creative "self-accommodations" could easily send an unintended signal of disinterest to a professor, when her desire and intentions are the opposite.

Of course, the ideal/normal academic life extends beyond the classroom to relationships with faculty and interactions with peers. These too are affected, according to Miranda (Flagship). When we asked what sort of student she would be if she was financially secure, she lists off her perceptions of what the Good Student does: "I definitely would go to office hours. A lot of the times I can't go to office hours 'cause I work or it just doesn't work out. And I'd study a lot more. I'd probably go to study groups. I'd definitely get office hours, actually talk to my TA, actually study. I would do my homework on time. Probably I'd get better grades."

Miranda recounts how her first semester she did not have a job and "her family was a little bit more comfortable" financially. Then, she went to office hours and studied more, keeping all her grades above a C.

> But then I started working the next semester and every semester since, I've gotten at least one C. And I rarely go to office hours if I can. I sometimes can't go to the study sessions or the groups that they have 'cause I work or I'm too tired from going to work or I have class or something else. I'd be able to prioritize more and probably have a higher GPA and be able to focus on what I want to do after school. I wouldn't have to worry so much about now.

The tyranny of the present is an effect of hunger several alternative student guides discussed. Selina (Lib Arts) reflects on the way it claims her attention while in class: "If I'm hungry I can't focus. It'll just . . . my notes are super sucky for some of my classes because if I am hungry, or sometimes when I sit with my friends in one of my classes and we'll just hear each other's stomachs go off and we just stare at each other like, yeah, we heard that but we're going to ignore it for now. Maybe that, that it's really hard to focus sometimes." Carli (PRU) echoes Selina's point, emphasizing the drain on concentration that hunger produces: "Sometimes I literally have food on the brain. Like in last class when I was in Arts Management . . . I was trying so hard to pay attention and all I could think was you know, a juicy cheeseburger or just something like filling. And it's like 'No Carli, you need to study, you need to focus.'"

The effects of basic needs scarcity robs the brain of the ability to focus on complex concepts and reduces the supply of willpower needed to stay on task, making a rigorous academic schedule additionally taxing.[2] As we exit a classroom building, Ariel (Lib Arts) describes the forced choice that has compromised her academic performance:

> My life did not allow me to get the 3.5 GPA or be the best at something; or speak up every day in class; or communicate as much as I needed to with my professors; or spend as much time as I wanted to on that paper because I wanted to. There were so many things that I was like, "If I could just sit down and actually do what I wanted to do . . ." or let's say I found the time to sit down and actually do what I wanted to do, I was so busy rushing to get it done because I was so tired all the time, that it just wasn't good. I still got the B, I still got the 89%, I still got what I needed to get out, but it's just like *my life didn't allow me to be the best.*

The irony of Ariel's experience, shared by many others, is that highly capable students are undermined by basic needs in an environment of abundant resources. In part this is because the unspoken ideology of college resource allocation fails to connect institutional imperatives for "student success" with allocation of resources in ways that help students with extensive needs succeed. Students, recognizing this, sometimes take action on their own. At Lib Arts, the dearth of affordable food, particularly in academic spaces, led to a student advocacy organization mobilizing around the food needs of students. According to Nicole (Lib Arts):

> And then also, just a little tidbit, there's also a club here called Undocumented and Unafraid . . . and they were the first ones who started a food co-op at Lib Arts. In one of the buildings you can donate, you can leave off food and you can donate food. And then you can also just pick up some if you're ever hungry. And they have a bunch of stuff like oatmeal, cereal bars, cereal, sometimes ramen. So, it's like things you can, if you're feeling really hungry, you don't have to worry about it. So, that's helped me a lot of the times, being food insecure during college. So, that is another resource, but it is student started.

Following Nicole into one of the sciences buildings, we climb the stairs and turn the corner into what appears to be a student lounge or breakroom; windows on the left cast afternoon sun on several circular tables and chairs, with more casual seating in the corner. A bank of vending machines, a fridge, and an economy kitchen lined with cabinets flank the right. Nicole extolls the virtues of the student initiative that has co-opted this space into a student food pantry: "Undocumented and Unafraid kind of created that sort of environment that it's okay to get food. Like you shouldn't feel bad about getting it, because also people are just donating what they have extra too."

The combination of respectful access and reduced social stigma for receiving help is an important factor in the success of the food co-op, but visibility seems to be an issue, as with food pantries at the other universities. Later, on a tour of the same building, we ask Paloma (Lib Arts) about her awareness and use.

> I actually did not know about it until recently. My sister took me up there one time, and then she's like, "Do you want snacks?" I was like, "What? They have snacks in there?" And then she was like, "Yeah." And I was like, "Wow." But now I know, and I go there all the time. So, it's pretty cool.
>
> —What does an organization like that tell you about Lib Arts?
>
> It tells me that the students care about everyone, and we look out for each other. People notice the problems that occur on campus and try to do things to fix it. So I guess food insecurity was a problem for a lot of students, and they saw that and wanted to create an organization that helps students have food. And I think it's kind of amazing.

The value and significance of a student-run food pantry, though operating at a more modest scale than those of our other two campuses, shows through in the sense of shared concern and agency that results. Nevertheless, as at PRU, those overseeing the Lib Arts food pantry struggled at times with making the resource sufficiently visible. The price of concern, real or imagined, that students might misuse or overuse free food (we did not hear any accounts of students abusing this resource), is often invisibility among those who need it. Selina (Lib Arts) expresses her frustration with institutional support for students in dire need of food:

> I guess I would say Lib Arts would find you the resources if you really need it to. But then I would also say I have no idea what those resources are because I've never been made aware of them at least. Like when it comes

to that, I've never been told, "If you're ever running low, this is where to go." I don't know if there's . . . I know universities sometimes have a pantry where students, whoever, running low on food they can go get food there. I don't know if we have anything similar to that. At least I haven't heard of it.

Lib Arts administrators were proud to encourage this independent student initiative. However, the scale and pervasiveness of student hunger challenged the organization and communication of the food co-op. The placement of the Lib Arts food pantry offered several advantages of proximity and convenience, at least for students in the sciences. The virtue of convergence between free food resources and time-intensive academic labor was increased productivity, as convenience food on campus is supposed to yield. Yet the strain of food needs across the three campuses was often most acute in spaces, such as academic buildings, that require the greatest expenditure of focus and energy.

Administrative Buildings

As we traverse the three campuses with alternative and official guides, we pass by a variety of buildings with minimal comment. "This building houses institutional research." "That one is where the bursar is located." "Over there is the development office." An organization as vast and complex as the modern university cannot exist without a great deal of mostly hidden bureaucratic machinery typically lumped together under the title of *administration*. For most students, this network of professionals is only episodically apparent, usually tied to a need for the intervention of a specialist. In our alternative tours three such specialized functions came up with regularity, with a fourth specific to Flagship University: health services, counseling services, financial aid, and the campus food pantry.

Health Services

We push through a set of large double doors, trailing Leah (Flagship) as she enters a multistory structure of brick and glass that houses an assemblage of student services offices. Veterans services, student emergency services, as well as a health clinic and pharmacy are among the many specialized spaces tucked into the various splintering hallways of offices that emanate from a central atrium. The bland forgettability of these buildings belies the urgency that often accompanies the students who visit these spaces. Leah lists off the reasons for her occasional presence:

> I come here for the medical center, the pharmacy.... That's the Health Services doctor's office. Whenever I have issues, it's free nurse consultations, so that's the main reason why I come here. My family's insurance is real tricky, so sometimes I just get my medical help here, and I pay like a relatively cheap-ish fee.... It's at a discounted rate, which I appreciate, because I, honestly, I could not afford it otherwise, because I needed to get a physical for my study abroad.

Low-income and working-class families often do not receive comprehensive health insurance as an employment benefit, resulting in students' reliance on governmental programs, high-deductible policies, or no insurance at all.[3] Expenses (e.g., required physical and shots) associated with student experiences such as study abroad are nearly invisible to those who are accustomed to the benefits of employer-provided health care or have the means to pay out of pocket. With the escalating cost of health care, universities often create an economy of scale to control prices by requiring students to carry a university health care plan if they are not otherwise covered. This strategy is understandable in part because of the dire effect an unexpected emergency can have on a student's experience. For example, Anali (Flagship) put a great deal of care into planning her semester budget. Her efforts at financial planning were undermined by a major injury and a paid internship that did not come through. "I had to pay a thousand something up front just to get seen, and that really set me back." Similarly, Gavin (Flagship) reflects on how a skateboarding accident and ensuing health care costs resulted in him losing his walking-intensive political canvassing job and his financial stability during his first year.

> And so it was just like that . . . kicked in that survival mode for sure. . . . Yeah, so I was just literally like . . . my family would send me $10–$20 sporadically. I would just have to extend that. I was just eating bread. I was just eating bread with jelly on it and peanut butter for protein. I was just like, "Let me get my . . ." It would be a joke with my roommates because I would be like, "Oh, let me just get my brain juice. I just need brain power. Let me eat a slice of bread."

Alejandra (Lib Arts), recognizes that between costs and resources, she can strategically manage her university's insurance requirement in a way that helps her cover her basic needs costs:

> Even in previous semesters, even if you don't have your insurance, they charge you the school's insurance, which is not cheap. And then, I try to get my insurance, because it's a couple dollars a month, and then they turned that, refund the money that they would be charging you for the school's insurance. So, then I can use that money to buy rent and food and all these other expenses that I have outside of school.

Alejandra's insight, that if she picked up inexpensive outside insurance, her university would refund her the amount required for her university health insurance plan, represents both creative financial navigation and a calculated risk, given the high deductible associated with her low-cost plan. Not surprisingly, scholars have found that basic needs—food, shelter, health care—are often intertwined and comorbid, meaning that a crisis in one area creates an echo crisis in the others.[4] Anali's example above illustrates this risk, when her well-planned financial model that facilitated a coveted unpaid internship was blown apart by an injury and out-of-pocket health care expenses.

Counseling Services

Although many of our participants singled out physical health services offices for praise or derision, it was help with the psychological aspects of life through counseling services that received more mentions. Leah (Flagship) includes these resources in her tour, detailing the number of free sessions (six) she can receive and the crisis hotlines available to students. Her evaluation is summatively positive: "They're really good here about getting you the physical amount of help you need."

Leah's regard for Flagship's mental health resources is notable, and a meaningful sign of change in the higher-education landscape. Across the United States, efforts to destigmatize mental health issues have succeeded in significantly normalizing use of counseling services with 18- to 22-year-old young adults.[5] The outcome of this generational sea change of attitudes has been a proliferation of demand for these services, often outstripping the capacity of staff, particularly at smaller colleges and universities. Nevertheless, increased acceptance of counseling services as part of the normal student experience means that students are more likely to identify their need for, and proactively seek, help, which Tia (PRU) highlights from her own experience:

> So, now I've noticed just in the course of all the changes and stuff that's been going on in life. I've just noticed that I need it. I need it. And . . . and I noticed that the changes in my mood and how I talk to people and stuff like that is—hasn't really been the best so far. Especially this semester, I've noticed it a lot. I've noticed my withdrawal from my friends and stuff. And even how I talk to my girlfriend sometimes, and my mom. And I'm like, "Oh, my god, no. I need to get some help." So, yeah.

For some students, this voluntary help-seeking provides a safe space to talk, sometimes for the first time, about their struggle to afford food. For Ariel (Lib Arts), reengaging with counseling has been instrumental in her psychological well-being: "I had a really bad experience with therapy when I was really young and it just made me not want to go back. Eventually going back is a really big source of comfort. A place where I would talk about all of my relationship with food and my relationship with feeding myself and nourishing my body and not wanting to."

Likewise, Vera (PRU) recalled overcoming her hesitations to begin counseling where she both received—and dispensed—information about food resources on campus. "So I started going [to counseling] to see, like, how it is. I've never been to counseling services, but they kind of helped with giving me more information about, like, my food insecurity. So I told them about the food pantry. They didn't know about it, either."

Despite occasional frustrations over cost and insurance coverage, mental health services were instrumental to the persistence and success of quite a few of our food-insecure students. However, counselors varied in their knowledge of collegiate food insecurity and their awareness of associated resources. As a result, in some cases counselors were conduits for needed information about basic needs resources, and in others, students were informants.

Financial Aid

Like counseling services, the offices that oversee student accounts and financial aid are, in some cases, the source of stress and anxiety, and in others, a location students turn to in their moments of desperation. Few other offices are so emotionally fraught for students, in part because it is here that the ideal of the student experience that has been tacitly promised meets the reality of students' dire financial situations. In these moments, financial aid advisors are either heroes or villains; there are few other options. Carli (PRU), a transfer student, stands outside the financial services building, recalling her rough entry:

> In the first two weeks I ended up going to my financial aid advisor, the bursar, everyone, anyone I could think of, because I basically didn't have two pennies thrown together. I talked to the bursar and I am, I consider myself a strong person. I don't cry unless I'm very frustrated or if there's something really bad. And here I am sitting in front of a guy, asking him if there's anything that could be done, if there was a different payment plan. And the tears are falling from my face because I felt stuck.

By the second semester, Carli found that the combination of persistence on her part and competence on the part of her financial aid advisor created a path for her, though not on the terms she preferred:

> In the spring, because I went to them almost constantly because I was fairly new to everything, they would be like, "Hey! There's this work study.

There's this. There's X, Y, Z." So I was like, "Okay." But then it was constantly about loans. And I was very headstrong—I don't want to do loans. Then I realized I kind of have to because how else am I going to get into classes the following semester, because they put a hold on your account.

The emphasis on taking loans as part of the "normal" college experience is often a shock to students who have been socialized to avoid them, as Chelsea (PRU), a first-generation college student, tried to avoid loans based on the advice of her parents: "All my parents told me was a loan is terrible. 'Try to get as much financial aid as you can get' and things like that, but even our . . . even the people in our financial aid office are advising us first-generation students to take loans."

The emotional turmoil brought on by going against valued parental advice is further accentuated by the dire consequences should the aid puzzle prove to be unsolvable.[6] Students frequently voiced frustration that their financial aid officers projected such an apparently cavalier attitude toward loans, as if there was no risk and questioning them was naïve. Vera's (PRU) frustration is palpable as she recalls how she explained to her financial aid advisor that her $30,000 gap in aid was the same amount as her dad makes in a year. Vera pleaded for help to identify scholarships, work on campus, or other alternatives: "She just straight up told me, 'No, just get out a loan, it's fine. You can pay it off later on.' I told her that I still had three more years there. That amount was going to accumulate and at some point it's going to be too much for me, and she told me, 'No, there's no other way.'"

Vera and students like her arrive at financial dead ends, hoping the black box of financial aid will produce a solution that they are not sure they can find on their own. In some situations, these desperate needs are met with almost miraculous solutions, as Carli testifies about in a turn of events since our prior conversation:

> Remember when I was struggling last semester, and I didn't have enough for my tuition? I actually ended up talking to some people and I found myself meeting this one woman and she said, "Let me see what I can do for you." And I found they changed the $20,000 that I initially owed, to like $6,000. And I was like, "How did that happen?" And she goes, "Well, it's

because of what you've done. You had a 4.0 in community college. You're a great community leader. You've went through all these outlets. And so, you've proven that you can do this." And they said that the rest somehow got paid and they said, "If you get a certain GPA this semester, then you don't have to worry."

Stories of aid interventions of this sort are just frequent enough to project the sense that aid offices have the power and discretion to help students when sufficiently motivated, and just infrequent enough that students are unsure what financial interventions they can count on.

From the outside, financial aid as a process might seem to be highly proscribed and procedural. However, as Carli's story illustrates and other student guides suggest, securing financial aid is perceived by students to be a matter of cultivating personal relationships with administrators who employ their knowledge of systems to look out for students' interests. When we asked what advice she would give to new students, Chelsea (PRU), echoed by others, said, "I would tell you to get with your financial advisor. Try to get some of the resources as much as you can." Alec (PRU) has an administrative advocate that has been key to their access of resources on several fronts:

> There's this woman here named Susan. She's just this super cool administrator. And she kind of just picks out kids that she sees that have potential and that she sees something in, and so, I guess she chose me as one of them. And she just kind of keeps an eye on me, making sure I'm doing okay, sending me to my disability coordinator if I'm having extra problems. Or sending me to financial aid people that can possibly get me a refund on something, you know, that kind of thing. I have some people that are looking out for me in certain interests.

Alec's and Carli's experiences of unexpected financial relief and care stand at dramatic contrast to Vera's dead ends at the same institution (PRU):

> And it's really just pissed me off and I even talked to the financial aid advisors. But they suck here. She said, "Well, I'm sorry, I can't find any other support that you can have here. You're just going to have to pay

everything off, but I have a list of loans here that you can get out." And I even told them my situation. Both of my parents are immigrants, or any of my other relatives here. I don't have anybody to co-sign on my behalf, and I even told her about that situation. She said, well she didn't say this exactly, but she kind of made it seem like that, well, "Sucks to be you, but just go find something else. You have to pay." And I've not been the only one. I've heard different stories from different students, that they've experienced things in the financial aid division from advisors. But it just sucks. It sucks.

From a student perspective, the apparent discretion of financial aid administrators to use their invisible power and access to resources is bewildering; elating when it works for them; devastating when it does not. Students grasp at the few mechanisms of control they have identified: building relationships with their financial aid advisor, looking for outside grants and scholarships, and appealing to as many advocates as they can for assistance. As Kelsy (Lib Arts) summarizes, "The financial aid is really good, but don't let it blindside you," implying that however available aid is in general, students have to pay attention for the gaps that can swallow them up.

The link between insufficient financial aid and money to pay for food is fairly straightforward: when students are stretched thin by tuition bills, food money is one of the first budget lines to go.[7] Far more invisible are those students who *are* eating reasonably well because they have taken out extensive loans, and the potential struggles waiting for them after college when monthly payments come due.[8] Quite a few of our participants were attending their prestige-oriented university because of a full-ride scholarship, yet it was all the additional expenses that sank them into food insecurity. Student guides expressed incredulousness that campuses with such extensive resources allow some students to struggle, even while supporting students not experiencing the same intensity of need. On this, Kelsy (Lib Arts) asserted:

I feel like there's almost a division sometimes of like, we have the really wealthy people here, who are almost, like, stealing our scholarship money, because they get need-based grants as well as merit-based grants and it does feel like they could pay for this, but we still have to pay out of pocket when we need more financial aid. So, I feel like that's a lot of issues in regards to, like, they're taking away opportunities that we would probably need.

This frustrated bewilderment of university priorities plays out practically in the apparent noblesse oblige of food resources intermittently abundant when they further organizational aims, such as a club looking to attract new members or an office holding an open house, but scarce when it comes to providing consistent meals that would buttress a student's basic needs. In the case of financial and food aid, students learn that this dependence is like a river crossing on thin ice: anxiety-producing when it holds but disastrous when it does not. Given that tenuousness, resources such as the campus food pantry would seem like a no-brainer to use, yet the details of its implementation play an important role in the function and symbolism students perceive.

The Flagship Food Pantry

At Flagship, the one form of direct food aid most consistently supplied is also situated in an administrative building: the campus food pantry. More than half of our eleven Flagship alternative tour guides reported using the food pantry at least once; two admitted that they had never heard of it before. Leah is among those who has made use of this resource, a geographical convenience to her campus work-study job. Approaching what appears to be an aging multistory apartment building, Leah outlines her initial experience in this converted office space:

> I heard about it . . . it's like you see those signs around campus, no one really talks about it, but there's signs everywhere. And one day I saw that they had the little doorbell out and I was like, "I don't have that much food in my house right now," so I was like, "I'm going to push it and see what happens . . ." Because I work for student services I have to be literate about all of the resources that the school has for everyone. So, I knew about it, so I was like, "Okay, it's here, I'm going home anyway, I might as well grab it."

Leah's situational advantages—work location, prior knowledge, plans to travel home afterward—all proved to be barriers for other students. Nevertheless, among those who had used the pantry, the actual experience was uniformly positive, as DeShauna recalls: "It was really nice. I walked in and they greeted me warmly, and they were just like, 'Take whatever you need, we have tons of stuff,' so that was nice." Lacey offers a similar account, noting some of the discomfort that can come with accepting this sort of aid:

—*What was that experience like for you?*

I kind of felt embarrassed, I'll be honest. But I think that's normal. Maybe. But any interactions I've had with them have been very nice. They smile and they're like, "Are you here for food?" And I'm like, "Yep." And they have me fill out this form . . . and it's like, "Check everything you would use,"'cause they obviously don't want to give you something if you're not going to use it.

Over the course of nearly two years of our data collection, the Flagship food pantry underwent something of a metamorphosis, first changing locations, then receiving extensive renovations that significantly improved the aesthetics and functionality of the interior. This investment, however, further ensconced the food pantry in a space and location that many of our students felt neither met their expectations for basic convenience nor university standards for presentation. Standing in front of the building on a hot summer afternoon, Terrence offers his bleak assessment:

Yeah. I'm surprised this building looks like this. Like we have so . . . like Flagship has so much money.

—*Yeah. What do you think about this building?*

It's old and raggedy! It looks sketch. . . . Like let's say this was like an apartment complex. I'm not gonna lie—I'd be embarrassed to bring my friends here, you know? Like, I would honestly. Honestly, I would because I've lived in apartment complexes like these that kind of look, like, rundown. . . . Yeah. I think if it were in another building like towards the middle of campus, it'd be a lot better.

In his analysis, Terrence transitions from exterior condition to the relative geographical placement of the food pantry, a frequent topic. Situated on the edge of campus away from the main flow of foot traffic and student housing, the location of the food pantry was often critiqued. When we ask what she would change, Anali responds: "Oh, definitely the food pantry. I wish that it was closer to central campus." Layla describes the food pantry building as in "a part of campus they never really showed us," and indeed, the official campus tours we attended did not extend to this part of the grounds.

Students give mixed responses as to whether the food pantry's peripheral location is an advantage—providing some measure of privacy—or simply an unwarranted inconvenience. Terrence initially found the Flagship food pantry through the method most available to college students: "I googled. I was like, 'I *know* this "bougie" university has a food pantry. I just need to know where' [*laughing*]." When we press him on whether a location in the middle of campus might discourage some students from using it, he considers the factors: "Yes. I feel like they'd have, like, their pride. Yeah, they'd just [*pauses*] they want the help but they don't know how to accept it. Yeah. But I don't know. Maybe if it were like closer in the middle . . . it'd be better, instead of all the way back over here. That's ridiculous."

The tension between the potential stigma of using the food pantry if it were located in a convenient and highly visible space, versus the inconvenience of its current location in a space with more privacy, was a topic that produced consternation among many of the administrators we interviewed as well. Despite the legitimacy of these concerns, Phillip and others were certain that students need to be a more prominent part of the decision-making:

> [Administrators] need to listen to students a bit more about how to do things, because we are the students. We navigate the campus every day. So, we kind of know what could help the most people. So, they have the food pantry, right? But it's . . . way in the corner of campus. . . . Nobody wants to walk to [that building]. I walk there for organization stuff, but that's a long ass walk just to . . . that's the truth of it.

The long walk that Phillip emphasizes points to Leah's logistical advantage working right next to the food pantry: synchronizing one's visit with hours of operation that reflect administrators' schedules rather than students' schedules. Miranda's reflection hints at her appreciation of a judgment-free experience but then focuses on the challenges of logistics that reduce the viability of the food pantry as a source of aid: "There's, I think it's called the Flagship food pantry, and they give you groceries once a month and they don't ask questions. You just go pick them up. But because the buses are really limited right now to get to Flagship, they are really far apart, I have to walk pretty far to get to the bus."

More than just the inconvenience that Miranda notes, Layla, a past user of the food pantry, suggests that administrative decision-making related to logistics reflects a lack of commitment to genuinely prioritizing student needs. Observing that the food pantry is only open 9 to 5 on weekdays and stocked by volunteers, she concludes that these commonsense organizational decisions reflect a deeper failure: "So they don't really . . . the institution doesn't really respond, though I think they have an obligation to." When we asked how these and other experiences have colored her perception of the campus over her years at Flagship, she continues: "I've changed my way that I view campus, as I view it as a more inaccessible or just bureaucratic place, which is something I don't think I thought of as a higher-education issue. I thought it was just like a place you did a degree."

Expanding on this point, Layla observes that Flagship's pursuit of prestige creates internal administrative pressure to respond in ways it might not have otherwise:

> Yeah. I mean I think that it's a lot of the pressure that comes with attending, like, a prestigious "Public Ivy," is what they like to call themselves. Like, I think that puts pressure on both the students and the administration and vice versa to excel and to push. I think it has potentially put pressure in some respects on the administration to start becoming aware of the issues of which their students are facing . . . so that way they can be more academically excellent.

Layla critiques the quality of response, arguing that the university has been pressed into responding to food issues just as it has been pressed into responding to mental health issues. Neither, in her view, the university does well. When we inquire whether Flagship's motivation matters to their response, Layla reflects: "Probably. I mean, like, if your motivation is just to help Band-Aid over any problems that way students can get good grades, then you're never gonna address the systemic issues that cause those temporary lapses in income or food access or whatever."

Accurate or not, Layla's accusations raise several key points about how the market position of the prestige-oriented university affects how students perceive services. First, that just as serious involvement in the prestige game rachets up the expectations on students, so also raised are the expectations *of* students and their families. Second, that fair or not, institutional prestige-seeking brings with it the perception that administrators have an instrumental view of students as a means to an organizational end and are not otherwise focused on what most benefits the student in crisis. And third, as Layla's final comment suggests, that "lapses" in food access are in fact the *outcome* of a university's unwillingness to take on broader systemic issues of cost because of status-seeking, and not merely a student problem to which the university has failed to provide adequate support. In short, it may be that a cost of engaging in competitive status-seeking that sets a high bar for achievement and campus image is an intensified student expectation that such standards extend to all facets of the university experience, including student support services such as the campus food pantry. In part II we turn our attention to administrators and the ways that they construct a view of the student, often based on their own backgrounds, that shape organizational responses to food insecurity.

PART II

ADMINISTRATING THE DREAM

CHAPTER 6

Dreaming of More
The Historical Convergence of Food and Prestige

Although growing attention to collegiate food insecurity by scholars, practitioners, and policymakers alike may suggest that the struggle to afford food has recently emerged as a pressing problem for college students,[1] issues of food access and affordability have long marked the college-going experience. The role of food in higher education, from the first universities in Europe founded nearly a millennium ago, to America's nascent colonial colleges, to today's myriad two-year, four-year, technical, baccalaureate, research, and for-profit institutions, reflects not only efforts by universities to satisfy students' basic needs but also institutional pursuits of status and lifestyle concomitant with the upper echelons of American society. A persistent undercurrent to this history is the ever-emergent tensions between students and administrators over education's purpose and who bears responsibility for certain aspects of it—including food.

Food in the Medieval University

In its earliest form, the European university in medieval times was a physical and intellectual space for master teachers to converge with devoted learners. Initially, the students hired and paid the instructors, often per class session; their authority was soon undermined by faculty who organized for self-protection, and administrators installed by state and religious authorities.[2] Many of the dilemmas and dynamics that beset universities during this time are still present today. Eager charges frequently hailed from wealthy, aristocratic families, able to afford the high cost of rare hand-copied texts of the Roman and Greek masters.[3] Other students were the children of laborers who scraped together paltry sums with the hope of social and economic emancipation, as sliding-scale tuition and fees at these universities made entry possible.[4] As students flocked to faculty in emerging centers of law, medicine, and theology—like Bologna and Paris—peers together organized to secure stable costs for housing and other necessities, including food and books.[5]

As university townspeople often sought to profit off of these growing student economies,[6] room and board were the largest expenses of the medieval student, over and above tuition and miscellaneous fees paid to their faculty and institutions.[7] Dining costs varied across European institutions: a penny per day at Oxford; two to three pennies per day in Vienna; two pennies per meal in Erfurt in Germany; and four *sous* per week in Paris for three meals a day.[8] At such rates, the well-heeled student could enjoy a standard of living similar to (and sometimes better than) the general populace and could easily meet their dietary needs. Students from poor and working backgrounds faced more difficulty in satisfying their bodily hunger and thus turned to a variety of food-seeking strategies. These practices included stealing food from dining halls and peers, seeking funding from parents or the local parishes, begging, and working in manual labor jobs.[9] At Oxford and Cambridge, the dining hall, shared by all students, revealed these divisions in wealth among student scholars. Tellingly, those from less affluent backgrounds donned shorter robes and served their peers in the Commons. The status of *Servitor* or *Commoner* not only stigmatized a portion of the "Oxbridge" student bodies but also reinforced the plethora of institutional rules and regulations related to dining at the time.[10]

Despite the availability of food in these early college towns, as well as the provision of two to three daily meals at European universities,[11] medieval students were known to rail against both the quality and quantity of food provided—and its price.[12] In this letter home, a thirteenth-century student pleads with his parents to send additional funds to sustain him: "This is to inform you that I am studying at Oxford with the greatest diligence, but the matter of money stands greatly in the way of my progress, as it is now two months since I spent the last of what you sent me. The city is expensive and makes many demands; I have to rent lodgings, buy necessaries, and provide for many other things which I cannot now specify."[13] As hinted at by this young Oxford scholar, who noted the "many demands" of his sponsoring city, medieval university students often desired to eat and drink off campus—although doing so was forcefully restricted by faculty masters hoping to avoid quarrels between the matriculates and townspeople. Despite such restrictions, medieval students often entered local pubs, resulting in both minor scuffles and escalating violence between persons of the town and the gown.[14]

University efforts to both provide for student needs and contain student initiative highlight a burgeoning institutional concern for the student experience and finances. Yet the struggle to access food of sufficient quality and quantity existed within these first places of higher learning for a subset of students, as did tensions between the broader student body and those tasked with tending to their learning and well-being.

Food in the Colonial Colleges

Efforts to structure college students' lives increased in the American colonial colleges, as the social contract enacted between youths and institutions catalyzed administrative control over all facets of a student's life, including when they studied, socialized, and slept. In these first American institutions, like Harvard College and Yale College, scholars note that "one of the most heavily regulated, and subsequently fraught, arenas of daily practice was *dining*," as much of the student experience revolved around food.[15] At many of these colleges, students were required to take meals together in the Commons, where the Steward—a staff member tasked with managing the campus kitchen and dining room—could keep a watchful eye on the rituals of prayer and eating in the hall.[16] The Steward also oversaw the portions and variety of food offered, which slowly increased in size and quality from meager provisions of game meat and vegetables to multicourse menus that included appetizers, desserts, and drinks.[17]

Outside of mealtimes, colonial college students could purchase stationery and groceries (called "sizings") like bread and beer at the Buttery, a campus commissary common to colleges throughout the eighteenth century. Here, students could supplement the food provided at mealtimes, which was often derided as monotonous and inadequate. The Butler, who ran the Buttery, was tasked with not only ordering and stocking the marketplace but also keeping tabs on student debt and their class standings, which were prominently displayed in the Buttery for all to see. As such, the Buttery functioned as a site of both administrative regulation and student independence.[18]

However, colonial college presidents established a variety of "Laws and Orders" that regulated food and drink on campus, restricting students' options in some cases and in others requiring certain offerings in the Buttery and Commons. In doing so, these administrators sought to extend the formation of institutional virtues, like moderation and morality,[19] among the student body. Campus records highlight how colonial students bristled at and often resisted such oversight, particularly in relation to wine and spirits. Not hesitant to subvert rules perceived as oppressive, students would bring regulated items from home, such as strong drinks, chocolate, and tea. Administrative responses to these actions were far from proactive, as new food-related regulations were passed years or even decades after the emergence of such informal student economies.[20]

Such tensions existed in the Commons as well, which most notably came to a head in the 1766 Butter Rebellion at Harvard. Frustrated with the rancid butter served at dinner, students elected a spokesperson to address this poor food quality with a college Tutor, or young instructor. However, the lack of response by the Tutor and the Steward's provision of the same rancid butter at the following day's meal led the student body to walk out of chapel en masse to find breakfast in nearby Cambridge.[21] More than just an expression of frustration with foodstuffs, the Butter Rebellion also marked an escalation in student resistance to administrative control rooted in a vision of these young scholars as children needing tending through corporal correction, while students envisioned themselves as autonomous, capable adults possessing associated rights and privileges.[22] Administrative attempts at suppression through various draconian punishments were met with intensifying rounds of guerilla tactics by students. These responses included throwing stones through lecture hall windows, stealing the Harvard Hall chapel Bible, and ultimately, dislodging and hurling the chapel bell through the adjacent library roof. Eventually, tension was resolved through a joint student and administrator committee that concluded that the rancid butter should be thrown out or used in sauces only. No further punishments were meted out for the month-long rioting.[23] In sum, the conflicts over food in the colonial college were of opportunity and restriction, through which students both followed the daily rhythms of their institutions and intentionally pushed back against such regulation, individually and collectively.

The development of dining spaces and administration in the eighteenth century also laid the foundation for continued development in the American university. The colonial Buttery echoes today's campus convenience stores. The roles of Steward and Butler have transitioned into an array of food service managers and dining administrators tasked with providing students with wide-ranging meal options, from decadent buffets in dining halls to grab-and-go options in campus libraries and student union buildings. And yet the dynamic between administrative regulation and student autonomy would be a reoccurring theme that took new forms in the twentieth century.

Food on Campus in the Twentieth Century

Throughout the 1900s, the role of food in campus life shifted as colleges and universities began to more explicitly cater to both students' food needs and wishes. The establishment of the campus dining or eating club exemplifies this transition in food services, as students and their institutions volleyed the responsibility for food provision back and forth throughout the first decades of the century. Much like the medieval students who went before them, the twentieth century college-goer sought not only food but social engagement as well. In conjunction with local townspeople and college alumni, students thus founded eating clubs as private dining options in houses on and around campus, which catered to students' desires for increased quality of food, as well as fraternization. Membership requirements in such eating clubs—like the Ivy Club at Princeton University (c. 1879) and the Breakers Club at Stanford University (c. 1909)—varied: some clubs accepted freshmen, while others were open only to upperclassmen. These eating clubs predominantly served only male students, even through the 1990s.[24] In their foundation and management at the beginning of the century, student autonomy reigned supreme, as they acquired buildings, hired cooks, invited speakers, and added entertainment options (like the eponymous billiards table) for their clubs.[25] As wryly noted by a founder of the Ivy Club, "The fact became apparent that undergraduate Princeton could govern itself."[26]

Increased college access and enrollment in the postwar period further crystalized shifts in dining management and services, most notably observed in outsourcing. As the doors to higher education swung open during the "massification" of the university midcentury—albeit more fully for White, male, affluent students—institutions could not internally keep pace with the demands placed on their services, like the dining hall.[27] Although the cost of food services and paucity of facilities meant that dining demand frequently exceeded campus supply, universities (private and public alike) reestablished on-campus eating in residence halls, standalone cafeterias, and student union buildings.[28] By returning to the food-purveying business, colleges and universities took renewed responsibility for this central facet of college life: here, they sought to combat the perceived elitism of the established dining club model in part by offering dining commons, particularly for poorer students.[29] Despite these original motives, institutions ultimately co-opted the dining clubs' inclinations toward luxury, branding, and exclusivity in their remaking of on-campus food services.

In the 1950s and 1960s, the self-service model became the norm of college dining as a faster, cheaper alternative to the formal eating rituals of years past.[30] Cafeteria-style eating replaced waited tables in the campus dining halls, although menus at the time were often constrained in flavor and variety.[31] Vending machines, soda fountains, and multiple entrée choices were introduced in the years that followed, as campus administrators sought to balance the bottom line of food costs with persistent student requests for increased options and quality.[32] More and more campuses turned to contracted food service providers like Saga (now Sodexo) and ARA (now Aramark) in the 1970s, especially among small and private institutions.[33] By relying on outside vendors to procure and provide food, administrators pursued cost savings through the economy of scale, freeing them to focus more fully on academic offerings, while still ensuring high-quality services that catered to students'—and later parents'—desires.[34] Although outsourcing did not eliminate student complaints altogether, this action did result in two major innovations in the campus dining scene, both of which reflected the emerging priorities of expedience, convenience, and choice: the all-you-can-eat buffet and food court models.

A far cry from the paltry staples cobbled together in the colonial colleges, the buffet and food court–style options introduced in the 1970s and 1980s increased the selection and amount of food available on campus, as multisite contract providers could operate on economies of scale unavailable to self-directed campus dining managers. Mirroring the revolutionary academic elective system introduced by Harvard president Charles Eliot some hundred years earlier,[35] the contract-managed cafeterias prioritized student choice and personalization, as diners could select between a broad array of cuisines to suit their tastes and preferences. In this same period, contractors also introduced the debit meal card system as an alternative to the allotted meal plan. As with buffet and food court innovations, students embraced the newfound ability to spend their dining funds in a variety of locations on and off campus, rather than eating all of their meals in the dining hall.[36] This gradual transformation from *food as sustenance* to *food as experience* also created new opportunities in campus dining for social engagement, expanded exposure to new and diverse foods, and even campus belonging.[37]

The essential elements of the buffet model—quantity, choice, taste—thus continued to take root in the college dining scene. By the end of the twentieth century, food offerings that reflected upper-middle-class lifestyle expectations were increasingly integrated into the American college-going experience. Such food services came to be expected by parents—baby boomers who themselves had witnessed increased quantity and quality of food options on campus.[38] Whereas the organizing principle of campus food in the nineteenth century was administrative control and the twentieth century was convenience and variety, lifestyle and brand recognition began to emerge as the new priorities of the twenty-first century. The *student-as-consumer* model was reified by campus food services and structures, as institutions established full-service convenience stores, remodeled student union buildings to include upscale coffee shops, and brought national chains and local retail eateries onto campus.[39] Structural changes were accompanied by shifts in the items administrators began to stock: organic, locally and responsibly sourced options, and vegetarian, vegan, gluten-free food selections, along with a multitude of snacks, beverages, and nonmeal offerings.[40]

By the end of the twentieth century, collegiate food service was a multibillion-dollar industry,[41] fully reentrenched in college administration and student life. This renewed centrality of food in the lives of college students is particularly evident in promotion and marketing at prestige-oriented institutions: university websites are rife with images of local and chain restaurants stationed across campus; "foodie paradise" was even a catchphrase in one of our study university's promotional materials. Official college tours often include stops (and time for samples) at niche coffee shops, newly remodeled dining halls, and campus convenience stores replete with snacks fit for late-night studying sessions and 8 a.m. classes. Together, these eateries signal to students that the collegiate lifestyle of selective universities is more lobster dinner than ramen noodles,[42] and that food is more amenity than basic need.

Summary

Thus, the story of food in the university is more than what was (or was not) offered at the campus dining hall or commissary; it is also a tale of persistent tensions between administrative regulation and student agency, institutional responsibility and student desire, cultural expectation and university provision. The role and function of food provided on campus grew and shifted in aims and ends as campus administrators sought first to mollify student hunger, later to increase student satisfaction, and presently to leverage food to attract consumer- and lifestyle-oriented prospective families.

Campus food offerings are, more than a convenience or indulgence, intertwined with the heart of higher learning itself:[43] universities' commitments to equal access and opportunity, to formation and engagement, and to self-governance and service are deeply tied to food, materially and symbolically. Yet where food access, expectations related to eating and dining, and shifting responsibilities for the provision of food in college become exclusionary under the umbrella of status striving, such ideals are compromised. The history of this core aspect of college-going adds a new layer to the environmental context of collegiate hunger, which affects both a student's physical well-being and their full participation and belonging in college as a whole experience.

CHAPTER 7

The Logics of Administrating Hunger

As food insecurity has come to the fore as a pressing national and institutional issue in the last decade,[1] administrative roles and responsibilities have shifted, demonstrated in large part by the advent of the campus food pantry and related administrative roles.[2] The creation and implementation of these solutions was not happenstance, however.

The origins of basic needs staffing and support can be located within the larger story of expansion and specialization across collegiate administration. Once the responsibility of the college president, recently graduated "tutors," or students themselves, services are now managed by a dense and interconnected structure of coordinators, directors, deans, and vice presidents.[3] Our study institutions are prime examples: the campuses of Flagship, Lib Arts, and PRU are dotted with centers, departments, and offices dedicated to all manner of student subpopulations and issues. Food insecurity is thus one focus among many for administrators in these selective, affluent universities, as the confluence of national attention, institutional concern, and student financial and material needs make the struggle to access food an unavoidable administrative issue.

The Rise of Modern Scientific Management and the Student Affairs Profession

A central shaping force on the development and direction of the college administrator and the field of student affairs was the rise of modern scientific management, a twentieth-century organizational paradigm that emphasized the principles of measurement, efficiency, and a focus on the individual.[4] Walter Dill Scott, who served as the tenth president of Northwestern University from 1920 to 1939, was one of the pioneers who applied this approach to the experiences of students.[5] Prior to his collegiate presidency, Scott used psychological concepts like motivation to study organizations, beginning with businesses, the US Army during World War I, and later, American colleges. Scott's work in higher education, conducted by Northwestern's Personnel Office, was guided by three core assumptions: that campus personnel should be interested in individual students; that scientific methods and knowledge were more beneficial to personnel work than personal feelings or inclinations; and that personnel services across a college should be coordinated and collaborative in nature.[6] The first task of the Personnel Office—namely, meeting with, testing, and tracking every entering Northwestern student—illustrates this juncture of student care, assessment, and efficiency. As Scott's scientific practices were adopted by other institutions, including Columbia University, Wabash College, and Rutgers University via departing Northwestern staff in the 1930s, the American Council on Education (ACE) took notice.

The 1937 Student Personnel Point of View (SPPV), a report commissioned by ACE to clarify the purposes and tools of college personnel, affirmed and expanded upon the foundational assumptions of modern scientific management made popular at Northwestern. Central to the SPPV was the emphasis on "the student as a whole." By shaping students intellectually, socially, physically, emotionally, and spiritually, college personnel could produce mature citizens and in turn fortify American democracy.[7] To catalyze the holistic development of college students, the SPPV encouraged colleges to make available curricular and co-curricular assistance, including admissions counseling, physical and mental health services, housing and food offerings, recreational and educational activities, student conduct services, and financial and employment aid.

Although the SPPV recognized students' role in their maturation, the report also included management principles aimed at promoting this development by college personnel: an interest in the interconnection of campus services, clarity regarding assigned responsibilities, and assessment about the effectiveness of programs.[8] Consequently, an SPPV-aligned campus personnel program was to include trained administrators who worked within departments of shared specialty, as well as partnered with other offices across their institutions. Ongoing assessment of administrative interventions and student outcomes was paramount. Ultimately, college personnel work shifted from "regulatory and disciplinary" in nature to "dealing with the total needs of the total student personality" through the SPPV as a profession-wide guiding document.[9]

Updated in 1949 and 1987, the SPPV continues to define the philosophy and practice of student affairs through a sustained focus on educating students as whole persons. As student affairs administrators and departments proliferated in the last century, in tandem with the post–World War II massification of higher education as a whole, this commitment functions as a continual ethos in an otherwise quickly changing field.[10] Throughout, one additional constant has been the centrality of evaluation metrics, which have evolved from rudimentary personality tests and nascent academic aptitude tests (which later became the widely used SAT exam) to national-level instruments and data clearinghouses like the National Survey of Student Engagement (NSSE) and the Integrated Postsecondary Education Data System (IPEDS). Student assessment has thus grown into a key feature of higher-education administration, shifting from Scott's simple demographic intakes at Northwestern to complex federal, institutional, and departmental measures of retention, learning, and development. As a result, student affairs administrators have a wealth of tools and information at their disposal to tailor and improve their services for college-goers. Together, the enduring concerns for whole persons and commitments to measurement and evaluation within the field of student affairs reveal how the principles of care and efficiency still foundationally shape administrative practice—including services for students struggling to afford food.

Two Approaches to Administrating Food

Administrative efforts to address collegiate food insecurity, flowing from the confluence of scientific management and the SPPV, are seen in administrative logics. "Logics" in this context refers to accumulated modalities of administrative thinking and practice, which function as implicit frameworks that guide administrators' definitions of students, their needs, and solutions for them. Personnel logics are foundationally shaped by socialization to the field through work and schooling, personal and professional experiences, and administrators' own conceptualizations of their role and work.[11]

The ways administrators at prestige-oriented universities defined and addressed the struggle to afford food reflected two approaches to fulfilling their role. The *logic of efficiency* reflects administrative prioritization of processes that maximize resources through standardization, structure, and data use. This logic is evident in the technical language of "food insecurity" and the strategic implementation of the campus food pantry. The *logic of care* illuminates a professional commitment to valuing students as complex persons with individual needs. This logic is marked by one-off responses to college hunger often offered in relationships between administrators and students. Both of these logics and their corresponding responses can also be read as answers to five central, implicit questions of higher-education administration and administrators:

- How do I best understand student needs?
- How do I best respond to student needs?
- How do I understand my own role?
- How does the environment shape my work?
- How do I envision and include students in my work?

Table 7.1 summarizes these administrative logics and captures the intersection of the logics with foundational concerns of campus personnel.

The efforts of administrators and campus leaders at PRU, Lib Arts, and Flagship reveal the simultaneous use of both of these administrative logics. This dual usage was particularly evident when we asked administrators what they would want students experiencing food insecurity to know about their place on campus. Janis's (library administrator at PRU, where the campus food pantry is located) response captures the combination of the logics in administrative action: "I would tell you that you have a strong support network of people who care. And that we don't want this food insecurity to get in the way of your success. And that here are all these resources and in fact if these aren't enough, tell us what else you need and we'll provide it." Hinting at commitments from both logics—care, relationships, measurement, management, equity—Janis's reflection typifies the co-existence of the principles of efficiency *and* care in the administration of college hunger at the prestige-oriented university.

These logics ultimately help to explain how *and* why particular campus responses to collegiate hunger, most notably the food pantry and one-off food provisions, were pursued and promoted in the prestige-oriented university. The "Good Administrator," then, embraces both of these logics (and their complementary solutions to student hunger), motivated by institutional status-striving and competition that direct administrative attention to marginalized students *and* to the structures of student services.

Table 7.1 Administrative Logics Questions

Administrative Concerns	The Logic of Efficiency	The Logic of Care
How do I best understand student needs?	Measurement	Autobiography
How do I best respond to student needs?	Institutionalization	Individualization
How do I understand my own role?	Management	Care
How does the environment shape my work?	Isomorphism	Locality
How do I envision and include students in my work?	Representation	Solidarity

Food Responses Shaped by the Logic of Efficiency

The campus food pantry as a solution to college hunger is an understandable outcome,[12] in the light of the history of professionalized collegiate administration and the concomitant efforts of institutionalized student services. Across all three study sites, the food pantries shared notable features: a variety of food options made available in a single institutional space supplied via donations and institutional bulk purchases. Whereas the Lib Arts food pantry was student-run, the pantries at Flagship and PRU were professionally staffed within their respective divisions of Student Life. Despite some key differences in staffing and location, the logic of *efficiency* can be seen in the ways administrators created food distribution locations, defined the struggle to afford food via standardized terminology, made and maintained rules for the distribution of food from their pantries, and involved students in solutions to collegiate hunger in limited ways.

For many of the administrators we spoke with, the language of "food insecurity" had fairly recently entered their professional lexicon and imagination. Despite the relative newness of this term in the higher-education sector—and administrators' perceptions that such terminology was not used by students themselves—"food insecurity" still functioned as a lingua franca among those serving students' basic needs. In their common usage of this language, administrators often spoke of the magnitude of food insecurity with regard to a student's experience. Andrea's (financial aid administrator at Lib Arts) definition captures these effects and their consequences:

> Yeah, it could go from having absolutely... "I don't know where I'm going to get my next meal." All the way to, "Well, I have groceries in the house, but I'm choosing that I want to save that for dinner instead of eating it at lunch time." And I mean, either one of those cases affects the student's ability while they're here at school. You know? Either... Both of them could have a health impact on the student. Not being able to focus in class. Not being able to do well. Then you top that on top of the food insecurity if you have a student that is worried about other forms of bills that they have, it just compiles.

As campus leaders and administrators acknowledged the potential negative impacts of food insecurity, many sought metrics that would demonstrate its presence on their campus and justify the outlay of resources in response.

Consequently, staff relied on national survey data and campus-level survey instruments to evaluate the prevalence of food insecurity at their institutions. At Flagship, administrators reported approximately one in four students experienced food insecurity, based on an internal student health survey; Lib Arts and PRU did not have population-wide data apart from pantry use statistics based on the number of student visits and the pounds of food distributed. Such institutional data was triangulated with extant scholarship on collegiate hunger, often learned by administrators from professional journals, conferences, and conversations with peers. Together, the standardized terminology of "food insecurity" and efforts to collect empirical data about the number of students experiencing this phenomenon reveals an administrative commitment to the practice of *measurement,* an extension of the logic of efficiency. By succinctly capturing the struggle to afford food in language and in data, administrators were able to make the case for resources to respond to food insecurity as a real student need.

From Data to Response

Equipped with data suggesting the prevalence and magnitude of student hunger on their campuses and within the larger college-going population, many administrators and campus leaders sought to meet these food needs through new or expanded services. Grace, a mid-level administrator at PRU, explained how efforts to address food insecurity have shifted since she started about a decade ago, culminating in the centralized campus food pantry:

> I think back then we had some emergency funding that we would make available to students, but to have something like the pantry on campus wasn't something that we were actually thinking about.
>
> —Mm hmm (Affirmative). So, what kind of made that shift, or what forced that to become a different kind of response?

I think probably seeing it more, having it be an issue that more students are talking about, rather than it being kind of just a one-off or every now and then having it be something that more students were talking about that they were struggling with.

At PRU, administrators pointed to the rising local and national awareness and pervasiveness of food insecurity as the genesis for institutional responses. Similarly, Ben connected campus data with campus efforts: "I think again it comes back to we saw a need [food insecurity]; we had data to support it." As Ben explained, even limited internal survey data was compelling enough for Student Life leaders at Flagship to then secure a space, funding, and staffing for an on-campus food pantry.

As administrators directed services to students with unmet food needs, most prominently in the form of the food pantry, the twin themes of *institutionalization* and *management* underscored their efforts. At Flagship and PRU in particular, the newly created pantries were operated by professional staff, with the backing of campus leaders like university presidents, vice presidents, and deans. The institutionalized nature of these pantries is also seen in their departmentally sponsored budgets, the space devoted to them on campus, and the campus-wide promotion of these services. One result of this data-driven, centralized effort was institutional legitimacy of food insecurity as a "real" issue, reflected in the minimal resistance administrators reported to the creation of food pantries on their campuses.

Institutional services were often benchmarked against the same services at other institutions, including peer and aspirant universities, as well as nonpeer universities who are leaders in addressing campus hunger. Ben explained this process regarding the Flagship pantry:

> But kind of the questions we were looking at is how are they operating their food pantry in like a 30,000-foot viewpoint? Let's see, we're looking at how do they track their students? 'Cause a lot of our software we're using is wanting to see how we can better track data. What are they reporting out to? 'Cause we need to continually justify our cause. Inventory was the other thing we were looking at. My big thing with the inventory is right now we track all the donations that are coming in and

going out. That is the capturing, but is there any other groups scanning like barcodes to say, "We got—these are the items that are coming in, these are coming out, these are the more popular, least popular," to be more a business model like actually running a grocery store, to better target our students' wants and needs?

For Ben and his supervisor Grant, campus comparisons and national resources like the College and University Food Bank Alliance (CUFBA) offered a "blueprint" for the Flagship pantry. Scholars term this kind of institutional mimicry *mimetic isomorphism*,[13] or reducing risk by patterning services after campus peers within an uncertain and competitive marketplace. With regard to the campus food pantry, mimetic isomorphism helps to explain administrators' desires to provide a comparable service to their peer and aspirant institutions, as well as the popularity of the campus food pantry as a solution to student hunger.

Food Aid as a Logistics Problem

For many administrators, management of the food pantry was labor-intensive, as they considered not only the logistics of providing this service but also the potential consequences for students utilizing it. Grace narrated these concerns in her reflections on opening and sustaining the PRU pantry:

> And there was a parent who wanted to donate money. And we were trying to figure out, well, if they were going to donate money, how is this going to happen? I think it just sort of organically happened that [the PRU food pantry] is what we came up with. So, we knew that we wanted a food pantry, trying to figure out what to call it, so that people would use it and not feel embarrassed. I mean to a certain extent, you have to make it sexy, right? So, people are like, "This is a thing, and this is something that I want to be a part of." On both ends, where a student is willing to go and get what they need but also so we can sustain it because it was a donation . . . a one-time donation, so how do we sustain this? And so, that's where the [food pantry] came from.

As Grace hinted, the processes involved with running a campus food pantry, from receiving donations to monitoring student usage and satisfaction, were core concerns of administrators tasked with managing such services. Despite these difficulties, many administrators viewed the pantry as *the* site of institutional support for students experiencing food insecurity. Tonya, an administrator in student emergency services at Flagship, summarized: "We know that our students are struggling sometimes with food insecurity. This is a real thing that happens to people. We have a resource [the campus food pantry] for that."

To aid in the management of their on-campus pantries, administrators often turned to students to elicit both input and buy-in. At Lib Arts, the campus pantry was student-run; at Flagship, a student advisory council of five was hired to promote and improve the campus food pantry; at PRU, student government endorsed the campus pantry, marketing the resource among peers. Across this work, students functioned as representatives for administrators and administrative services and of the issue of food insecurity, justifying university investments by the urgency of their presence. In this *representative* role, students also spurred forward on-campus conversations, served on steering committees and task forces, and helped to operate the pantry and related services. Notably, it was not a requirement for these roles that students struggled to afford food, and often they did not or had not. However, student representatives did possess an interest in the issue of hunger in college and beyond and were willing to advocate for food resources with both peers and administrators.

Across our study institutions, the logic of efficiency undergirded administrative solutions to student hunger as campus personnel sought to empirically define this struggle as food insecurity and effectively manage this type of student need via the campus food pantry and other initiatives. By revealing how this logic guided responses to college student hunger, the food pantry in particular can be viewed not simply as a singular answer to food insecurity but rather as a popular solution aligned with prevailing administrative operational preferences for measurement, management, institutionalization, isomorphism, and representation. For some administrators, a different modality marked their responses to the struggle to access food in college, one directed instead by the logic of care.

Food Solutions Informed by the Logic of Care

Whereas the structure and function of the campus food pantry reflects the culmination of the logic of efficiency, given its function as a site of management, measurement, and monitoring, the *logic of care* is most visible in administrators' situational responses to hungry students. These individual-level solutions for students struggling to afford food included giving students money directly, stocking snacks in offices, providing food at meetings, and distributing grocery store gift cards to those in need. Within these various professional spaces, administrators also invited students to share their stories of getting by on panels, in meetings, or as committee members. Meeting individual needs and harnessing individual relationships thus represented an essential mechanism of motivation and change under the logic of care. Consequently, this administrative modality sits at the confluence of commitments to autobiography, individualization, locality, and solidarity.

As administrators formed relationships with students through programming, teaching, supervising, and mentoring, those struggling to afford food often confided in them about their experiences and needs. Charles, a senior-level student affairs administrator at PRU, narrated how conversations and relationships between both Hannah (director of student support), Nancy (director of family services), and students with unmet food needs illuminated the magnitude of the issue on their campus: "They [Hannah and Nancy] are the ones who are the initial true champions of this who said, 'Look this is something that we've heard enough students, usually a one-off type conversation, who are dealing with some kind of food insecurity. This issue is more widespread than most of us believe it is, and we need to do something about it.'" Individual students showing up at offices was often the launch point into a wider awareness of food insecurity as a campus "issue." Henry, a center director and professor at Lib Arts, reflected on his own experience in which a student revealed such struggles:

> I co-taught another class with an art historian and I had a student who had a bohemian look—we'll just call him Darren. And he was in my office one day and he said kind of off the cuff that his parents had been living in his dorm room because they're homeless and they lost their business. And he's hungry. He's just not getting enough food because they're eating on his meal plan.
>
> —Wow.
>
> And [I'm] so shocked because you know, it's my own lack of education, but there it is. I've been here long enough to know what offices you call. The dean of students put me in touch with the president's office, which has sort of a discretionary fund for students in exactly this position.

The revelation of food struggles to trusted administrators not only magnified the issue of collegiate hunger but also spurred administrative action, often by activating existing organizational relationships, offices, and systems.

Personalizing Campus Hunger

A number of administrators explained that they too had personal experiences of hunger in their own lives, which fortified their connections with students and motivated their efforts to address students' needs. Alyssa (financial aid administrator at Flagship) was one such administrator whose own difficulties accessing food catalyzed her work: "And I think about my experience where I wasn't talking to anybody about [my] food insecurity. So, I think that students that have food insecurity are stressed, perhaps more isolated, less engaged, maybe working more . . . and I also am afraid that it can be a compounding experience and sort of a vicious cycle. So as all of these things occur that students can just get further and further down this isolated path." These markers and outcomes of the struggle to afford food shaped Alyssa's own financial advising, as well as the ways she trained other academic and financial advisors to recognize and connect with students in need. As we continue to explore in the next chapter, the *biographical* knowledge of hunger deepened administrators' awareness of food insecurity as a campus issue, which they cared about personally and professionally.

For campus personnel at prestige-oriented universities, relationships with students struggling to afford food also served as a medium for tailored, immediate responses to such needs. In contrast to providing structured office-based services, many administrators also acted out of a sense of personal empathy and *care*, often in the form of one-off responses that came out of their own pocket. This sort of administrative tending was also inherently relational, directed toward students with whom they had personal connections. Margaret's (associate provost at PRU) actions to address college student hunger illuminate this kind of administrative action and concern:

> And it was in the classroom that I first realized there is a student who I had who... she was hungry. She came to office hours and we were just sort of talking about different things and she shared what was going on, and that's when I decided to have a basket of snacks in my office. Then as a department we have a basket of snacks, and there's a basket of snacks in this office. So, when students come in for meetings, now, regardless of who they are, I just put the snacks on the table because if she hadn't told me about that, I would never have known.

Similarly, Stephanie (faculty member and student organization advisor at Lib Arts) listed the food items she makes available for students, which she keeps stocked in her office: "Granola bars, nuts, dark chocolate, candy... lots of tea, things like that. And even personal hygiene products." Informed by the logic of care, administrative actions were *personalized* to the students they knew who entered their sphere of influence, rather than centralized administratively through official policy and structures. Administrators who practiced these forms of care were not necessarily critical of the food pantry as a response to food insecurity, but they also opted to tend to the students in their vicinity through individualized provisions of food and financial resources.

Contextualizing the Struggle to Afford Food

As an extension of this administrative practice of personalization, staff also considered the particular campus context in which students' food needs were unmet. Across our conversations with administrators, the topics of cost of living and tuition expenses, grocery store and restaurant locations, on- and off-campus living opportunities, institutional culture and rankings were highlighted as major features of the student experience on these campuses. The affluence and discretionary income implicitly expected of students at these prestige-oriented universities was a noted concern of campus administrators, who recognized the environmental and financial features that intensified the costs of food insecurity on campus. At Flagship, Bret reflected on the potential shame and stigma faced by students from nonaffluent backgrounds, like many of those with unmet food needs: "There may be issues of shame or embarrassment when you're at a place like this where the majority of the students here are from middle and upper income. And then being immersed in that environment and not coming from that background—is there shame or embarrassment or humiliation of trying to cover that aspect of one's life?" Bret's concern—which was shared by campus personnel across our study sites—points to an administrative commitment to both *equity* and *locality*, or the meaning and effect of campus context. Sensitive to the normative realities of campus life, administrators articulated the hidden influence that expected economic stability and surplus had on this subset of students.

In their reflections on hunger as an inequitable student experience, a few campus administrators expressed a desire to be in *solidarity* with those students on the margins of their selective, affluent institutions. Illustratively, Charlotte, an upper-level student affairs administrator at Lib Arts, described the importance of mutual relationships in caring for students, especially those marginalized in higher education institutions:

> We're called to that role [campus leaders] because we care about students and we're student-centered. Nobody as an [upper administrator]

lasts if they don't care about students and they're not student-centric. And in a small community you feel called because you have relationships with people. And food insecurity is one of those things where I can't fix that. I can't make that go away. And that's hard. So, standing in solidarity with our undocumented students who happened to have taken up that cause as theirs ... to be able to really be with people ... it's a pastoral engagement. We walk with folks. We get to know them. We get to know their families. We want to help them be successful and meet their goals. We're not pushing stuff on them. This is about a relationship and fostering transformation over time.

For administrators like Charlotte, caring about the struggle to afford food in college meant developing relationships with students and recognizing their concerns as whole persons, with rich lives and needs outside of the classroom. This commitment to relationship-building is especially evident in the practices of administrators who relied, even implicitly, on the logic of care, as one-off food solutions were often provided in the context of one-on-one connections between students and campus staff.

In sum, the logic of care, like the logic of efficiency, shaped administrators' definitions of and responses to student hunger. Although less prevalent, this approach to supporting students reveals the presence of noncentralized alternatives to the campus food pantry that may be more responsive to the particulars of individual needs.

Prestige and the Logics of Hunger

The presence and influence of both logics within the administration of hunger was amplified by administrators' simultaneous pursuits of prestige. Most clearly, under the logic of efficiency, institutional commitments to prestige augmented the orientation to efficiency toward a pursuit of excellence. Within these status-striving universities, isomorphic tendencies were not isolated to the campus food pantry. Rather, institutional comparison, benchmarking, and the implementation of already-established student services broadly marked administrative efforts. However, simple mimicry of competitors was not the end goal. Desiring to fit the ethos of their institutions—which messaged to students that world-changing experiences happened there—campus personnel instead sought to provide the *best* support to students. Such administrative strivings toward excellence in the context of prestige were especially evident in the operation of the Flagship campus food pantry, which purposefully looked more like a J. Crew store than a church basement, to use Ben's language. Excellence was not solely a mechanism to address students' unmet basic food needs; it was also a channel to remain competitive with other institutions in the higher education marketplace. Ben (food pantry personnel at Flagship) aptly summarized: "We're definitely concerned with what other institutions are doing. I think that comes down to the competitive nature ... we want to be at that level too."

Institutional prestige pursuits also shaped the logic of care, as shifting methodologies of highly publicized college ranking lists pressed campus administrators to care for low-income and first-generation students[14]—many of whom struggle to afford food. Although our conversations with campus administrators like Charlotte and Maxine revealed preexisting awareness of students' basic needs, food issues and their resulting services were made legitimate in part by these national prestige metrics. From presidential commitments (Flagship) to strategic plans (PRU) and mission statements (Lib Arts), administrators and leaders across our campus sites directed resources, spaces, staffing, and money to allay students' food access struggles. Moreover, many campus staff commented on the speed at which institutional responses to students' food needs were made, further hinting at the level of commitment (and the lack of pushback) to address hunger in the prestige-oriented university.

The struggle to access or afford food has long been a feature of the college-going experience. Guided by the professional principles of efficiency and care, administrators and campus leaders at PRU, Lib Arts, and Flagship sought to address this pressing student need through services and relationships, drawing on the logics of efficiency and care. The context of the prestige-oriented university transformed and legitimated these approaches to administrating hunger, as excellence in student services and sensitivity to marginalized populations marked administrators' responses to unmet food needs. By uncovering the confluence of food, administration, and prestige, we see how hunger in college fits within and expands administrative modalities to serving students.

The Good Administrator's Logics

In the prestige-oriented university setting, administrators are tasked with tending to institutional commitments to prestige and to serving students, like those struggling to afford food. The Good Administrator thus leverages growing field-wide sensitivity to marginalized student populations and creates or borrows solutions to student needs by providing excellent services. In doing so, the Good Administrator utilizes *both* the logic of efficiency and the logic of care to institutionalize solutions to collegiate hunger (e.g., the campus food pantry), recognizing through the lens of whole personhood how unmet food needs constrain student experiences in an opportunity-rich environment. The dual usage of these logics is made possible within this particular higher-education context, which values both individual care and institutional status—and can direct resources to both.

Yet the interwoven application of the logics is not without tension. The constitutive elements of these personnel approaches, including measurement, institutionalization, individualization, care, locality, and solidarity, can constrain and otherwise redirect administrators' commitments to efficiency or care. Across our conversations, campus personnel hinted at these tensions, narrating the complexity of administrating students' food needs within selective, affluent campus environments. Illustratively, Isaiah (administrator at PRU) describes how "practical problem-solving" on behalf of the university may not equate to full student care:

> We want students to be here. We're aware that most of our students don't fit that kind of profile [basic needs difficulties]. So what do we do?

And I'll just be honest with you—I don't think we do a great job at that. Still trying to figure it out. There's a lot of interest and concern and the [campus food pantry] is definitely a step in the right direction. But figuring out how to provide a more institutional, cultural sort of support and modification where students feel more welcome and at home here like they actually do belong, that's a big challenge.

Isaiah expands on the experience of students with unmet food needs in the prestige-oriented university setting, one marked by struggle not only in terms of food access but belonging as well, precisely because of the university's cultural identity. He then diagnoses a gap between *student needs* and *university responses*. Isaiah's concern for students' resource challenges and feelings of being unwelcome reflect the logic of care. In turn, Isaiah points to the campus food pantry as a helpful starting point for addressing students' unmet food needs. However, as Isaiah implies, the on-campus pantry and its complementary logic of efficiency do not fully address the institutional and cultural aspects of hunger in the prestige-oriented university.

The prevailing administrative focus on the campus food pantry as the centerpiece solution to collegiate hunger, undergirded by the logic of efficiency, may thus become myopic in focus and function if a holistic concern for student care is not also embraced by campus personnel and leaders. This was a reality at Flagship, PRU, and Lib Arts, as food pantries were incomplete or insufficient at meeting students' food needs—a reality students themselves narrated. The Good Administrator in the prestige-oriented university, whose role sits at the junction of institutional prestige-seeking and the Opportunity Paradigm, must ultimately hold in tension both status-striving and serving students, although each of these tasks may constrain meaningful progress for the other.

CHAPTER 8

Administrating Hungry Students

Administrators responded to their growing awareness of student food insecurity on campus by evaluating its prevalence at their institutions, creating and promoting on-campus food pantries, and building relationships with students struggling to afford food. Across these efforts, campus personnel implicitly developed and conveyed visions of studenthood, or the anticipated identity and experiences of those enrolled at their prestige-oriented places of higher learning.[1]

These administrative images of students—who they are, how they engage on campus, how they utilize campus resources—coalesced into two archetypal visions, which we name the *Good Student* and the *Needy Student*. Whereas the Good Student fully maximizes their experience within an environment rife with resources and opportunities, the Needy Student participates in campus life in constrained or otherwise alternate ways, in part a consequence of the challenges to access food in college they experience. Our use of these terms is intended to be tongue-in-cheek, but in a way that reflects administrators' own implicit bifurcation and valuation of students and student experiences on their selective, affluent campuses.

Administrative Visions of Studenthood

The lens of studenthood offers a new window into the administration of hungry students, as food insecurity is typically studied organizationally rather than relationally.[2] Using this lens uncovers how institutional and administrative efforts to address the struggle to access food often inadvertently aligned with the Good Student, rather than the Needy Student—to the potential detriment of those with unmet food needs.

Ideal and Alternate Campus Experiences

Foundationally, administrators described the Good Student in reference to the ideal/normal campus experience they embraced. For Andrea (director of financial aid), such an education is well rounded, and Good Students take advantage of the possibilities of Lib Arts toward their greater purpose: "I would say it's a student that really values being . . . having an experience that is going to help them be successful in a career after college. I mean, they really want to know 'when I'm coming, what I'm studying is going to make a difference in my life and in the community,' and like I said, having those connections of, 'if I come to Lib Arts where is that going to take me in life?' I think students are now driven to that purpose."

The Good Student, a stereotype implied, promoted, and sometimes critiqued as an ideal by administrators like Andrea, seizes upon the many opportunities offered on their campuses to grow personally, socially, and academically. Administrators reflected on the strong feelings of affiliation that the Good Student carries with them for their alma mater, as well as on the value the institutions place on these students. Julie, a former student emergency services administrator at Flagship, summarized: "There is so much pride in being a student and being a graduate from this institution. . . . And I think again, the reputation that comes from it is that people also hold this institution very highly regarded. So, people want to hire a Flagship graduate, they want to work or do other things with our alumni."

Across our conversations with administrators, many highlighted the financial resources of students on their campuses, which equip them to engage in campus life fully and readily. The Good Student, then, often met cultural expectations of student affluence, which enabled their extensive involvement in campus opportunities. Brad (associate vice president) expanded upon these campus-wide assumptions: "Because there's a certain expectation about what a PRU student is or has access to, there was sort of a blanket assumption that *all* PRU students have those kind of resources available." Although some administrators were abundantly clear that a lack of financial capital did not preclude students from engagement in these prestige-oriented communities, the experience of the Needy Student was shaped in part by a persistent lack of discretionary funds.

Many administrators pointed to the magnitude of hunger as a disruptive force in the lives of Needy Students. Campus personnel recognized how food needs constrain students from the maximized, ideal experience of the Good Student, one promised and promoted by their status- striving campuses. Ben, a food pantry director, expanded upon these implications in terms of involvement, a key feature of the Good Student experience:

> So you could see student involvement, maybe students are involved because that's where the free food's at. You could see a lack of student involvement, especially if there's a cost associated with that. While there is a business school, there is a free career development opportunity. But you have to have a suit. "Well, I'm not gonna buy a suit. I have $1,100 rent. I got electricity. I gotta pay for gas. I can't get across town to buy a suit, let alone get on campus. Not happening." So that would limit that opportunity. . . . So there is definitely financial security, insecurity kinda overlap with food insecurity. So I can definitely easily imagine that translation very well.

Ben's reflections, echoed by many of the administrators we met with, connect financial constraints, unmet food needs, and limited or alternative forms of campus involvement in the experiences of the Needy Student. Although the Good Student was also not without struggle, administrators evaluated them differently than those of the Needy Student—a reality to which we now turn.

Student Challenges and Crises

As we explored previously, there have always been students who struggle with material needs in college. However, the notion that the right kind and amount of challenges are productive in college-going has become endemic to student development literature and the practice of student affairs.[3] Psychologist Nevitt Sanford is credited with first introducing the language of "challenge and support" into the study of college student development,[4] where growth occurs for students when environmental difficulties and support systems function in a productive, dynamic tension. For administrators, such collegiate challenges were present for both the Good Student and the Needy Student at their prestige-oriented campuses. However, whereas the Good Student managed environmental struggles toward growth through the use of existing campus supports, Needy Students experienced crises administrators' perceived as their own responsibility, which often required extra administrative effort to address.

Administrators described the challenges that the Good Student faces, adeptly manages, and grows from, including time management, prioritizing involvement, and dealing with the pressure of their prestige-oriented institutions. Tyler, an administrator at Lib Arts, described how students who maximize their campus experiences work through such issues: "I think that is a part of the maturing process that happens when you're in college. So, I think it is just about trying some things out, getting involved in a number of different organizations or a number of different classes. You know, even changing your major or trying things out in a couple of different majors to see which really, you're interested in and then going for it." The student Tyler describes struggles in expected ways that produce development along psychosocial continua.[5]

Managing the opportunities present at their prestige-oriented institutions pays off for the Good Student, who can then grow in maturity, discern their passion and interests, and ultimately position themselves well for future careers and postcollege plans. Administrators narrated the struggles of the Good Student in tandem with the resources offered by their campuses and used by those who maximized their experiences there. Bret, an administrator at Flagship, summarized how these Good Student issues have corresponding administrative departments to provide solutions and support students: "Now, students are challenged in many different ways. Some have mental health issues. Some have personal family issues. Some have substance abuse issues. Some have issues related to food insecurity, housing issues, you name it. And we've got services here to help you figure your place here. We may not have all the answers, but there are offices, there are services here to help you figure that out." On one hand, Bret's comments helpfully highlight that most students come with human issues that require university attention, often in the form of a specialist's intervention. Part of the challenge of the campus administrator is to familiarize students with these services and their corresponding campus resources. Students are introduced to these structures through campus tours, orientation, marketing and outreach, referrals, mentoring, and advising. These campus resources and administrative relationships coalesce as a safety net for the Good Student, whose needs fit within the scope of acceptable type and severity.

Whereas the Good Student navigates challenges in a supportive environment, the Needy Student deals with crises and ongoing difficulties that administrators and administrative systems were not always set up—or willing—to handle. Administrators in financial aid and student emergency services roles often pointed to these serious financial- and food-related struggles with students as representing needs beyond their ability and mandate to solve. Angelica, a dean of students, used the language of "foreseeable" and "unforeseeable" to describe those areas of need that are the responsibility of the university versus those that are the responsibility of the student:

> I think the perception of a lot of students is we're this university that has all kinds of money, [so] "can't you do this for us?" . . . If there's an unforeseeable expense comes up, we can help them [students] with those kinds

of things and expenses. But foreseeable expenses—housing, food, books, things like that—those are things we want to help students prepare for, and while we can offer financial aid and things like that, those are things that they're ultimately responsible for.

Angelica followed her distinction between "foreseeable" and "unforeseeable" with an example of a student parent struggling to afford food who sought administrators' help with securing childcare and kitchen items for a new apartment. The administrative response was to direct this student to resources, including those outside of the university, but not to provide them directly. Angelica summarized, "We don't do it for them, but we can try to help them learn how to advocate for themselves and get connected to resources." Locating personal responsibility for solving needs by using the language of self-advocacy has the virtue of recognizing the agency of students. However, this framing also serves the dual function of absolving administrators of the moral burden of care in the name of encouraging student development, and subtly suggesting that students are not already taking such actions and should not see their university as a place obligated to help them through their extreme or chronic crises.

When student needs do not fit administrative definitions for what is an acceptable "ask," administrators demonstrate this misalignment through questions that suggest to the student that culpability for the situation rests with them. Alyssa (director of financial aid) summarized the questions that are triggered by a student's request for additional financial aid. These inquiries understandably reflect concern about how students are managing their resources but also implicitly suggest that severe needs are a product of financial mismanagement:

> When they come to us and they ask for additional assistance beyond what they've received already, we really have some very serious conversations with them. "What happened to your money? How are you spending it? Where is it going? Show me your budget. Let's talk about wants versus needs." We spend some pretty significant amount of time with them regarding all of this 'cause we're trying to assist them in understanding what it means to be financially responsible.

Financial responsibility is, like student self-advocacy, an unquestionable good. The suggested message from some administrators, however, was that needs of this magnitude are a product of Needy Students failing at financial management, rather than larger structural or systemic factors that have placed students in fiscal jeopardy.[6]

Situations where extensive aid is made available sometimes came with administrative cautionary tales. At Lib Arts, Charlotte (a student affairs leader) summarized how campus administration institutionalized a student government effort to donate and distribute unused dining swipes; students in need could access these swipes by stopping by a campus office to receive $50 in meal plan credit a week through the end of the semester, to tide students over. However, Charlotte concluded that this effort "did not go so hot": "We ended up dropping 30,000 unplanned dollars, university dollars, and not very many people donated. And everybody went in . . . I say 'everybody' but when they were out of their meal plan . . . Right, let's go get some money. Rather than say, 'Hey, mom, I need some more money for my [dining dollars],' right?" Charlotte noted that this effort created an "internal dialogue" on campus where students and administrators alike questioned who truly counted as a Needy Student—and thus deserved the funds provided. However, administrators did not seem to question their systemic responsibility for the culture of expensive food and beverage access expectation they had constructed and imbued into many students' unsustainable daily practices, in part through the required freshman "big" meal plan. In sum, many administrators worked from the assumptions that the struggle to afford food was often self-inflicted and that their prestige-oriented institutions had limits to the services and support they could provide to Needy Students.

Administrative characterizations of challenges for the Good Student and the Needy Student, as well as their efforts to support them, thus differed not only in the characterization of such struggles (i.e., productive challenge versus self-inflicted crisis) but in the responses as well (i.e., offering existing administrative resources versus questioning student resources). Moreover, these varied responses hint at a third core administrative assumption: that student agency must be protected and encouraged above all.

Student Agency, Advocacy, and Activism

To maximize their campus experience, the Good Student curates a broad set of choices within an opportunity-filled environment, deciding what clubs to join, which internships to pursue, and where to meet up with friends after classes. Consequently, administrators at prestige-oriented universities sought to encourage and protect the agency of the Good Student, stepping in to provide support in established modes and continually promoting the wide variety of experiences available on campus and beyond. This administrative commitment is most readily seen, however, in administrators' responses to the Needy Student. Recall the following instances of administrators' purposeful limitation of provisions for students struggling to afford or access food, done in the name of spurring on student action and agency:

- At PRU, Angelica and her colleagues pointed a student parent experiencing food insecurity to a local thrift store to purchase pots and pans for their new campus housing accommodations when pressed by the student for such resources, so the student and those like them could grow as advocates for their own needs.
- At Flagship, Alyssa and the financial aid office focused on developing students' financial responsibility and decision-making, rather than extending aid in a time of crisis for food-insecure students.
- At Lib Arts, although the student affairs office created a meal plan fund for students in need—who first had to find the right campus office and self-identify as struggling to afford food for these resources—the overwhelming usage of the fund led to programmatic critique and assumptions of student abuse.

Notably, even as professional commitments to helping students expand, these agents often implicitly overlook the vital fact that many students who experience food insecurity in college have already spent a lifetime navigating a lack of financial and food resources. And further, that these difficult challenges have produced in them the maturity, capital, and know-how to be successful in systems like the prestige-oriented university.[7] The prioritization of "agency" (albeit in a narrower sense) by administrators thus often unintentionally served to constrict rather than honor the resourcefulness and determination of food-insecure students, leaving them in a lurch when the resources requested did not fit the existing administrative set of solutions.

In their commitment to student agency, many administrators differentiated between the *productive advocacy* of the Good Student and the *critical activism* of the Needy Student. Whereas administrators viewed the navigational capital and advocacy—both for themselves and others—of the Good Student as generative skills to be honed in college, the requests of Needy Students for funds, services, and support to meet their basic needs were more often met by administrative critique and frustration. Thus, although campus personnel were generally committed to "student agency," the unanswered petitions of the Needy Student whose requests did not fit the extant mental models of administrators reveal the occasional limits and consequences of such ways of thinking.

Lindsey, an assessment director, described the development of productive advocacy at the juncture of administrative structure and students who are just beginning to learn how to navigate organizational systems:

> But really, I think, the biggest challenge we're facing with students is getting them to understand . . . metacognitive piece of, like . . . How do I connect my experiences here, and how do I purposely plan what I'm doing here even if I don't know . . . even if I come in, and I'm a 17- or 18-year-old kid, and I'm going to college because I know that that's what I'm supposed to do. . . . So I guess that's kind of getting them to be active partners in that as well, but having the structure set up for them, so that they know how to navigate and advocate for themselves in that way. So that whatever they do while they're here, they both enjoy it, learn from it, grow

from it, develop, and then ultimately are able to achieve whatever their set markers of success look like once they leave us.

In conversations with administrators like Lindsey, campus personnel characterized student services as a kind of scaffolding for students on their journeys through college and into maturity. The Good Student recognizes this administrative structure, using it as a launching point to follow their own interests and fulfill their own needs.

As narrated by administrators, once students begin to grasp a sense of how to advocate for themselves, Good Students also use that power under the banner of "leadership" to advocate for others. Consequently, students who were not personally struggling to access food, but spread awareness or created solutions for this pressing student issue, were lauded by administrators on the campuses we visited. At Flagship, Ben (food pantry coordinator) and his colleagues hired a student leadership team to run the pantry. He shared how empathy was a central posture valued in the selection process:

> I wasn't too concerned if they were an expert in food insecurity. We can train. That's trainable. But a lot of the folks that we ended up hiring did have a pretty solid understanding. Thinking about [a student who was hired] who mentioned that he didn't have personal experience with food insecurity, but I don't remember exactly what it was, but he definitely had a lot of understanding of what that impact would be. [He] could think in someone else's shoes.

The Good Student, then, engages in advocacy not only for themselves, but for others as well—including Needy Students.

The administrators that we spoke with explicitly expressed a desire to develop student advocacy, especially in times of need. Kathryn, who worked in student emergency services, reflected on how she wanted the students she served—like the Needy Student struggling to afford food—to develop this skill and posture:

> I think in this particular role, it's learning to be an advocate and support students, but also because my [professional] background tells me that they have within themselves to get it done. It's not me doing it for them.

And so self-advocacy and instilling in the student that they know what they can do. They just have to maybe get an extra referral or resources or whatever to get it done is really important to me. I also think that helps me recognize that even in some of our worst crises that there's only so much I can do as my role.

Self-advocacy, then, is an important outcome that can be supported by administrators, though as Kathryn suggests at the end, positioning administrative systems as "supports" distances and shields them from intensive crises when it would seem students are most in need of aid. Like Kathryn, Charlotte (a vice president for student affairs) desired to form students as advocates, particularly when problems arise:

> 'Cause we don't talk about problems at orientation, right? We don't have problems at . . . Jedi mind trick [*waves hand imitating a Star Wars Jedi*]. "There are no problems here, this is like Walt Disney World." So, thinking about within the systems here how do we acknowledge this is a thing? How do we say, "There's nothing wrong with you because you are food insecure, you are hungry, let's help each other. It's okay to ask for help. We want you to be able to advocate for yourself, advocate for one another. Be in community with each other about this."

As Charlotte hints, however, such institutional desires for advocacy are not always explicitly communicated to students, despite deep administrative commitments to this posture.

When the Needy Student *did* engage in agency and advocate on behalf of their needs in ways similar to the Good Student, such efforts of critical activism sometimes garnered administrative critique and reminders of institutional resource limits. At Lib Arts, a student campaign for institutional attention to hunger on campus was met with frustration by some personnel there. Chad explained how the university was already having conversations about campus hunger and supporting groups working on this pressing issue before the student-led campaign, thus contributing to feelings that students did not recognize the university was already organizing around the problem. Jennifer, also an administrator at Lib Arts, reflected on institutional responses to student activism and requests, describing the need for students to accept something less than they initially demanded: "So, there's compromise, there's usually some way that we can figure something out. It doesn't always often look exactly like the ask from the student. So, it's an ongoing challenge and it never won't be. But you kind of have to get comfortable in that space and just always make sure that you're always trying and that 'no' isn't your first answer." Jennifer suggested that part of what students have to adapt to is getting less than they want, even in a context where agency is seen as a virtue. This "cooling out" of student expectations for the outcomes of student activism was paired with a general administrative posture of desiring student engagement,[8] even if it led to a certain amount of disappointment for the ends achieved.

The administrative challenge of addressing the student activism of Needy Students was punctuated by questions of institutional responsibility and resource limits. Grant (dean of students) summarized the state of institutionally available resources, asserting the need for students to have resources outside of what the university provides:

> And if it's a short-term crisis that they're having, we're able to get them through that. We have other resources in student emergency services we provide. We provide [grocery store] gift cards, not as part of the [food pantry], but just a part of our regular interactions with students. So the goal is to help students learn and be able to be self-sufficient and sustained, right? So I would say with that, our program is really hopefully a supplement to them. They also need to be doing other things. And we have other places we can help them, but they need to be doing other things to help whatever their position is, right?

Administrators' visions of agency for the Good Student were of students in temporary need of aid, who worked within the expressed limitations of the university. This vision did not align with the sorts of advocacy for ongoing or severe needs expressed at times by the Needy Student, whose activism challenged campus structural limitations.

Administrators at prestige-oriented universities broadly valued student agency; yet particular modes of agency (namely, advocacy versus activism) were variously encouraged or critiqued by these campus personnel, depending on their alignment with administrative practices. Agency exerted within existing institutional structures and norms ultimately corresponded with the Good Student. In contrast, the Needy Student—like those struggling to afford food—was often framed either as deficient in their agentic capacities or directing such capacities in institutionally inappropriate ways. The Good Student, by enacting agency through making choices about campus engagement and seeking existing administrative support, maximized their undergraduate experience at the prestige-oriented university. The Needy, hungry student, despite similar capacities, was instead perceived as experiencing ongoing crises and seeking solutions outside the purview of the institution.

Resource Claims in the Prestige-Oriented University

By exploring administrators' implicit visions of the college students they are tasked to serve, we reveal how the food services and resources provided at these three prestige-oriented campuses make sense to administrators, while sometimes not adequately serving students' food needs, at least from the students' perspective. Offering resources that do not align with the needs, experiences, and values of students risks contributing to further marginalization of those already on the economic and social periphery. As the chapters that follow reveal, students struggling to afford food are adept at engaging in campus life by navigating systems and structures not built with them in mind, though often at a cost. Yet the design and management of food resources primarily intended for the Good Student makes such navigation even more difficult. The combined result of the struggle to afford food and narrowly focused administrative supports contributes to Needy Students' sense that their place in the university is on the margins and that their presence primarily serves institutional status gain.

One way to understand these mechanisms of marginalization that undergird administrative support systems and student experiences in the prestige-oriented university is through the nature and success of their *resource claims*.[9] A "resource claim" is any action in an organizational context that attempts to secure or direct financial, material, or human resource assets in a way that will be recognized as legitimate. As administrators and students at Flagship, PRU, and Lib Arts requested campus resources—from budget lines for a campus food pantry to a seat at the president's council—those that most aligned with university commitments to student agency and prestige were approved, promoted, and institutionalized.

Relational Inequality Theory (RIT) describes how resource claims are made in organizations, like college campuses, as organizational actors jockey for funding, power, and respect.[10] Material, cultural, and social resources are limited within organizations, however, requiring arbitration: resources are negotiated between actors, and the most legitimate claims are granted.[11] In the prestige-oriented university, the legitimacy of administrators' and students' claims on resources is staked on administrators' desire to develop student agency and to further institutional efforts to maintain or increase prestige. As claims are formally and informally "approved" by campus leadership or even administrators themselves, institutional resources are then directed toward these ends as well, reifying their legitimacy within the prestige-oriented university context.

The missions and mottos of our study campuses reflect the administrative commitment to *agency*, all three of which encourage students and alumni to change the world through or because of their education. As discussed earlier, students practicing agency in nonpreferred modes, like critical activism over productive advocacy, were critiqued and often resisted, as were their enactments of agency (i.e., requests for financial aid or food resources) that did not fit existing administrative solutions. Instead, administrators championed and protected a vision of agency where students were free to make choices that engaged them in their opportunity-rich campus environments. As such, "inappropriate" resource claims, such as one student's request for pots and pans, were rejected, while "appropriate" claims for one-time emergency funding were typically approved. The latter aligned with administrative notions that such support would put students back on their feet without minimizing their agentic capabilities, whereas the former was assumed to undercut student development. Certainly, administrative concerns about resource limitations have some legitimacy, even within resource-rich and opportunity-rich campuses. And yet, the evaluation of resources claims—both those legitimated and rejected—illuminates how this distribution is not random but rather implicitly and explicitly aligned with institutional values that may or may not serve students' actual needs.

Joining "agency," prestige was the second guiding criteria for legitimate claims across our study sites. Definitions of prestige rested on institutional selectivity and rankings, academic rigor, endowment size, students' academic and personal successes, and competitive advantage over other institutions. For a few administrators, status was not the only goal of increasing these facets, however. Charles (upper-level administrator at PRU) explained how easing the burden on students at the financial margins may happen indirectly:

> As we seek to become a more selective institution, high-ranked, more prestigious institution, then we'll be able to grow our endowment, which will allow us to offer far more competitive financial aid packages.... Hopefully, that would mitigate some of the challenges that we experience with regards to just financial hardship in general, amongst a small segment of our student body population. But that's not part of the narrative, if you will, of improving the academic stature of the institution.

As Charles notes, the pursuit of prestige is more often motivated overtly by status gains, rather than improved services or support. In the context of unmet food needs, Mandi, a director of multicultural affairs, suggested that leaders who function as "claims" evaluators largely can avoid focusing on students who struggle the most. Instead, the story told about the university reflects those with the readiest access to resources:

> So, while I think that there is absolutely a responsibility, just because I think we're a community, so we need to care for the "least of us," they [campus leaders] don't have to if they don't want to.... And so there's no incentive, I think, for any institution to... besides out of morality or ethics,

you know? But we don't always operate on morality and ethics, and so when you're thinking, again, about the bottom line and kind of what . . . who comes out of this university, who's going to go abroad and wherever to promote this university, it's more of those students who aren't facing food insecurity than those who are. And so we just rely on the bulk of them because they can . . . to the victor is the spoils. They can tell the story of the university.

However, as recognition of food insecurity in the field of higher education as a pressing student need has increased, the function of prestige has become twofold: to direct administrative attention to a popular issue too visible to ignore, in terms of reputation; and to influence, even implicitly, the creation of services and staff to address hunger in the college setting. At Flagship, for example, the president of the institution introduced a multipillar effort for increasing retention and success, which included a commitment to support low-income students. In tandem with new metrics for institutional rankings that measured support of Pell-eligible students,[12] Flagship's strategic plan not only served students from low-income backgrounds on campus but also bolstered the standing of the university. Even the food pantry at Flagship relayed the effects of prestige: as it was built in reference to resource offerings at peer universities, administrators in emergency services, student life, and communications offices experienced the press of prestige expectations to create a pantry reflective of its image and aspirations.

The interest convergence catalyzed by striving toward status and prestige, through which institutions could serve both students in need and their own aspirational ends, ultimately informed solutions to food insecurity issues via the legitimation of particular resource claims, like the campus food pantry. And yet, the assumptions that justify and shape these pantries—agency and prestige—often poorly served Needy Students, for whom opportunities and engagement were costly, financially, socially, and academically.

Some administrators, recognizing the ways in which their prestige-oriented universities and colleagues did not fully see or serve Needy

Students, offered alternate visions of students struggling to access food and innovative practices of support. These campus personnel, who worked across all three study institutions, shared a formative experience: they themselves had faced food barriers as children or in college, or closely observed others who had.

The Role of Administrative Biography in Managing Hungry Students

Stationed in a quiet office in the center of a bustling campus, Maxine, a director of diversity and inclusion efforts at PRU, sits pondering the question we've posed to her: "How does she define food insecurity?"

> I think, interestingly . . . so, one of the things that you asked me was about food insecurity personally, and I had to really think about that, because in undergrad I didn't experience food insecurity. So, I grew up in Section 8 housing, on food stamps, and Medicaid and free reduced lunch at school. And so college was the first time I was financially independent. Because, surprise, at the time [*laughs*] if you were really poor then you could go to college for almost free [*laughs*]. So, it was kind of amazing. There were some loans, but the interest rates were better and there were more grants, et cetera.
>
> I found myself richer than I'd ever been. Suddenly I had food and I had money. . . . So, it was very surreal.

Maxine's story shifts, however, as she recounts her experiences in graduate school:

> I was paying out-of-state tuition. I was a first-generation and so I don't think I really understood how to look for money during grad school [*laughs*]. So, I was 100% loans, I think. And so I was living off of about $15 a week after all my bills were paid, because my rent was $1,100 and I was sharing an apartment with three other people, and I was still paying $1,100. And, yeah, I remember making bean and cheese quesadillas and I remember making peanut butter and jelly sandwiches. And the grocery store near my house, because it was right next to [prestigious state

institution], was expensive; so I would drive ten miles away to find groceries that were more affordable. I never did the math to see if that was actually reasonable, but it just felt less astronomical. I would skip lunch and just have breakfast when I went to class.

For administrators in our study like Maxine, food insecurity was not solely a burgeoning national issue that required administrative attention but also a struggle experienced personally, as children or as college students themselves.

The results of this biographical orientation to hunger were multiple: administrators with personal histories of and exposure to food insecurity offered more nuanced visions of students struggling to afford food in college, beyond the dichotomy of Good or Needy. And, these same campus personnel often provided prompt and direct support to students with unmet food needs in their midst, often long before formal, institutionalized efforts. These perspectives and practices were undergirded by personal experiences that granted them a complex and empathetic understanding we call *administrative critical distance,* through which administrators from and familiar with the margins defined and addressed hunger in ways outside of the primary dictates of prestige.

Administrators' Own Experiences of Food Struggles

Recent scholarship on college administrators from working-class backgrounds complements existing work on the experiences of students and faculty from lower socioeconomic classes and racially minoritized groups.[13] Broadly, this genre of literature highlights the dissonance often felt by those who do not enter the gates of the academy from middle- and upper-class families, as well as the navigational strategies and alternative forms of capital held by first-generation, low-income, and minoritized students, faculty, and administrators. Despite growing scholarly interest in college administrators' backgrounds, identities, and experiences, few scholars have focused on the intersection of biography and role, or how student and academic affairs professionals draw on their own histories to guide how they understand and respond to student needs.[14] Consequently, questions remain about the ways in which professional and biographical aspects of identity may be intricately merged for those tending to students' basic needs.[15]

Across our conversations with administrators and campus leaders at Flagship, PRU, and Lib Arts, some two dozen campus personnel revealed that personal food struggles shaped their knowledge of this collegiate issue, motivated them to serve students with food needs, and directed their manifold responses to hunger in college. Joy (dean, Lib Arts) revealed this deep connection between her professional concern for college hunger and her biographical struggles to afford food:

> I think that, personally, food insecurity is very clear to me. You know, you just hit on something that I hadn't even thought about or realized, but one of the reasons that this is so personal to me is because I was reared by my grandparents. So, I came from very limited means myself. And I just had a flashback of going to the grocery store with my grandmother and watching her calculate how much money she had in her purse to spend and what she could use that money to spend it on. And how she could make that last for the three of us, my grandfather and her and myself, for a week at a time. And I just had a flashback of watching her do that and feeling that sense of a little bit of shame, embarrassment because I realized that we weren't like everybody else in the store, being able to pick up the meat that we wanted to pick up. We had to go for the beans and the rice instead because it would go further. So, I guess that's one of the reasons why I'm drawn to this, because it's so very, very personal for me.

The richly personal connections to the struggle to afford food shared by college administrators shaped their definitions of and concern for food insecurity, an experience marked not just by hunger but also by stress, anxiety, embarrassment, and navigational strategies.

These administrative biographical reflections both undergirded their definitions of collegiate food insecurity and expanded their imaginations for the experiences of students with unmet food needs. Marissa, a dean and professor at Flagship, referenced her upbringing and family strategies related to food in describing how students deal with hunger in college today:

> I came from a middle-class family but single parent. And I worked all the way through college, so there were just lots of choices to be made about when to eat and what to eat, and trying to eat as late in the morning as possible and as early in the evening as possible so I would only have to pay for two meals a day. Making huge batches of food that I could eat for a week at a time. And I hear the same thing from students—students saying they want things that they can make fairly quickly that are somewhat healthy that are cheap and will last them awhile. And so skipping meals, eating on the run, not eating healthy foods, and then definitely not being able to afford to eat healthy foods.

Devin, a director in admissions and campus visits at PRU, also conveyed insights about students' food difficulties, grounded in his own college experiences. He shared,

> I was someone in college who paid for my own food all throughout four years and I ended up working a lot and taking away from my study time and taking away from my other roles and my extracurricular so I could pay for food. So, that . . . you know. There's not a lot of grocery stores around here, so I think a lot of students struggle with food insecurity because there's not a lot of food availability, like food deserts is a big part of that. I would consider PRU's campus to be partly a food desert because of the restaurants and areas around here are generally expensive.

As these narratives illuminate, the experiences and effects of food insecurity were not foreign to some administrators, who themselves struggled to access food as children or during their own time in college. Instead, these campus personnel recognized how their universities' expectations and contexts added pressure to the college student experience, requiring careful navigation in the pursuit of food.[16]

Campus administrators further shared the ways students with unmet food needs strategically maximized their experiences in college, much like the Good Student. As Maxine (director of diversity at PRU) suggested, such striving was possible "because they're fasting and they're resourceful, they're going to programs and they're making friends with people who have meal plans." Ellen (enrollment management administrator at Flagship) also pointed out the resourcefulness and perseverance of students struggling to access food, as they pursued a full campus experience: "You don't have food. That doesn't mean that you're not getting up every single day and going to school and performing. And you're doing it against the odds. That student is demonstrating resiliency, initiative, and responsibility and maturity at levels that are very different than other students and I don't want us to discount that." Despite this recognition by campus personnel of the navigational strategies and resiliency of students with unmet food needs, such challenges were often evidence of the prevailing Needy Student archetype.

Campus personnel who had secondhand experiences of hunger, of financial difficulties, and of marginality often also arrived at perspectives similar to marginalized administrators. Charlotte's childhood environment contributed to her current empathy for low-income students: "I would say personally I have come from an, I would say middle-class, family. I did grow up in Appalachia part of my life. So, I grew up with poverty around me, but my family was educated and so we didn't suffer at the same pace as some of my peers did growing up." In reflecting on the experiences of her undergraduate peers, Grace, an associate dean of students at PRU, highlighted how unmet basic needs have long been a part of her campus life:

—Yeah. Does it surprise you that this is like an issue for college students?

Mm hmm [negative].

—No?

No, and I guess it doesn't surprise me because one of the things that I talked about was when I was in undergrad, knowing people who were on public assistance in order to be able to eat. So, it was like they could take care of books and all of their tuition type stuff with whatever money they received but just some of the basics were what was falling through the cracks. So, I mean, I guess no, it doesn't surprise me, just because of the people that I knew when I was in school.

From having childhood friends who lived in Section 8 housing to seeing struggles with limited budgets in undergraduate and graduate programs to observing free and reduced lunch offerings in grade school, many administrators we met with described a personal, though secondhand history with the struggle to afford food, long before the term "food insecurity" entered their professional lexicon.

Administrators' personal and witnessed connections to food insecurity not only sensitized them to this need in the college setting but also shaped their rationale for why students may sacrifice food and food resources in opportunity-rich environments. Timothy, an enrollment management administrator, described how his own experience as a "typical ramen kid" in college expanded his knowledge of why students may opt out of university food resources, like a dining hall meal plan, even though in a larger sense, they benefit the student:

> I can point to research where there are benefits to requiring that kid to have a meal plan. And to the extent that it can then be built into a financial aid package—great. But the reality is that the financial aid package will tend, because we don't meet full need, financial aid package will tend not to cover the full thing. And any student, I mean that's the reason I dropped my meal plan when I was in college after the conversation we had is if I've got to get $5,000 towards food and a meal plan, can I make that $5,000 go a lot farther if I am spending it myself? I was the typical ramen kid [*laughing*]. I could make that go a lot further than I can paying Aramark or Sodexo or one of those companies. Now would I have eaten better? Absolutely [*laughs*]. Not a doubt would I have been more successful. Absolutely. But at the time, that wasn't what was in my mind. I didn't know the research around nutrition and student success. I knew what my bill was, and I had to pay for food.

Brad (associate vice president) similarly offered insight into student food choices, with careful recognition of how institutional identity and prestige shapes the food sacrifices students are willing to make to capitalize on their experience:

> So I think part of it just having a personal interest based on where I came from and always wanting to be cognizant of the struggles or challenges. And trying to understand at the different institutions I've been at what people prioritize over food. And at PRU, it's something very different than

other institutions I worked for based on sort of the status, desire, social capital that students are looking for here. They prioritize different things over food than other institutions I've been at.

Some administrators thus articulated how the social, cultural, and even geographic features of their institutions shaped students' experiences of and responses to food insecurity.

Within the growing institutional and national concern for students' struggles to afford food in college, administrators' biographical experiences of hunger, including financial distress, social and psychological effects, and navigational strategies to access food thus functioned as a source of additional insight into this issue and the students affected by it, by virtue of the perspective it granted them.

Biography Shapes Administrative Action

In conversations with campus administrators, many cited their broad experiences of marginalization—and the ways they learned to navigate them—as sources of motivation to enter the field of higher education and as deep influences on their actions as administrators. Charles, an upper-level student affairs administrator at PRU, articulated the influence of his upbringing on his professional career:

> So, I very much consider this work a calling. I'm a first-generation college student. I grew up in a working-class community, I attended a predominantly White institution, and struggled to find community and just felt like a fish out of water. And have since then kind of devoted my career to ensuring that this incredibly significant period in students' lives is maximized to its fullest potential. That students not only survive their collegiate experience, but they actually thrive while they're here.

Across our study institutions, staff members like Isaiah (PRU), Maxine (Lib Arts), and Zoe (Flagship) echoed Charles's commitments, narrating how their experiences as individuals from historically marginalized groups in relation to class, race/ethnicity, and gender/sexuality catalyzed their aspirations to work on college campuses.

In their current roles, campus administrators also drew on their personal and witnessed struggles to afford food, an experience of marginalization that directly influenced their perspectives on and practices for students with the same struggles. Ellen, a vice president of enrollment management, explained how her biographical food experiences have long shaped her approach to serving students in need: "Well, I was a Pell student and I had my own issues with when am I gonna eat; where am I gonna eat; how is that gonna work; am I gonna eat in a healthy way or not? I just encountered a student last week who said she didn't have money for food. And students tell you about it. I mean they're gonna be upright and honest about what their experiences are." Ellen directly connected the strategies she adopted to get by to those she observes in her students today, both of which inform the ways she creates food opportunities on campus:

> I was on leadership groups and I would say, "Can we provide dinner? We're expecting people to come here after class. Can we do that?" As a young supervisor, I was really concerned about when we had trainings for student staff that we would provide food. I mean things that seemed really minor but are a big deal for our students—that we always had a break room for students, that we always had a microwave, that we had access. So, if we had student employees and they were on campus and not working that day, they could still use the facilities. Making sure there were no restrictions for students—that was important.

These personal experiences of food struggles oriented professional concerns and conversations, particularly in ensuring that "minor" food resources, from a free meal to a microwave, could be provided to students. Rachel (upper-level administrator, Flagship) connected her food and financial challenges in college to those faced by students today:

> But I can identify with it as a student, I was a first-gen. [My] parents just didn't have the money. I made some of the same choices that I see students making now, [which] is to skip the meal. Just skip the meal or try to . . . and one of the things . . . second semester sophomore year I found out if you can get an excuse to get exempt from having to eat in the dining

center. They give you the money [from your student loan], right? And I did that my second semester cause my parents needed money. I'm telling my mom, "I got it. It's cool. Blah blah blah." I was hungry. And so, I didn't do that again 'cause that was a lesson learned. I didn't do that again. But I understand it because I was that back in 1978 . . . I was that student, which is why I will work extremely hard if I can.

Rachel's experiences as a struggling student decades ago still shapes small practices that reflect her heightened sensitivity to the burden and stress of lacking adequate food, which included making snacks she personally purchased available in her office for any students. She noted that these items are usually gone "by the end of the week," as students know that they can find food there. Rachel concluded, "And I'm sensitive to that [food struggles] because I know what that's like."

Zoe also made food available in her department, using personal and professional funds to keep snacks and tea stocked for the students who frequent the common area:

> The students we call lovingly "the regulars" that are here every day—they're more likely to stick their head in. I mean like I keep a little stash of snacks and stuff there too if I'm meeting with someone and they're like, "Ooh! Feeling a little woozy." Or, "I just didn't have lunch today." I always offer tea and snacks and stuff just to have that around. And if I have, like, leftovers and stuff, I usually will bring it in too and it gets gone like that.

As with Ellen and Rachel, Zoe's provision of foodstuffs was deeply rooted in her own exposure to basic needs struggles as an undergraduate RA, including food and housing insecurity among her residents. Stephanie, another administrator without personal experiences of hunger but who had witnessed food insecurity among the migrant farm workers she supported before becoming a higher-education professional, connected these experiences to her ritual of bringing donuts and coffee to meetings with students in the campus organization she advised and purchasing coffee and snacks for other students. She recalled that her colleagues accused her of "infantilizing" these students in such efforts, to which she responded: "But the ethos of care I think is compromised and then reframed with a deficit perspective. When it's about recognizing reality for students." The biographical experiences of and exposure to hunger thus led some administrators to offer both informal support and more programmatic resources for students struggling to access food in college.

Many of these practices predated official campus food pantries, although this set of administrators also supported such institutional efforts as well—including Marissa, Grace, and Maxine. When questioned about the feasibility and institutionalization of an on-campus food pantry, Maxine deadpanned: "I don't know, but I'm bringing boxes of granola bars over there right now [*laughs*]."

Personal experiences of food insecurity ultimately sensitized administrators to the struggle to afford food among students on their own campus, perhaps in ways hidden to administrators who have not navigated this issue. These divisions of biography between those who personally knew the struggle to afford food and those who did not sometimes became a fault line, which then separated administrators taking initiative to address collegiate hunger from those who are unsure if it is a legitimate problem. Maxine surmised, "So, it's difficult to get administrators who have not experienced food insecurity to understand that it is a given that it's happening. I know it to be. I've experienced it."

Administrative Critical Distance

For this subset of administrators, biographical knowledge and experiences of food struggles complicates the seemingly neat division between the Good Student and Needy Student. Campus personnel including Maxine, Timothy, Rachel, and Ellen drew upon their own struggles to afford food in their envisioning of hungry students, offering a kind of witness to the lived yet often hidden experiences of food insecurity in affluent spaces. Here, they also recognized the strategic navigation of students with unmet food needs, practices made necessary by the status-striving institutions they occupied.

More than affirmation of struggle and strategy alone, these administrators also offered direct support to food-insecure students on their campuses, from leaving baskets of food near or in their offices (Rachel, Zoe, Marissa) to dropping off goods for campus food pantries (Maxine) to ensuring that student workers had access to microwaves and meals during trainings (Ellen). Administrators' personal knowledge of food insecurity thus emerged as an influential factor in their approach and response to this pressing need.

The concept of *administrative critical distance* further frames some administrators' ways of knowing and modes of addressing hunger in the prestige-oriented environment. Critical distance refers to the perspectives of those with personal identities and experiences outside of the dominant cultural, organizational, and institutional paradigms.[17] From the periphery, individuals and communities have special access to insights and critiques about the invisible and influential norms and expectations of such systems which are often difficult for those entrenched in these spaces to perceive.[18] Thus, experiences of marginality are a valuable source of orientation and evaluation. As well, they enable imagination for alternate forms of agency, affiliation, and support in higher education and beyond.[19]

Biographical experiences of hunger instilled campus administrators with this critical distance in the context of their prestige-oriented universities. Critically Distanced Administrators were sensitized to students' own struggles to afford food and the systems that contributed to those difficulties—even before institution-wide efforts to address food insecurity were created. Rather than waiting for overt signs or the explicit revelation of students' food struggles, Critically Distanced Administrators recognized that campus cultural expectations of disposable income and the normality of expensive campus food together exacerbated food access difficulties. Such foresight is particularly potent in the prestige-oriented university, which implicitly promises that students' basic needs will be met, in part through the proliferation of food options on and near campus. As a result, these administrators responded with small but meaningful actions to put food in the paths of students.

Critically Distanced Administrators' imagination and practices within prestige-oriented environments thus exceeded and rejected implicit institutional expectations and offered new avenues of student support, often informally. These personnel were not deterred by the normative framings of Needy Students on their campuses (e.g., Stephanie's rebuttal to infantilizing hungry students) nor the questions of sustainability and institutional fit and backing (e.g., Maxine's support of the new campus food pantry). In holding these alternate perspectives and actions, Critically Distanced Administrators extended the logic of efficiency *and* the logic of care: they provided new ways of understanding the prevalence and experiences of food insecurity on campus (measurement *and* biography); they promoted singular and campus-wide food efforts, including the on-campus pantries (institutionalization *and* individualization); and they directed personal and departmental resources to provide food for students in their areas (management *and* care).

Critical distance, then, did not remove campus personnel from the prestige-oriented university system but instead equipped them with alternative modes of seeing, and ultimately, administrating. Such alternatives can be viewed as channels of critique and resistance, whereby Critically Distanced Administrators implicitly and explicitly challenged the status quo perspectives and practices of their campuses and sought to transform the management of hunger and hungry students. Purchasing snacks or coffee for students, then, was more than a random act of kindness by campus personnel; rather, such actions—rooted in the biographies of Critically Distanced Administrators—point to deeper and more expansive forms of solidarity and care, which counter the modus operandi of prestige-oriented institutions otherwise concerned with image, status, and affluence.

Summary

Our analysis of prevailing administrative visions of studenthood, namely, the Good Student and the Needy Student, reveals a mismatch between administrative services and student needs. From the campus food pantry to emergency aid departments, such services often assume particular modes of engagement and advocacy that can tacitly invalidate the resource claims of students struggling to afford food. Focusing on resource claims also illuminates how this mismatch of services and needs came to be: claims aligned with institutional pursuits of student agency and prestige were affirmed and promoted by those tasked with tending to student needs. As a result, student services were largely shaped by an idea of a particular type of student who makes particular sorts of claims that utilize resources of specific kinds, shaped by a particular vision of institutional visibility. Students—and their claims—that fall outside of this relatively narrow band of acceptable "asks" are easily invalidated in terms of the acceptability of their identity and their needs. Worse yet, the failure of Needy Students to align with the desirable identity categories and structures of aid available to them represent a threat to university prestige claims by symbolically insinuating that the university is not excelling at some aspect of its function.

The important exception is administrators whose own experiences give them an imagination for expanding the legitimacy of nontraditional student pathways in the prestige-oriented university, often outside of the structures and policies that dominate their time and work. Critically Distanced Administrators drew on their own experiences on the margins in recognizing the struggles and strategies of food-insecure students, as well as the systemic features that exacerbate and necessitate these realities. In doing so, this subset of campus personnel implicitly and explicitly rejected the dichotomous framing of students as Good or Needy, and they instead envisioned those with unmet food needs as both limited by their circumstances and environment, and yet persistent in their maximization of campus opportunities. Moreover, in their critiques of the prestige-oriented university expectations and norms, Critically Distanced Administrators rebuffed the false promises of the Opportunity Paradigm; that is, they could see the ways in which this status-striving system did not serve all students, as clearly evidenced by students' food struggles in an otherwise opportunity-rich environment.

Our portrait of administrators managing hunger and hungry students in prestige-oriented universities is ultimately marked by conflict and contradiction. Prestige, agency, care, and biography interweave in the lives and work of campus personnel who are responsive to student basic needs, although sometimes in modes that serve the ends of prestige, instead of students themselves. The aim of our interrogation of the Good and Critically Distanced Administrators, then, is not to simply demonize the former and valorize the latter. Neither is our work aimed at relieving prestige-oriented institutions and those who tend them from the burden that food insecurity is often a problem that results—at least in part—from administrative decision-making.

Rather, we interpreted our task in part II as revealing the constraints and possibilities of administrators in the prestige-oriented university. Administrative critical distance is one such channel of possibility, as new ways of thinking about students, their needs, and institutional practices rooted in administrators' own backgrounds can offer innovative and humanizing institutional responses for those struggling to afford food on campus. For administrators *without* these biographical experiences of hunger, empathy for students with unmet food needs and sensitivity to how the prestige-oriented environment intensifies these challenges can be gained from those on the margins and from personal experiences with those who are marginalized—including colleague administrators. From this empathy and sensitivity, the Good Administrator entrenched in the paradigm of prestige can imagine new visions of studenthood and new forms of student services, to more fully honor students' own imaginative initiatives in the context of prestige and affluence.

PART III

NAVIGATING THE DREAM

CHAPTER 9

Navigating Pathways through College

Why do young people in college make the choices that they do? The simplicity of this question belies the complexity of factors that influence what a student chooses to spend their time, energy, and money on, and what comes of it. Making sense of students' choices in college has led researchers to ask different sorts of questions, each laden with its own assumptions. Are choices of friends, courses, activities, major, and career the result of a strategic calculation about what options lead most directly to a set of desired goals? Or might decisions in college really not be decisions at all, but outcomes of lifelong socialization to the value of certain kinds of activities that reflect one's social standing, friends from particular social and demographic categories, and majors believed to deliver desirable and attainable status and lifestyle in the future? Or is college a kind of random opportunity generator in which students bounce around collecting friends, courses, internships, and eventually, majors as a product of timing, circumstance, and preference?

The above sets of questions represent three important ways that higher-education scholars interpret how students make their way through college and the particular route or "pathway" that they follow. The first reflects a "rational choice" perspective most common to economics, rooted in the assumption that people make decisions based on an evaluation of what means will produce the most desired ends.[1]

The second is sociological and draws on theories of social influence and reproduction to describe the ways that an individual's imagination for what is possible for them is shaped and constrained by family, culture, and socioeconomic position.[2] The third option is socioenvironmental and emphasizes the power of context and serendipity to explain how a college experience is accumulated from the opportunities available.[3]

If you attended college, each of these approaches likely says something that might resonate as true. And yet, each is strikingly incomplete without the others. In combination then: most students do enter college with goals that are influenced by precollege socialization based on family and community values, priorities, and experiences. These expectations, along with recognized and unrecognized constraints, inform why a student might interpret certain aspects of college as more desirable, worthwhile, or even possible. For example, is an evening at the coffee shop studying with friends an essential part of the social and academic experience, or a waste of money spent on lattes and time that could be spent earning money? Once on campus, the vast array of courses, activities, organizations, and social events create their own set of haphazard encounters and opportunities, even as structural, social, and economic realities reduce or shift the actual set of options available and, perhaps more importantly, the set of possibilities one can imagine. This assemblage of options intersects with an emerging sense of purpose and expectation to result in the way a person navigates through college.

Decades of concern for issues such as student persistence through college, integration into college life, social and psychological development, and choice of major and career[4] have coalesced around the umbrella concept of *student pathways navigation through college*.[5] As set forth by sociologists Elizabeth Armstrong and Laura Hamilton, a "college pathway" describes an organizationally structured set of options—curricula, organizations, social groupings, and experiences—that reflect and reproduce class-stratified opportunities.[6] Although these scholars suggest that student backgrounds heavily influence which of these pathways a student tends to follow (such as the "business pathway" or the "party pathway"), other researchers emphasize instead the role of student agency in navigating these pathways despite constraints.[7]

In the past decade a subset of scholars have focused specifically on student pathways navigation in an attempt to illuminate why students make the decisions they do.[8] Prominently, Chambliss and Takacs emphasize the dynamics of opportunistic choice.[9] The authors argue that, rather than college functioning as a sequence of rational decisions toward a preplanned goal, much of what produces a student's winding trail through college is serendipitous, "based on immediate conditions [and] often idiosyncratic" because student preferences were "neither fixed nor always decisive."[10] Nevertheless, these and other authors emphasize how student social identities (e.g., gender, race, class) and early choices in college (e.g., where one lives, first-year connections with faculty) can encourage "path dependencies," or settle a student into a predictable sequence of choices often related to their social and economic positions, from which they tend not to deviate.[11]

Recently, scholar and educator Theodore Cockle has argued for an approach that is profound in its simplicity: pathways navigation is the product of students *pursuing what they care about most*.[12] Not what they *say* they care about most, but what they actually care about most—as demonstrated by what they actually do. In this way of thinking, students' college experiences are simultaneously rational and opportunistic, emotional and quasi-coherent, but they reveal in the patterns of their choices a set of central priorities, or "cares." A "cares" approach does not negate research which demonstrates that pathways navigation is significantly influenced by university structures and policies, such as required courses or on-campus residency, as well as by interpersonal relationships including with peers, faculty, and student life staff. Of course, students experience a range of unequally distributed constraints and opportunities that may impede or facilitate their efforts to pursue what they care about, including difficult or beneficial financial and familial situations, often related to the social demographics categories with which they identify. However, Cockle found that students themselves pointed to choice as a persistently central feature, leading him to conclude that "agency lies with the student, even in the face of very real social structures."[13]

We find these approaches, with their varying emphases, nevertheless coalesce into a vision of opportunity and constraint. A student's coherent sense of identity, then, emerges from the process of pursuing a set of potentially conflicting "cares," such as honoring parents' desire for a medical degree (which might press them toward a particular professional pathway) while exploring a new passion for theater. This pursuit plays out across a range of bounded "decision points" that are mostly small and incremental but occasionally large and consequential. The result, Cockle names "identity momentum," or the accumulating tendency to make choices that align with priorities one associates most closely with, that gradually coalesce into a distinct but still fungible sense of one's self and one's purpose.[14] For our purposes, "cares" are a helpful entry point for identifying the patterns of decisions that emerge among our participants in response to constraints of background, opportunity, and environment.

The "Cares" of Food-Insecure Students

All students, including those we interviewed, manage an onslaught of decision points that contributed to their particular trajectory through college: Party or study? Work or attend class? Exercise alone or join a fitness class? Attend an organization meeting or hang out with friends? Within our conversations with food-insecure students, participants pointed to two collection points of what Cockle describes as "ultimate cares" or higher-priority motivations into which many other smaller cares feed.[15] This process of sorting out cares across time based on behavior also reveals the "intrusion" of food needs as an aspect of the college experience that students must decide how much "care" to assign to, and how that "care" might be managed alongside less tangible priorities.

In the first, students described moving through college to graduation as an act of *overcoming barriers that honored and benefited those close to them, in addition to themselves.* Most of our participants experienced extraordinary life challenges prior to and during their college careers, such that completion was a major milestone. Kelsy, Vera, and Jill expressed that they had been through too much in life to just quit now. Jill, a senior, recalled nearly dropping out the prior year after her mother was gravely ill, her brother had been shot, and several extended family members died. Engaging in positive self-talk, she reflects, "But then I'm like, 'No, you know, you came all this way. You went through all this stuff. To not finish would just be the greatest regret of all time.'" The importance of graduation was not just for her: "It's important because I think my family has seen me through this all and to not have an end result would be a slap in the face, almost." Similarly, Anali and others articulated the shared sacrifice that made college completion imperative: "My parents have struggled for 40-something years of their life. But I hope that I can make the next 40 for them comfortable." She summarized, "I'm basically their retirement plan." Rather than view this obligation resentfully, Anali embraced the opportunity to use her academic abilities and experiences to improve the lives of her family.

Benefiting loved ones was a theme that took the form of concern for subsequent waves of friends and relations that might follow as well.[16] Many of our participants, including Brooke, Carli, DeShauna, Gavin, Kelsy, and Nicole, were the firstborn of several siblings or the oldest among a close extended family and felt the responsibility of educational trailblazing. Of this task, Nicole commented that "there's, like, a first-gen [college student] quote, that's to remember that 'you're the first so that you won't be the last.' And that's really what I hope to model." Establishing a legacy of not only college access but imagination for life possibilities was a frequent point of emphasis. Nevertheless, communities of origin played a complicated role in the desires of participants. In some cases, they were a constraint to be overcome or separated from due to limitations of resources and imagination for who the student could be. In other cases, they represented vital sources of identity and purposes to which students wanted to then contribute.[17]

Second, in this vein, students want to *maximize the opportunities of a high-quality education in ways that made contributions to themselves and their community.* Despite challenging life circumstances before college, our participants gained access to their competitive universities in part because of their academic achievement, ability, and motivation. These factors contributed to their interest in and efforts to take full advantage of the rich opportunities afforded by their campus, despite a sense among many that they did not belong in the affluent culture of their university. Anali observed of her fellow honors students: "So I can never relate to them in any way that like, 'Oh, yeah, I love Paris.' And I'm like, 'I've never been out of the country.' I can never relate to them on a lot of things." Nevertheless, the idea of using college to grow in ways that were personally valued was reflected by Anali, as well as Beth, Carli, Jules, Tia, and Valeria. Jules observes of his university experience thus far: "I've experienced myself grow here. And it's like a big thing for me. It's what I want to continue to do." Brooke describes her shift from a survival mindset to one of enjoyment and excitement:

> Definitely I think my motivations have kind of shifted as I've grown as a student. Definitely, like I said, in the beginning in my freshman year there were a lot of days where it was like, "I have to do this because I have to, like I just have to do it. I have to do it for my family." . . . And I think now I have really kind of shifted gears a little bit because I love what I'm studying. . . . I love talking about it and thinking about the ways that I'll be able to engage in my career that are really exciting for me.

Brooke's emerging passion for her major altered her sense of collegiate purpose and resulting experience from one focused primarily on others out of a sense of duty, to one also focused on her ability to grow in a field and career.

Growth, as Brooke's story hints, is also a matter of preparing for a future self and contribution. Lucas, who struggled with fitting in as a low-income transfer student, reflects on the advantages he foresees: "I just feel like once I come out of here with a degree, I will be a force. I'll definitely be a force of nature. I'll have a lot of opportunities, and a lot of knowledge, and just general skill set. And I won't have to settle for—it will get me a head start. It will put me a little higher on the ladder of starting out my career, whatever that might be."

Lucas, whose professional goals are to do nonprofit human rights advocacy work, focuses his education on what he wants from life: "I've literally tailored my whole thing to getting to jobs sectors where I have a lot of freedom. . . . so my personal idea of being a good student is gaining the skills to make an actual difference in the world." Similarly, Gavin describes the opportunities he can capitalize upon through strategic use of his education in a place of immense resources:

> The resources. Just . . . I know that . . . I could literally be trapped on this campus and be given a task, I could complete it. Literally any task. You can . . . probably besides presidential shit where it's like "Save the world," or nuke something, but it's like . . . you want to solve cancer? That could happen in these fucking city blocks. And that's why I'm very happy I'm here, 'cause I'm very big on fixing socioeconomic inequality. Change the world; that can happen here. So, that's what I feel about Flagship.

Gavin's confidence that he can leverage his opportunities despite challenges points toward a desired end shared by other participants: to contribute to their communities and to the world in addition to achieving a stable economic life for themselves and their families. Despite the frequent convergence of "cares," basic food needs in an environment of affluence represented a wedge driven by circumstance between the ideal/normal and the real/possible, requiring students to develop coping strategies of various types, each with its own opportunities and consequences.

Campus Navigation Strategies Typology

Students' pursuit of "cares" in the context of food insecurity resulted in five general strategies for navigating the opportunities and constraints of their collegiate experience. Phrased as a question, recognizing that they cannot fully experience the ideal/normal college life of the Good Student, how do students navigate the tension between meeting their basic needs and taking advantage of what their university offers? The navigation strategies typology that emerged from our analysis in response to this question is important in part because food-insecure students tend to be treated as an undifferentiated group across and within higher-education segments.[18] Researchers do recognize that demographic subpopulations, such as Students of Color and first-generation students, are disproportionately likely to experience food insecurity.[19] However, the way particular students navigate the opportunities and demands of the college environment has not been considered.[20]

The Typology: An Overview

The Campus Navigation Strategies Typology emerged from our close reading of student interview transcripts, focused around three pivotal questions related to the tension between the constraints of finances, food, and environment, and the expectations and resources of their prestige-oriented university:

1. What do students prioritize, or care most about?
2. How do students work at having the ideal/normal experience of the Good Student, despite obstacles, as they define and understand it?
3. What opportunities and consequences result from their choices?

Comparing our students' responses to these questions revealed five archetypal approaches:[21]

1. *Adapting*—is the attempt to align one's experience with that of the ideal/normal through engagement with the structures—typically housing and dining—expected of them. These students, often in their first or second years, find the struggle with the cost of food so surprising and frustrating because college for them is so similar to the expectations created by administrators and peers. Adapting is for many students a starting point from which they move into other strategies. Adapting students are Alfredo (Lib Arts), Corbett (PRU), Tia (PRU), Margaret (Lib Arts), Cadence (Lib Arts), DeShauna (Flagship), Gina (Flagship), Jules (Flagship), and Gabriela (Lib Arts).

2. *Sacrificing*—is a strategy whereby students give up more extensive campus involvement in favor of paid employment to cover college costs and basic needs. These students choose to work to pay for college, bills, and food, but their overall dearth of resources means that their food budget is still tight, resulting in careful grocery shopping, limited eating out, and strategies for getting food similar to students in other categories. Food insecurity for this group, in the form of skipping meals, tends to be episodic, occurring due to life crises such as job loss and helping family members financially. Some Sacrificing students live on a thin enough margin that even with employment they eat fewer than three meals a day and often eat inexpensive low-nutrition foods. Sacrificing students are Alejandra (Lib Arts), Anali (Flagship), Beth (Lib Arts), Kelsy (Lib Arts), Valeria (Lib Arts), and William (Lib Arts).
3. *Prioritizing*—makes engagement with campus the motivating and organizing goal. As a result of this orientation, food is a bodily necessity that is given attention only when required but ignored to the fullest extent possible. The result is that students who are Prioritizing may eat only semiregularly and poorly from a nutritional standpoint, worsened by their tendency to eat whatever is fast, available, and does not get in the way of their many commitments and activities. Students engaged in Prioritizing are Camila (Lib Arts), Carli (PRU), Gavin (Flagship), Jill (PRU), Lacey (Flagship), Mandy (Flagship), Nicole (Lib Arts), Paloma (Lib Arts), and Selina (Lib Arts).
4. *Maximizing*—students are focused on capitalizing on the resources of their environment and have learned to do so fairly successfully, although their specific approaches vary significantly. Similar to those Prioritizing in terms of extensive engagement, these students bring the same entrepreneurial spirit to finding food as they do to their general university experience. In some cases they miss meals when this strategic gamble fails to pay off. Maximizing students are Lucas (PRU), Phillip (Flagship), Layla (Flagship), Terrence (Flagship), and Vera (PRU).

5. *Surviving*—students experience the most dire of personal and financial situations. Surviving exemplifies what it looks like to just hang on through college, highlighting how food struggles, often the by-product of other personal and financial challenges, undercut the ability of talented students to maximize their abilities. Surviving is a strategy that students move in and out of as they figure out solutions to difficult circumstances or when those circumstances improve. Surviving students are Ariel (Lib Arts), Chelsea (PRU), and Miranda (Flagship).

As with all typologies, these five categories are generalizations based on commonalities. They do not completely explain the behavior and priorities of any one student. The types do not represent "stable states" but semifluid strategic positions that change as students adapt to their collegiate environment, to new life circumstances, and to their emerging sense of how to manage demands and priorities. Nevertheless, the typology demonstrates how "student food insecurity" can be parsed out into specific strategies used to navigate college under constraint. Further, reflecting recent scholarship, it contributes to the shift away from damage-centric modes of understanding the experiences of marginalized persons and toward asset- and desire-focused approaches that emphasize the typically unacknowledged resources and navigation strategies they employ.[22]

CHAPTER 10

Navigating the Dream I
Adapting

Our first strategic approach, "Adapting," describes students who are doing their best to fit with the social and economic systems embedded in their universities. These nine students' experiences (Alec—PRU; Alfredo—Lib Arts; Cadence—Lib Arts; Corbett—PRU; Gabriela—Lib Arts; Gina—Flagship; Jules—Flagship; Margaret—Lib Arts; Tia—PRU) are the most "normal" of the campus navigation types for how closely their lives almost—but not quite—mirror the archetypal "Good Student" experience. None of the students who are Adapting are desperately food insecure. Often, their times of struggle are isolated to particular circumstances. None of them work extreme numbers of hours or have particularly dire family or relationship circumstances, at least at the point when we talked with them. The gaps in food access they do experience, however, reveal how even in nonextreme scenarios, the environmental expectations of affluence and harmony with campus resource structures, such as the dining hall, can leave students scrambling who are just trying to fit in with what is expected of them. The student profiles below show how fairly ordinary students making ordinary college decisions still can result in costs that exceed resources. In other words, relatively stable students can easily find themselves on the verge of food crises in an environment of affluence expectancy.

Through our analysis we develop a short portrait of featured students in three thematic areas where food insecurity appeared: meal plan gaps, meal plan structures, and transitions from the services bubble. Into each featured student profile we integrate the narratives of similar students to illustrate their apparent "normality" and bring to light how the assumptions of the environment thrust underresourced students into periods of struggle.

Meal Plan Gaps

Three Adapting students who lived on campus with "big" meal plans experienced food insecurity when the tacit promise of the services bubble met the implicit expectation of surplus resources at specific moments in the academic calendar. Tia, an African American sophomore at PRU, attended public schools she described as being more invested in its athletics than academics. Her early passion for dance and theater continued throughout high school. Participation in a national nonprofit arts organization led to a serendipitous connection with a woman who would become an important mentor. Tia's mentor pushed her to consider colleges that had not been on her list, particularly PRU. Tia was initially uncertain: "So, I was like, 'Okay. I'll go to PRU.' And I was looking up the prices and stuff for it. And I was like, 'Oh, this is a pricey school!' I was like, 'This school is expensive!' My mentor was like, 'No, they give out a bunch of scholarships and you're a woman and you're Black.'" Despite earning the "huge" scholarship predicted by her mentor, Tia still pays $16,000 per year for room and board "which sucks," in her words. Of this, Tia finds the meal plan requirements particularly frustrating: "I'm paying for my meal plan. I have to pay out of pocket for it. Plus the flex, which is like you have to do that. Your freshman and sophomore year you have to. Even though I cannot afford it, I have to do it."

Tia notes that PRU's "unlimited" swipes arrangement offers all-day entry into the dining hall but not necessarily the consistent promise of the same food at all times:

> That's another thing that irritates me, too. They just have food out when no one's there. And then they take the food up in the middle of the day. I have

class from 12:30 to 2:00-ish, 3:00-ish, sometimes. And at 2:30, 3:00, there's no food. And there will be no food until 4:00 or 5:00. And it's like, "What am I supposed to do for lunch?" And I understand that some people, other majors and stuff, they're able to do that. But not everybody can.

Her struggle to afford food was not surprising to Tia as a general feature of college, but it was a surprise given the impression of food availability she received from PRU. "They made it seem like, even during breaks, that places would be open. And so, I didn't realize how difficult that would be. How difficult getting access to food when I don't have money and I don't have time. Or when the only thing that's open is all the way across campus would be. I didn't think it was going to be that difficult."

Making her situation more difficult is PRU's location. The university is situated in an upscale residential area bordered by several shopping areas with stores that largely reflect the normative socioeconomics of the neighborhood. Boutiques and niche eateries abound. For students on a tight budget, this means either finding transportation to a less expensive shopping area, ordering food for delivery, or paying the cost of convenience, often in full-service pharmacies or gas station shops with food. Tia feels trapped between these options and frustrated that her university keeps the residence halls open for students but cuts off campus food options:[1] "I'm staying on campus for spring break. I stayed on campus fall break. But there's no food. Everything's closed because everybody's on break. But they don't think about—my thing is, I mean, people, yeah, like me, and my friend. We're both from the east coast. So, we live really far. So, it's not like we have a whole bunch of money to just fly home and be home for the break." The social and logistical support of friends similarly struggling offered some buffer as together they shared the cost of pizza, swapping a few dollars on Cash App. Occasionally, one friend would cover for the others: "And I'll be like, 'Are you sure? Thanks, because I'm broke.' Yeah, that's how we do it most of the times." With spring break upcoming and her friends planning to be gone, Tia is already anxious about managing on her own without the emotional and logistical support that got her through before.

Tia, as a second-year student, is still in the process of figuring out how to manage the apparent inconsistencies of food access at PRU despite her on-campus housing and meal plan. Corbett (PRU) and Alfredo (Lib Arts), both seniors who live on campus and also have full meal plans are seasoned veterans, and yet not beyond the reach of the gaps in the stream of services that come with seasonal academic breaks. Corbett's intersection with the social and cultural norms of PRU is a stark contrast to Tia's. Although he comes from a low-income background, Corbett is a White male whose familiarity with pastimes usually associated with wealth has created connections and opportunities, but also the hazard of potentially revealing that he does not completely fit.

Growing up in New England, Corbett's mother learned to snow ski and sail a boat. From an early age, she had her boys on skis, getting the family free passes by volunteering as a ski instructor. When Corbett was in high school and his mother was able to scrape the money together, they would take a family budget ski trip. The recreational skills of skiing and sailing, typically upper-class leisure activities, created familiarity and comfort in spaces of affluence where lower-income individuals might feel out of place.[2] Once in college, Corbett saw how that familiarity paid off: "When I got to PRU there are other people that have done those things, and so it was something I could also relate to with them, you know? Going up to my friend's ski houses and stuff like that and they've had me there and I can keep up with all of them. Yeah. So, I mean, I think it's kind of an experience that I can relate to some other people with."

Corbett's ability to navigate important cultural signaling activities allowed him to "pass" as middle-income most of the time. One of the few moments of relevance from his perspective was when he joined a fraternity, which was treated by the university as on-campus housing. However, his share of the cost for the in-house chef who cooked meals for the fraternity could not be rolled into financial aid. Corbett knew he could not afford that financial obligation, so he worked out a deal with the fraternity leadership to do extra volunteering and work at house events: "I was good friends with the president and everything like that. He kind of understood my situation. I was like, 'Hey, this is where I'm at.' They loved having me around, so they were like, 'Yeah, we're not going to give you any penalty, just help out, set up, tear things down, do whatever.'"

Corbett was fortunate to leverage his social relationships and "insider" status to get a break on the expected costs of dining with his fraternity. Nevertheless, life among financially well-off friends places Corbett in situations where he needs to avoid the expenses that come with a comfortable financial margin:

> So, I've had plenty of situations where people have a birthday or something like that. And, yeah, they want to go out and, of course, a lot of my friends through my fraternity, you know, are from pretty financially well-off families, and so they'll go out to a nice steak house or something like that. I'm like, "I just can't afford to go to the steak house." And so a lot of times I'll either just turn it down or just be like, "Oh, I've got some studying to do." Or "I'll catch up with you later for a drink or something."

In many ways, Corbett's success at integrating into upper-middle-class social circles, exemplified by Greek life, also places pressure on him to keep up the ruse. In contrast to Tia, whose friend group yields social solidarity and resource-sharing, Corbett's strategy isolates him. Although in most situations he believes his friends to be either unaware or unconcerned about his financial reality, neither does he discuss his situation with most of them. "I've never been extremely, like, open about my financial aid situation. If someone asks me I'll mention that I'm pretty self-supported and stuff like that. But unless you're a good friend of mine, probably never ever aware." The cultural taxation of being low-income, despite matching the ideal/normal of race, gender, and cultural knowledge, is the burden of maintaining a projection of financial stability that does not reflect Corbett's reality, particularly on a campus and in a social setting of normative affluence.

Aside from the need to vigilantly guard against situations where he might get pulled into expenses he cannot afford, Corbett's college experience has been one of resource stability within the services bubble, mostly. Between his financial commitment to on-campus housing and dining, Corbett's basic needs are covered within the confines of the traditional school calendar. Even though he is well versed in the financial aid processes at this point, several weeks prior to our interview a hitch in the system led to a cascade of circumstances that left him with almost no money for food: "My financial aid hadn't been fully applied to my account yet so I wasn't able to enroll in my summer classes, and I didn't have a meal plan. And so . . . and I'm also recovering from this brutal face injury. And so I was like . . . I hadn't worked in a few weeks. So, I was pretty much broke." Between a serious injury that kept him from working and the gap in financial aid that kept him from enrolling in classes so he could get a meal plan, Corbett managed for two weeks on $50. These interruptions are usually something he anticipates, a cost of the services bubble he's adapted to, until his accident removed his safety net. Corbett's close alignment with the unspoken campus ideal/normal includes academic success, extensive campus involvement, integration with the privileged social system of Greek life, and full participation in the housing/dining complex. Yet the apparent security of full engagement on so many fronts does not shield Corbett from the hazards of semester transitions when students are expected to shift their basic needs to their families. Without these financial safety nets, even those who have contingency plans can be thrust into food insecurity when faced with life crises.

Alfredo (Lib Arts) is in many ways the middle ground between Tia and Corbett. A biracial gay student and self-identified "socialite," Alfredo has had a campus career of extensive involvement and visibility. He has been president of the campus PRIDE organization, served on the president's advisory council, run on the cross country team, led training through the Health and Counseling center, and participated with the university spirit squad, among a variety of other activities. In short, he's lived a collegiate life of extensive and visible involvement.

On a campus that is easily navigable physically and organizationally, in a place where he is well known and is connected to many administrators, Alfredo seemed well positioned to avoid, or at least handle a gap in his food resources:

For the most part my meal plan was paid for by the school since I was working for them. Because freshman year they make you buy a meal plan unless you somehow convince them to let you live off campus, but if you live on campus as a freshman you have to have the biggest meal plan. Sophomore year, I just had to pay for a meal plan that year, and then the next two years mine was paid for. So, after... during the summer was my last... was my first chance of surviving on my own.

Alfredo's "surviving" moment, much like Corbett's, came in the summer when he was taking classes between a research internship and the start of the fall semester. Without a paycheck or a meal plan, Alfredo had to get by on the few dollars left after paying tuition and expenses not covered by his scholarship:

> It was like the summer that I was just trying to survive. I don't... I remember the first two weeks vividly because that was intense, but after a while I was just like, "Okay." I eventually switched up, I think, at some point I switched to tortillas instead of ramen, because I just couldn't do ramen anymore, so I started eating tortillas and water. So, that's what I survived off of after that, and then I think at some point I got mangoes to include in that meal so that was it. And then rice, too.

Because it was the summer and few students were around, Alfredo had limited resources at his disposal for food: "because no one was on campus so I couldn't scam or mooch." His only other source of food was the cookies set out for customers at the boutique where Alfredo put in a few hours each week. What surprised Alfredo was the rapid transition from food as an afterthought to food as an emergency, brought on by a fairly minor change in circumstances: "[It was] kind of wild how it happened so quickly. And no one notices. No one noticed that I wasn't eating as much." The invisibility of his struggle, though an isolated situation in a college career largely marked by food security, is to this day an experience he does not talk about with others: "No. Absolutely not. Because my family doesn't have any money. I can't even ask my mom for $20. So, if asking her would put strain on her, her worrying about me, doing this whole thing... I was like 'I can figure it out, I can handle it.' I didn't tell my friends because I just didn't want them to worry and try to figure out . . . I can handle this."

As we have noted in prior research, struggles with food are often the price paid for a student's pursuit of independence and responsibility.[3] Similarly, many students in this study accepted the burden of hunger as a kind of virtue of adulthood, as a way to indirectly care for friends and family who might have been willing to lend a hand but who would struggle in turn if they helped. Alfredo's own sense of bearing the burden of hunger for the benefit of others is reflected in a moment he observed, and learned from, as a child:

> I remember very specifically there was one time when my mom made some kind of white rice, something else, meat dish—something. And I eat a lot. So, I always ate a lot as a kid. Even now, to this day, I still eat a lot. She cooked us this, whatever it was, and then she served us a bowl of it or whatever and then there wasn't anything left in the pot and I was like, "Mom, what are you eating?" Because she was like, "Oh, I'll just get something later." I was like, "Okay," but I knew that was a lie. So, essentially, I ate, like, half of my food and then just, like, left it to not finish it, because I knew she was going to eat that, or whatever was left.

Although missing meals because of the cost of food might seem like a choice to avoid at all costs, food insecurity in some situations gained a kind of nobility when students framed it in terms of the virtues of responsibility and care, often learned from observing their own parents struggle on their behalf.

Like Alfredo and Corbett, Tia has chosen the "virtue" of proving she can be independent, even though unlike them, she believes she could have received help from family if she asked.

> Yeah, fall break, for sure. And even winter break. I was with my dad, but even in that, because I went back a little earlier. And I had money for maybe one chili bowl that I would have to make sure I didn't eat the whole thing in one sitting. Because I needed it for the next day type of thing, and I didn't tell my dad. And I kind of regret that now, knowing that, I mean,

he's my dad, he would have paid for it. He didn't care. I was like, "I'm an adult, I have to figure this out type of thing." And I don't always want to rely on my parents to fix my issues for me.

The features that shape the unsteady transition to adulthood differ substantially depending on a student's resources. For upper-middle-class students, parents may participate in "launching" them by providing a starter car, tuition payments, or help with rent.[4] For many students we talked with, this transition looked much more like recognizing how they could reduce the financial and psychological burden on their parents, even at the cost of hunger.

Tia recognizes her struggles with food are situational, and she is grateful for most of what she has experienced as a student at PRU. Yet she envisions her food access issues affecting her more deeply than occasional bouts with hunger and hard decisions. Food insecurity is reshaping how she understands herself:

> It's rough, because it's like everything here, for the most part, I feel has been positive . . . [but] *it makes me feel like I'm half of a lucky person*. I mean, I can be. And for the most part I am. And it's, like, with struggle comes a lot of stuff. And I feel like that tears at your character. And that tears at you as a person. And yeah, so, I feel like it's hard. And there's a pull-and-give with me having to sacrifice food and me having to sacrifice money in order to continue to be this person. And also, me sacrificing these things in order for me to get the money that I need, and to stay healthy, and stuff like that.

The image of a food-insecure student as "half of a lucky person" and hunger as something that "tears at your character" dramatically describes the unseen effects not merely of experiencing hunger but the reminder of cultural alienation and outsider status that hunger in this space of plenty represents. Even for Corbett (PRU) and Alfredo (Lib Arts) who have had engaged, traditionally successful college careers, the cost of hunger has been a certain level of social isolation and hiding their experiences from others.

Meal Plan Structures

Margaret loves her Lib Arts experience. A sophomore art major with a mental health diagnosis that has significantly shaped her life since birth, she effuses about her sensitive faculty ("I couldn't ask for more!") and the accommodation support she receives through a dedicated case worker ("They help guide me through a lot"). The second of four children in a family she describes as "Mexican-Irish," Margaret is close with her father but often felt uncomfortable and isolated at home due to a strained relationship with her mother. For this reason, she describes Lib Arts as "more homey to me than even back where I used to live. So I love this campus."

Because she knew money was tight for college, she applied herself in high school and was awarded a full scholarship to Lib Arts. Nevertheless, Margaret and her family have at times struggled to understand what a "full ride" implies, in terms of what is and is not covered.

> Last year I took out loans for my books and my supplies. And this year, I didn't take out a loan for those things, because my dad inherited money from my grandmother, who passed away this summer, and he had some of that put away for my supplies so we wouldn't have to take out for that this year. But he didn't know that my meal plan wasn't included, and what my scholarship covered this year. So, he was just kind of caught off guard by that, and that's why we took out a loan last minute.

The "simple" solution of taking out a loan to cover the cost of food (about $2,000 for the year) and sometimes art supplies (around $200 per semester) punts the costs for services down the road, which is a relief in the short run. However, this choice functionally has the compounding effect of increasing the cost of food directly, since on-campus dining costs more than shopping and cooking, and indirectly, since Margaret and her family will need to pay interest on top of the principal from the loan.

The gamble that Margaret—and many other lower- to middle-income families make—is that taking on this debt burden to enter the full campus services "bubble" of housing and dining will pay off in the long run because the student will be taken care of and be able to focus more fully on their collegiate experience.[5] Although this desired effect is achieved in some cases, the waiting gauntlet of postcollege debt threatens to drag young adults into a spiral of expenses that is unsustainable.[6] But future debt is not the only liability of this choice.

What Margaret and her family find confusing and frustrating is the inconsistency of what is provided with institutional language like "full ride" and "full meal plan." The bundle of services promoted on the campus tour that includes meals (and "extra" flex cash), housing, mental and physical health care, campus recreation, and athletic events, can seem like a complete "all included" package. However, what is actually covered is often piecemeal and varies from place to place, such as printing, laundry, parking, and access to athletics and arts events. Much like the added expenses for services provided at high-end hotels, these added costs can seem bothersome to those who are economically secure but represent budget-breakers for those who expect these resources to be all inclusive to the high price already paid.

Cadence, an African American first-year student at Lib Arts, also lives on campus with a meal plan, but her residential and dining experience reflects a different strategic approach: minimize costs. As a participant in the honors program, Cadence is required to live in the honors program residence hall. Because her residence hall does not have a full kitchen, she also pays for a meal plan. Opting for the least expensive option provides her about $100 per week to eat in the dining hall, coffee shop, and on-campus convenience stores. The limitations of her meal budget are clear to her: "I have to be intentional with what I get when I get it, stuff like that, because it's supposed to last the whole semester. But if I eat three times a day, it'll be gone by the middle of November or the end of October." Since Lib Arts charges per item in the dining halls rather than a buffet style, Cadence has learned that she can afford one meal "and probably a snack, like fruit or something" per day if she wants to stretch her money to the end of the semester. Because she has, with careful budgeting, the very basics of a sustainable food source, she does not engage in some of the food access strategies of her peers, such as attending events just for food, unless she is really interested in the club. However, she admits that "if one of the clubs I go to, if they have food, then I'll eat."

Margaret's struggles with food access reflect the expectations of the college environment that she maximize opportunities and align her life with the structures of the university. Although she has the "big" meal plan, the schedule of dining services at Lib Arts means that food is available during certain hours that do not always dovetail with the rhythms of intensive majors and activities. In her case, as a visual arts major, Margaret loves—and at times is consumed by—the extensive studio time her courses require: "Some days I'll remember before the dining hall closes at eight to go and get something before they run out. Or I'll . . . that's probably twice a week. The rest of the time I kind of just forget about it until I'm in bed and my stomach is growling." In some ways, Margaret's food needs are already met, and she simply needs to be better at scheduling her life around when food is available. However, in addition to an environment that expects constant engagement, Margaret's relationship to food and her passive prioritization of meals is a product of a childhood that set these patterns in place. When we ask about the role of food in her family growing up, she admits,

> I honestly think it was kind of an afterthought. There weren't really a lot of planned meals. It was more like oh we . . . it's kind of the same way for me now, which is kind of hard, but it's like, "Oh, we forgot to eat today, so let's go to pick something up off the dollar menu at McDonald's." Or like, we don't have time to eat, we need to . . . because we'd calculate how . . . okay, so how much would . . . how much work would it take to eat this and is it worth it? Like in terms of a paycheck.

The compounding effect of family socialization that minimized the importance of meals and eating—an experience in stark contrast to most middle- and upper-income persons for whom meals provide enjoyment and social connection—and the engrossing experience of college life produces patterns of inconsistent meals for Margaret.

Alec, a first-year student at PRU, is astoundingly involved on campus already: residence hall executive council, student senator, founding member of PRU's first-generation student organization, freshman chair of the East Asian Student Association, PRU Democrats, and an active part of the women's/LGBT center, on top of working two jobs. Alec's personal descriptors include "ambitious," "self-motivated," "passionate," "activist," and "dreamer"—"I've got big dreams." In short, Alec checks many of the boxes that the PRU admissions tour promoted as reflective of a desirable student. Alec lives on campus with a "full" meal plan, but like Margaret and Cadence, their struggle finds its source at the intersection of Alec's history with food and the structures of the meal plan. Unlike Margaret, who finds the available hours of food too constraining, Alec struggled at first because food of some sort is available almost all the time. When Alec was a child, food was inconsistently available and Alec had trouble establishing a healthy relationship to food. "Growing up without food, kind of translated into the first part of my college experience, for like the first half of my first semester I was still just very like, 'This is so strange. There's so much food. Why? How?'" Coming to a campus where traditional "three squares" were expected was one part of Alec's food struggle:

> So, the first week I was trying to figure out, "Okay, I'm going to eat. Yeah? I'm going to eat. Go to class. Am I going to eat again? I guess I'm eating again. And then, dinner. And I'm like, am I supposed to eat one more time? Yeah? No?" and then kids are all walking to the dining hall and I'm like, "I'm going to follow them, because I guess that's how this goes!" So, I just kind of had to learn how to schedule eating, because I didn't have that before.

The invisible normality of food access corresponding to particular times of day was a new experience for Alec. As their sense of confidence that food access is reliable has grown, Alec further deals with their food discomfort by staying busy enough not to think about it: "But for me, my struggle is 24 hours is not enough time in a day. And so, there are a lot of times where I have to make the compromise of, is food worth leaving work and making a few dollars less than what I could make on my next paycheck? Or is food worth not studying and getting a lower grade on tests?" Alec's process of "learning food" in college has set a trajectory of moving from initial Adapting toward other forms of navigation where campus engagement is more important than eating.

Similar to Alec, Cadence (Lib Arts) skipped meals in high school and as a result, doing so in college does not seem like a big deal to her. In part, this is because she has developed adaptive strategies that normalize being hungry in her mind. When we ask how she deals with her busy days when her first meal is at 8:30 p.m., she asserts:

> Sometimes I'm like, "Dang," because sometimes I just want to eat. And then I'm like, "You know . . . can't always . . ." So I'll eventually dive into something else, like work or working on a project or something, you know, forget about it.
>
> —*Yeah, you work to distract yourself from being hungry?*
>
> Yeah.

In a kind of twisted, reverse-Maslowian pyramid, Cadence's food needs make her a more productive student, at least in the sense that she spends more time on her academics as a way to take her mind off of her hunger. And yet, despite this adaptation that many students would find unimaginable, Cadence is determined to have the college experience she came for, even given her food difficulties that she calls "dumb": "I think it's honestly dumb that people have to struggle to pay for food while they're trying to pursue an education. But for me, I'm still going to pursue my education no matter, so, yeah."

Whereas Cadence does her best to ignore food for the sake of academics, Margaret's academic schedule and obsessive working style result in a low prioritization of scheduled meals. Consequently, Margaret's food insecurity occurs at the intersection of food systems that do not take into account students whose entire food budget is committed to their meal plan on one hand, and on the other, students like Cadence who operate from a position of benign neglect when it comes to food needs. Margaret's response is piecemeal and reactive: "Usually before the dining hall closes—it closes Friday night—I try to get a couple frozen mac and cheeses or pretzels as a snack, and I'll use the money that my Dad got me for . . . like we'll run to the store, me and my roommate, we'll run to the store and get a few things." The occasional $20 her Dad is able to send her represents most of her non–meal plan food budget. As a result, Margaret tries hard to save her personal funds for occasional trips to the grocery store for staples (such as laundry detergent) when her roommate can drive them: "I try to go to the store because everything on campus is so overpriced. I've never spent, like, money, money that wasn't part of my meal plan unless I was completely out of my meal plan on campus because it's overpriced."

The struggles that Margaret, Cadence, and Alec experience with food illustrate the mismatch between structural expectations and student resources. Meal plans and dining halls are embedded with organizational assumptions about when and how students should eat that may not be clearly communicated, nor consider factors such as student background, financial limitations, and scheduling expectations. The financial flexibility to travel home or eat out presses middle-class mobility and dining privileges upon students whose "generous" financial packages and meal plans tacitly promise that students will be cared for.

From Meal Plan to Independence

Gina, a junior biology major at Flagship, is determined to be a surgeon. She credits her high school biology teacher for helping her apply for scholarships, pushing her to excel academically, and aiding her college search process. Gina is proud to be a student at Flagship but feels the gulf between classmates who have friends who are doctors and lawyers and can help them make connections and her own family, who has only the vaguest notion of the challenges of her academic path, let alone how to support her:

> So when I go to my dad's side of the family I just say, "Oh, I'm going to college in [metro city]," just 'cause, yeah. And when they ask me what I'm studying, I don't say "biology"'cause then they're like, "Oh what's that?" I just say "medicine" just to like, yeah.
>
> —And how do they respond?
>
> Oh, they're just like ... well they're always like, "Oh! Wow! That's long!" And they're like, "Oh, I've heard it's long!" They don't know because they know someone. They just heard. And I'm like, "Yeah." And they ask me

how many years and then just give me this face like. And it's not like the face . . . I don't know. It's the kind of face where it's like they're like, "Can you do that?" You know? Like that kind of face? And that just . . . yeah.

Gina senses the divide between her family's lack of perspective on her academic journey and her own deep desire to feel supported, even though she believes she is capable of reaching her goals.

Differently from Gina, Jules, the son of immigrants from Rwanda and a junior at Flagship, was fortunate to attend a private college prep high school on scholarship. College was always a family expectation. Although his school provided counselors, he found watching "a day in the life of" vlogs about students' individual daily experiences greatly informed his perceptions of college generally and the specific colleges he considered attending.

Now a junior with his sights set on dentistry, Jules attributes most of his food struggles to the transition from the protected life of the residence hall and meal plan to the relative independence of living off campus his sophomore year, with no prior experience grocery shopping or cooking: "It was like the first month of living on your own. It was just like, yeah, it was very different. 'Cause we bought food from the grocery store and stuff like that, but I was still eating out a lot. So, it was like, 'Dude, this is not . . . I'm not going to be able to sustain this.'" Once off the meal plan, Jules found the typical expectation of his campus environment—and the trendy city neighborhood that flanks it—was for him to eat the convenience and lifestyle food easily available to him, which quickly drained his bank account. In part, his prep school socialization and middle-class friend group made spending money he could not afford on food that was environmentally "normal" seem like the obvious choice.

Like Jules, Gina lived on campus with a meal plan her first year and has found the transition off campus and the time required to plan groceries and cooking to not fit well with her busy student life:

> So I feel like everything is kind of, like, I have to schedule everything just so I know how much time I need and stuff like that. And also it's really hard to find time to eat as well 'cause I wake up and then I always . . . when I wake

up like I'm not hungry. So then I don't eat. But then I realize in class, my stomach starts to, like, rumble and so I'm like, "Oh my god. I should have ate or I should have brought something."

Managing food as the nontypical aspect of her life within an otherwise fairly typical college experience means guessing at what meals she can skip or how to plan her food needs in the space of an unrelenting social, organizational, and academic schedule.

Also opting for the "normal" college experience, Gabriela, a sophomore Mexican American from west Texas, was attracted to Lib Arts for the forensic science major, but the financial aid package she received was the clincher. A combination of scholarships, grants, and loans pay her way, adding to her budget awareness, particularly at the end of the month: "I'm constantly having to remind myself to be able to budget what I have and eat what's in the house already." Part of her financial and logistical calculus was deciding to live on campus: "I felt like living on the campus apartments would be a lot cheaper than it would be out of campus. And it's pretty convenient to live on campus and be able to just go to my classes next door or go to the dining hall if I need to." Gabriela's strategic decision to be part of the on-campus experience, long recognized as endemic to the small liberal arts college, comes with opportunities and costs.[7] Beyond the question of whether on-campus housing is actually the cheaper option, the easy access to food her first year when she was on the "big" meal plan shapes her sense that her busy student life could best be maintained if food was readily available, even if budget-threateningly expensive. Now learning to make do on campus without the reassurance of a meal plan, Gabriela and her roommate share the struggle to afford food, shopping together and making joint grocery decisions. Nevertheless, by the end of the month she is often stretched thin after paying nonnegotiable bills, such as electricity.

Gabriela also skips meals to make sure she doesn't run out of money later. To her, prioritizing academics means making sure she has a financial margin for unexpected expenses: "I think I tend to skip meals just in case I need to buy something for a class, because I don't want to get a hit to my grade just because I don't have the money to be able to get what I need." Nevertheless, academics sometimes does take a "hit" because she is skipping meals and running low on energy: "There are tutoring sessions that I would like to attend to be able to improve in some of my classes, but sometimes I'm too tired or other times I'll find myself feeling really tired during classes."

Similar to Gabriela and others, most of Gina's food cost issues happen toward the end of the month when, after bills are covered, her remaining funds are meted out carefully over the week until her next payday. She has learned as well, like Cadence and Gabriela, to cut back earlier sometimes in anticipation of one-time expenses, such as special occasions like birthdays or other unavoidable hits to her budget. Currently, she's saving money to make sure she has what she needs for gas to drive home for one of her siblings' birthdays ("We don't do a lot for that, it's just being there, singing 'Happy Birthday'") and for a cousin's upcoming wedding.

Opportunism is part of Gina's strategy. When she's home, Gina stocks up on favorite foods that she can bring back to supplement her food budget: "I told my Grandma to make extra tamales so I could bring some. So I brought 36 back. So in the beginning of January I was eating all of that." At her internship is a small kitchen often stocked with ready-made snacks that she's been told are free for the taking. "Sometimes they have like mac and cheese things in there, and I like mac and cheese, so I'm like, 'Oh, I'll take those.'" As with other students, the generosity of friends with meal plans, roommates cooking dinner, and organizations offering free food are important parts of "making it" financially.

Like Gina, Gabriela has learned to keep a close eye on her budget and keep some money in reserve for emergencies by skimping on food, and the effects of these choices shape how she sees herself in this competitive affluent environment. Describing times she lies to her friends about what she has eaten, Gabriela concludes, "It feels bad to lie to them, but I'd also feel really embarrassed to tell them I was struggling." Probing further on this comment, she elaborates: "Like, I guess everyone just seems to be doing perfectly fine. They'll ... everyone seems to be able to go spend money on coffees or going to eat somewhere fancy, and it's kind of like putting pressure on people who don't really have the opportunity to do that, to not talk about stuff like that."

Despite Gina's premed major and many points of engagement, she seems to be managing it all fairly well. However, the costs of college mean that struggling to pay for food (and preparing it) is her specific source of frustration:

> Well, if I didn't struggle to pay for food and if I knew how to cook, I would probably be living a good life. Yeah, 'cause other than that I'm not bugged about having to travel all the way to campus, having to wake up early. I'm not bugged about that. I feel like food is definitely like, when I'm stressed I do like to eat. So it's like school can wait a little while I eat. So I feel like food is definitely . . . like if I had it and if I wasn't struggling, then I'd be living good.

When we ask how she deals with stress but does not have much money for food, Gina replies, deadpan: "Oh, I go to sleep. Yeah. I go to sleep. I tend to sleep a lot when I'm stressed just to like de-stress. Kind of like clear my mind." A number of students described some variation on the theme of "eating sleep for dinner"—managing the difficulty of hunger by going to bed. The lack of enough to eat forces students like Gina who are fitting much of the student mold to take on some behaviors that are far from normal, even while they often appear to peers, professors, and family as if their student experiences are completely typical.

Gina, Jules, and Gabriela are not far off from the vision of the Good Student college life their environment invisibly presses upon them through norms of housing, participation, and food access. All three students are deeply involved academically, make time to participate in on-campus events, and have a social circle important to their college experience. And yet, part of the burden of "not quite" is the physical toll of not having the energy to fully engage academically, and the psychological toll of not being able to engage fully—and honestly—socially.

Summary

The students engaged in Adapting strategies are making it reasonably well. They are invested in their majors, often employed, and engaged in organizations and with friends on campus. Yet to describe them, as Tia offers, as "half of a lucky person," highlights both the rich opportunities of enrollment at a prestige-oriented university and the incompleteness of their experience. Most of this group—Alec, Alfredo, Cadence, Corbett, Margaret, and Tia—are engaged in the partial student experience even though they have taken on the cost burden of on-campus housing and meal plans. The sales price of total care in the services bubble is accompanied by the "fine print" of institutional expectations of financial reserves to cover food during breaks and days when schedules do not align with dining hours. Valeria (Lib Arts), who previously engaged in Adapting, highlights the contrast between what she—and others—feel they were sold, and the reality they find: "And it's really frustrating because schools sell you this idea of, like, you'll be taken care of. 'You can come to our program. It will be paid for.' But, like, people now have learned to read the fine print that says, 'Tuition is covered. You have to look for housing.'" Learning to "read the fine print" and coming to terms with the mismatch between the ideal/normal tacitly promised and the reality of financial struggle is often what transitioned students away from their efforts at Adapting and toward one of the other strategies detailed in subsequent chapters.

The other three students—Gabriela, Gina, and Jules—all experienced the shock of a rough exit out of the shelter of the meal plan as they were functionally thrust into the challenges of operational autonomy. This new state of self-management outside the seeming abundance of the services bubble nevertheless subjected them not only to the full cost of on-campus convenience food but also to the inconvenience of a near-campus environment geared toward the apparently well-financed student. On this point, statistics asserting that roughly 40% of college students experience some form of food insecurity can seem gaudy and exaggerated.[8] That is, until we recognize how the for-profit aspects of the food industry in and around campuses has developed in tandem with the ease of interest-deferred college loans that fill the pockets of unwary undergraduates with borrowed money to spend. Students of modest means who are concerned about submergence in college debt find that they are priced out of participating in what have become "typical" food consumption practices: grabbing lunch with friends at a trendy food truck, going to get dessert at a craft ice cream shop, or hanging out around afternoon coffee at a hipster café.

Some students (Alec, Margaret, Gabriela) in the Adapting strategy struggle at the intersection of precollege experiences with food that have resulted in responses ranging from eating disorders to benign neglect of food. The most stable students employing the Adapting strategy (Alfredo, Corbett, Tia) are generally food secure, but they hit their crisis moments when their lack of the expected safety net of family wealth leaves them without resource during university breaks. Other students whose experiences are outside the services bubble face choices more dire and complex, resulting in strategies that are similarly more extreme, in terms of their cost-benefit analysis of what is worth caring about in college.

CHAPTER 11

Navigating the Dream II
Sacrificing

Students who engaged in Sacrificing recognized the possibilities for networking, involvement in organizations, and preprofessional engagement offered by a competitive university that went beyond basic academic quality. This environmental recognition made them similar to peers using other navigation strategies. We call this understanding "buying into the Opportunity Paradigm." According to Alejandra, "Maximizing your time here at Lib Arts is also making good use of all the resources available to you." Anali (Flagship) similarly names specific forms of engagement as central to taking advantage of all the university has to offer: "definitely building a network of people and that's obviously through being involved in organizations and being friendly with your professors." For many of our participants, the full spectrum of college opportunities and related expectations was unknown until they arrived on campus. Valeria (Lib Arts) points again to the collegiate totem of the unpaid internship as attractive but not universally available:

> So, we have some students who have really great experiences with either service opportunities or internships, but both are usually unpaid for. And those are a lot of the kids who have more funds to do that. And so, you have other kids, like me, for the most part, and this is a reality amongst most Latino communities, on campus at least. Maybe you're part of a club,

but you're also working. You either have one part-time job. I know some people who have three. And usually they live off campus, because they can't afford to live on campus because their scholarships don't fulfill that. No one really talks about that specific grind versus the ideal, "Oh, you don't have to worry about it, just get an internship."

Valeria's description of the "grind" of working outside employment to make ends meet but still not having the time and resources to engage in the most desirable experiences reflects the situations of many students who choose Sacrificing as their strategic approach. For this reason, Sacrificing students keenly feel the tension of college as a place of choices. For them, some choices—such as employment—are less choices than they are requirements, and other choices, such as unpaid internships, are seldom ones that they can afford to make.

Employment

The defining characteristic of Sacrificing is the belief that working to pay for college-related expenses is nonnegotiable, and by implication, the rest of college life is arranged around the priority of employment. The six students who best fit the Sacrificing strategy (Alejandra—Lib Arts, Anali—Flagship, Beth—Lib Arts, Kelsy—Lib Arts, Valeria—Lib Arts, and William—Lib Arts) worked, on average, 20 and 40 hours per week while attending classes full time. Often, they took on more hours during breaks in the academic calendar. As their experiences reveal, "employment" is a false monolith disguising considerable variety: Kelsy (Starbucks), Beth (Urban Outfitters), and Valeria (school district paid internship) had "steady" work, in the sense that they benefited from the continuity of employment at the same location. The other four students in this type described moving from job to job, sometimes because of short-term employment (e.g., Alejandra's jobs in the hospitality industry; Anali's paid internships), sometimes because of the undesired loss of a position. Kelsy worked a combination of on- and off-campus positions, including at a work-study "desk job." William paired regular hours at a local grocery with a psych services consulting gig that paid more but with less predictable hours.

Students found that the decision to prioritize paid employment quickly cascaded into the series of branching streams of logistical decisions carrying forward the compromises of college choices. In this, Beth's (Lib Arts) experience highlights important features. After her required first year on campus, Beth chose to live across the city to save money on rent, where her share is about $500 a month. Although she is fortunate that her scholarship covers most of it, the "cost" of trying to fit her housing expense within the amount allotted from her scholarship means an hour commute each way, including several bus changes to reach campus.

Finding a job that works within the constraints of an academic schedule poses challenges that often make flexibility of work times a high priority, even if it did not pay very well or yield as many hours as students might find otherwise. Beth's job downtown at Urban Outfitters, a trendy clothing retailer, comes with costs and opportunities: "I would love to have a better-paying job, but they are so lenient with availability, which is hard, I know. If need be, they'll let me take, like, the entire summer off. Like, when I first started, they're like, 'Oh, are you going back home for the summer?' which I didn't because I wanted to make some money. So yeah—that's really why I chose that job." Kelsy's (Lib Arts) job at Starbucks offers early morning work hours that fit with her academic schedule, is close by campus, and includes "really good benefits" in the form of health insurance, free food, and Spotify Premium.

The Campus Experience

Because of her working and transit schedules, Beth is on campus at Lib Arts only three days a week this semester. Packing a full load of classes into a Monday/Wednesday/Friday schedule means maximizing her time on campus, including fitting homework in between class times, touching base with friends, and making any stops to talk to faculty that she requires. The morning bus that leaves at 7:20 a.m. returns her home on "school days" at 8 p.m., leaving little time for the sorts of campus involvement often envisioned as part of a small college experience. When we ask Beth if her expectation of college matches her experiences, Beth laughs and says, "Ooh, my experience is definitely much different. I was given false information by movies." When pressed, she elaborates: "I thought it was going to be so awesome, but it's definitely more 'real life' than I was expecting. . . . I really didn't think I would have to work more. Growing up, I guess I thought you'd be more focused on the actual experience of it, but now because of it you have to work a lot more, which makes you miss things." Beth's comment highlights the compromise between gaining "access" in terms of admission to the university versus "access" as full engagement in the Opportunity Paradigm.

Valeria (Lib Arts) echoes Beth's perspective and the vision of the college experience where she could be both a fully engaged student and carefree, or "dumb," to use her term:

> I thought living on my own, being a college student, I can just be dumb. I can go out on the weekends. And I'm like, "No, you have to work on Monday." Or "You need to do this internship, or this research project over the summer." So, I couldn't really hang out with my friends last summer. It was just so much more being a good, responsible young adult, rather than being what I deemed, you know, going in here, being a college student. Being really relaxed, having very few things to worry about, for the most part.

Describing her vision of what elsewhere we term the "Good Student"—relaxed, carefree, few worries—Valeria focuses on professional opportunities missed; Beth (Lib Arts) and Anali (Flagship) express a kind of collegiate FOMO (Fear of Missing Out) related to the social experiences that are the stuff of memories. Beth explains what working is costing her: "Opportunities to meet people and to mingle and things like that, because a lot of times I'm at a shift while people are going out to party or going to do this, I'm working." Anali (Flagship) observes peers joining spirit organizations and going to sporting events, and she reflects wistfully: "So they get to do things like, I don't know, take fun

Instagram pictures, you know, *Instagram-able moments*, just like really enjoy things that come with college. And I feel like I'm just like, 'I have to focus on school.'" For students who engage in Sacrificing, committing to living within their limited financial resources means watching the ideal/normal college experience like a kind of parallel universe, similar to but apart from their own.

Despite the tension between schoolwork, employment, transit logistics, and maintaining some semblance of a social life, Sacrificing students often do want to be involved on campus, though success at this goal varied. Alejandra (Lib Arts) made time for a Latine student organization, intramural sports, and "a couple political kind of clubs"; Anali (Flagship) joined her university's color guard, an organization for immigrant advocacy, and student government. Kelsy (Lib Arts) holds leadership roles in PRIDE (the campus straight-gay alliance) and a sexual assault education/prevention organization.

Others Sacrificing have either not found ways to engage as they wish or have found involvement elsewhere. William (Lib Arts) was involved with the campus radio station as a first-year, but his activities now mostly take place off campus, living with several friends in a house, playing in a band, working several jobs, and dreaming of starting a nonprofit to support musicians' mental health. Beth (Lib Arts) intended to join an arts club and even signed up at an activity fair but has not been able to make the travel schedule work:

> I wanted to be [involved]. Technically I am on paper, but I haven't been able to go to meetings 'cause the times are so inconvenient, especially with the bus ride. It would be like an all-day affair.
>
> —*Yeah. How do you feel about that?*
>
> I'm disappointed 'cause I was actually really excited to be a part of them and some of them seemed really cool.

Despite her participation in the McNair Scholars program that supports graduate aspirations for low-income and first-generation students, Valeria (Lib Arts) says, with a laugh, that food insecurity is "the one club I'm in on campus."

Academic Costs of Employment

Although "involvement" often signals attention to what happens outside of class, Sacrificing students are very aware of how working changes the way they engage with academics. Classes that Beth (Lib Arts) finds less compelling sometimes become a casualty of financial pressure: "Sometimes I [ask myself], 'Oh, can I just skip class today and pick up an extra shift for more money?' Then there's the stress from work that blurs into school, and also stress from school affects my work."[1] For these high-ability students, the compromise of working is also a compromise of achievement, a part of their life and identity that has been a constant until now. As scholars have found, although the solution to the cost of college seems to point to concurrent employment, often students find that the demands of school and work are incommensurate, each its own "greedy" institution demanding priority that students find difficult to reconcile.[2]

Managing Food

Because of the press of an expensive campus environment and the unpredictability of life crises, students engage in a cost-benefit game between the "cares" of financial stability, social and academic involvement, and eating, where one of these important investments is often losing out. Valeria (Lib Arts) articulates this tension in terms of being "responsible," a kind of extra burden that does not fit her vision of the ideal/normal college experience, but one that is required of her just to get by:

> I realized that if I was not responsible, I would not get what I want. And if I wanted to be selfish and if I want to afford the things that I want to afford, if I want to be able to afford necessities and the extra stuff, that meant being responsible. Especially budgeting—it's just completely shaped the way I think of things. As in, "Oh, that's so many groceries right there." Or, "Do I really need that textbook? Because I could use that money because I got sick." It's totally—*my strict finances have really made me the adult that I have to be when I really didn't want to be.*

Fewer groceries, fewer textbooks, a bit more margin in case of emergencies—these are the "adult" compromises that employment salves but does not heal. Beth (Lib Arts) describes the demands of working paired with the hard choices of what to do with the time and resources that remain: "So I would say I sacrifice doing recreational activities a lot so that I can work to afford food. So I know that my friends have brought it up. They're like, 'Oh, you're always busy.' And it's 'cause I'm like, 'I have to work. I have to get food and stuff.' So I sacrifice that a lot."

The struggle between needs—for food, for relationships, for mental health—involves ongoing calculations of what price is worth paying. However, the battle of priorities also frequently plays out in real time as opportunities for free food come up and decisions must be made quickly. Kelsy (Lib Arts) recalls a recent situation when study time was preempted by the inconvenient convenience of free food events, complicating what it means to be "responsible":

> So, I know me personally, if I see something has free food, especially free pizza, I'm like, "Ooh, I'm not interested in going to it, but I want to now." And actually I just had a thing about that today. I'm a Religious Studies minor and we have an end of the year religious studies party and I was like, "Oh, I don't really want to go, 'cause I'm busy that day, I could study instead," but they were like, "Oh, we're going to have free tacos from this nearby Mexican restaurant, and drinks and dessert." I'm like, "Okay, I'm going to go now." So, I feel like a lot of the times when I decide to go can be dependent on what they're offering, especially at the end of the year.

As Kelsy's example highlights, life on the margins requires a constant evaluation of how to best use the time not taken up by employment to pursue other important priorities.

The decision to rely on employment as a route to increased financial security also creates a double-edged sword of dependence on jobs that were often undependable, in terms of hours or even continuous work. Anali (Flagship) set out to save up enough money to embrace that symbol of privilege, the unpaid internship, if for just a semester, though events did not pan out as planned:

> The way that I had budgeted out my money for the year was that I was supposed to have enough for everything, like food, like rent, and everything. But what happened is that I got injured, and so I didn't have insurance. I had to pay a thousand something up front just to get seen, and that really set me back. And so I thought I wasn't going to have to work. I had an internship. I had an internship already, and it was going to be unpaid.

Anali's undocumented, non-DACA status means that federal work study on campus and most jobs off campus are unavailable to her. Combined with commitments she has made to her internship and other organizations, Anali felt stuck and overwhelmed. Her injury derailed a careful plan, plunging her into chronic struggles to pay for food. She reflects on how this unexpected change affected her mentally, as well as logistically:

> I remember I just didn't want to think about anything else. I was just stressed all the time. I was like, "How am I going to get the money for this?" Because I was also stressing about how to pay for my last month of rent for the academic school year. So I was just very worried all the time about, like, "How am I going to do this? How am I going to do that?" I was so busy also that semester, and I was like, "I can't even go out and try and get a job, or I'm going to fail my classes, or I'm going to get kicked out of my orgs." I just feel like I had all these other responsibilities that I had to take care of that I couldn't just drop to go and try to make these ends meet. And so I was trying to make the best of whatever resources that I already had.

As stories of situational crises illustrate, the selective university ideal/normal experience has a narrow tolerance for variation. Constructed around the expectation of financial security and full engagement, the rollercoaster of employment simultaneously provides a form of access to these campuses even while full participation is often tantalizingly out of reach because of the hours of work required to pay for it, or when it is in reach, comes at the cost of stressful choices between living into the coveted activities of college and meeting basic needs, such as food.

Working, Food, and Creative Solutions

Although employment is the most direct (and in a few cases, indirect) means to accessing food, Sacrificing students, as with other strategies, engaged in a range of innovative and resourceful approaches to meeting their food needs. In some cases, jobs offered avenues for food access. Kelsy (Lib Arts) capitalizes on the free food and drinks offered by her position at Starbucks:

> I think that's helped me save a lot of money because you get free drinks. And, like, for me when I drink coffee, it kind of counts as, like, a meal for me because I don't really get hungry. It's probably, like, the caffeine. And you also get one free food item while you're there. So, like, for the first few weeks, I ate, like, nothing but spinach feta wraps. They are so good! And then now I eat just the plain bagels with cream cheese. Like, that's been my past, like, two weeks. So I felt like I've saved a lot of money doing that, even though I'm still working and eating there.

Similar to Kelsy's double win of making money and reducing her food costs, Valeria's (Lib Arts) workplace offers free food, though she primarily uses it as her fallback plan when she misses meals: "I learned that at the school I work for, they offer free meals even to, like, employees. So it was pretty cool. So I had that sort of safety net if I really needed to eat."

Other students engaged in Sacrificing are not so fortunate but still maximize available resources to reduce direct food costs. Anali (Flagship) found that a local grocery chain offers free delivery on the first four orders, which reduces the stress of trying to find a ride to the store. After the first one ran out, she created a series of new email addresses to secure ongoing free deliveries. Similarly, Beth (Lib Arts) signed up for multiple food delivery apps that offered free credits and delivery as inducements, which she stockpiles. Like students across the strategies, nearly all Sacrificing students rely on friends with meal plans to swipe them in or use campus dollars to buy them food. Cooking and shopping also represent opportunities to maximize financial resources in ways the general student population might not consider, as Valeria (Lib Arts) says:

> I've learned to get really creative with groceries. So, learning celery can work for a snack, it can work in soup, it can work as this, as that. The peanut butter, it's great. Whatever I put in a salad, I can usually put in an omelet, you just add some eggs. So, I've grown really creative in the kitchen. And my friend is always surprised. She's like, "I thought we had nothing." I'm like, "No, you just throw it all together in a pan and you add different spices." And she's like, "You're right!"

Reflective of these students' creative use of resources, scholars from a critical race perspective have worked to shift perceptions of students from marginalized backgrounds as bereft of the resources necessary to succeed in college to holders of particular *forms* of knowledge, or "capital," that are endemic to various racial and ethnic communities. Most prominently, the concept of Community Cultural Wealth (CCW), originally articulated by Tara Yosso, identifies and celebrates features of environmental knowledge and strategic engagement.[3] Among them are *navigational capital*, or knowledge of how to work with and around organizational systems, *familial capital*, or the support and resources of deep and extensive family connections, and *aspirational capital*, or the ability to maintain one's hopes and dreams even in the face of significant obstacles. The capacity to use resources imaginatively, engage with university bureaucracy strategically, and persist despite the ongoing friction between the college experience promised and the one available reflects these forms of capital.[4] Nevertheless, students expressed that this environmental "turbulence" did come at a cost, not only physically because of meal skipping, but coming to grips with the experience available to them, yet persevering. Valeria (Lib Arts) reflects: "I mean economically, it's like either car, food, or any necessities, other necessities that I need. Mentally it's the anxiety for sure—me picking at my cuticles while I'm talking about anxiety. But it's just mentally draining constantly thinking about it at night. Or, like, just beating yourself up over enjoying either, like, a night out or something like that. And it gets really overwhelming after some time."

The use of these alternative forms of capital, though often sustaining, still place Sacrificing students in an intersection of stresses as they try to manage work, school, friends, and family simultaneously. In this, the place of food is not straightforward: though clearly employment provides food directly and indirectly, students still struggled with a choice that failed to completely solve their food needs even while it separated them from the ideal/normal experience. Brooke (Lib Arts), considering advice she would give to incoming students, confesses to the costs of her campus navigation strategy that frequently separates her from campus, both physically and psychologically:

> There's a lot of support there for you that you could utilize and I mean, obviously I don't think it's perfect. There are a lot of gaps in services for students, but there are definitely a lot of things that I didn't know existed and I was nervous about reaching out to professors and asking for this or that and so I definitely would tell you that there are people there who care about you and that it's a place where you can really be yourself and there's a lot of opportunities for you to get involved. And there are so many different organizations and even if you're not a part of them you can go to the events that they host and things like that to still be . . . to feel a part of the Lib Arts community, because sometimes I felt really disconnected from the community because I haven't been on campus at all. I think I'm telling you to stay connected to the community.

Brooke's recognition of the "goods" of her selective university environment that includes involvement and support, is bittersweet as realizations hard earned yet not fully actualized in her own experience. These are the costs of the Sacrificing strategy, where the modicum of financial security gained simultaneously distances many students from full access to the ideal/normal experience so close at hand.

CHAPTER 12

Navigating the Dream III
Prioritizing

Talking together as a research team after our first interview with Paloma, we are not entirely sure why food insecurity is a struggle for her. A junior psychology major at Lib Arts, Paloma lives at home near campus with her mom and sister—who is also a student at Lib Arts—to save money. A McNair Scholar, she spent the summer doing research with one of her professors: "I was able to form a relationship with her and it was as simple as me going to her office and asking: 'Can I do research with you?' It was as simple as that." We are a few weeks away from spring break, and Paloma is looking forward to going on a service trip to Peru. Last year she went on a similar trip to Colorado on an urban poverty experience. During the semester, conferences with McNair Scholars, involvement with a religious campus ministry organization, and an officer role with a Latine student leaders association keep her busy, in addition to her job at the campus bookstore and tutoring at a city high school. Although she's interested in taking a job off campus, she has held off for other priorities: "I don't want to get a job and then I'm going to get an internship soon, so I have to think about that."

Sitting in a library study room ringed by windows, Paloma projects the calm and confidence of a student who understands her campus and her purpose on it. She reflects on her shift from expecting college to just be about going to class to college being about involvement as the priority: "Yeah, because I know some people who aren't—who just go to class and aren't involved. And I kind of think about that, and I would be miserable. I love being involved and being part of these different communities on campus. Because you really learn from them and you kind of build your own college career through that." Paloma's investment in "building her own college career" speaks to a high level of agency and ownership, which she learned in part from the modeling of a student ahead of her at Lib Arts:

> Yeah. So, that girl . . . she got the presidential award, which is only given to 10 people. And you get that by being involved, and kind of being, not "well known" on campus, but making a presence on campus. And she was also a leader in many different things on campus. And so, seeing her make a presence maybe inspired me and made me want to do that as well. And so far, I've been trying to maximize my time here like she did. Because it seemed to do well for her. And it's been doing well for me, too.

And yet, nearly three-quarters of her journey through higher education, Paloma has not figured out how to manage her food needs in a sustainable way. Mostly, this is because she does not think about food until she has to. In fact, just knowing that she was interviewing with us motivated her to rethink how she plans and eats:

> So, I didn't realize how hard it was to feed myself every day until I came to college, because before I was used to being fed by school or my mom. But since I'm a commuter it's especially hard because we don't get as high of a meal plan, like it's only $160. And that usually runs out by, like, my second week, because the prices, food prices here at the university are, like, super high. They make . . . they purposely raise the prices because we are using our meal plan. But commuters don't get a lot. So, you run out by just drinking coffee at The Grind every day. Which I spent it on.

Shifting from a focus on campus food prices to her packed schedule, Paloma confesses the heart of her struggle: "So, sometimes I forget to eat and so I'm like, 'It's 5:00 p.m. and I'm already home' and I'm like, 'Oh, I didn't eat. I just had a coffee in the morning.'"

Paloma's embrace of the college experience—building fruitful relationships with faculty, getting involved in research as an undergraduate, engaging with student organizations, taking advantage of study abroad, investing in social connections with a range of communities on campus—doing all the things she has heard and seen that the Good Student does, somehow has left out parallel lessons about eating. Curiously, Paloma talks about meal plans as something students "get," as if the university gifts meal plans to residential students. At the same time, Paloma expresses frustration that her small plan only provides her with expensive drinks from the on-campus coffee shop for a few weeks. Even as she has adopted a vision of college that aligns with the environmental press toward involvement, her inability to afford the "big" meal plan means she just tends to skip over the part of life that centers on food.[1] In this, Paloma is the poster child for Prioritizing: students who are so committed to engaging in the Opportunity Paradigm that they neglect their basic food needs and find, with shock and frustration, that the very environment that generally rewards them for their full embrace of involvement seems to punish them for their inability to fit the financial ideal/normal.

The Priority of Involvement

The ten students who best exemplify the Prioritizing strategy (Camila—Lib Arts, Carli—PRU, Gavin—Flagship, Jill—PRU, Lacey—Flagship, Leah—Flagship, Mandy—Flagship, Nicole—Lib Arts, Paloma—Lib Arts, Selina—Lib Arts) all largely order their college experience around involvement, though defined and pursued differently. Selina (Lib Arts) is extensively engaged in activities that connect to her ethnic identity, major, and future aspirations, including co-founding a Latina political advocacy organization chapter, participating in a health occupations group, taking on research as a McNair Scholar, and volunteering at a local hospital. Extensive involvement has been baked into the expectations of her educational experience throughout, as necessary elements of future educational and career access and success:

> Because I've been so used to "if you want to succeed you need to do more" sort of a thing. Like, that's why I was so involved in high school. I volunteered so much, too, because I was always told the more holistic of a good student you are the better chance you have to getting anywhere. And so I feel like especially if you continue on to grad school, life is all about trying to make yourself look better on paper, to make yourself look appealing to these programs, and say, "Yes! Pick me, I'm a good choice!"

As with many students, Selina's motivation reflects her understanding of college as a time when one accumulates a body of evidence in the arms race of qualification signaling through standard forms of involvement, such as preprofessional organizations and community volunteering. Selina reflects on how she ended up in so many organizations, and she comes to the realization that her social circle has much to do with it: "But yeah, I don't think I've ever applied to something and got in it just because I knew about it, at least not on campus. It's all been through somebody else saying, 'Hey, I don't want to do this by myself. Do it with me.' It's like, 'Okay,' and then just sort of going with it afterwards." The pressure to engage that originated in high school for Selina dovetails with the expectancy of her collegiate environment, manifest not only in a breadth of opportunities for involvement but a social environment where similarly prepared students reinforce these values among one another.[2] Functionally, this most often looks like the social support of friends inviting one another to events, though this characterization can mask the alchemy of environmental opportunity and normative pressure to be a "joiner" that pervades competitive campuses.

The broad virtue of involvement on these campuses can disguise the true variety of engagement strategies. Nicole (Lib Arts) and Gavin (Flagship) exemplify this variety. Nicole began her college career by approaching involvement via joining almost anything and everything of interest to her. Now a senior with a double major in global studies and computer information science, she has a paper trail of involvement that is extensive and wide-ranging, including study abroad, organizational leadership, and serving as a campus tour guide.

Like Nicole, Gavin (Flagship) entered his university with an enthusiasm for the potential of his new educational environment:

> At first whenever I first got in I was like, "Holy shit, I'm at this school!" 'cause everyone was trying to get in. So, that's how it was at first. But now it's like, these resources, they just make me excited, because I feel like I've played my cards right to the point where hopefully at the end of the day or in a couple of years and maybe even a couple of months I can just like back-to-back to-back-to-back use these resources to do whatever I need to do.

Yet Gavin's perspective and priorities are oriented toward Flagship as a place of *human* resources, rather than a place of *organizations* as resources. Oriented personally and professionally to entrepreneurship, Gavin is foremost interested in creating networks of networks that can serve his big picture aim of "solving socioeconomic inequality," as he puts it, without a hint of hyperbole:

> But like I said, my end mission is to solve socioeconomic inequality. Because I like so many things and this has been a constant theme throughout my life 'cause like I said I have so many siblings that taught me about x, y, and z—I was able to connect with my friends in middle school and high school because of x, y, and z. Now I like x, y, and z *and* a, b, and c and d and I can hopefully, at the end of the day I want to combine it. I have a friend who deals specifically in being a lawyer or wants to be a teacher, perfect—let me tap into that. Because I'm genuinely interested in this thing but I'm not an expert in it, but I have a friend who is. So, boom, let me connect that with a kid who doesn't have a teacher, or maybe wants to be a teacher, or wants to be a lawyer, or someone wants to be an . . . I'm very big on dreaming as much as you want, but just helping the kid understand they have that opportunity.

Students engaging in Prioritizing, like Gavin, Nicole, and Paloma, are inspired and motivated by the opportunities of their environment and as such, they align closely and enthusiastically with the preferred modus operandi of the prestige-oriented university.

One result of this hard push toward maximum involvement that Prioritizing embraces is the tendency to not just participate but to create and lead organizations in line with student aspirations and interests. Nicole (Lib Arts) is co-founder and president of an academic club focused on international politics and activism. Selina (Lib Arts) collaborated with friends to bring a Latine student organization to campus that promotes voter awareness of political issues.

Leah (Flagship) is an officer in her campus spirit group, a position that gives her joy and responsibility: "I'm really excited! I've been looking forward to it—it's like my beacon." When we press her on the importance of being part of what is essentially a Latina-focused student tailgate club (with occasional community volunteering activities), Leah explains:

> I don't want that to be my regret, like, I didn't get as involved as I could have.
>
> —Why do you find involvement important?
>
> I think it's important because it kind of like validates why I'm here. It gives me more of a purpose beyond my studies.

The campus virtue of involvement, preached by tour guides, promoted by student affairs staff, and modeled by the most lauded of exemplar students is to some, as Leah suggests, the true mark of a successful college experience, but one attained at a high cost by some students.

Challenges to the Involvement Ideal

Leah (Flagship) has a dilemma. The opportunity for leadership in her student spirit organization energizes her, but her aspirations to be a doctor mean hard decisions between embracing the full experience of college and making time for the checklist of activities she has learned are important to med school admissions. She anticipates that the career of a physician in part means squeezing more out of the hours of the day than most people can: "I have a job, so kind of putting my job into my study hours, scheduling everything together with my organizations, with my internships, my volunteering, trying to make sure everything comes together and I still get sleep at night [*laughs*]. 'Cause there are necessities and trying to be a doctor, you have to basically wear 80 hats."

Nevertheless, pursuing her desired professional path and having the complete college experience as she defines it has come to a head, with some hard choices to be made. Leah is contemplating taking on a second job to pay for MCAT study materials, and we ask if that means cutting back on her involvement:

> I think so. I had to for this semester just because it didn't fit in my schedule. I gave up volunteering at the hospital. I really enjoyed it. I worked at the NICU. It was very sweet. The lady I worked with, she was so nice. I didn't want to do that, but my schedule, just it didn't work very well. And they were just like, "You can come back next semester!" And I'm like, "This is what I have to do." So if I did [take another job], I would have to give up volunteering. Maybe scale back on my organizations because I don't want to give them up fully because I, like, still want to be involved and have friends and not just do school and work because it's going to make me go insane. But also I need money [*laughs*]. And it's just like the worst juggling act and *the only person that I hurt is myself.*

Leah's conviction that cutting back on organizational involvement means undercutting the very opportunities that make all her efforts worthwhile leaves her with choices between maximizing her present and preparing for her future. Leah's current on-campus desk job offers her a flexible, academics-sensitive schedule. She is well aware that fast food employment, which she has worked in the past, is not so accommodating. Her ideal scenario, if she must work more, is to work an entire weekend day:

> But I would love to if I could find a place like, "We just need a Saturday, Sunday worker." I'm like, "I'm right here!" I'll get up and I'll do it and I'll come home, because I try to keep my Saturdays and Sundays free just because I need to keep sane. I run myself into the ground Monday through Friday and then Saturday, Sunday is usually my recoup time. But I'm good to, like, work for five hours of the day.

Leah's admission that "I run myself into the ground" to make a packed academic and social life work is also reflected in Nicole's thoughts about how her life would be different if she were economically stable. The mere conversation about it seems to send her into a reflective headspace she seldom allows herself to occupy: "Oh, so many things. I would be able to be sustainable. I would be able to eat better. I'd probably be vegetarian or something [*laughs*]. I don't know. I would [*sighs*] yeah [*pauses*]. Yeah. I just . . . I don't know. Yeah. I would just be a healthier person, for sure. And just more, I don't know, like *my reality would definitely just match more with my capabilities.*"

At the heart of the struggle for most students, and particularly those Prioritizing, is the sense that the burden of basic needs and the stress related to it means not performing up to their full academic capacity, that despite "running themselves into the ground" to paraphrase Leah, the juggling act that is full engagement at a prestige-oriented university means there are always too many balls to keep in the air. Gavin sees this too, describing the cost in comparison to peers who are freed from this inevitable compromise between basic resources and involvement:

> Other students don't have to worry about the things that I have to worry about so they can get ahead. And it's things like that that can continue to create these inequalities and inequities and opportunities and things like that. Even though we are at this school, "All right what's the next barrier? What's the next barrier?" It should be, "You're at this school, you paid for it." Boom. What's going down to help me besides me having to, like . . . sometimes you have to bend over backwards. And I'm not in these organizations, because luckily I do other things, but some students . . . that might be the only thing that they can be in that's social or, like, is helping them proceed or go forward in their careers, but they can't even focus on that because the meetings are always from 6 to 7 but they always got to work at 6 to 7.

As Gavin describes it, "college constrained" means operating from a barrier-oriented perspective of attempting to anticipate what the next impediment will be. Simply not having that to worry about, he suggests, *is* a fundamental inequity that the university should actively work to remove. Because that burden largely falls on students, the negotiation of time and opportunity means for some students choosing not to eat, as Selina (Lib Arts) concludes:

> If you're not involved it's just... I need to work, so there's no way around that. Because I help my mom pay for what's not covered by my federal loans on my semesters. So, I need work to pay for the next semester and it's always been like that. Work, save, and then pay for the semester. So, I can't stop working because I can't depend on my family to give me money or an allowance or anything of that sort. And I also can't stop going to classes. So, I really can't not do either. So, I just have to find a way to make it work and sometimes that means I don't eat properly for one or two weeks. Or I have one meal here and another one there every other day, and it's just something that I kind of had to figure out ever since I started working.

Because Prioritizing builds the college experience around involvement, eating becomes a burden that these students must navigate, or like Paloma, simply try to ignore.

Navigating Food

The hallmark of the Prioritizing is that the high virtue of involvement supersedes and displaces the inconvenience of attending to food needs. Remarking that students are more susceptible to food insecurity than the general population,[3] Camila (Lib Arts) enumerates why she believes this to be the case, unintentionally outlining the Prioritizing perspective:

> I think it's a combination of three things. It's time. We just don't have the time to actually go out and actually cook. No one has time for that. Then money. Yeah. I think money is the main one. We just have to be smarter about where we allocate our monetary funds and we'd rather spend it on doing fun things that college students do. We want to go to these tailgates and we want to go to these events. Food is such... it's just food. We'll be fine. I think it's kind of like, we're young, we'll be okay. And then... see it's just time, money and we just don't really know how to manage it maybe. I think that's why. Just convenience.

The intersection of money and time/convenience produces the Prioritizing approach when added to the deep desire to engage in the collegiate ideal—experiences. Following up on her assertion, we ask what makes her want to prioritize events like this over food. Camila responds quickly:

> Oh, it's experiences. You're never going to get that back. You can always be like, "Oh, I'll try to be healthier next year. I'll focus more on health and I'll try to eat better." But these experiences are now, and they're never going to come back. And you won't remember the fact that you had to eat a tortilla with cheese instead of a chicken burrito. That's just . . . nobody cares about that. Now, the pictures that you're going to take, the memories, it's very cliché. . . . It's definitely experience-centered. You'd rather take those with you than have to, like, spend time at home just to make sure you have enough to eat for the week. It just sounds so ridiculous.

Perhaps as a spin on the old college saying that "you can retake a test but you can't retake a party," the Prioritizing strategy makes a gambit that in a land of plenty, there will always be just enough to get by—and these students are sometimes correct.

That said, Prioritizing is frequently less a strategy than it is inertia: students who Prioritize typically arrive at their response to the "problem" of eating somewhat organically, as an offshoot of their internalization of the high value of involvement and their particular path through college. This organic sensemaking tends to clump into two approaches to food we call *extreme organization* and *extreme negligence*.

Students using Prioritizing strategies usually did not begin college highly organized but arrived at this modality through a series of dire circumstances that made plain the unsustainability of their current food practices. Camila (Lib Arts), who had lived on campus with a full meal plan her first year as part of a university requirement, began college with a typical Adapting strategy. However, her epiphany came when the convenience of food disappeared:

> I was so used to having, like, full three meals a day with so much food. . . . So, when I kind of lost that big meal plan and I was on the senior plan, so it

> took about $600 a semester, which is more than I had this year. Well, my third semester, my sophomore year, I just kept those same eating patterns and when I ran out, I think within a month and a half, I was like, "Woah, this is different." So, I think my third semester here was the hardest in terms of how I eat and where, and just things like that, and with who. And so, it was a lot harder. That was a really hard semester. . . . I didn't know how to cope with that.

From that hard year of just getting by, Camila realized she needed to adjust:

> I had to learn to be smarter about my shopping trips. So, I had to go, "Okay, if I buy fruit, this is how long it's going to last me and I'm going to eat that fruit and I'm not going to go out." And that's kind of when I stopped going to the dining halls and I realized I can't be going to Taco House every Friday because it's expensive. So, yeah, I've just been a lot smarter. I became a lot smarter. But that was a tough transition though.

Now, Camila is much more careful about how, when, and where she eats. She anticipates the temptation to eat on campus and plans ahead, both in terms of food and her class schedule: "I live a ten-minute drive away. So, I try to schedule my classes so I don't have such a big gap. Because I'll know I'll be hungry, and I'll be tempted. So, if I just have them back to back, just go home to eat and have something there. Or I can just stop by somewhere on the way and grab a taco or something like that."

Similarly, Leah (Flagship) has had to work hard to shed her attraction to the Starbucks lifestyle, making a plan to avoid expensive convenience food on campus part of her morning routine:

> My days are usually long, which sucks, because if I don't pack a lunch and I'm starving, I usually have to eat out. And that means five dollars a day, which adds up to a lot. I've gotten better on my coffees. I've bought instant coffee and I keep a little baggie of something. And then I just get water from the fountain, because I like iced coffee better anyway. Or, like, I like cold coffee so much better. Because I have powdered creamer, I have some sugar and I have instant coffee all in a baggie just already mixed up.

And I just pour it in there and then I just stir, and I already have coffee. So that's kind of how I cut down on my Starbucks.

As Leah's experiences illustrate, the cost of exclusion from the convenience economy of the campus food scene comes in two forms: the extra time required to cobble together workable food solutions that partly meet one's needs, and the steep cost of failing to do so, in terms of budget-crippling expenses when one gives in and buys what is most easy to access. In response, Prioritizing for these students means learning to become almost militantly organized with their food choices in ways that maximize their opportunities and their budgets.

In the *extreme negligence* substrategy of Prioritizing, the primary mode of navigating food is by trying not to think about it. Paloma's initially mystifying food insecurity, described in the opening of this chapter, reflects a way of dealing with the cost and inconvenience of food centered on a kind of forced improvisation. When we ask Nicole (Lib Arts), a student who is highly strategic about her professional development, about how she manages financially difficult weeks, she reflects, haltingly, that food is less about strategy than it is about willful neglect:

> I think I would just probably . . . I honestly would not eat . . . I don't know . . . it's not on my mind. I'll probably get something like a Pop Tart from a vending machine on campus. Trail Mix, like a soda, like ramen for sure. Ramen is the biggest one. I feel it's hard to describe because I'm still doing it. But I'm not like . . . it's not like . . . I probably will eat this bagel . . . Okay, so I have class from 11 a.m. to 2 p.m., and I have another class at 3:30, and then I leave at 4:45 and I get on my two-hour bus to my class at 7 and then I get out at 8:20, but I don't come back home at 9. So, it's kind of like . . . I don't know . . . it's just not . . . on my mind. I just get it, if it's there. And if I'm feeling very, very hungry . . . I think yesterday . . . I don't even remember what I ate because it's not . . . it's hard to . . . I'm sorry. It's just that like . . . I don't know. Like, today's meal I guess, will probably be this bagel, this banana, I have coffee. But, yeah, it's not on my mind.

Nicole struggles to recall what she ate yesterday and has almost no plan for food today because her financial inability to afford food primarily represents a distraction from the aspects of college she *can* engage in—class, internships, organizations, and relationships. Reflecting on her overall mode of life, Nicole concludes: "Yeah. So, whenever I'm hungry, I'm like 'Okay, time to eat.' Like, I don't really schedule meals. Only when my body feels like it needs it."

Similarly, Carli (PRU) places food at the bottom of her priorities. Mostly it is those moments when she slows down enough to think about it that she really faces the extent of her discontent and struggle:

> Sometimes I just don't have the funds, so I don't get the food because I do have to save that money for other issues. Like what if my parents need it for home, for something? I think I don't really take care of myself on that as much because I just think if I keep going, then I don't have to worry about it. But then when I do get home, it's like, "I don't want to just, I really want some actual substance. I really wish sometimes I had more funds just so I wouldn't have to be like this." Other times, I'm very, I'm happy with who I am because then I've learned, you know, I can't really ask for anything. I know the difference between getting and earning something.

Carli's intense work ethic and commitment to helping her parents, as with other students who view their struggle as a virtue, means eating what she wants has become a kind of unearned privilege that she rejects.

Paloma represents several other students who, in the course of our series of interviews, came to realize that they were neglecting attention to their food needs at a cost to their health and well-being. Paloma is attempting to adjust, and to be aware of when and what she is putting in her body:

> But this year, my schedules have been really weird. Every day is really different for me. So, I never really have a set time that I could eat. So, because of that, I've kind of been neglecting my meals and not eating and forgetting. And if I do have a little time, I just buy something that's really bad for me, like chips or something from the vending machine. So, kind of doing this study, I've realized that I've been doing that. Because I don't think I've been realizing how bad it's been. Because it hasn't really, well,

the only thing that's really been affecting me is my headaches and concentration, but other than that, I haven't really been noticing the effects that it has been doing. It's probably doing really bad damage to my body. But I just haven't been realizing it yet. Yeah, I've been considering that lately.

The rollercoaster of a packed academic and social schedule makes time for food a liability, which Paloma is realizing cannot be a long-term strategy. Paloma reflects on her emerging awareness that more deliberate use of the resources already around her can improve her eating: "So, I've been kind of preparing what I'm going to eat and going home sometimes when I have time to go eat. If I don't pack my lunch, then I go home. And also, realizing my resources on campus with access to food. If there's an event going on and there's food, I go to it. Or if my friends have extra meal plan, I ask them." As with Nicole, Paloma's default disregard for food as an inconvenience and a distraction allows her to approximate the experience of engagement she recognizes as the environmental ideal, though at a cost she, and others who are Prioritizing, would rather ignore. In these cases, the irony is clear: food insecurity is the price paid by some students who enthusiastically embrace the collegiate ideal advanced by the university.

Food for Expedience

Prioritizing, like Sacrificing, reveals the struggle between the opportunity costs of free food on campus and the time required to make use of it. When we ask Selina (Lib Arts) if there are ways other than buying food that she eats, her response suggests she is wise to the free food "system" and to some degree resents it, even if she does rely on it:

> Yeah, events on campus. Like, if I knew there was an event on campus and they were . . . I feel like they bribe us with it. Like, "If you come we'll have food," and it's like, "I'll be there!" Even if it's . . . like, they have the little cheese sandwiches or some places have pizza. So, if I know there's an event on campus where they're giving out food I'll be there. Normally that will replace me having to buy lunch on campus or something.

Food as involvement inducement, highlighted in the campus tour chapter, exerts a different kind of influence on students who struggle to pay for food than those who could just as easily eat in the dining hall or at a nearby fast food restaurant. Where free pizza might just entice those mildly interested in the event but able to eat elsewhere, for food-insecure students interest takes a backseat to the opportunity to eat for free.

Although most participants took advantage of free food on campus, the importance of expedience and engagement to Prioritizing students resulted in some slightly different adaptations. The press of Nicole's schedule means that while she is willing to take a detour to an organization meeting or special event offering free food, it does not mean she will stay if it is not a meeting essential to her involvement commitments:

> So, but it's funny because like a lot of the events that we have on campus—they'll usually offer free food as like the biggest incentive for people to come. And usually, and I think it's pretty, like, good quality stuff. Like they'll cater, like, Taco House and stuff to get people to come to an event. Or just pizza, you know?
>
> —Do you go to events because there's food?
>
> Oh yeah [*laughs*]. If anything, that's probably like . . . like I'll go . . . I shouldn't say that, but [*laughs*]—I'll go and like get food and then leave [*laughs*].

Nicole's response hints at her awareness that she is, on some level, violating the unspoken terms of the "free food for attendance" exchange relationship. Nevertheless, the environmental virtue of extensive involvement trumps whatever discomfort she feels with this grab-and-go strategy. This same commitment to maximizing opportunities takes others who are Prioritizing to more extreme adaptive strategies. Jill (PRU) found a guy through the Tinder dating/hook-up app that became an unhealthy means for accessing food: "I got involved in a very toxic type of relationship because I knew that if I went over there that I would get to eat and that they would have drinks and weed and whatever—but it was a very manipulative and not good type of relationship and I stayed in it for way too long, but it was a way that I knew I would eat."

By our final interview with her, Jill had separated herself from this "bad scene" (her words) with help from her roommate. Where students differently oriented might seek employment, Prioritizing students seek maximum flexibility, even when it occasionally results in risky behavior. Jill was also among several students Prioritizing—and more than any other subtype—who occasionally resorted to theft to meet food needs. Camila (Lib Arts) outlines the origins of the student-run food pantry, which in part came about from stories of students stealing food from the dining hall. With some hesitation, she admits that she was among them: "Yeah, I used to do that too. I used to just take the wraps, and they were $7 wraps and I was like, 'I can't afford that, and I don't know where else to buy food, so I'm just going to take the wrap.'"

Although Camila clearly felt shame for her actions, Gavin is far more sanguine about it:

> Hopefully . . . I don't want to blow their cover for people. I'm stealing here, too, just because I literally have to. . . . I'm now living in North Campus, if I want to eat something I can't just go and, like, grab a granola bar. It's like, "I'm starving, I know I want to be here for another three or four hours, what do I do?" I have to go to the campus shop and like get some food, 'cause that's just the way it is.

Across our three interviews, Gavin expresses mixed emotions about stealing to eat, not wanting it to be part of his life but feeling defiant that in a place he pays so much to attend he should not still be struggling to pay for food:

> Maybe I'm fucking over a family business, probably not, but you know, I'm going to take that risk. You're Flagship, you're a big-ass institution, I'm paying you a lot of money, man, I'm going to take it. It's a lot of money. Whatever, man. I'm going to, just fuck it, I'm going to just take it. I'm going to just take it. It's what I have to do. And sometimes I do feel bad and it's like, "I don't want to do these things. I don't want to have to steal." I want to get to the point in my life where I don't have to worry about money or worry about . . . maybe if I am worrying about money if it's to pay something big off, like not my next meal. So, it was just, "Whatever man, just survive."

In the context of the Prioritizing mindset, stealing food takes on new meaning. Theft presents one avenue by which students wanting to maximize their time and energy for involvement can mimic the time-use patterns of the ideal/normal student: when you are hungry, walk in, get food, and get back to your busy life.

Ironically, Prioritizing leads to a variety of extreme behaviors—ignoring food completely, stealing food, accessing food in psychologically unhealthy ways—all in an attempt to maximize flexibility and time to approximate the ideal/normal university experience they have been sold from the tour forward and observed closely in the lives of their classmates who can afford to inhabit the role of the Good Student. The Prioritizing approach is thus driven by the virtue of expedience in a college setting where fast, convenient, expensive food greases the skids for a student lifestyle of extensive involvement, only fully available to those who can financially afford it.

CHAPTER 13

Navigating the Dream IV
Maximizing

The students engaged in Maximizing (Lucas and Vera from PRU; Layla, Phillip, and Terrence from Flagship) have figured out how to leverage the resources of their environment in ways that students using the other strategies do infrequently or inconsistently. Some of these Maximizing students are exemplars of extensive involvement and goal-driven attainment. Others are not "joiners" in terms of campus organizations but seem comfortable defining involvement in their own way. Unlike Adapting students, those engaged in Maximizing are largely independent of the residential and dining services bubble; Vera is the only one of this group who lives on campus, and she does not have a meal plan.

Like students who are Sacrificing, those Maximizing all have jobs, but their jobs do not seem to crowd out other activities and priorities. In fact, a hallmark of Maximizing is that work is a place where students find resources beyond the obvious financial benefits. Most of the students who are Maximizing are extensively involved, like those Prioritizing, but their ability to find food and financial support means that they have (mostly) risen above the desperate daily strain to feed themselves.

In short, students Maximizing are succeeding in many ways that students operating from other strategy types are struggling. Their learned adaptations are effective because they combine strategies employed by others, such as going to meetings that offer free food, yet they creatively leverage their networks and environments to find food in ways that minimize disruption to their busy student lives. Still, for all their cagy college navigation skills, food insecurity is a lingering threat because Maximizing is an adaptive strategy that does not completely align with the ideal/normal college experience. As such, Maximizing is less an optimal environmental response, and more a situationally effective way of operating within resource-rich systems where food-insecure students do not fit.

From Slow Starts to Creative Engagement

Contrary to what might be expected given this glowing introduction, students who are Maximizing developed this strategy as they learned how to navigate the resources and social contours of their campus. Layla (Flagship) began her college career unaware of the places food was available and "nervous" about taking advantage of places where she could get it for free. Gradually, she gained a broader awareness of campus resources and the confidence to use them thoughtfully:

> Learning about more opportunities helped me strategize. Like in the beginning I was kind of nervous to go to "party hop" organizations [for food] or realize that I didn't work at the Civil Rights Project or I wasn't comfortable to stay in the evening when I realized they were ordering pizza and everybody was just kind of staying until eight and working. I didn't know that really happened. And so things like that, things like the food pantry, things like navigating whenever people would be doing new member pushes. Like, those are all things that kind of changed as I learned about them. But in the beginning it was kind of just if my roommates cooked extra and I was there and they were being nice, I would sneak a thing of soup that they cooked. 'Cause they cooked a lot and it was ironic. But yeah it just changed as I learned new opportunities.

As with other students using this strategy type, Layla's acclimation to college was a process of figuring out the "hidden curriculum" of campus opportunities that were often not immediately apparent or required initiative on her part to access.[1]

Gradually, Layla learned that opportunities beget opportunities. Describing her internship with a civil rights nonprofit, Layla notes with pride that she "recently convinced them to now pay their interns." The long hours she invests—more than 20 per week—provide her with new social and resource opportunities, in addition to valuable professional experience. When we ask who she spends time with, Layla outlines her shift from high school friends to new connections formed through her internship:

> I make friends at work, so some of my closest friends that I didn't get in high school, even my high school friends, I spend less time with them than I do our law clerks at the office. Or even my 20-something-year-old staff attorney bosses. We all go to a restaurant downtown and they will pay 'cause it's on the company credit card, which is great. Yeah, I spend my time probably at work or with people at work to some extent every day. Where I'm going to at 9:30 p.m. tonight is to a lobbying dinner. So wherever I can I will spend my time working.

Layla's internship experience produces benefits four times over: professional experience and recommendations she will leverage toward graduate school and future employment, income which she uses to pay for housing and food, access to young professionals who offer social support and social capital that will benefit her navigation of the professional world, and food and coffee paid for from the company credit card.

Layla's second paid internship at a university research institute and her work as a high school debate coach and competition judge on the weekends combines to occupy much of her non–class time to the tune of 30–50 hours per week. Although she enjoys her work and internships, Layla names the university Quidditch team as one activity she would check out if she had time and money. Despite her crafty navigation of opportunities, hers is still a college life defined by choices that eliminate desirable options, and she feels pressure to focus on "productive" activities that help her toward her professional goals. Two other students strategically Maximizing, Phillip (Flagship) and Vera (PRU), both premed, also have university experiences significantly shaped around their career aspirations. The variety and intensity of their involvement forms reflect the consuming and demanding nature of their majors but also overlap with their strategic, and altruistic, methods of accessing food.

Intensive Engagement Meets Extensive Opportunity

Health professions majors across the strategies typology (DeShauna, Gina, Leah, Phillip, Vera, and others) were, as a group, the most intensively involved students in our study. The nexus of a high-status, highly demanding professional track at a highly competitive university populated by highly capable and motivated students resulted in an extraordinary level of engagement expectancy on the path to medical school. Whether premed students were explicitly instructed or simply picked up from others that volunteering, preprofessional organizational membership, and broad campus and community leadership were part of a competitive medical school application was unclear, yet this message was certainly received and embraced. Vera (PRU) rattles off a list of nine clubs and organizations she's joined, two African study abroad trips she's taken, three other roles (teaching assistant, wellness champion, resident assistant) she's applied for, and a chapter of a health human rights organization she's starting with a faculty member's encouragement. Many of these groups represent some combination of preprofessional purpose and racial/ethnic focus reflective of her Hispanic heritage and identity. Two others—an outreach program that helps local students from underperforming schools prepare for college and a second similar program focused on college aspirations for underserved populations—are motivated by her frustrations with the lack of guidance she received during her own college application process:

> In particular with my [school guidance] counselor, she didn't want to write letters of recommendation on my behalf, because she thought that I didn't have the potential of getting into privileged universities. She told me that I should just consider going back to a community college. I graduated from an early college high school. I graduated with my associate's degree ... and she told me that it would just be best if I went back to a community college, and she just didn't see any potential in me.

In defiance of her guidance counselor's discouraging advice, Vera applied to 15 schools, mostly in-state, and chose PRU, turning down several full-ride scholarships. Like many who are Maximizing, Vera struggled at first to find her place in a university that is geographically close to home but socially and culturally foreign. As with other students, Vera's transition out of the convenience of a full meal plan as a first-year student thrust her back into food insecurity, which had been part of her life before college. This experience also affirmed in her mind the impression that the tacit promise that her needs would be met was a false one. The stress of trying to figure out food outside the safety of the "unlimited" meal plan, combined with helping her parents financially, placed her on the brink. However, unlike many Adapting students, in the time since she departed the full meal plan, Vera has seen her perspective on PRU shift, or at least become more expansive, as she has gained a new understanding of the breadth and depth of resources available on campus, and how to leverage them:

> So, before I came here I would always rely on the stereotypes that the university had. That it had a lot of students that were wealthy and stuff like that. I mean, that's stayed the same. I still have that message, that's true. But I didn't realize that this school does have a lot of resources, it's just that, you just have to speak up on it. And again, from my experience of going hungry here on campus . . . just having issues with financial aid, or anything like that. You can always find someone, either a student or a faculty member or even a higher-up, so a dean, that you can talk to. They can actually help you with that. But it's just a resources aspect that has really changed because I personally did not know that I could find this many connections, even within alums of school that could help out like that. I've actually had a few alums help out other students regarding their financial situation. So, it's just that perception of the networking connections that you can get here. It's just great.

Vera's transition from a stereotype of PRU as a place that serves only wealthy students to a place packed with resources that *anyone* can access if they know what to do or who to ask informs her current navigation strategies. In part this has meant dedicating time each week to plan out how she will maximize her resource-rich campus:

> Yeah, so I usually try to take at least two hours during the whole week to kind of set everything in my planner to say, "Okay, so these are the events that I can attend, or even ask other students to attend on my behalf and just take the food and bring it here." That's what we do here on the Service House. . . . In the Service House it's usually for a lot of students who are from low-income families and they don't have enough money to come here or just in general they don't have enough money to buy food. What we do is we let each other know, hey, we can't go to this event, but this other friend can go for us and she can bring food for everybody. So, we can share food. All of us can share food here.
>
> But even with that, sometimes we run a little bit short. Because the thing is we . . . sometimes some of them have specific food for each other and not all of us have food for all . . . well, for everybody.

Unlike students engaged in Prioritizing who are similarly committed to the intensive campus experience but ignore food needs or do not see them connected to campus opportunities, Vera intentionally maps out the free food she can utilize for the week. More than that, she thinks collectively about gathering resources to benefit her on-campus community-oriented housing unit. This entrepreneurial approach leads her to join organizations in part because they regularly give away food:

> So, with Program Council they actually host the biggest events here on campus and that's another reason why I joined, because of the food. They're the ones that provide the most food here on campus. . . . I started [gathering food] this semester for this past event, that they had a lot of food left over, they had . . . I believe they had more than ten boxes of pizza left, five boxes of wings, and like three or two boxes of, like, desserts, and they were going to throw it away. They were just going to throw it away, so I told them that, "Hey, could I just bring it here to the Service House?" That's something I was able to help myself and the rest of my peers here with their food.

Gathering surplus food generated from large-scale campus events and conferences has been a point of focus on many campuses, as students and administrators have developed Twitter ("X") handles, GroupMe text chains, and even custom apps that send alerts about leftover food that otherwise ends up in the dumpster.[2] Several students at PRU and Flagship mentioned using such student-run communication forms. In many other situations, informal arrangements and social networks, such as Vera described, are important avenues of food access for students at the financial margins.

Although food is still a struggle for Vera, ironically, she finds that the wealth of free food available makes steady meals on campus more reliable than off of it. Even as many students (and some participants) head home and stock up on groceries on their parents' dime, at times Vera has reversed this flow, using campus food to benefit her family during difficult stretches. Over Christmas break, Vera's family pulled together to help cover her remaining financial need, which strained their food budget: "That's why I was just really looking forward to coming back to campus. Because I know that even though a lot of the events that go on here, they tend to give out a lot of food. And I even bring it back to where I live here. I tend to take a little bit of that food to my mom and my little brother." The surplus of food on campus, nearly invisible to those for whom food is a matter of what to eat and not if, becomes a lifeline for students—and sometimes their families—whose financial margins are thin.

Like Vera's community engagement-themed residence hall, for Phillip (Flagship) the Multicultural Affairs Office (MAO) is a physical and social space on campus that has become his hub for identity, community, support, and food. Phillip's mentor, an administrator in the MAO named Jackson, has been a significant influence on the way Phillip experienced campus since the isolation he felt his first year:

> If you ask anybody in the Black community here, they'll say Jackson is an angel.... I am grateful to have him in my college experience. I feel like he shaped a lot of it. Helped me get involved in a lot of things and pushed me in a direction to do things. Like, I'll be hesitant, but he'll tell me like, "You

don't see the good in it now, but you'll see it later." And he hasn't been wrong since.

At Jackson's encouragement, Phillip studied abroad in China, applied for a variety of scholarships, and took on leadership roles within the organizations the MAO houses. Many students from across the typology found important mentors and gained strategic allies who helped them navigate college.[3] These relationships happened less often among our participants at Flagship due in part to the sheer scale and number of students. Where these relationships did coalesce, it often happened around specific organizations, research internships, or on-campus jobs that brought students into close contact with faculty and staff.

As the hub of Phillip's on-campus experience, the MAO serves as the intersection of employment, engagement, and free food access: "I spend most of my time there [the MAO]. I get paid for the work that I'm doing there and that's stuff I want to do. I can maximize my time in there and do a lot of different things in there while I'm getting paid." Using the most effective strategies, students who found ways to simultaneously meet multiple kinds of need maximized the precious hours of the day not spent in class.

Part of what makes Phillip effective at Maximizing, and a contrast to Prioritizing students who are similarly very involved on campus, is that he is constantly on the lookout for food as part of his daily routine. His strategy is significantly aided by the scope of resources at Flagship as the university's orientation toward promoting student organizations.

> Flagship is always doing something. Some org is doing something. I'll... The things I would do is like if I see a group of students walking with a bunch of pizza boxes, they're going to some meeting. So, I'd be like, "Hey, what are y'all doing with that food?" and they'd be like, "Oh, it's our meeting, do you want to come?" Everyone invites you to their meeting. They don't care who you are or what your interests are. If someone shows up to the meeting, they sign in and it helps them look good. So, I'll go, I'll sign in, and I'll sit in the meeting of something I don't care about, just so I can get some food. So, I'll eat good. I'll do that every day, twice a day.

In addition to his general campus awareness, Phillip recognizes how his relationship to the MAO and premed interests lead to connections that lead to free food. "Ironically, I stumbled upon a few premed orgs I didn't know about. I ended up at one of their meetings. So, these agencies . . . I would stumble upon these agencies randomly and I would go to their events and I would get free food." What sounds from Phillip's explanation to be a kind of organizational serendipity reflects deeper constructs of the Opportunity Paradigm at Flagship: opportunities beget opportunities because involvement is an incentivized priority. Reflecting in our final interview, Phillip identifies the advantages of his resource-rich environment, in concert with his own efforts to make use of it: "People know a lot of things, there's a lot of resources, opportunity that's here for me. So, I have been able to look back and I've been able to see that it's a really good place. [But] it's only as good as you make it. And it's the fact that *there's so much laying around the edge,* it doesn't take that much to make it good for you. You just have to apply yourself."

Phillip's description of resources "laying around the edge" highlights his keen awareness of the surplus built into the prestige-oriented university. This excess is particularly available within those functions, such as STEM preprofessional student organizations, that align with university priorities. Whether serendipitously or intentionally, Phillip's various clubs, organizations, volunteerism, and relationships seem to connect him to free food. Additionally, his mentors in the MAO send him emails about organizational events with food, his friends sometimes swipe him in to the cafeteria, and he is also friendly with the workers at the campus market, who hook him up: "A lot of times, the people working there are really nice, like the Black and Brown people that recognize, they know how it is, so I can get food on my plate and they'll scan the cheapest item and I'll have four or five things on my plate. So, I get a $10/$12 meal for like $2—so that's really helpful when they do stuff like that." Phillip finds similar sympathy and aid at the hospital where he volunteers: "When I volunteer at the hospital, they have snacks. I love that. You can get a . . . if you go you can get a free drink too. So, that's really helpful too. And the lady there, she's really nice, she gave me some free meal cards. So, I have free meal cards when I go to the hospital so I can use that to eat. That's extremely helpful."

Phillip's social network—on full display in the number of people who shout his name and wave as we traverse campus together—is considerable and seems to channel resources his way. Through his hospital shadowing internship Phillip got connected with an informal mentorship event hosted by a local surgeon who invites both students and other medical professionals to his house: "Yeah, he has a really, really nice house. He has a lot of doctor friends, so he invites all of them, he brings food—like food trucks, he has a house and a guest house. He brings 20+ doctors, we're just networking." Phillip is one of those rare students who moves through their university experience in a "preferred pathway,"[4] making connections that grant him access to campus and community leaders and their associated networks. Prestige-oriented campuses are places where faculty and administrators are particularly geared to identifying and plugging in talented and eager students like Phillip, Alfredo, and Ariel. Nevertheless, some combination of mutual interest, student initiative, and serendipity produces exclusive opportunities, such as serving on presidential advisory committees (Alfredo), forming personal, informal relationships with high-ranking administrators (Ariel), and gaining access to valuable mentorship programs and events (Phillip).

The environmental opportunism that motivates Phillip to engage Flagship so extensively has also sensitized—and emboldened—him both to recognize free food and, like Vera, to draw it into his social circle of other students who are also struggling. Phillip recalls a meeting with leftovers where he was resourceful but careful not to be greedy: "I was like, 'You all want pizza, but you go first and make sure . . . take whatever you want and . . . I'm not going to stop you, take what you need.' But what did anyone take? No one took anything, so I took the boxes back to my office and they're sitting in the MAO right now. I sent a picture to my friends to say, 'Hey, there's pizza here!'" The strength of Phillip's network and the way it effectively circulates opportunities within and among its members reduces the daily burden of finding food for himself and others. His combination of resource awareness and opportunism redefines the role of students in the success of others. This empathetic altruism results in a largely hidden subeconomy of recirculated resources within systems that, because of surplus expectations, often simply discards leftovers. Although Phillip and Vera emphasize food resources they leveraged on campus, other students extend that beyond the campus gates through their own networks and innovations.

Opportunism on and beyond Campus

As much as Phillip represents many aspects of the prototypical ideal student—STEM student, hyper involved in clubs, organizations, and volunteering—Lucas (PRU) does not. A lanky White guy with long, bushy unkempt hair, ripped jeans, and worn vintage jacket; Lucas's pride and joy is a late model van he bought despite his father's wishes. Lucas is about as far from the PRU stereotype as a person can get, which is also part of his goal. Growing up with an emotionally unstable mother, Lucas spent his young life channeling his considerable energy and anger into an antiestablishment identity punctuated by petty crime, vandalism, and drug use. And yet almost despite himself, his academic abilities and the dedication of a few educators pushed him through high school. His *very* conflicted feelings about PRU are rooted in the extreme contrast between the life he knew attending high school nearby and the projection of affluence and put-togetherness PRU conveys: "I've had two of my friends die from gun violence within a couple miles of campus. So, then I went to PRU and suddenly that doesn't exist here. It doesn't . . . not only does it not exist, 90% of people here, from what I've gathered, anecdotal evidence, have never even been exposed to anything like that. I grew up very differently. But it was very . . . I felt like an outlier, to the maximum extent of being an outlier."

Nevertheless, Lucas has discovered that there are people worth getting to know on campus. People who defy the PRU stereotype like him, and others who *fit* the stereotype but are still okay. As we cross toward the library on our tour, from a distance Lucas spies a distinctive-looking student sporting a cowboy hat and boots, and he jumps into an animated response:

That kid's legit. He was in my Human Migration class and that class kind of, it was cool, but there was some sucky people in there. It was about immigration and there was kids that wore Trump shirts and shit. He was in there. He'd wear his cowboy hat and his boots. And he'd always throw his opinion: "Well, all of my relatives are Confederate soldiers, and a lot of them are also Union soldiers, and every year my family, we go visit the graves of the Confederacy *and* the Union." And he just had such a unique, he wasn't just your mainstream Trump conservative. He was definitely conservative, but in a very educated way about it. I was like, "I like this kid."

Though Lucas came to PRU with strong feelings against a campus culture with a reputation for being White, wealthy, and conservative, encounters with students like this one has nuanced his perception of who falls into some of those categories. Lucas's pursuit of free food on campus has also challenged his preconceptions of roles and persons in ways he has not expected:

Actually, I met some minister though the other day, she was offering cider and donuts. I'm very anti–established religions, for the most part. She was really cool though. She is running the only accepting LGBT ministry on campus. She does a lot of work focused on anticolonialism and anticapitalism, and I was like, "The fuck? Y'all are like a religious organization that's anticolonialism? I've never heard of that in my life!" . . . She's actually a genuinely cool person.

Lucas, like many of our participants, has found that his food-seeking has produced unexpected educational moments, exposing him to new ideas and to people he did not expect he would connect with. In his case, part of these educational situations are their effect on his perceptions of who is part of PRU.

Gradually finding his niche on campus has given Lucas increased confidence in his efforts to recognize and seize upon the opportunities of his environment. Nevertheless, he struggles to embrace the role of "joiner" so endemic to the expectations of the prestige-oriented university, even though he recognizes both the expectation and the benefits.

I'm going to try to join a club soon, just really not sure which one. Yeah, there was one called, there's a political club that I thought was interesting. It was a very left-leaning club, which I thought was interesting for PRU. I met with the president and he was a cool person, cool ideas. But he was almost too political. And then they wanted us to pay dues to be in a club. And I was like, "Oh, no thank you. I'm not paying any dues."

When we press Lucas on why he wants to join clubs when he clearly does not want to join clubs, he reflects:

Well, it looks good on resumes, obviously. It's easier to meet people in a club, because there's more discussion going on, rather than being in a class with a bunch of cool people, but you're all listening to the teacher. You have five minutes before and after class to talk to each other. That's about it, really. Just to meet people. And because you're supposed to be in a club, I guess, to have a good resume and shit. Make connections. Everybody tells me PRU's really the place to make connections. I'm literally a little bit antisocial at times.

The powerful environmental press of involvement expectation symbolized in "everybody tells me . . ." is a feature of campus noted by sociologists Peter Kaufman and Ken Feldman.[5] These scholars emphasize that rather than seeing college primarily as a place where young people develop psychologically (which is also the case), we need to recognize that college presses normative messages about student identity upon students, influencing their priorities as a result.[6] Messages about the importance of joining as an essential part of studenthood were clearly affecting Lucas. Though Lucas was openly critical of PRU in our first interview, several months later at our final conversation together he seemed to be finding acceptable "joining" avenues:

And then the other day, yesterday, actually, a new opportunity arose where I'm going to be taking, where I'll be working with a pretty big law firm. But they just opened up a section where they're taking pro bono cases for LGBTQ youth caught in the immigration bullshit going on at the border and being stuck in camps, where they're at really high risk. So, they've been taking on those cases for free. And that's right up my alley.

That's like disenfranchised people, in more than one way, and being fucked by the US government. That's what I want to be involved in. Advocating for people like that. And I'm going to be working with them now doing research and sitting in on consultations. And they're very fast-moving cases. So, that's exciting. That's just an example of the opportunities I get here, and how I take advantage of it.

In many ways, Lucas's approach to finding opportunities for engagement mirrors his approach to finding food, the sense that although campus spaces are important, engagement means looking beyond it as well. Like Layla (Flagship), who also grew up in the same city as her university, Lucas finds much of his food off campus, due to his existing connections and knowledge of the area. For someone who portrays himself as antisocial, Lucas is remarkably people-oriented. His willingness to strike up a conversation with anyone who might interest him combines with his distinctive look to make him a memorable persona with a wide social circle. However, his reticence at joining (rather than simply skimming food opportunistically from organizational meetings) means his opportunism related to food does not dovetail the way it has for Phillip and Layla.

Instead, Lucas takes ample advantage of his social network off campus in parallel with his food opportunism on campus. Lucas's regular late-night employment at a bar a short drive away meshes with his social circle full of people willing to give him a discount or a free meal. "Yeah, so, I wind up eating out a lot. I usually go to Ringo's because I know everybody there. Actually, I usually go to [a nearby suburb] location because that's where they really hook me up. Sometimes I don't even pay for anything over there. I just hang out with them and they feed me and give me drinks and it's great." PRU's neighborhood, a combination of upper-income residential enclaves, clusters of boutique shops and eateries, and a ring of expensive chain stores a bit farther out, creates a bubble of affluence that makes inexpensive food-getting challenging on and around campus. Navigating the nearby food scene through his social connections is one way Lucas manages the higher prices: "I go to the Starbucks near me that my friend works at and she just gives me free coffee. That's honestly how I do a lot of eating out. It's that I work in the service industry and all my friends are in the service industry. So, I either get heavy discounts or I just don't pay. People usually like to see me when I come in, so, I don't even ask for it." Because of his local knowledge and social resources, Lucas finds the prices and quality of available on-campus food to be unacceptable: "I'm not a taco snob, I promise. I go get my junk tacos for $1.25, but at least they're authentic Mexican tacos. I feel like a lot of the stuff that they sell here, while it's not insanely overpriced, I feel like it's bumped up a dollar or two. I'm just like, 'I'll just not eat here and just wait until I'm off campus.'"

Terrence (Flagship) holds similar feelings about on-campus food, especially given the variety of options off campus. His response, in contrast to Lucas's engagement with his social network, is to leverage corporate systems intent on capitalizing on college students' tendency to rely on and socialize around convenience (such as fast food chains) and lifestyle (such as coffee shops) food through discounts, memberships, and loyalty programs. In short, Terrence is the master of extreme couponing, college-style. Throughout our interviews, Terrence's phone dinged and buzzed with push alerts promoting specials and deals from a bevy of retailers. When we ask how much time he spends thinking about food, he explains his perpetual alert strategy:

> Well, I spend a lot of time thinking about deals. But I also think, I mean that also counts. I'm looking, that's the main thing. It's like food . . . It's like a constant thing because I get those alerts from, like, the Slick Deals app. I'll show you. . . . Like, here are all my deal alerts. I have Door Dash. I have Chili's. I needed toothpaste so I was looking for a deal on toothpaste and Walgreens has a lot of deals on, like, detergent and toothpaste. . . . But yeah, when it comes to food it's like a constant thing, yeah.

This is just the beginning. Throughout our two interviews and tour, Terrence peppers us with deals he's found—a free salad with the Wendy's app, a T-Mobile/Dunkin' Donuts cross promotion for a free latte, bonus Starbucks reward points that get him free food and drinks, a free scoop of ice cream from Baskin Robbins, an Apple Pay promo with Qdoba—the vast array of vendors near campus make possible Terrence's perpetual deal-maximizing. However, the *big* fish is Amazon.

Amazon has masterfully capitalized on the college student demographic. Among its many perks and offerings for students are discount Prime memberships and food delivery services through Amazon Prime Now and Amazon drop sites on major college campuses that expedite delivery and accessibility. Add to that 500 polo-wearing student "brand ambassadors" on more than 250 campuses across the country who promote Amazon products and "lifestyle" associations.[7] This combined push to capture the spending habits of future professionals has produced what marketing commentators call the "Amazon Effect," or the student expectation that products and services be delivered fast, free, and at low prices.[8]

Amazon is at the center of much of Terrence's economic strategizing, and he's not shy about exploiting the incentives offered by the online retail behemoth. His efforts take two primary forms. First, Terrence creates multiple accounts to leverage new member benefits:

> So, like, with Amazon Prime Now, I have literally a hundred accounts. I'm not joking. They've banned me a few times [*laughing*]. I'm very serious. . . . So back in high school I started using Amazon Prime Now when it came to our area. Basically, the order minimum was $15 and you'd get $10 off your order. So you'd end up spending $5 for $15 worth of food or products. And that's what I mainly did during high school and then, like, I kept doing it throughout college.

Once he's navigated Amazon's blocking system for his additional accounts, he uses the Amazon app as a price comparison to shop locally:

> So what I would do is I'll make out a list in the Notes app and I'll look at the website. I'll go to, like, Walmart or go on the app and look at how much a certain item is and then I'll go on Amazon Prime Now and I'll look at how much it is. And then I'll decide where I want to purchase the item because I know I'm gonna get ten dollars off, right? But I don't want to pay more for the item on Amazon if I can get it cheaper, right? So I'll do that.

Books and school supplies get the same treatment. In particular, the ease and generosity of Amazon's return policy provides a window for managing the high cost of textbooks:

> Oh yeah—when it comes to school supplies this is what I do. This seems so bad. But this is what I would do. I'll buy the book on Amazon. I'll pay the full price, right? Then each month before the 30 days is up, I'll return it and then buy it again, and then have to return and buy . . . or I'll take photos of it, right? That's what I do. I don't even rent it. I just buy it and then return it.

Terrence's hedging "this seems so bad" conveys the sense that he knows some of his practices stretch, if not outright cross lines of ethical behavior. And while he makes it clear he is not okay with outright theft, he views taking advantage of a corporate promotion as a slightly different issue . . . mostly:

> I think when it comes to Amazon, that's maybe unethical—creating multiple accounts and getting $10 off each order, right? That's . . . I guess it's unethical. But the thing is, they wouldn't offer if it would hurt them. Because corporations, they're not gonna offer things that are gonna make them go bankrupt, you know? So they have an allotted amount of promotional money they want to give out to these customers, right? And I'm just the person doing it three times a month, you know?

However his actions are viewed, Terrence's navigation of his food needs in college is made possible by an economic infrastructure that merges corporate and collegiate interests. Over the past half century, higher education has weathered reductions in state and federal aid, the shift from college as a public good to a private good, and the transformation of a college degree to an essential element for social mobility or status maintenance (depending on the position one was born into).[9] As a result, competitive universities have become increasingly market-oriented and friendly with for-profit interests, particularly on the student services side.[10] In this collaboration, convenience and expedience are implicit cultural values that dovetail with and promote a student consumer mindset.[11] The cyclic effect created by these various elements reinforces middle-class consumptive habits that function as the justification for lavish residential housing, lazy rivers, and upscale on-campus coffee vendors. Amenities that reflect the twin priorities of expedience and lifestyle ideation also reify classed orientations to goods and services as not just desirable but normal and necessary.[12]

Terrence represents an extreme response to this resulting resource *largess,* but he is not alone in recognizing that resources are there for the taking and sharing. As with the other students who are Maximizing, Terrence's strategies are individualized modes of operation that spill over into his social relationships. However, whereas Vera and Phillip's friends benefit directly in terms of food gathered, Terrence's compatriots receive a constant feed of deal opportunities, whether they want them or not: "Yeah, like my friends get annoyed with me when I tell them, literally I'll always text them about, 'Hey, Door Dash has this deal. You could, right? You could do a pickup order and spend like $2 on like an $11 meal or $3, right?' And I'm just like, 'You could do this instead of spending all this money!' And they're just like, 'Terrence, stop.'" Across the board, Maximizing students connected to resources through people, and connected people to resources, as an implicit aspect of their emergent food strategy. In part these strategies are a matter of students simply trying to find enough food to get by. In other ways, messages about the sorts of consumptive experiences students should be having are laced throughout campus and the environment beyond, shaping expectations as well as opportunities. Nevertheless, attempts to maximize the campus environment and its opportunities came with some liabilities.

Gaps and Compromises

Recognizing and capitalizing on environmental opportunities on and off campus did not completely remove the struggle for food from any of our students using this strategy. Sometimes there were no meetings to attend, no app deals that day, or a friend who usually provided the hook-up on discount food was not working. All students relied, to various degrees, on serendipity and opportunity to get by in environments where food resources were plentiful but inconsistently available. But Maximizing students engaged in a different kind of calculus about what experiences were worth investing in, and at what cost. A question posed to Layla about prioritizing food caused her to reflect on her implicit ordering of needs: "I guess I'd never looked at food and/or food insecurity as a priority or as, like, a priority in myself and a priority in the decisions that I make.... Like, I would probably make more money just serving at a restaurant near campus, but that's not best to get vocational practice. But then that contributes to food insecurity. So I never really thought about the syllogism of that or the way that I didn't prioritize [food] access." For our Maximizing students, internships, leadership roles, research positions, and other opportunities that sometimes arose from their compelling personal narratives, identities, and aspirations connected them with positions and relationships that also yielded food. However, as Layla notes, sometimes those opportunities came at the cost of the more consistent financial resources that motivated Sacrificing students to work multiple jobs.

The reliance on free campus food to fill the gaps in financial resources came with its own risks. Prior to our interview, Phillip conserved food he had at home by not bringing lunch to campus because he was attending an interest meeting for a student group. He noted, "But [the organization] kind of played us. There wasn't enough. I actually need to eat later." Free food events came without assurance of amount or availability, and for each experience that yielded a free meal, the possibility of investing the time to attend and not getting to eat was a real risk.

The occasional gaps in resources Maximizing students' experience, despite their learned food navigation strategies, highlights the compromise that "making it work" represents: specifically, that the ability to leverage a resource-rich environment is not the same as fully engaging in campus life from the protection and convenience of normative affluence. In *The Privileged Poor*, Tony Jack makes the closing point that access is not inclusion and inclusion is not equity.[13] Described with other marginalized populations as "cultural work-arounds," laudable efforts by mentors, faculty, and administrators to connect struggling students with food through organizational events, internships, and other contexts still represent partial and incomplete solutions so long as the normativity of student affluence persists.[14] Whether these redirected resources represent a rising tide of changing attitudes across campus that will result in large-scale cultural transformation, or whether these increasingly accepted accommodations will leave the expectation of student wealth largely unchanged remains to be seen.

Making Sense of Maximizing

Short of the larger systemic question, the relative success of students engaged in Maximizing can be attributed to a few recognizable patterns that highlight the strategic types as adaptive learned behaviors. Maximizing students were late in their academic careers—juniors and seniors—whose strategic campus resource management neither descended from heaven in a moment of epiphany nor was endemic to them as persons. Rather, Maximizing strategies were the culmination of students figuring things out for themselves, shaped by childhood experiences of necessary innovation and their socialization to the core functionality of the Opportunity Paradigm as a space where relationships (with individuals or corporations) yield resources. For example, Phillip (Flagship) not only paid for many of his high school expenses but also for his study abroad trip to China by selling candy on the side. Although he struggled to connect socially his first year, finding his "home" in the MAO taught him to lean on mentors and leadership roles to provide food as well as professional development. Phillip's experience, as with many others, reinforces how students use situational adaptive strategies that can and do change throughout college. Given their accounts, it is likely that Layla and Lucas started out Sacrificing as first-year students and Phillip, Terrence, and Vera were Adapting until they formed the connections and habits that serve them as upper-division students.

All of these students struggled out of the gate to adapt to the dynamics of their new prestige-oriented environment. Yet all of them had experienced significant struggles before college, including financial hardship, family dysfunction, food insecurity, and homelessness, which although certainly distressing and difficult, had also contributed to their life navigation skills and their confidence that they could figure things out.[15] The social sciences give us a variety of conceptual tools to help us make sense of Maximizing behaviors. Popular concepts such as "grit" and "resilience" could be applied to describe these students.[16] Both of these ideas have gained broad national attention in the past decade as character virtues that contribute to an individual's ability to cope with and overcome difficult circumstances.[17] In response, social scientists and educators have developed a wide range of interventions designed to boost the grit and resilience of young people.[18] However, these concepts have also been critiqued as an after-the-fact explanation. That is, rather than grit and resilience representing the *capacity* that allows an individual to persist despite obstacles, they might simply describe a socially desirable outcome that other factors produced. Grit in particular has also been critiqued for functionally blaming children born into poverty for not overcoming their circumstances.[19]

By contrast, asset-based approaches emphasize how individuals from marginalized backgrounds leverage the knowledge and resources of their social and cultural backgrounds to identify and pursue what they need to succeed.[20] Maximizing, as a strategy, reflects *navigational capital,* or learned approaches for moving through and finding resources embedded in organizational structures. The combination of prior experience of struggle and the social support of important networks, particularly for Students of Color, buttressed students for a campus environment that was socioeconomically foreign but still culturally manageable given their predilections for developing community and sharing resources. Maximizing students, then, opportunistically take advantage of and share the excesses of their environment in ways that utilize their social networks effectively. They also represent the culmination of environmental learning—the construction of opportunity—possible in an environment tacitly made to encourage student entrepreneurship and autonomy, even if it is not quite the variety that administrators intended.

CHAPTER 14

Navigating the Dream V
Surviving

Only three students we talked with fit the Surviving strategy; we wished it were fewer still. "Surviving" occurs when a student's fragile web of already limited resources begins to unravel, often initiated by a particular crisis moment that challenges the stability of the support system that has mostly worked for them up to this point. Nevertheless, the texture of each student's situation, resources, and responses reveals variations of navigation decisions in which choices between employment and involvement are present as they are for other students, even within this collegiate context of extraordinary difficulty. And so, we profile each student—Miranda (Flagship), Chelsea (PRU), and Ariel (Lib Arts)—separately and at length to illustrate how circumstances can converge to push students to the edge of basic sustainability but more so, to highlight how, even in this space of desperation, students engage their environments with agency, purpose, and determination.

Miranda

Miranda, a rising junior at Flagship, grew up in a rural town 30 minutes from a large metropolitan area. Her great-grandmother survived a life of prostitution in Mexico, later bringing her grandmother and her siblings to America for a fresh start and new opportunities. Each of the children were given to a different family in the United States. The story of her grandmother's journey to and in America is very important to Miranda, functioning as a kind of family legend that has inspired her before and within college.[1] Miranda's hometown had "no more than 3,000 people ever. So it was literally one of the towns that if you looked away for a minute, you would really pass it." Food options in her community were limited to a very small grocery store, "but it was weirdly overpriced and not good food. If there was any fresh produce, it was not good. It was just kind of the last things that you would want." Her family would make a trip every two weeks to the city to get groceries. Despite her parents working multiple jobs, they struggled financially, resulting in careful and creative use of resources: "So when we didn't have light [electricity], we'd have to keep the fridge closed at all times so nothing would go bad." Her family stretched their food options as far as possible, in part because features of their cultural identity lent themselves to doing so: "But a lot of Mexican food was just very cheap, so it wasn't . . . we'd have a lot of variations of things that were basically the same, but just depending on what we have. It was never a lot. It was always really the same things. And we used tomato sauce on everything." Watching her family get by with very little and innovate around a few inexpensive ingredients formed Miranda's perception of how to successfully navigate situations of minimal financial resources with minimal stress.

Miranda is a first-generation college student, which shapes much of her college-going experience. A few of her cousins had attended college but did not finish. Miranda had always planned on going to college to create options for her future: "I just always knew I wanted to go to school. I knew there wasn't anything in the town for me. There wasn't anything that just piqued my interest. Unless you learn a trade or you become a wife to someone, then there was really nothing else there for you to be." Her high school was very small and underresourced. She notes, "We had really bad teachers who were underpaid and overworked and they would never last more than a year. Sometimes not even a semester." She did have the opportunity to take dual credit college classes and almost finished her "basics" before college. Miranda educated herself about college-going, reading on her own about loans and applying—"the whole process of being here and applying here and finding housing and doing FAFSA was just really hard. I did it all my own. I did all the paperwork on my own." She came to Flagship for three reasons: they gave her a scholarship, it was far from home, and "it felt right" when she came to visit. When we asked her to explain what she meant by "it felt right," she reflected, "Flagship was somewhere where I could not only start fresh, but where I could just come into who I really am."

First Year Adapting

Miranda began her college career living on campus with a meal plan, pulled into the services bubble by the same first-generation student anxiety that motivated other students to make similar "Adapting" choices. Although housing on campus was about twice as expensive as her cheap shared apartment off campus the year after, the knowledge gap about how college works and navigating a new city made it the right choice, in her mind: "But . . . it was worth it for the experience and to just kind of get the gist of how things work and learn how to budget more. I definitely don't think I would have been able to find housing on my own or how to manage it on my own." The steep learning curve Miranda and her family faced meant paying additional money for convenience foods on campus as part of the meal plan, compared to living off campus and buying food from a grocery store:

> When I stayed [on campus] . . . things were a little pricier, but considering it was already a part of my tuition, it didn't feel the same as me actually having money. It just clicked as, "Oh, I have that as a part of my tuition." But I paid, but it's still in a different form. It's easier for me to spend five bucks on that little fruit box and four bucks on a smoothie when you have, like . . . I think I had $1800 or $1200 around there. So, it was easier to say okay this is for the whole year. And just because things got so expensive and things come up where you need something, and you don't really have another option to go to.

Adapting her first year, Miranda benefited from the ease of access and apparent irrelevance of the high cost of on-campus food and other necessary supplies.

Second Year: Shifting Circumstances and Strategies

Although she began college Adapting like other students, Miranda's friendship with a few older students clued her in to the benefits of off-campus living and how to navigate it. Miranda's perspective that the move off campus is a "learning experience" frames her willing adaptation to college in her best moments. Still, the virtues of off-campus living in the aggregate—saving money, primarily—are hard earned in the particulars of daily decision-making. Miranda especially found this to be the case managing food while living in an apartment with strangers: "[Living off campus] has got its pluses and minuses. It's harder now because I have to buy groceries. I have to make time to go do that. And I have to budget that into my money, and I have to find time to cook, and then considering I have a really bad roommate situation it's not always the easiest to do."

In an effort to save money and minimize debt, Miranda's second year she adopted Sacrificing strategies, focusing on employment supplemented by free food she could scrounge from campus organizations or mooch off of friends. The combination of feeling uncomfortable using her shared kitchen, the lack of time to shop and cook, and the cost of food meant Miranda often resorted to snacking—or simply not eating—as her central food strategy: "Especially since I haven't been comfortable enough to cook in my own home, a lot of what I've been buying is just snacks. I also don't eat as much, because I've trained myself to not be as hungry. So, I can . . . usually I won't eat until around four to six. And then I'll eat a little snack maybe, but that's it. Just one meal." At times during her second year, Miranda combined the worst elements of Sacrificing and Prioritizing: working long hours that kept her from unpaid internships and organizations but still eating very poorly, if at all:

> I used to work as, like, a barista. And I'd be on my feet for, like, five, six hours sometimes. And then we wouldn't really get, like, a break or, like, a lunch. When we weren't busy, we could get things and I would just go to the place next door and get tacos, 'cause it was decently priced and it was good food. So that was just the easiest thing to do. And then I'd get home so late and then I just didn't want to eat. I'd just go to bed even if I was a little bit hungry if I didn't get to eat at work.

Miranda's learned practice of ignoring hunger, a vestige of childhood food insecurity, meant that she also often neglected preparing to eat by not planning ahead for groceries, which reinforced her reliance on vending machine food and whatever happened to be left in the fridge.

But Miranda's second-year experience was not all bad news. Miranda was fortunate to be hired as a mentor in the same scholarship program for low-income students that had oriented her to Adapting her first year. She quickly found that being a mentor benefited her indirectly as well:

> It was beneficial in a way because being a mentor and technically working for Flagship, we would constantly have presentations on resources around campus on departments that were in campus and had to navigate those. So that's how I learned a lot of resources and that's how I learned a lot of places that were actually helpful that a lot of people didn't know about. So that helped me a lot and I was given the opportunity to learn more about that, and now I share it with other people who I think might be struggling or who might need it. So that's been really beneficial.

Once she was in charge of her own batch of new students, her position gave her access to a regular stream of ideas and guidance about programs, offices, and events that, although intended for her charges, enhanced Miranda's own ability to navigate campus. The scholarship role brought her into closer relationship with her supervisors "and they helped with class schedule and they helped finding jobs and things you needed. So having that support system in a different way was really nice."

Working two jobs and armed with a better sense of how to navigate the organizational behemoth that is Flagship, Miranda edged close to

Maximizing strategies, relying on friends, attending free food events, and capitalizing on start-of-the-year giveaways at nearby businesses. Miranda harnessed her newfound campus knowledge and resources to aid herself and her students:

> But I was constantly trying to provide them with resources, whether that was on campus or not. I kept reminding them that if they needed a meal, we could always go eat. I was at a point since I was working two jobs, I was at a point where I was fine with that. I was offering help for them 'cause I knew I could. And there were times where . . . it was finals time and it was rough for them, so I would buy them just like a pizza and we would eat and have our meetings. So I try to remind them that it wasn't something to be ashamed of and that it was okay to struggle and that they didn't have to do it alone.

Offering emotional support—as well as food—to her mentees reflected Miranda's understanding of the range of needs students on the financial margins often have, and her particular ability to help meet them. Even on a very thin budget, occasionally springing for pizza gave her the good feeling of doing more than merely surviving; she was contributing to the success of others who were trying to "adapt" just as she had the previous year.

The relative stability Miranda achieved her second year began to evaporate as the academic year came to a close. With her mentorship position ending, Miranda struggled paycheck to paycheck, which "was not great, but it worked." Still, periodic unexpected expenses and her own admitted difficulty with budgeting left her short on some occasions, causing her to dip into her financial aid, which she described as "my savings," to cover food and rent. When that money ran out in May things were tight. And then she lost her job as a briefing clerk for a law firm. "I really like the job. It's the only job I ever really liked," explains Miranda, verging on tears. "My parents actually don't know I lost my job. I'm gonna keep that away from them as far as I can. I'm just gonna refuse that tension. Just gonna delay it." Like many of our participants, Miranda has worked very hard as a first-generation college student to fill in the gaps in her parents' financial and logistical knowledge, proving to herself—and to them—that she can manage mostly on her own. As she talks, Miranda reveals both frustration that her parents are not able to be more help and recognition that they try to support her in the ways they can.

> I think my parents... don't really realize that I do a lot of this on my own. And they didn't really realize that they're literally not paying anything unless I ask them for money. They thought they were gonna pay the parent loan, which I guess essentially they would like legally. But in real life, I know I'm gonna have to pay that for them. Which is fine. I've already known that. But that in itself, having to rely on them for rent is just, especially when I know they already do not make as much 'cause my dad doesn't make as much as they used to. So that in itself is just rough. Which is why I don't want to tell them I lost my job.

As with many low-income families, college for Miranda is only possible through a federal government Parent Plus loan, a program financial aid experts note is often both a lifeline and a debt trap for overborrowing.[2] Miranda understands that while her parents assume the financial liability for the loan, it will be up to her to repay it, a situation that potentially imperils them both.

Miranda details the confluence of situations that led to her unemployment, and as tragically to her, her inability to prove that she can get by without her parents' support. Miranda's already precarious financial situation since her financial aid ran out had forced her to ask for help from her parents, which cascaded into a blow-up about college and finances and all the topics Miranda very much did not want to talk to her mom and dad about. She was already struggling with mental health issues, and then the situation spiraled out of control:

> I took two days off right after I had to pay rent because I had an argument with my parents. I took two days off 'cause I just didn't want to cry at work all day, and I told my boss. And then the next day, there was a scam with my account. So there was a whole problem with my bank and then having to do that. So I got too caught up in that and I didn't get a chance to email my boss about that situation. And then they fired me.

Now with $18 in her wallet (plus the gift card to a local grocery chain we provided at the start of the interview) and facing a largely empty campus with few resources in the summer, Miranda is in Surviving mode:

> Now it's just, I'm looking for food that I might have bought a long time ago but I forgot and finding that some of it is expired. Or I think yesterday I just ate a bag of broccoli. That was just it. I just ate a bag of broccoli. And then now that it's a little bit tighter around money, I'm just eating once a day usually. I'm used to—I never really eat breakfast. Now that I don't have work or even when I did work, I didn't have to go in so early. So I wouldn't get hungry around lunchtime. Maybe I'd eat, like, a granola bar if I was. And then I'd eat something at dinner.

The rollercoaster of living on a thin margin in college has its highs and lows, and perhaps for that reason Miranda is remarkably sanguine about her prospects.

> Yeah. I never really thought I'd be in this situation. I knew I'd have a rough patch. That's just how life is when you don't have the stability of money. You're just gonna have rough patches. And that's fine. I've learned how to work with that. . . . Being put in that situation now is a little bit harder than I expected. But it's something that I think is important to be able to do and to have that system of support. So it's not ideal to not be able to know when your next meal is coming, or making something stretch a lot longer than it might, or not completely eating to just 'cause you want to. Just eat because you know you haven't eaten in a day or two or you haven't really drank that much water as you should have. So focusing on that more is harder but it's . . . I know it could be worse. So I work with what I have.

Miranda has learned to think about enduring an extremely challenging college journey as an important skillset she has developed. The refrain she ends with—"it could be worse"—we heard from several students who faced extreme circumstances. Perhaps this phrase functions for them as a kind of reassurance that as bad as it seems, it helps to remember that there are others whose lives are yet more difficult. Perhaps as well it is a mantra that adds nobility and virtue to such an acute struggle in a space awash in surplus resources for those who are able to pay the price to be "normal."

Chelsea

Very differently from Miranda, Chelsea, an African American junior transfer student at PRU, is making it through college by holding administrators' feet to the fire of their own rhetoric about caring for students. Her story of learning to bend systems of privilege toward her needs began long before she entered PRU. Chelsea grew up in an RV across from her elementary school with her parents and eight siblings. Having to "share everything" made her family very close relationally as well as spatially. The second youngest of the bunch, she always felt that school and college-going were priorities, and she credits her parents for preparing her through "their confidence in me and their encouragement, and just believing in me." Although Chelsea is a first-generation college student, the seven siblings ahead of her all attended college, making the path easier to imagine and navigate.

Chelsea's sophomore year of high school she decided to move in with her older sister, who lived in an academically strong public school system near PRU. In a foreshadowing of her PRU experience, her new high school did not have the federal free/reduced-price lunch program in place because so few students needed it. Instead, she recalls, "the liaison of my school would pay me $30 each week so I could have food." Operating on the margins became a way of life.

In high school, Chelsea had to adjust to a faster academic pace and expectations beyond what she had experienced before, in addition to the social challenges of making her way in an affluent, majority White school: "Yeah, well I dealt with a lot of racism and a lot of students not understanding my background, so I had to kind of assimilate but still understand where I came from and stuff. And you know, I just . . . it was very difficult." The dance between needing to "kind of assimilate" or learn what to say and do, or not say and do, while trying to "still understand where I came from" or resist potential marginalization and shame from her socioeconomic and racial background, was a daunting process. But as a student gaining the advantages of becoming "privileged poor," even by degree, Chelsea recognizes the academic and organizational lessons she learned that now serve her well:[3] "[High school] helped me become a better person by its hard coursework and being able to not assimilate, [it] helped me become just a little bit more social and understand what the majority of this population also does, too, because this is a majority White population and a lot of the students are privileged here. So, it just taught me how to kind of maneuver around."

Chelsea's second mention of "assimilation" highlights a long-running point of tension for scholars who study the transition into college. For decades, prevailing theory held that students are most successful when they set aside their precollege identities and integrate into the campus culture, often using the language of "integration."[4] More recently, researchers who focus on the experiences of historically marginalized groups have pushed back, arguing that campus cultures are not class- and race-neutral. As such, "integration" means Students of Color, those from low socioeconomic–status families, and others who do not reflect traditionally served populations must leave behind their preestablished identities to become part of the campus culture. Meanwhile, upper-middle-class White students enter a campus environment invisibly aligned with how they have been raised and racially identify that affirms rather than separates them from their cultural identities. The unspoken implication of "integration" is that other-than-White and upper/middle-class identities are a detriment to student success. Subsequent researchers have contested this assumption, asserting that historically excluded racial and classed identities are actually vital resources for campus navigation and support.[5] Chelsea's induction into an education of invisible White/wealthy normativity was a lesson not only in valuing her own background but also in how to make her way in a culturally foreign environment.

Chelsea began her college career at East Metro, a nearby community college, where she felt a much higher level of support than she experiences at PRU: "I feel like East Metro was more resourceful towards students who were first-generation. I guess it was because of many people where they're coming from their background, you know, we were able to get loaned textbooks and stuff and we just don't have that program here. It's a lot of programs missing that we should have." In addition to the textbook loan program, East Metro had a well-stocked food pantry and childcare resources. The irony is that PRU, for all its famous alumni, vast array of student organizations, and impressive buildings, is not structured to serve Chelsea nearly as well as the modest community college down the road where she began. That financial and staff resources are so apparent in Greek life, athletics, and the residential college system—all elements where tradition and organizational orientation toward prestige have had their say—makes the reluctance to help a student like Chelsea confounding but perhaps understandable, in light of the type of student PRU has traditionally served.[6]

Parenting at PRU

The additional element of Chelsea's experience that accentuates PRU's lack of preparedness for a student like her is that she is also parenting her 5-month-old son, Jacob. Chelsea decided to live on campus to be close to her classes because nearby rentals are expensive, and because she views renting as a waste of money. She would prefer to buy a place that needs work, but she lacks the resources at this point. At the time of our first interview, Chelsea was living in a residence hall for juniors and seniors with a roommate, but the housing director caught wind that Chelsea's son was living with her there—apparently a violation of the overnight guest policy—and she was told Jacob was not allowed to stay. So most nights, Chelsea and Jacob sleep in her car in a nearby park (she can't afford on-campus parking). In the morning, she uses her expensive on-campus housing to shower, change, and get ready for the day. Sometimes they sleep on a couch in one of the buildings, which the custodial staff accommodate: "I never have any problems. It's janitors, they're like . . . 'It's the usual, just Chelsea and her baby' and they'll come by and say, 'Hey,' speak to me and I think that is what makes my transition helpful, too, because they give me a lot of encouraging words."

Ironically, at the start of her PRU experience it is those employees with the least amount of organizational power—hourly custodial and food service works—who are most notably supportive and encouraging.[7] For the couple weeks prior to our first interview, Chelsea's 11-year-old niece had also been staying with her in her car and helping out with Jacob. Chelsea would begin her day at 5 a.m. bathing Jacob and getting ready for the day with the help of her niece before running her to school and getting herself to class. Chelsea also gets by with the flexibility of faculty who are understanding of her needs as a single mother and student: "I take him to class with me every day, and the teachers are very accommodating towards it."

Navigating Food

From the start, food has been a major challenge, and Chelsea has relied on the campus food pantry for basic subsistence: "I've been struggling since I was pregnant. I was pregnant when I entered school here as well. And you know the resources were very low. I was eating canned goods every day. I was eating noodles every day and it was really making me sick. We didn't have any fresh foods or nothing. And that is just the majority of what I was eating and it was very difficult." As with other students we talked with, finding the food pantry was a considerable ordeal. Knowing nutrition was important during her pregnancy, she saw a poster advertising that the African Student Association was collecting donations, but she was unsure where the food pantry was actually located. "Yeah. I thought the pantry was in the African Student's meeting, but it wasn't in the African Student's meeting, so I had to go to the library, but I didn't also know it was at the library, I had to go to the Dean of Students to ask, 'Is there any programs that can give us food?' And they're like, 'Oh yeah, well we have the pantry.'"

On a typical day, Chelsea starts her morning with cereal, noodles, or canned goods—whatever the food pantry has available—"and maybe some water." Usually, she will skip lunch and eat dinner when she can: "Sometimes I won't eat until 6:00 because I have to tote my child around. I have to complete my homework and you know I'm back on campus, can't get really far with that." The WIC government program provides formula for Jacob and some baby care staples, but when it comes to her own eating, the lack of campus childcare that would free her up to earn money means she depends on the food pantry and the generosity of friends and employees to eat:

> Well, you know, with my funds its difficult, but sometimes I won't have any funds, but what really helps is a lot of the school employees will look out for students who don't have any funds. So, one day I used to just go in and go get water from Chick-fil-A and then you know a lot of the employees were helping me pay for my food. I have a friend, she actually works at the dining hall, but she only gets ten passes a day for free food. So, you know, when I have to use it sometimes I use it and . . . I'll stack up my food from the dining hall and, or she'll bring some and I'll just have it . . . like, separate my food between the days, like, maybe grab two sandwiches for the week and some pizzas on top, like, piling it up. And I'll try to make it equal through the day so I can be able to eat.

As we've seen with Phillip (Flagship) and several others, the empathy of food service workers, often Persons of Color, creates a "soft economy" for those they recognize are struggling. Chelsea, likely nearly all our participants, has also learned to glean the excess food available through campus organizations and events, a practice that brings her into contact with other students who are doing the same thing:

> Honestly, I'm at every event that has food. If they have pizza, I try to be there. If they have sandwiches, I try to be there for everything. Everything that has refreshments. A lot of the students, I see the same students go, you know? I see a lot of the Asian students, a lot of first-generation students, always at the same thing as I am. They're not really there for the program, they're really there for the food.

A significant part of Chelsea's struggle that sets her apart from Tia, Lucas, Corbett, and other PRU students is that her needs are not the episodic sort that hit at spring break or when car repair bills take over the food budget. Getting by on almost nothing is her daily life. The pantry at PRU, though an important lifeline for her, is set up to meet occasional needs, not chronic ones. Students are limited in how often they can visit; supplies include shelf-stable foods as well as a few toiletries. Compared to the sort of needs administrators expect students to have, Chelsea's situation is almost beyond imagination: "You know what would also help? Is if we had items for our dorms. Like, maybe something to make us more accommodating at home. I don't have a blanket and I had to use my roommate's blanket, and she let me borrow it. Thank you, Jesus." Chelsea came to college with few possessions and in need of basic college resources that Miranda (Flagship) was fortunate to receive from her first-generation student scholarship program. No such program is in place at PRU. Even basics, such as clothes and school supplies, are often beyond her financial resources:

> I wish we had clothes, like maybe a thrift store on our campus, or something, you know? I didn't have clothes coming here, either. I didn't even have maternity clothes. I was walking around with my pants unzipped the whole nine. Every day . . . I didn't have warm clothes. I didn't have umbrellas. You know? I didn't have school materials. I didn't have pencils. I didn't have notebook paper. I didn't have anything. And I didn't have a jacket and you know I came in January, it's very freezing. I didn't have anything.

Chelsea notes, with frustration, that PRU students donate food, clothing, and dorm room supplies to Goodwill at the end of the year, but these resources leave campus: "Instead of just having a drive here so people can . . . we can keep it within our community, whatever we donate. I see Goodwill here at the end of the semester when students move out. . . . How is it a donation center if it's not staying within the community? And I think that we need to keep those things within our community to help our students that need it." Administrators at PRU who are involved with the food pantry also express frustration that canned food drives and other charity-oriented evens, often hosted by fraternities and sororities, send resources out into the nearby urban community without a thought that students on campus might also need these items.

Advocating as Surviving

Despite the social, economic, and racial marginalization Chelsea feels at PRU, her experiences at the nearby wealthy public school contributed to her belief that administrators will help her if she persistently advocates for her needs. Several months after the first interview, we sit together on a cold spring morning to catch up. Chelsea's housing situation has improved dramatically. She and Jacob are now living in an on-campus apartment for the same cost as her shared dorm room the prior semester. Part of the reason things have changed for the better is her belief in the responsibility of organizations to respond to her. "I expect the institution to change," Chelsea says, but she has also come to expect that those tasked with helping her will not necessarily give her the help she wants. When we ask how she got in her apartment, Chelsea lays out her process:

> Usually I write letters, I speak very well, I'm able to get my... I'm able to talk [well] and I'm well-mannered in the way I speak, and I've been pushed down a lot, however, I just keep persisting. "Yeah, you're pushing me away, but how can we fix my issue? Because I don't want to walk out of this door without my issue being fixed. So, how can you help me?" I'm always trying to find a solution. "This is your job to help me, so how can we find a solution? What can you do?" Even after that, the way I speak right now, I still get pushed away, but I keep... if that doesn't work then I go up the chain.

Chelsea is unequivocal about the added labor advocating creates for her: "I had to work very hard. I had to talk to a lot of people. I had to work hard for that... but I did make it very known that I am a student who has a child staying in a dorm with another person that's small, very small. I had to make it known. I had to talk to a couple supervisors."

Chelsea's willingness to escalate her concerns "up the chain" points to the power that students hold in a consumer-oriented student services environment that embraces "caring" as a professional virtue. Nearly all PRU administrators believe that limits should be set on student aid in the name of "taking responsibility." However, the power Chelsea wields, whether she recognizes it or not, is that her actions effectively leverage

Surviving   293

the organizational commitment to caring by using the hierarchical power structure of the university to appeal to those for whom denying the needs of a first-generation African American single parent attending on a full scholarship is politically if not morally untenable. As such, Chelsea actively rejects the implicit administrative definitions of a Good Student and acceptable agency through the hard truth of her needs and circumstances.

Among the items Chelsea pushed PRU to provide were textbooks, which administrators strongly resisted. Chelsea's experience with a textbook loan program in community college made some sort of textbook support seem obvious to her at a well-funded university. Chelsea went to two different upper administrators and heard the same thing: "And the lady literally, from her mouth, it sounded the same as the other woman. She was like, you know, 'Who recommended you here? What do you think this is? We don't pay for books here.' Things like that." This response surprised Chelsea, who anticipated a spirit of cooperation and problem solving: "I thought they were going to be like, 'Okay, well you know, I understand—what can we do? Maybe I can find some resources for you, . . .' but it wasn't the case. It was more threatening. You know? They didn't want to really help me and they treated me like I was stealing from the school."

Ultimately, the administrators relented and funded books for Chelsea. Even then, the process of buying the books was dehumanizing to her, and she felt treated with suspicion. Chelsea was required to sign a paper saying she had received the books, which she interpreted as a move to make sure she did not try to sell the books for money. "They just treated me like I was a thief or just some student coming from a poor class." Chelsea's frustration and determination are palpable, so much so that she encourages us to make her identity known to PRU:

> I wish you could put that on your thing so they can . . . whoever hears it, whoever hears [this story], they know it's me. I'm going to get somewhere.
>
> —*You want them to know it's you?*
>
> Yeah, I want them to know it's me, and I want to succeed because that is the thing that motivates me.

Much of Chelsea's PRU experience has been defined by her relentless demand that her university honor her admission by supporting her success in ways that make at least some PRU administrators uncomfortable. In the course of our interviews with administrators at PRU, several people described, in vague terms, a student situation that sounded very much like Chelsea's. One administrator directly identifies Chelsea when describing how refusing her request for pots and pans was done to protect Chelsea's agency. Whether about her or not, administrators' comments point to the challenging dialogue about managing resources organizationally versus meeting the needs of any one particular student. Grace, a student affairs administrator at PRU, reflected on a question we asked about "limits" to PRU's responsibility: "What are . . . what are . . . when do we say 'when'? What are some of the limits to the help that we can provide? So, I will say that that is a conversation that we've had in our office. But it's a larger conversation that I've had with other colleagues across divisions of the University."

A senior administrator, referring to a student who "had a child but the child did not have a place to live," described conversations with colleagues about how the twin goals of accessibility and mission should play out when those students in need of basic resources are also Students of Color:

> Yeah. I mean, I think that is one of the tensions, you know, that you want to be accessible and you want to recruit the best and the brightest, regardless of what background they're coming from. But that can also make it cost prohibitive for those populations that are disadvantaged in society. So, often those are People of Color. So, I know that's something that we think about a lot and how can we be accessible and when a student gets here how can we also create an inclusive culture here, so they feel like a part of the community and are a part of the community? So, that's a continual struggle at a place like PRU.

The discourses of "accessibility" and "equity" in higher education are challenging for prestigious universities because "prestige" as an institutional attribute includes with it a range of expectations from various constituents that are difficult to simultaneously manage. Some of these expectations, like athletic success, are broadly attractive. Others, like financial resources prioritized for Greek life, are attracting increased scrutiny.[8] The slippery math that catches administrators is the transition from "limits to what we can provide" to "not a place for everyone" to, often unintentionally, "not a place for certain kinds of people," which is code for students from low-income backgrounds who are often also Students of Color. When we ask Grace, herself a Person of Color, if there are limits to PRU's responsibility for students' food needs, she pauses,

> Yeah. I mean, because resources aren't unlimited. It's one of those things that I really struggle with sometimes, because I think everyone should be able to be educated. Everyone doesn't have to be educated at PRU. So, I do struggle sometimes with the price tag of the institution where I work, because it's steep. It's very steep. So, there are times when I struggle with students . . . and this is going to sound harsh, and I don't necessarily mean for it to, but students know the price tag, and so how do you balance, "this is what you signed up for and now it's not a possibility, and I realize that people go through a variety of things." You know? We've had students come in and say, "When I applied my dad had this job and this was completely possible, but I'm a junior, I'm getting ready to go into my junior year, my dad doesn't have that job anymore." As we know, as you progress the aid that you receive is lessened, so it does put people in harder situations, so that's . . . I think that's where my struggle is. When I talk about people, I feel like everyone should have the opportunity to be educated, but it doesn't necessarily mean it has to be a PRU education.

Grace does not set her department's budget. She works with real constraints among the students who are most desperately in need of aid. For her and many others who attempt to work conscientiously in the thicket of administration, prestige often functions like a set of golden handcuffs, casting the university in the best light possible as a place of resources and possibilities but constraining response to student needs because of the financial priorities prestige implies. When students buy into the prestige image but find there are real limits to what the university believes it can provide, administrators become defensive and students become incredulous and frustrated.

But Chelsea is not concerned with the misgivings of administrators. She and other students who are engaged in Surviving have immediate and pressing needs that strip well-meaning organizational jargon like "accessibility" and "equity" of their virtuous veneer. Whether through her practice of leaving notes in the food pantry about items she would like them to stock, or her persistent meetings with administrators advocating for services to meet her basic needs, Chelsea has endured considerable hardship to get where she is, and the reluctance of a system not designed to meet her degree of need does not deter her. Concluding our interview, she gave advice to other students similarly struggling that reflects her important life theme, that being resourceful and receiving aid should not come at the cost of changing who you are: "I would tell them definitely go to the school programs, or different clubs are hosting so you can get food. Try to remember who you are, don't change who you are, and don't be afraid to ask for help." "Surviving" can seem like a low bar in an environment of aspiration and accomplishment. But, as Chelsea's story shows, Surviving can also be a considerable achievement, one that reflects deep inner resources and a willingness to challenge how administrators interpret the limits of "care."

Ariel

Partway through our very first conversation, Ariel's phone rings. She glances at the number: [*to us*] "Give me one second" [*answering phone*]. "Hello? Hey. Oh wow. It really is the second, the third. Wow. No, I'm sorry. I've been very stressed. I had no . . ."

We stop the recorder at this point to give Ariel privacy to finish the call. Later she tells us that it was from her landlord. She's late on the last $317 of her rent; money she does not have. Composing herself, she puts on a brave face about the situation:

> It's okay. It really is. I'm like compartmentalized enough to still have a good day. I'm just like, "Bro! Why does the world have to run on money?" But yes. Being broke sucks because I don't have enough money and I don't

have enough money and I can't have enough food. And if I don't have enough food, I go crazy, therefore needing more money to have more doctors, to have more time.

And it's incredibly exhausting because it just feels like I can't do anything to catch up and my mom will be like, "Don't live paycheck to paycheck!" "Make sure you're saving . . . blah, blah, blah." But, like, I literally have no money to save and I literally cut it down to the wire every single two weeks. And most of my paycheck is gone by Sunday after I've been paid because I pay bills immediately.

So that is my life.

***

As with Chelsea, the desperation of Ariel's situation thrusts her into interactions with administrators. But in contrast to Chelsea, who has battled for resources from the social margins of campus, a central theme of Ariel's college journey at Lib Arts has been community. A senior communications major and daughter of Middle Eastern immigrants, Ariel defines "immediate family" expansively, including her parents, two younger sisters and a brother who are actually cousins, as well as an additional "sister" who is a friend from childhood and her current roommate. Summing up this group, she reflects with a smile: "Yeah, and then here I have some friends that I love a lot, so add all of them. I collect people." Holding the door as we head into an administrative building, Ariel informs us, "You're going to meet more of my parents." As we wind our way through a variety of hallways and offices, Ariel introduces several administrators as her "Lib Arts mom" or "my Lib Arts dad." With each introduction comes a brief description of their qualifications for what anthropologists call "fictive kin,"[9] or family beyond bloodlines: "This is my Lib Arts dad . . . he's the one who helped me change my major, and largely saved my life because I hate science." Her enthusiasm for the variety of staff who have helped her along the way ends with Ariel connecting this space of emotional and logistical support to basic needs. "In this building in general I haven't had any bad experiences, even by accident! Oh, they also make sure that we have food. . . . Like, midterms and finals, they will just always have snacks. They'll have fruit, they'll have snacks, they'll just have everything."

But positive vibes are a dramatic departure from where she began four years ago as a first-year student. Walking us down the hill on the back side of campus, Ariel takes us toward a pair of nearly identical modest multistory residence halls. Wingert and North Halls are showing their age. The physical wear, the basic cinder block construction, the small windows, and the low ceilings together produce an impression of a well-used space likely to be excluded from campus tours and promotional brochures. Ariel, however, sees none of that. She sees community:

> This is my favorite place. This is Wingert Hall, it's 100% freshman housing. And when I was a freshman, sophomore, and junior this is the hall that if you were a freshman and you wanted a true college experience, this is where you wanted to live. . . . It was a very communal living. Everybody has to come in through the same door. So, you're in the lobby. It's like coming in through the living room, and so you build really strong relationships in there.

It was in these modest residence halls that, as a socially isolated first-year student, Ariel experienced the initial embrace of community initiation. On the day of her birthday just before Thanksgiving break, Ariel had almost convinced herself that she didn't care:

> So I was like, "I'm not expecting anybody to know what is happening with me or anything or, like, say anything. And I'm not gonna be hurt about it because that's unreasonable. I don't know when *your* birthday is." And at midnight on my birthday, like, ten people came to my door and sang "Happy Birthday" to me. And I literally burst into tears because no one had ever done anything like that, and I just didn't expect it. Like, "How would you know when my birthday was? I don't understand!" And I'm friends with all of those people still. So even though I was actively uninvolved, everybody else was actively trying to be my friend and that was just great.

That birthday experience was a turning point in her social and campus engagement. Ariel spent three years living in the residence halls, two as a resident and one as RA staff. The friend group that developed around that first impromptu birthday party put her on the radar of an administrator looking for new leadership for the campus PRIDE organization. Ariel and two of her friends took on this new responsibility with gusto, reinvigorating PRIDE's mission from "largely a social club" to an education, visibility, and advocacy organization.

Mobilizing around campus issues quickly expanded beyond PRIDE's traditional focus when a series of administrative decisions combined to push frustration among students to a boiling point:

> It's, like, we have well-meaning administrators, we have well-meaning professors, we have well-meaning everybody—nobody has malice in their heart for these students. They just don't know that they're not doing anything. They don't know that they're not being helpful. They don't know that food culture sucks and then representation sucks and then having affordable housing sucks. You don't realize what your trickledown consequences are by doing or not doing all these things.

As a small social justice–oriented campus, Lib Arts has a tendency to both attract and foster student activism. Administrators admit that this culture of social activism naturally—and rightly—gets turned back on the university at times, leading to confrontations over issues related to funding, student group access, and representation on campus committees. Ariel gives some credit to administrators for their responsiveness, including adding students to the president's advisory council. This body eventually developed 15 action steps; among the items were demands for support systems to aid students who struggle with the cost of food.

Ironically, as Ariel began to do research on food insecurity in preparation for meetings with administrators to lobby for a meal plan emergency fund, she started to understand her own experience differently:

> Honestly, I didn't realize I was struggling to afford food until I studied food insecurity. I didn't know that I was food insecure until I really talked about it in the context of other people. And then even after that, I'd have to be like, "Oh, wait a second . . . I understand because I've done this" [*imitating*

a survey question]. "Have you asked your friend to buy you food every day of the week because part of your budget is to ask your friend for food?" "Yes." You know, if I was eating on campus, I literally had a rotation of people that would feed me lunch so that I could buy groceries to feed myself for breakfast and dinner.

The intersection of advocacy, visibility, and Ariel's awareness of her own food insecurity brought about what she calls "my identity crisis," as she struggled to decide whether to use her personal experience in her conversations with administrators and students:

> Because I was just like, "Am I wrong for not sharing . . . ?" But I have a personal stake in this. Like, is it wrong? Is it less successful because I identify with this and I'm not telling anybody that I identify with it? Like, doing a disservice by not saying, "I'm a part of the people that need this, make this a thing!" But on the other hand, not sharing is a better idea because then everyone is going to think that you're selfish and that you're not really being genuine about wanting this for everybody, you just want this for yourself. So, it was just easier to deal with the quiet internal struggle than to actually voice it and the outward struggle of sharing.

Ariel's "quiet internal struggle" with food insecurity was present her sophomore year, when she was no longer on the big meal plan and lived off the generosity of friends. Her junior year, when she worked as an RA with a free meal plan, food was no longer a problem, and she frequently paid for other students' meals. Now in her senior year living off campus, Ariel's food struggles have become acute. Uncomfortable using food insecurity as a platform during her sophomore and junior years, she has now turned over most of her roles to a new generation of student leaders. Despite her close circle of friends and warm affinity for some administrators, her resistance to accepting help continues. When we ask who she has told about her food struggles, Ariel is unequivocal: "No, I didn't tell anybody." Consequently, Ariel lies to her friends even though they know she loves food. She lies to her parents when they ask, "Do you have everything you need?" because she knows they cannot afford to help her. When she was finally confronted by a campus mentor who pressed her on why she didn't reach out about her problems paying for food, she reacted,

> And it's just like, "I don't know! I can't tell you why. I just didn't want to . . . I just didn't want to talk about it." And like I said, I don't think it was a shame thing. I'm not embarrassed about it now; I wasn't embarrassed about it then. It was [*pauses*] . . . too tiring to tell people what was going on. And I just didn't have the energy for that, so I chose not to share it.

Although shame, embarrassment, and pride were frequently cited by other participants as their reasons for keeping their food struggles to themselves, the burden of "the conversation" and the incredulous surprise she earned from her mentor reflect the hidden psychological costs of food insecurity, especially for high-ability students.[10] Indeed, one of the "tells" of a social stigma is the effort an individual makes to avoid having to explain and process it with well-meaning people.[11]

Like Miranda, Ariel has experienced various phases of engagement with the campus navigation strategies: Adapting as a first-year student, Prioritizing her sophomore year, and Maximizing her junior year. But at the point of our first interview Ariel was in full Surviving mode, and the efforts she had made to avoid conversations about her challenges were coming to a head at the intersection of financial and mental health crises. Recently, Ariel missed a test because of her mental health struggles and now has a failing grade on a class she needs to graduate this spring. Now she faces the prospect of needing another $5,000 to retake the class. Worse than that, her grandparents are scheduled to fly to the United States to see her walk across the stage, but Ariel has not told her family about the situation. On the verge of tears, Ariel is defiant that she has the ability but has been robbed of the opportunity to show her best:

> I am smart. I am *big* smart. And you can ask anybody on this campus. I'm brilliant. I have an incredibly bright future if I have the time for it. And I don't right now. I don't have the time to be brilliant. I don't have the time to be 3.75 GPA smart. And I don't have the energy, either. And so it's incredibly unfair when your parents kill themselves to put you in school

and you can't come through because you're busy worried about money or you're busy worried about food.

Now crying, Ariel continues:

> And it just really is disappointing. 'Cause my dad didn't have a heart attack because he's unhealthy. He had a heart attack 'cause he's stressed out. So I have four grandparents and they're all coming to see me walk and because one man [her professor who gave her the grade] didn't care, I don't get to really feel ownership over that. And I can't tell my dad because I don't want him to be disappointed, because it's not that I'm worried about him being mad at me or whatever. It's that he's gonna kill himself to try to find $5,000 for me to take one class. So it doesn't feel fair. And that's the frustrating part, because I have all the tools and I literally just don't have the time to be good enough. And that is, like, the worst. That is the worst part.

• • •

Five months after this initial encounter, we meet again to catch up on her life. Ariel looks back with some perspective on that stressful day when her landlord called. She is still struggling to pay for food as she nears graduation. Part of what made that day so emotional, she tells us, is the realization she had about what her food insecurity has done to her ability to live up to her potential, which includes confirming the confidence her family has had in her.

> I want my parents to be proud of me. And I want my grandparents to be proud of me. And I want them to speak highly of me, and I want to be able to say I did all these things and I have a 3.5 GPA and I'm going to do this, I'm going to do this, and I'm going to do this. It's not like that, and I'm not saying that if I had a 3.5 GPA I'd be doing anything differently right now, but the fact that I don't get to know because . . . because I was hungry is just crazy.

Students like Ariel see the trajectory of life, the Good Student, that their academic ability points them toward—academic honors, success in the classroom, admission to graduate school—but live with the burden of outcomes that often do not match it. Though food is one of several factors impeding her, food is a tangible symbol of all that pulls her below the surface of a sustainable college life and leaves her straining to make it another month, another week, another day. Ariel has little choice but to either give up, which is clearly not an option in her mind, or to make peace with the constraints of her situation:

> I was a perfectionist child. I did well at . . . I excelled at things very quickly. And so, everyone was like, "Oh, if you just push yourself imagine how great you would be!" All those things. And it's just like, I get very triggered when people say stuff like that to me now, because it's just like, "Well, I literally can't do anything more than I'm doing now. This is not my best, this is not what I'm capable of, but this is what my life is allowing me to do." *And that is the discrimination of food insecurity.* You have to choose between what you're capable of doing and what your life allows you to do. My life did not allow me to be the best.

Ariel's phrase "the discrimination of food insecurity" draws attention to a further facet of "choices" as an undesirable aspect of living on the financial margins in college. In crisis situations, "choices" are not simply campus engagement dilemmas, such as between working and joining an organization. "Choices" are sometimes also between accepting a lesser version of one's identity and ability as a student, or not continuing in college at all. The ripples of such dire choices reshape college experiences as well as the relationships that Ariel values so highly: not living up to hopes and aspirations of her family; concealing her hunger from friends and parents; taking on the stresses of her mother and father, who she knows would do anything to help her succeed.

Reflecting back on that previous interview and time of crisis, Ariel turns from frustration at the twists and turns of her college experience to determination to view what she has made of her situation as its own kind of success:

> So many people along the way weren't even . . . couldn't even fathom that that's what my life is like, and that I'm not even close to the only person who experiences life like that, in college or otherwise. And so, I was once

very emotional about it, and disappointed and just very defeated by it. But I'm not defeated by it anymore. I just really recognize that the worth of my actions is not invalidated because I had to do what my life let me do. I can only work to where being able to do what I can do, instead of letting my life determine it for me.

Summary

Ariel's ability to identify the dignity and worth in her struggle, or Chelsea's commitment to overcome the reluctance of administrators to help her, or Miranda's capacity to connect the lessons of her family's struggles to her own collegiate crises, all reflect Surviving as a mindset as much as a resource management strategy. In each of these three cases, students chose *not* to take options that might have reduced the strain of their situations: asking for help, seeking different employment options, even transferring to a different institution or dropping out. In this sense, Surviving is not simply a matter of making decisions that are most likely to remove the source of difficulty. In part, this is because being a college student, and one at a place that is socially and economically challenging, is an *elective* decision. And, because college is a choice, Surviving as a strategy sometimes means students made choices that allowed them to protect and preserve what they most cared about even at the cost of serious difficulty: the perceptions of friends and family, the future opportunities of a prestige-oriented university degree, and the commitment to themselves to see their college experience through to the extent of their ability.

The Dream Revisited
Opportunity, Confluence, and Contradiction

In this book we have operated from a two-part claim: to fully understand these students' navigation of food insecurity, it is first necessary to understand the prestige-oriented university. And understanding the functional and symbolic roles of food in these students' experiences exposes otherwise hidden features of the prestige-oriented university. As we have argued throughout, the material and social features of food give it an important and complex role in higher education. This complexity arises from the basic physicality of food as a bodily necessity: students must eat, but food access is costly in terms of time and money, making food quality, quantity, and accessibility a reflection of a student's financial means. Part of the significance of food in college is the effect of proper nutrition on educational performance.[1] As such, eating is both a matter of human survival and maximizing human potential in a learning environment.

But more than that, food is imbued with social meaning that conveys a great deal of information about a person's social and economic position in society and knowledge of preferred cultural forms. This means, for example, not only a student's appreciation for freshly rolled sushi and their knowledge of the terms associated with its various forms and ingredients but also their ability to connect with peers over their preferences and prior sushi experiences. As French social scholar Pierre Bourdieu described it, this sort of "cultural capital" can be converted into economic capital by those who understand how and where to leverage it.[2] At the institutional level, the type and quality of food a university provides symbolically communicates basic competence by providing something like "a decent cup of coffee"; sensitivity to student needs by offering gluten-free options; awareness of social trends, as exemplified by the presence of a campus sushi bar or upscale food trucks; and status lifestyle affiliations, such as easy access to a beloved local gourmet coffee shop / hangout spot or ethically sourced food. Most of these layered meanings are invisible in their obviousness, which is an important aspect of their power. Paralleling this invisibility of social meaning is the largely hidden daily navigational task required of some students whose financial resources make cultural immersion in the consumables du jour impossible, at least on a consistent basis. Thus, food is a valuable lens because its ordinary-ness conceals so much layered social meaning in the prestige-oriented university, where meaning management is embedded in nearly every facet of daily activity. Reflecting on these environments and what they represent as spaces of opportunity and contradiction related to food and food insecurity illuminates some of the hidden challenges and possibilities contained within them.

Revisiting Opportunity

The word "opportunity" takes on a range of meanings in the context of this study, in reference both to students and administrators. Prestige-oriented universities clearly represent opportunity for students of modest means, many of whom have excelled academically despite challenges such as attending underfunded public schools. Often, key mentors and caring teachers provided the encouragement and intellectual stimulation that pushed them forward and kept them on track. In this sense, almost all our students have long been outsiders, as the ones getting good grades, hanging out with teachers, or staying after school to put in extra time on projects while their friends struggled or were caught up in other teenage diversions. Those students lucky enough to attend good schools by the fortune of scholarships, strategic housing decisions, and their parents' sacrifices, were also outsiders. Growing up, they were the ones who achieved in the classroom but lived on the social periphery, not able to afford the consumer goods and travel experiences of their peers. Often these students learned adaptive strategies, such as buying name-brand clothes at thrift stores to blend in and making nice with wealthy friends' parents who might include them on family meals and trips without a thought for the additional cost. As Chelsea (PRU) discussed, it was in these kinds of educational environments that she learned how to get what she needed from administrators by advocating for herself and how to blend in without losing her identity.

As such, college, as a long-anticipated opportunity, often represented something different depending on students' K–12 experiences. This demarcation is one that Tony Jack describes as the difference between the "privileged poor" (those who had the advantage of socialization in good schools) and the "doubly disadvantaged" (those who were not only poor but attended poorly performing schools).[3] Because of their socialization experiences, the privileged poor arrive at their selective universities better equipped to navigate spaces of status and affluence but still as outsiders because of their financial resources and family background.

Doubly disadvantaged students are more likely to be shocked and overwhelmed by how much of college life has little to do with academics, driven instead by status hierarchies embedded in social networks and activities, such as Greek life. Some of our participants, like Gavin (Flagship) and Nicole (Lib Arts), entered college with a pretty keen sense of the resources available and knew that their task was to figure out how to leverage them toward their goals. Others, like Lucas (PRU) and Layla (Flagship), developed their own approach to integrating their interests with this campus mode of operation over time. But the contradiction *in* the opportunity foisted upon all of these students, regardless of K–12 preparation, was the additional logistical, physical, and emotional labor of managing employment, skimming resources, borrowing off of friends, and strategizing about every dime. This burden not only undercut students' efforts to achieve the ideal/normal experience that seemed so fundamental to the university as it had been sold to them, but it also added stress and anxiety to an already challenging educational and social environment.

The majority of our participants fell into the "doubly disadvantaged" category. Different from most of their peers, for whom college was a rite of passage into the upper-middle-class lifestyle of their parents, the students we talked with were sometimes surprised that they felt alienated in a space that seemed to have been made for them—that is, for smart kids.[4] As Devin, the PRU campus admissions tour administrator, highlighted, the prestige-oriented university is not intended merely for good students but for smart students who are ready and willing to engage in a campus environment marked by the Opportunity Paradigm and who have the resources to do so.

Yet in contrast to Jack's analysis, which implies socioeconomic and educational background as collegiate destiny, understanding the prestige-oriented university as opportunity means recognizing ways that students learned social and organizational systems, cultivated relationships, and leveraged the organizational desirability of their marginalized status to pursue their goals, despite difficulty. In most cases, their paths through college were very different from those of their upper-income peers, but in a system of resources primed to reward initiative, students on the social and economic margins often found ways to have at least a partial version of the experience they came for.

How students managed and navigated the added labor of hunger was in part revealed via the Campus Navigation Strategies Typology. However, using the language of "opportunity" highlights how students perceived and approached the resources of campus differently. That is, one aspect of students' campus navigation was the ability to see or imagine opportunity, in terms of knowing which persons, activities, or experiences could help to provide for their food needs. On a broader level, all participants engaged in identifying opportunity as they cultivated relationships with faculty mentors who could write them letters of recommendation, took on internships that could lead to jobs, and joined organizations that built social networks beneficial now and in the future. To some degree, these behaviors were the product of the convergence of precollege socialization to engagement and a college environment set up to draw students into deeper forms of involvement and interaction.

Specifically related to food, the capacity to identify the opportunities of food access often began before college. This socialization came from watching family members and peers get by with very little, "hack" their way through inexpensive meals, and generally ignore food for the sake of other priorities. Scholars use the term "funds of knowledge" to refer to lessons students learn from their families and peers that help them navigate educational spaces.[5] Terrence (Flagship) learning to exploit Amazon and GrubHub for cheap groceries, Phillip (Flagship) learning to leverage leadership roles to create food access, and Ariel (Lib Arts) learning to eat leftover event food in the Student Life office fridge were some of the many examples of students' capacity to see opportunity in places they were not "supposed" to see it, often rooted in their childhood experiences. To a great extent, the tension between the Good Student and Needy Student archetypes was a result of how administrators viewed the claims on resources that students made based on their imagination for what resources were "for" them or should be available to them. In this, administrators also had a role in shaping "opportunity" by legitimizing or denying creative student claims. Here again, administrators with experiences of marginality—first- or secondhand—were often better able to identify the signs of students struggling and imagine how to leverage care and efficiency for their benefit.

Yet in most of their efforts to imagine and maximize resources, students were walking into the wind, facing the invisible resistance of campus cultures, practices, and policies implicitly established to serve a different economic stratum. In a conversation about food insecurity at competitive universities, the language of "opportunity cost" takes on new meaning. As Anali (Flagship) and others reflected, the easier choice, and one recommended by some family members, was to stay close to home and attend a community college or regional state university, which would reduce or eliminate their food insecurity risks. Many of our students, and especially the young women, had a clear sense that they needed to pursue their educational aspirations away from their home communities or they would be pulled into the social expectations of marriage and family that would undermine their academic and professional goals.[6]

As such, the double cost of opportunity was the strain of separation from one's social support system (often extended families), coupled with the daily struggle to pay for food in a space where opportunity also meant the constant temptation to engage in the attractive but budget-destroying lifestyle practices of affluent peers. That food can satisfy both physical and social desires, however temporarily, made it a particularly able seducer. The fact that choosing or not choosing to indulge both came with costs made the multitude of decision points even more psychologically wearing.[7] Further, that food is a perpetual decision point meant that the "opportunity" to experience the consequences of either choice was ever present. Nevertheless, by deciding to enroll in a prestige-oriented university, students had inadvertently made choices, in the sense that theirs was an educational journey of bargains, compromises, and partial access despite their best efforts. In doing so, knowingly or unknowingly, students engaged in an opportunity bargain in which going hungry might occasionally be the price of their aspirations. That students in some sense chose this struggle should not shroud the fact that their universities also made choices of how to craft the student experience that exacerbated the difficulties experienced by these students.

Thus, another facet of "opportunity" is one held by these universities: that they have the resources, cultural and financial, to significantly reduce—if not eliminate—the basic food needs of the students they admit but choose not to make that a priority. This is a hard claim and one that many compassionate but pragmatic administrators we interviewed would deny, in part because few of them were in the position to enact the degree of change this would require. Nevertheless, students (and some administrators) strongly asserted that the prestige-oriented university has a moral burden to fully support students in need. However, even assuming the will to eliminate the food access deficits of underresourced students, the tension between the Needy Student and the Good Student exposes another unintended consequence of leveraging consumable class markers (again, upscale coffee, food trucks, convenience items) as a tool of admissions and student life. Namely, when luxuries become necessities imbued with upper-middle-class values and consumptive habits, redividing luxuries from necessities in order to determine what the university has a responsibility to provide for all students, and what is "extra," becomes not just impossible but nonsensical. The resulting outcomes fit the logic of the system but not a logic that would hold up outside of it: administrators willing to provide midnight nacho bars for students without basic needs but not pots and pans for a student whose basic needs are overwhelming. This pointed critique should not imply that administrators are not concerned and not taking action, only that the nature of the task is encumbered by the largely invisible structures and commitments embedded in the prestige-oriented university and the competitive marketplace it inhabits.

Beyond the care and justice orientation of administrators, the pressures of the prestige-oriented market segment have also spurred responsiveness. Nationally, the shift toward meeting basic needs as an opportunity for visibility and prestige, in part due to shifting rankings metrics, is evident in university efforts to be the best at treating students with humanity and respect. To a great degree, this imperative was operationalized through the familiar structures of food pantries and free clothing "closets."[8] We found that many administrators were very aware of the larger prestige game that their work fed, and more still, were critical of it. Yet the pervasive influence of market competition and public-facing image often combined with the implicit standards of the Good Administrator (caring, justice, efficiency, rationality) to undercut the effectiveness of programs and imagination for solutions that could actually improve student academic success, sense of belonging, persistence, and engagement—all outcomes these universities pursue. Given the high stakes of institutional reputation, attending to institutional prestige as a broad organizational priority is likely a permanent feature. However, administrators perhaps can attend to institutional status while also centering equitable opportunities by shifting the implicit operating question from "Can we leverage this for prestige?" to

"Do the markers of prestige in this area serve our most vulnerable students well?"

Practical Lessons and Implications in Two Sections

We now transition to recommendations with two sections of advice, both subdivided by their two intended audiences: students who might struggle with the cost of food and faculty/administrators. The first section of practical lessons are the authors' ideas that emerged over the course of this study; the second are responses from our student participants, who we asked to give advice to faculty/administrators and to students who might navigate college on the financial margins.

Lessons from the Authors for Students Struggling with the Cost of Food

1. The number one lesson is this: Do not feel ashamed of struggling with basic needs in college. The systems that create the high price of higher education are not of your making, and the lack of university support you may experience is an organizational failure, not a personal failure on your part. Be responsible with your resources and seek ways to maximize them, but do not internalize the tendency of the environment to want to shame you for what are essentially lifestyle and prestige expenses embedded in campus operations and practices.
2. Especially if you attend a university with competitive admissions, understand that your campus is orientated toward maximizing opportunities for student involvement but that these opportunities come at a cost, in terms of time and often money. Generally speaking, involvement is still worth the investment, with some caveats. If you have limited resources and time, recognize the categories of possible involvement on campus, and strategize your time carefully: preprofessional programs, clubs, organizations, and internships are valuable, but different activities offer different kinds of value. Interest

organizations focused on a hobby, social identity category, or activity you enjoy or want to learn can be important points of connections that widen and deepen social networks and increase your sense of belonging. At the same time, there is no merit badge for participating in the most organizations and activities. Consider, as Nicole (Lib Arts) did, how opportunities scaffold and can build on each other toward more significant internships, organizational leadership, and relationships with faculty and staff who can help you enter the professional world.

3. Understand that high-ability students from historically underrepresented and marginalized groups represent a kind of valued organizational commodity for the prestige-oriented university. At the same time, these universities, regardless of current intentions, have long served racial, gender, and economic power majorities, and many systems are built to advantage those backgrounds. This uneasy union of organizational history and current motivation requires awareness of the places and spaces where marginalized identities can be leveraged advantageously. For example, all three of our universities had orientation programs dedicated to supporting marginalized subpopulations. Often, the gold of those programs are the associated faculty or staff, who are passionate about promoting student success and in many cases, experienced college as marginalized students themselves. Finding and connecting with these individuals can be vital to learning how to navigate spaces of privilege and affluence.

4. On this theme, advocacy and "claims" on resources are your central task as you work at creating the time and space for campus involvement. Some administrators are supposed to help you because of their role on campus (e.g., emergency services coordinators). Others want to help you because of their own background, values, and general student success motivation. Identify faculty and administrative allies and do the work to cultivate those relationships. Often these individuals can be identified by talking to other students who similarly struggle.

5. Be aware that how administrators might define "acceptable" self-advocacy may not align with the needs you are actually experiencing. That difference should not discourage you from making "asks"; persist in your asking, and move up the administrative ladder to find a responsive administrator. The tension administrators feel between wanting students to honor and follow the organizational systems they have constructed and wanting to help and support students at the margins will often work for you if you continue to articulate your needs and connect them to their desire to promote student success. Not every administrator will be sympathetic (often a lower proportion of these persons work in financial aid),[9] but there are people in the system who can help you, even if finding them requires perseverance.
6. Recognize that there are many grants and scholarships designed for you from inside and outside the university. These require legwork to find and apply for, but faculty and administrative allies can also help this process.
7. Be reflective about your own background and the expectations about food it creates. Consider how that history does or does not fit with campus food systems constructed around lifestyle and convenience, often at a high price. Universities, and many financially secure families, assume the ability both to eat regularly scheduled meals and to afford food whenever it suits them throughout the day. If you grew up in a household where formal family sit-down meals were infrequent, where inexpensive fast food or ready-to-heat meals were regularly an afterthought solution, the expectations of eating baked into competitive universities may be a surprise and an adjustment. Being a student of modest means in these universities is difficult, but a few insights can help you make it through:

— Make full use of the aid the university does provide, even if it is sometimes inconvenient. Making an hour to stop in the university food pantry once a week can take the edge off your grocery bill. Find out what days or times they stock their shelves and try to visit immediately after for the best shot at the items you need. If there are opportunities to provide feedback about what items or services you need, such as comment cards, take them. Also, stop in to see the administrators who oversee these resources and give them feedback. They usually want to serve your needs but sometimes need help knowing how to do so.

— Struggling to pay for food can be very lonely and isolating, but there are many others also struggling. Make an effort to find them. Some of the most successful students we talked with were those whose peer relationships provided camaraderie around their shared struggle, and as importantly, provided a network of resource-sharing. Often these persons are found in racial/ethnic organizations, first-generation student support offices/organizations, and other programs that target resources and staff toward marginalized populations.

— Strategically engage with campus "lifestyle" foods—it is okay to occasionally stop at Starbucks with a friend if you can work it into your budget—but also keep in mind that these "identity goods" are not intrinsic to being a college student. Many students we talked with struggled most when they gave in to the temptation to buy an expensive coffee or go out to unplanned lunches with friends. At the same time, those experiences are also places where students connect after class or for a study group. Having a small reserve fund for such occasions, or when participating, picking the least expensive option (buying sides instead of entrées is a way to eat cheap) provides the opportunity for engagement without destroying a budget.

8. Consider carefully the cost-benefit analysis of off-campus employment. As our campus navigation strategies highlight,

work of some kind is probably necessary, and each student's relative set of financial needs in light of scholarships, grants, and other forms of aid, requires a different consideration of employment. Working off campus can be more lucrative and can provide the side benefit of free food or other perks. Jobs that are close to campus, that can be done primarily on the weekend, or that have flexible hours are advantageous. However, off-campus employment often does not align well with the flow of the academic calendar, including class schedules and more intense periods of the semester, such as finals. Off-campus employment can also make participating in campus organizations difficult, since they often meet in the evenings and on weekends.

9. Self-evaluate your campus navigation strategy tendencies if you struggle with the cost of food at a prestige-oriented university. Do you live on campus with a meal plan? Do you tend to work a lot to pay your bills? Do you live close to campus? In what ways are you involved outside the classroom? College creates a range of decision points that pull students away or press them toward a more robust college experience, each with their own costs and benefits to weigh.

10. Similarly, recognize that especially on larger campuses there are many sources of unintended free food, often related to events and organization meetings. One way to combine campus involvement and sustainable eating is to get organized, as Vera (PRU) did in creating a weekly plan of free food events, or Terrence (Flagship) did in using apps and deal offers to leverage free food from businesses near campus. Here again, social networks can be a significant source of knowledge of where and when to find food, as well as sources of direct food access through meal swipes and flex dollars. On many campuses, students have already created GroupMe, Twitter, Facebook, Instagram, and other informal alert systems for finding food. The time finding these systems can be well worth the effort. Or consider starting them yourself if you cannot find them.

11. Finally, in summary, understand that although the cost of food may be a problem for you, it is not your problem alone. And, although you bear the primary responsibility for figuring it out, it is your responsibility in large part because of the dysfunction of much larger systems. As scholars have detailed at length, the combined expectation of college as a necessary step toward an economically stable adulthood and the skyrocketing cost of college due in part to the prestige and amenities arms race place individual students in impossible situations.[10] Financial discipline and strategy are necessary on your part. However, your university must also take responsibility for the ways it chooses to prioritize flashy events, impressive facilities, and other expensive investments over reducing student debt and helping students pay for basic needs.

Lessons from the Authors for Faculty and Administrators

1. The challenging reality is that if you are serious about providing a commensurate experience for all students, it will not happen without a major restructuring of financial aid priorities. Some universities, both public and private, have committed to making tuition free for students from families earning below a specific threshold.[11] This is a considerable step forward. Even so, the costs of participating in the Opportunity Paradigm mean that even students who attend tuition-free do not attend expense-free, and may still struggle financially, especially if the university is situated in an expensive urban area. Even tuition-free initiatives need to be paired with wraparound services to assure that student basic needs are still met. Failing to do so sets up a tiered system of educational access where for some students simply surviving to graduation is sufficient, while other students are engaging in clubs, internships, and social relationships that will pay off in better life opportunities after college.
2. The logic of administration requires revision to fully meet student needs. Most forms of aid, developed by conscientious and well-meaning administrators, struggled in their effectiveness because

they were constructed around the assumption that *if students' needs are acute enough, they will inconvenience themselves to access the services the university provides.* This belief is a fundamental fallacy of administrating hunger that ignores the priorities of the Opportunity Paradigm, a system that administrators construct, tend, and participate in. With that, reject the notion that creating inconvenience for students is equipping them with "agency." Most students on the financial and social margins already have plenty of experience managing difficult lives. Instead, embrace the centrality of convenience and expedience in your development of food aid resources. And, rather than castigating student "asks" that do not align with administrative systems, arm students with the knowledge of how to navigate administrative processes and take their extraordinary requests seriously.

3. If students are not using the aid resources you developed for them, it is not because your campus lacks students with needs. Find and pay students who represent populations you want to serve to participate in an advisory group and take their suggestions seriously, even if those suggestions may not fit how you would prefer to do things. These students can often be found through administrators who work directly with them, such as first-generation programs and transfer student programs, as well as through administrators who themselves struggled economically in college.

4. Make peace with and even encourage students "skimming" resources from organizations and events as a legitimate part of how many students get by. Instead of objecting, consider the volume of students who do this to be a barometer of the mismatch between student needs and institutional resources aimed at helping them. Consider providing free food at more events as a way to aid students who depend on them for meals and publicize where leftover food can be found and recovered for those who want it. As Lucas (PRU) and others found, educational experiences often result from pursuing free food, which was the goal of the initiative in the first place.

5. Recognize the importance of prestige lifestyle goods on campus and work at the problem from both ends: reduce centralizing and normalizing expensive goods, and at the same time provide nonstigmatizing ways for all students to participate. For example, consider bookstore credits that provide low-income students a free or "at cost" clothing item of their choice. Resist the urge to hand out a special shirt made just for them that might be then identified as the "poor student tee."
6. Shift your perspective on students experiencing food needs from a "damage" perspective that focuses on what they lack to a "desire" and "resource" approach that focuses on understanding how they are already strategically managing resources toward their goals.[12] Use of the Campus Navigation Strategies Typology as a framework for understanding students' implicit modes of operation can be valuable. Develop support systems that dovetail with the best of their existing strategies.
7. As many other scholars have noted, food pantries are important resources, but they are only a small part of meeting student food needs, and often assume a particular demographic (those with access to kitchens). Thinking in terms of a "web of resources" that captures the most students through overlapping sources of aid will increase impact and accessibility. These could include strategically placed mini-fridges with free grab-and-go foods, meal plan vouchers or scholarships, and low-cost, prepackaged meals in dining halls or convenience stores.
8. Recognize that many administrators, by virtue of their own social identities or personal experiences, have an extent of understanding of struggling students that should be paid attention to. Particularly for mid- and upper-level administrators, listen for the insights of experience among your staff and give them space to imagine solutions that may not fit traditional structures and practices. In other words, more fully leverage the empathy and knowledge that is often invisible and unheard related to students on the margins.

Advice from Students for Students

Toward the conclusion of our final interview with each student, we asked what advice they would give someone heading to college who was likely to struggle to pay for food. Some recommendations focused on the logistics and navigation of finances, food, relationships, and resources on campus; others provided encouragement aimed at shaping attitudes and approaches to college from the social and economic margins. Hearing the guidance of students for students is valuable for those in college facing similar circumstances. For administrators, faculty, parents, and others who have a hand in shaping the resources and supports available to these students, glimpsing campus life through the perspective of what students prioritize as recommendations for others is also instructive.

The list below represents the suggestions that received the greatest concentration of focus; students offered many other one-off recommendations as well. However, the intersection of frequency and insight give the following advice particular weight and value. What we found striking about them as a group is the time commitment these suggestions require. Following this guidance does provide students with agency, yet the time cost of doing so also pulls them away from having a "normal" campus experience.

Suggestion #1: Run Your Own Collegiate Race

I would take things at your own pace.... especially after living with these people, you're in class with these people and everything, it's easy to get caught up in what they're doing and not focus on what you're doing. But I feel like, if you just take things at your own pace and don't compare yourself to other people, that will set you up for success. (Cadence, Lib Arts)

Implicit within this advice is students' acknowledgment that most food-insecure students are, in various ways, social and economic outsiders in a campus space of normative affluence where financial security facilitates a range of precollege experiences, leisure activities, and consumptive practices that are foreign to students with modest financial resources. Terrence (Flagship) was more direct about how to relate to friends with money:

> Don't let having rich friends make you broke, okay? Don't envy your rich friends. Don't, like, resent them because they're rich. It's just the way it is. And don't let your rich friends make you feel bad even though it might happen because they have money. Just do your best.

Students extended the theme of resisting comparison to others to general guidance about campus involvement. Recognizing differences in collegiate preparation and familiarity, students offered encouragement to appreciate the magnitude of the transition underway and ease into it strategically. Camila (Lib Arts) connected these dots:

> Don't overwhelm yourself or don't try to do too much too soon. Kind of take it . . .'cause it's already a huge transition depending on what student you are. For anyone it's just like from a high school to a postsecondary institution and it's . . . especially if it's a private one it's a huge transition.

Camila followed this thematic suggestion with several specific examples, including to "take classes you really enjoy," "adjust to class life first," "start off slow," and "it's okay to cut back" if you begin to feel overcommitted. In short, implicit messages about what the Good Student does that are conveyed through the structures and resources of the Opportunity Paradigm and the engagement patterns of classmates set expectations that are not necessary to follow. Developing clarity about what you want out of college involves both a sense of one's own priorities and confidence to resist patterns of engagement that can seem like requirements.

> **Suggestion #2: Build and Maintain Your Support System**
> There are definitely a lot of things that I didn't know existed, and I was nervous about reaching out to professors and asking for this or that. And so I definitely would tell you that there are people there who care about you and that it's a place where you can really be yourself, and there's a lot of opportunities for you to get involved. (Brooke, Lib Arts)

Following from advice to "run your own race" is guidance about what that "running" should include: "getting out of your comfort zone" (Vera, PRU), "get involved with campus" (Beth, Lib Arts), and "take risks" (Carli, PRU) in terms of joining organizations, "because then you won't feel as stuck as you would." Valeria (Lib Arts) specified both emotional and logistical support to be gained: "I would say find people who are going to raise you up, like friends. Make friends who are really going to raise you up and who will be willing to be there when you're struggling."

Camila (Lib Arts) added an emphasis on maintaining family connections "because you'll need them in times of support especially if you don't have friends yet."

Jill (PRU) echoed the importance of building relationships, linking outsider status to the need for solidarity with others who are having similar experiences:

> PRU is difficult if you don't fit into the typical student that comes here, which is White, rich, and in a sorority or fraternity. If you don't fit into that you need to find people who are like you. . . . So you just need to find the people who are similar to you and find your people. It's kind of hard and it's a little hidden and it takes time, but it's possible. There are people like you, I promise. And just seek them out. Yeah. And talk to your professors.

This last bit of advice—getting to know professors—was the most common encouragement. As Camila (Lib Arts) put it: "Don't be afraid to talk to professors. They really do care." Beth (Lib Arts) agreed, "You should make relationships with your professors," then she confessed, "which I haven't done enough of." In sum, relationships can seem like the stressor most easily avoided in a new environment, but students (and researchers)[13] agree that the demands of navigating a new environment are exactly what makes these connections so essential.

Suggestion #3: Advocate for Yourself

> Don't wait . . . they say, "A closed mouth don't get fed," but like some of these mouths are closed because they're afraid they're not going to get fed when they do open their mouth. (Phillip, Flagship)

Closely related to making connections to faculty and peers is the general advice to seek campus resources and supports, or in the language of some researchers, make "claims" upon faculty and administrators.[14] Carli (PRU) agreed, listing off the offices she visited regularly to press for aid: "Take every opportunity that you can or to ask for assistance. I mean I've been told from the bursar, from financial aid, from academic advisors, they will do anything and everything for you." Similarly, Corbett (PRU) combined reaching out to administrators with taking advantage of known campus resources:

> Just speak to the financial aid office, the dean of student life, and stuff like that, I mean, if they are aware of your situation there's also resources that they can help you with, or they have more scholarships or find a way to make sure you're well supported. And so make sure you're actually utilizing all the resources we have available to you.

Student experiences of sympathy and aid varied greatly, but what those who got resources had in common was, they asked, and asked persistently, taking on the labor of explaining the details of their difficulties in ways administrators and faculty could connect with.

Suggestion #4: Get Serious about Financial Planning and Budgeting

How to budget. I think that's the number one skill that you really need to learn how to do. And whether it's you're getting steady income from your parents, or whether you're getting paid, I think you should have to balance what you need and what you want. (Valeria, Lib Arts)

Learning to budget was perhaps the most frequent single piece of advice we heard. Budgeting was important, as Valeria suggested above, because of the lure of opportunity to spend too much money on nonessentials, especially in an environment where so many students appear to have the resources to do so. Gaining budgeting and financial planning skills during college was a point of lament for a number of students who wished they had been taught this sooner. Alejandra (Lib Arts) reflected:

> I didn't learn about budgeting until my math class in college that really taught me stuff about mortgage and stuff like that, you know? So just kind

of high schools don't offer that, but I wish they did, you know? Bills are the essentials.

Developing the knowledge of how to budget and actually budgeting, however, are not the same. Several students quickly followed encouragement to budget with, as Leah did, the addendum "not like I do—like, actually stick to a budget."

Beyond basic financial management, students pressed the importance of maximizing financial aid, in particular by making use of the FAFSA, seeking scholarship opportunities, and meeting with your financial aid advisor. Valeria (Lib Arts) summed up much of this advice under the heading of "becoming financially literate":

> I would ask if they're financially literate, and I would encourage you to become financially literate. So what's the difference between these kinds of loans? Are you getting FAFSA? If you're not, apply for it either way. I had a friend who did not apply for FAFSA and I'm like, "Why wouldn't you do that?" And be willing to look for grants outside of [your university] because sometimes you'll find them. You know for housing, you'll find them. I didn't find out there was some grants for housing until this year.

Valeria concluded by lamenting, "It's like, people don't tell you these things," frustrated that it took her nearly to the end of her college career to figure out some of the resources available and how to access them.

Suggestion #5: From Having Resources to Strategizing Resources

> One of my thoughts is not counting so much on the institution to give so much to you, like also looking for cheaper things off campus, but I feel like I don't know if that's normal for colleges, I guess. I mean, things are going to be cheaper either way off campus, like, a banana in the grocery store would definitely cost less than, like, a banana in our little stores here. (Nicole, Lib Arts)

Students peppered us with logistical advice, such as buying cheaper school supplies or groceries at Walmart (Terrence and Kelsy), purchasing discount produce if you go to the 24-hour grocery at 2 a.m. when they are restocking (Layla), and avoiding spending money at on-campus coffee shops (Kelsy, Paloma, William). Although the truth of their wisdom is incontrovertible, much of it points to Nicole's opening injunction about how to approach college as a student of modest means: Do not count on the institution giving much to you. A dramatic departure from the implicit promise of the services bubble and total support assumption universities implicitly project, that the university is not a trustworthy partner was a hard-earned lesson about maximizing resources for many students. Meal plans, on-campus food (particularly coffee), and housing are all expensive traps of normality and convenience students should not expect to be able to afford. This reality requires a different sense of where and how to get what one needs. According to students this does include using the campus food pantry (DeShauna, Flagship; Anali, Flagship; Beth, Lib Arts; Chelsea, PRU) but also strategies like "make some friends who would be willing to swipe you in [to the dining hall]" (Anali), "learn to cook more" (DeShauna, Flagship), and "find really, really cheap apartments that have utilities included and make sure that there's a shuttle, like a bus that takes you there and back" (Layla, Flagship).

Strategizing resources requires making careful decisions about which opportunities justify the associated costs. Living on or close to campus is more expensive than living farther away but increases ease of access and involvement, which often separated students engaged in Sacrificing from those Prioritizing. Taking a job off campus may pay more than on-campus employment, but it also might demand work hours that do not consider the rhythms of academic life and might eliminate opportunities for internships. On the other hand, off-campus jobs might provide food or other side benefits. Corbett (PRU) reflected on these considerations, emphasizing prioritizing academics:

> If you're working, just make sure you know how to manage a schedule efficiently to never . . . the reason you're here is for your academics. And so make sure not to over extend yourself if you're working at the same time. I mean, this might be more of a bias for on-campus jobs . . . most people on an on-campus job they understand you have a major deadline or something like that, they'll hopefully be flexible with you if you give them plenty of notice.

As a group, strategizing and maximizing resources meant shifting from a mindset of personally holding all needed resources, or having resources, to constructing a personal "resource map," or strategizing resources in terms of learning how and where to get resources as needed. Rather than owning a car, knowing people with cars who are willing to provide rides to the grocery store. Instead of paying for a meal plan, cultivating a group of friends with meal plans who are willing to swipe you in on certain days. Cooking every day may be too expensive and time consuming, so sharing meals and meal preparation with a group of friends. Renting and borrowing books instead of purchasing and keeping them. Dropping by the office of a mentor around lunchtime or walking through departments that frequently host events to check for leftover food rather than expecting to buy lunch each day. Once students shifted from an expectation of resource possession to a mindset of resource navigation and maximization, they found ways to make their lives something closer to sustainable, even though it came with the daily risk that their piecemeal system might fail them.

Student Advice for Administrators

Student advice for universities and administrators was pointed and wide-ranging across four broad categories that offered guidance on how to approach food access and the student experience conceptually and practically.

> ### Suggestion #1: Adjust Priorities and Perspectives
> I hope PRU will stop allocating as much of its money as it does to grass and more to humans. Because we should be respecting our students and letting them learn and study with a peace of mind versus the anxiety and chronic issues that I've had to deal with because of my, I guess, lack of safety net. (Alec, PRU)

Students argued that to better meet their needs, administrators and faculty need to reorient their approach not simply to students but to the university in general. In the quote above, Alec characterized this as a tension between money for landscaping ("grass") and campus beautification versus contributing to the financial stability and emotional health of students ("humans"). From an administrative perspective this comparison is likely a false dichotomy: investment in grounds contributes to the experience of all students and is part of the symbolic representation of a desirable campus to prospective families. The financial and logistical diffusion of financial decision-making of universities also means that there are seldom financial forked paths of the sort Alec describes: more money for grounds versus more money for need- based student aid. Yet for financially struggling students who walk the grounds and observe the investments in buildings, landscaping, and amenities, the message that they are a low institutional priority is hard not for them to derive. Jill, also a student at PRU, expressed the tension between the joys of a beautiful campus and the student fees she pays that she's been told in part support the impressive visuals of campus:

> Campus is overwhelmingly beautiful. It is insane. It is so apparent how much money they put into it. They're constantly uprooting flowers and stuff. It's not going to be the same throughout the week, you know? . . . I like that it's pretty. Definitely. I think I wouldn't mind paying less money so it wouldn't have to be so pretty.

Grounds are only one of many features of the physical campus where the university makes a considerable strategic investment. Students had similar commentary for lavish athletics facilities and campus events that were an affront to those who were barely making it. In a prior study that focused on a single private research university, we found students not only resented how their university prioritized some if its financial decisions, but with it, students themselves were also deeply conflicted about some of the benefits they enjoyed that contributed to their experiences, such as the aforementioned grounds and athletics.[15]

Suggestion #2: Create and Improve Resources for Students Experiencing Food Insecurity

This was by far the largest category of student advice. Participants shared specific recommendations for increasing the accessibility of food. Many of the suggestions were practical, reflecting the sorts of solutions that are commonsense to students but do not easily fit administrative modes of problem-solving. Some examples include:

— Free food in the cafeterias: "They could probably afford to, like, let a cafeteria be open one day a week around campus for students to go through the lines for a meal a day. Like, I don't think they're making the food already. It shouldn't be an issue to let one plate go by for a student" (Layla, Flagship).

— A shuttle bus to grocery stores: "I know that there's a shuttle, there's a PRU shuttle that can take you from somewhere to somewhere, I've never taken it. But I wonder if they could like travel to grocery stores" (Jill, PRU).

— A shared meal system: "A community meal. You pitch in at the beginning of the semester, so they have all this money allocated so that they can plan all the meals out. Once a day, every day, maybe at night, for dinner, so students can come in, get food and go" (William, Lib Arts).

— More free food at events: "Like maybe catering more food 'cause sometimes we do have a lot of . . . the administration puts on a lot of events. Maybe if they could just bring some more in there, that could help a student out for a day" (Camila, Lib Arts).

— A support group for students struggling with food: "Maybe having—maybe even having a group, that as a minority, whatever minority, it is in this case for instance, the issue with food. Maybe having a group for that. You know, that, hey, everybody that comes here is dealing with this, so you don't have to feel shameful. We're all going through this" (Alejandra, Lib Arts).

— Make dining hall leftovers available: "With the dining halls. Again, they throw away a lot of food. I feel like if they were to have that food available . . . at the pantry, where students could just come and grab something, I feel like that would help out a lot" (Vera, PRU).

Beyond these very practical—and in many cases actionable—suggestions, the largest single recommendation from students was simply to make the resources that are available easier to access. Specifically, students noted the inaccessibility of the food pantries, in terms of location ("I wish that it was closer to central campus"—Anali, Flagship), hours, and the foods available ("What we need is a 24-hour public multilocational and accessible food pantry with healthy food options"—Layla, Flagship). Accessibility issues spilled over into the third recommendation theme that focused on transparency, visibility, and communication.

Suggestion #3: Acknowledge Food Insecurity Experiences and Communicate Clearly about Resources

First start out by addressing that they know that students experience food insecurity, instead of brushing it under the table (Cadence, Lib Arts).

Students asserted that administrators—and the public at large—need to do a better job acknowledging that struggling with the cost of food in college is a common problem. Camila (Lib Arts) declared: "People just kind of need to understand that the problem exists in every college. Public and private. And there needs to be more conversation at a more national level maybe." Layla (Flagship) described the need for a "social awareness campaign" by the university to sensitize students and administrators to the systemic issues of housing, food accessibility, and poverty in college.

Closely connected to this public acknowledgment was students' desire for administrators to then clearly convey what resources were available and how to find them. Brooke (Lib Arts) encouraged these connections from the start:

During orientation week, connecting people not just with resources but making those tangible efforts. Being like, "Hey, you all, these are the dates within the first week of school that we are going to take people to the food pantry to get supplies for, I don't know, like the first three weeks of school." Then having a plan in place that's not just a reactive plan.... Not something that's like, "Oh, come to us whenever you are food insecure." But, "We're going to go to the food pantry every three weeks for the entire semester. We are going to take a trip to the food pantry."

In addition to adding food resources to first-year orientation, students recommended emails, flyers, and other posted communication that instructed students on the aid available to them. Gina (Flagship) noted, as did many others, that students are used to this sort of promotion tactic for other sorts of events:

> I feel like you could probably publicly announce it or put up flyers and stuff like that. Like they sent out emails and they put a lot of their events on there. So probably putting out something like, "Oh, this week we'll have free this and that."

Camila (Lib Arts) summed this view simply, saying, "I think, yeah, the school just needs to communicate a lot better."

Suggestion #4: Reduce Financial Burdens

> Making food cheaper. Maybe even finding if they need outside resources, to grants, things like that. I mean, my public school that I work at, it provides free breakfast and lunch. I don't understand why a private school can't do that, you know, for certain things. Or if you, within your financial aid package, if you yourself either don't work or you're already receiving all this financial aid, that should also include your meal plan. (Valeria, Lib Arts)

The high cost of food on campus received extensive critique. Students simply rejected the premise of the underlying economic model in which the university and its for-profit partners capitalized on student debit or created conditions where students could not afford to eat on campus. As Valeria (Lib Arts) implied above, the National School Lunch Program (NSLP) that offers free and reduced-price meals for low-income K–12 students was a model several students pointed to as a reasonable expectation:

> They take your income, like, if you make under a certain amount, they have FAFSA records, the income, IRS records. They have to because we apply every year. So, based off of that, and hey, if you fall under a certain margin, like discount student rates. The prices, lunch prices and stuff. Just like they did in high school. (Alejandra, Lib Arts)

The logic of the NSLP model in which students below a certain income threshold receive either free or discounted meals reflected a common student mentality that both the university and the wider public has an interest in student success that food needs undermine. Camila (Lib Arts) articulated this connection between student support and the public good:

> We're like the next generation that are gonna go into the job markets and we want to make sure that we're well enough that we can succeed in college and get that degree and then contribute back to the community. But it's little things like overpricing or massive student loan interest that are keeping us back. And just addressing food insecurity maybe by I don't know, mandating, like, a free school lunch program.

Chelsea (PRU) expanded the conversation to meal scholarships generally, highlighting how her university's lack of food aid results in her social and academic exclusion:

> I would definitely issue more . . . scholarships for students who can't afford a meal plan to be helped. So they don't have any worries. Usually, I have study groups before an exam, all the students are like, "Hey, let's meet at the cafeteria," you know? In the dining hall, and I can't even go inside the dining hall. Yeah. Because I don't have a dining plan.

In addition to food scholarships, students recommended reducing the burden of the cost of food through vouchers for textbooks (Chelsea, PRU), requiring that internships be paid (Valeria, Lib Arts), eliminating costs for transcripts for low-income students (Layla, Flagship), and structuring campus jobs so they fit better with student schedules (Layla, Flagship).

Extending The Dream: Changing Perspectives and Structures

The sum of the injunctions offered by students are, obviously, not simply strategies for financial management or making the most of what the university offers. They are, more pointedly, indictments of the systemic biases built into prestige environments that undermine the success of underresourced students upon whom are imposed choices between trying to meet their basic food needs fully, and fully engaging in the incredible opportunities of their selective, normatively affluent university. Students were not alone in these critiques. Some administrators also rejected the implicit normality of this two-tiered system of educational opportunity, highlighting the resourcefulness of students while decrying a campus economic model that treats lifestyle goods and classed experiences as normal and necessary.

Yet the institutional commitment to the prestige game is virtually impossible to disaggregate from the tools of class reproduction that so powerfully unite the interests of upper-middle-class parents and competitive universities. Particularly given the vocal endorsement of diversity and access as institutional values over the past half century, seeing these campuses through the lens of the campus tour reveals how much prestige-oriented universities have remade themselves in the lifestyle image of their preferred clientele. As we highlighted at the outset, Mitchell Stevens asserts that the pressures of elite higher-education entry have redefined the activities of good parenting such that they align with the demands of admission criteria. The companion to that here is that administrators have remade these campuses to reflect the lifestyle expectations of the upper-middle-class families they are trying to attract. Certainly, it would be a flagrant oversight to ignore the hard work and advocacy of many administrators—often persons who experienced the difficulty of marginalization during their own undergraduate experiences.[16] But unfortunately, too many administrators, as the keepers of campus experience structures, seem to be unaware or unconcerned that expensive classed lifestyle goods have become intertwined with the normative expectations of the student experience such that to not participate in them is to not fully be a student. As students' navigation experiences attest, the choice to abstain is available. However, as administrators construct physical and organizational campus structures around consumption experiences, cultural and economic ostracism has been tacitly normalized for students who struggle financially.

If prestige-oriented universities are to meaningfully address these gaps in access, faculty and administrators will have to take seriously the uncomfortable process of redefining who the campus "dream" is for, including changes to financial priorities such as student activities programming, Greek life, student employment opportunities, tiered housing, and lifestyle-oriented campus dining options. Doing so, however, requires sober reflection about whether well-intentioned initiatives such as special orientation programs for students from historically marginalized groups and institutionally sponsored campus food pantries can not only give these students spaces and times to "bond" with others like them but to "bridge" into relationships with peers from different backgrounds.[17] In other words, initiatives to aid students at the margins, such as PRU's Tower Scholars program, carry with them the risk of preserving the status quo of lifestyle and status if they merely create a peripheral space for students who do not quite fit, rather than considering what more fundamental changes need to happen to make campus a more broadly inclusive space, socioeconomically and culturally. Certainly, increasing campus demographic diversity is an important part of the process, but as scholars have observed, changing representation has minimal impact if the campus climate does not also shift.[18]

In this sense, the change we call for is also to redefine what constitutes the ideal/normal; to revisit the substance of The Dream. Change of the magnitude necessary to create socioeconomically inclusive and equitable campuses that are also prestigious will require difficult parsing between the aspects of the Opportunity Paradigm that promote human growth and flourishing and those that primarily reinforce class advantage for a subset of wealthy students. Realistically, mechanisms of social reproduction and mobility are sufficiently embedded in prestige-oriented universities—and are sufficiently attractive to all students—that eliminating them fully is neither possible nor completely desirable. The goal, then, is not some system of cultural or socioeconomic matching that relegates underresourced students to less selective institutions that already value their classed backgrounds. Such a move undermines student agency and relieves prestige-oriented universities of their moral burden to address the full implications of equity and access. Instead, underresourced students can benefit from experiences in the prestige-oriented university by integrating their navigational knowledge and strategies with new insights (and critiques) about upper-middle-class lifestyle markers, thereby broadening their capacity to operate in a variety of professional and cultural settings. Administrators, then, must take an active role in validating diverse socioeconomic backgrounds and experiences, by substantiating resource requests that uncomfortably challenge preferred organizational scripts, by mentoring students toward more effective navigation of bureaucratic systems, and by harnessing the earned sensitivity of Critically Distanced Administrators[19] toward responsive relationships and reformed organizational structures.

Ultimately, for a shift in normative culture to occur over time, campus leaders will need to expand the canon of whose precollege experiences and forms of knowledge are valued, whose cultural practices have merit, and what consumptive habits are centered through campus services, activities, and programs. Toward this end, the agency and self-advocacy of students, combined with the empathy and student success orientation of administrators and faculty, gives us hope that this change is possible.

***

Honestly, just being where I'm at feels like a miracle and a movie and this triumph story, but it shouldn't be that way. It should never . . . it doesn't always have to be a struggle. It doesn't always have to be this other thing. Like a miracle doesn't need to happen for people to get their basic necessities or, like, it shouldn't be this rise or pull . . . crazy thing whenever, you know, things could be allocated differently. And even then, like, people . . . whenever other people are not complaining but are voicing their strife, people are so quick to say, "Well, you're not working hard enough. You're not . . . this isn't happening, you're not doing this, you're not exerting enough energy." But I'm a testament that I've exerted so much energy, this has happened, a miracle has happened. Like, I've had to work so hard and then I'm still kind of in this hole. And it shouldn't be that way. It shouldn't have to be a miracle.

—*Gavin (Flagship)*

APPENDIX

Participant Demographics

Pseudonym	Race and Ethnicity	Gender and Sexuality[1]	College Attendance Status	Socioeconomic Status	Academic Year	Institution	Typology	Other
Alec	Asian American Pacific Islander	Nonbinary, gay	First-generation	Low SES	First Year	PRU	Adapting	
Alejandra	Hispanic	Cis gender female	First-generation	Low SES	Fourth Year	Lib Arts	Sacrificing	Migrant farm worker family
Alfredo	Hispanic; Black; Caucasian	Man, gay	First-generation	Low SES	Fifth Year	Lib Arts	Adapting	
Anali	Hispanic	Woman	First-generation	Low SES	Second Year	Flagship	Sacrificing	Undocumented
Ariel	Asian American Pacific Islander	Woman, gay	First-generation	Low SES	Fourth Year	Lib Arts	Surviving	
Beth	Multiracial	Woman, female		Low SES	Fourth Year	Lib Arts	Sacrificing	
Brooke	Caucasian	Nonbinary, queer[1]	First-generation	Low SES	Third Year	Lib Arts	Sacrificing	
Cadence	Black or African American	Woman		Low SES	First Year	Lib Arts	Adapting	
Camila	Hispanic, Latina	Female, Woman	First-generation	Low SES	Fourth Year	Lib Arts	Prioritizing	Migrant farm worker family
Carli	Hispanic; Native American	Woman		Low SES	Third Year (transfer)	PRU	Prioritizing	Transfer student
Chelsea	Black or African American	Woman	First-generation	Low SES	Third Year (transfer)	PRU	Surviving	Single mother; transfer student
Corbett	Caucasian	Man		Low SES	Fifth Year	PRU	Adapting	
DeShauna	Black or African American	Woman		Low SES	Second Year	Flagship	Adapting	Second-gen immigrant family
Gabriela	Hispanic	Female, Woman		Low SES	Second Year	Lib Arts	Adapting	
Gavin	Hispanic	Male, Man		Low SES	Second Year	Flagship	Prioritizing	Second-gen immigrant family
Gina	Hispanic	Woman	First-generation	Low SES	Third Year	Flagship	Adapting	
Jill	Hispanic, Latina	Female, Woman	First-generation	Low SES	Fifth Year	PRU	Prioritizing	Transfer student; previously homeless

Name	Race/Ethnicity	Gender	Generation	SES	Year	Institution	Orientation	Other
Jules	Black or African American	Male, Man		Low SES	Third Year	Flagship	Adapting	Second-gen immigrant family
Kelsy	Caucasian, Romani	Woman	First-generation	Low SES	Second Year	Lib Arts	Sacrificing	
Lacey	Caucasian	Woman		Low SES	Third Year	Flagship	Prioritizing	
Layla	Caucasian	Female, Woman	First-generation	Low SES	Third Year	Flagship	Maximizing	Previously homeless
Leah	Black; Caucasian	Woman	First-generation	Low SES	Third Year	Flagship	Prioritizing	
Lucas	Caucasian	Man		Low SES	Third Year (transfer)	PRU	Maximizing	Transfer student; cultural outsider
Mandy	Hispanic	Female, Woman	First-generation	Low SES	Third Year	Flagship	Prioritizing	
Margaret	Mexican-Irish	Woman	First-generation	Low SES	Second Year	Lib Arts	Adapting	
Miranda	Hispanic, Latina	Woman, queer female	First-generation	Low SES	Third Year	Flagship	Surviving	
Nicole	Hispanic	Woman	First-generation	Low SES	Fourth Year	Lib Arts	Prioritizing	Undocumented family
Paloma	Hispanic, Latina	Woman		Low SES	Third Year	Lib Arts	Prioritizing	
Phillip	Black or African American	Man		Low SES	Fourth Year	Flagship	Maximizing	Second-gen immigrant family
Selina	Hispanic	Woman	First-generation	Low SES	Fourth Year	Lib Arts	Prioritizing	Migrant farm worker family
Terrence	Black or African American	Man		Low SES	Third Year	Flagship	Maximizing	
Tia	Black or African American	Woman, gay		Low SES	Second Year	PRU	Adapting	
Valeria	Hispanic	Woman, bisexual	First-generation	Low SES	Third Year	Lib Arts	Sacrificing	
Vera	Hispanic; Mexican–American	Woman	First-generation	Low SES	Second Year	PRU	Maximizing	Migrant farm worker family
William	Caucasian; Native American	Man	First-generation	Low SES	Third Year	Lib Arts	Sacrificing	

[1] In a demographic survey prior to interviewing, students had the option to select "woman," "man," or to write in a gender descriptor. During the interviews students were invited to complete an activity where they articulated important identity categories. Some participants named additional gender or sexual orientation descriptors in that context that we also include. Consequently, this column, while indicating student self-identification, is incomplete.

NOTES

Introduction to the Dream
1. Clare L. Cady, "Food Insecurity as a Student Issue," *Journal of College and Character* 15, no. 4 (November 2014): 265–272, https://doi.org/10.1515/jcc-2014-0031.
2. Cady, "Food Insecurity as a Student Issue."
3. Matthew P. Rabbitt, Laura J. Hales, Michael P. Burke, and Alisha Coleman-Jensen, *Household Food Security in the United States in 2022 Report No. ERR-325* (US Department of Agriculture, October 2023): 1–53, https://www.ers.usda.gov/webdocs/publications/107703/err-325.pdf?v=1429.3.
4. Kathryn Larin, *Food Insecurity: Better Information Could Help Eligible College Students Access Federal Food Assistance Benefits GAO-19-95* (US Government Accountability Office, December 2018): 1–62, https://files.eric.ed.gov/fulltext/ED594848.pdf; Katharine M. Broton and Sara Goldrick-Rab, "Going Without: An Exploration of Food and Housing Insecurity among Undergraduates," *Educational Researcher* 47, no. 2 (March 2018): 121–133, https://doi.org/10.3102/0013189X17741303.
5. Suzanna M. Martinez, Karen Webb, Edward A. Frongillo, and Lorrene D. Ritchie, "Food Insecurity in California's Public University System: What Are the Risk Factors?" *Journal of Hunger & Environmental Nutrition* 13, no. 1 (January 2018): 1–18, https://doi.org/10.1080/19320248.2017.1374901; Michael J. Stebleton, Crystal K. Lee, and Kate K. Diamond, "Understanding the Food Insecurity Experiences of College Students: A Qualitative Inquiry," *The Review of Higher Education* 43, no. 3 (Spring 2020): 727–752, https://doi.org/10.1353/rhe.2020.0005.
6. David Karen, "The Politics of Class, Race, and Gender: Access to Higher Education in the United States, 1960–1986," *American Journal of Education* 99, no. 2 (February 1991): 208–237, https://doi.org/10.1086/443979.
7. Larry D. Singell Jr. and Joe A. Stone, "For Whom the Pell Tolls: The Response of University Tuition to Federal Grants-in-Aid," *Economics of Education Review* 26, no. 3 (June 2007): 285–295, https://doi.org/10.1016/j.econedurev.2006.01.005.
8. James C. Hearn and Kelly Ochs Rosinger, "Socioeconomic Diversity in Selective Private Colleges: An Organizational Analysis," *The Review of Higher Education* 38, no. 1 (Fall 2014): 71–104, https://doi.org/10.1353/rhe.2014.0043; Jennie H. Woo and Susan P. Choy, *Merit Aid for Undergraduates: Trends from 1995–96 to 2007–08 Stats in Brief NCES 2012-160* (National Center for Education Statistics, October 2011): 1–23, https://nces.ed.gov/pubs2012/2012160.pdf.

9. Sara Goldrick-Rab, *Paying the Price* (Chicago: University of Chicago Press, 2016); Robert Kelchen, Sara Goldrick-Rab, and Braden Hosch, "The Costs of College Attendance: Examining Variation and Consistency in Institutional Living Cost Allowances," *The Journal of Higher Education* 88, no. 6 (March 2017): 947–971, https://doi.org/10.1080/00221546.2016.1272092; Rebecca L. Wyland, Scott W. Lester, Mark A. Mone, and Doan E. Winkel, "Work and School at the Same Time? A Conflict Perspective of the Work-School Interface," *Journal of Leadership & Organizational Studies* 20, no. 3 (August 2013): 346–357, https://doi.org/10.1177/1548051813484360.
10. Rabbitt et al., *Household Food Security in the United States in 2022.*
11. *National Postsecondary Student Aid Study: 2020 Undergraduate Students* (National Center for Education Statistics, 2023), https://nces.ed.gov/surveys/npsas/.

    The NPSAS survey was fielded in March 2020, during the earliest stages of the COVID-19 pandemic. The survey collected data from over 80,000 undergraduate students. We know from students participating in this study that the pandemic shifted their experience with food significantly, in some cases creating more stability as campuses and the government created structures to address food insecurity during the pandemic. In other cases, students faced additional uncertainty and increased food needs. Although not nationally representative, prior to the pandemic, single and multisite studies found that 33–42% of postsecondary students at four-year institutions experience food insecurity at some level, with rates even higher at two-year institutions. Prior to national measures, this high rate was contested by some scholars due to inconsistent sampling strategies, differences in postsecondary institution types, nonrepresentative samples, varying forms of measurement, and questions about the accuracy of the USDA food security measure among this specific population. We are eager to see the results from the NPSAS survey that is in the field as we finalize the book edits (Spring 2024) to understand the national rates of food insecurity as campuses shift out of COVID-19 pandemic responses and fewer federal social safety nets exist.

    See also Cassandra J. Nikolaus, An Ruopeng, Brenna Ellison, and Sharon M. Nickols-Richardson, "Food Insecurity among College Students in the United States: A Scoping Review," *Advances in Nutrition* 11, no. 2 (March 2020): 327–348, https://doi.org/10.1093/advances/nmz111; Craig Gundersen, "Are College Students More Likely to Be Food Insecure than Nonstudents of Similar Ages?", *Applied Economic Perspectives and Policy* 43, no. 4 (December 2021): 1476–1486, https://doi.org/10.1002/aepp.13110.
12. Meg Bruening, Stephanie Brennhofer, Irene Van Woerden, Michael Todd, and Melissa Laska, "Factors Related to the High Rates of Food Insecurity among Diverse, Urban College Freshmen," *Journal of the Academy of Nutrition and Dietetics* 116, no. 9 (September 2016): 1450–1457, https://doi.org/10.1016/j.jand.2016.04.004; Sara Goldrick-Rab, Jed Richardson, Joel Schneider, Anthony Hernandez, and Clare Cady, *Still Hungry and Homeless in College* (Madison: Wisconsin HOPE Lab, 2018); Broton and Goldrick-Rab, "Going Without"; Megan M. Patton-López,

Daniel F. López-Cevallos, Doris I. Cancel-Tirado, and Leticia Vazquez, "Prevalence and Correlates of Food Insecurity among Students Attending a Midsize Rural University in Oregon," *Journal of Nutrition Education and Behavior* 46, no. 3 (May–June 2014): 209–214, https://doi.org/10.1016/j.jneb.2013.10.007.

13. Nathan F. Alleman, Cara Cliburn Allen, and Sarah E. Madsen, "Constructed Pathways: How Multiply-Marginalized Students Navigate Food Insecurity at Selective Universities," *American Educational Research Journal* 61, no. 2 (April 2024): 328–365, https://doi.org/10.3102/00028312231217751; Diana Cuy Castellanos and Jeanne Holcomb, "Food Insecurity, Financial Priority, and Nutrition Literacy of University Students at a Mid-Size Private University," *Journal of American College Health* 68, no.1 (January 2020): 16–20, https://doi.org/10.1080/07448481.2018.1515762; Cara Cliburn Allen and Nathan F. Alleman, "A Private Struggle at a Private Institution: Effects of Student Hunger on Social and Academic Experiences," *Journal of College Student Development* 60, no. 1 (January–February 2019): 52–69, https://doi.org/10.1353/csd.2019.0003; Rashida M. Crutchfield and Jennifer Maguire, *Study of Student Basic Needs* (The California State University, January 2018): 1–53, https://www.calstate.edu/impact-of-the-csu/student-success/basic-needs-initiative/Documents/BasicNeedsStudy_phaseII_withAccessibilityComments.pdf; Anthony A. Jack, *The Privileged Poor: How Elite Colleges Are Failing Disadvantaged Students* (Cambridge: Harvard University Press, 2019).

14. Crutchfield and Maguire, *Study of Student Basic Needs*; Goldrick-Rab, Richardson, Schneider, Hernandez, and Cady, *Still Hungry and Homeless in College*; Larin, *Food Insecurity*; Maya E. Maroto, Anastasia Snelling, and Henry Linck, "Food Insecurity among Community College Students: Prevalence and Association with Grade Point Average," *Community College Journal of Research and Practice* 39, no. 6 (June 2015): 515–526, https://doi.org/10.1080/10668926.2013.850758.

15. Crutchfield and Maguire, *Study of Student Basic Needs*; Lisa Henry, "Understanding Food Insecurity among College Students: Experience, Motivation, and Local Solutions," *Annals of Anthropological Practice* 41, no. 1 (May 2017): 6–19, https://doi.org/10.1111/napa.12108; Martinez, Webb, Frongillo, and Ritchie, "Food Insecurity in California's Public University System"; Erica Phillips, Anne McDaniel, and Alicia Croft, "Food Insecurity and Academic Disruption among College Students," *Journal of Student Affairs Research and Practice* 55, no. 4 (Winter 2018): 353–372, https://doi.org/10.1080/19496591.2018.1470003; Cliburn Allen and Alleman, "A Private Struggle"; Monideepa B. Becerra and Benjamin J. Becerra, "Psychological Distress among College Students: Role of Food Insecurity and Other Social Determinants of Mental Health," *International Journal of Environmental Research and Public Health* 17, no. 11 (June 2020): 4118–4130, https://doi.org/10.3390/ijerph17114118; Kate K. Diamond, Michael J. Stebleton, and Robert C. delMas, "Exploring the Relationship between Food Insecurity and Mental Health in an Undergraduate Student Population," *Journal of Student Affairs Research and Practice* 57, no. 5 (October 2020): 546–560, https://doi.org/10.1080/19496591.2019.1679158.

Food insecurity research is a quickly developing area of scholarship, and likely by the time this book reaches press, important new studies will have been published that we were not able to include due to the publication timeline.

16. Cliburn Allen and Alleman, "A Private Struggle."
17. Kelly Stamper Balistreri, "A Decade of Change: Measuring the Extent, Depth and Severity of Food Insecurity," *Journal of Family and Economic Issues* 37 (2016): 373–382, https://doi.org/10.1007/s10834-016-9500-9; Kristin Blagg, Craig Gundersen, Diane Whitmore Schanzenbach, and James P. Ziliak, *Assessing Food Insecurity on Campus: A National Look at Food Insecurity among America's College Students* (The Urban Institute, August 2017): 1–16, https://www.urban.org/sites/default/files/publication/92331/assessing_food_insecurity_on_campus_4.pdf; Aydin Nazmi, Suzanna Martinez, Ajani Byrd, Derrick Robinson, Stephanie Bianco, Jennifer Maguire, Rashida M. Crutchfield, Kelly Condron, and Lorrene Ritchie, "A Systematic Review of Food Insecurity among US Students in Higher Education," *Journal of Hunger & Environmental Nutrition* 14, no. 5 (October 2019): 725–740, https://doi.org/10.1080/19320248.2018.1484316.
18. Katharine M. Broton, Kari E. Weaver, and Minhtuyen Mai, "Hunger in Higher Education: Experiences and Correlates of Food Insecurity among Wisconsin Undergraduates from Low-Income Families," *Social Sciences* 7, no. 10 (September 2018): 179–204, https://doi.org/10.3390/socsci7100179.
19. Alleman, Cliburn Allen, and Madsen, "Constructed Pathways"; Broton and Goldrick-Rab, "Going Without."
20. Elizabeth Aries and Maynard Seider, "The Interactive Relationship between Class Identity and the College Experience: The Case of Lower Income Students," *Qualitative Sociology* 28, no. 4 (December 2005): 419–443, https://doi.org/10.1007/s11133-005-8366-1; Georgianna LaNelle Martin, "Getting Out, Missing Out, and Surviving: The Social Class Experiences of White, Low-Income, First-Generation College Students" (PhD diss., The University of Iowa, 2012), https://www.proquest.com/docview/1030437183.
21. John Douglass and Gregg Thomson, "Poor and Rich: Student Economic Stratification and Academic Performance in a Public Research University System," *Higher Education Quarterly* 66, no. 1 (January 2012): 65–89, https://doi.org/10.1111/j.1468-2273.2011.00511.x; Simon Marginson, "The Worldwide Trend to High Participation Higher Education: Dynamics of Social Stratification in Inclusive Systems," *Higher Education* 72 (June 2016): 413–434, https://doi.org/10.1007/s10734-016-0016-x.
22. Aries and Seider, "The Interactive Relationship between Class Identity and the College Experience"; Elizabeth Lee, *Class and Campus Life: Managing and Experiencing Inequality at an Elite College* (Ithaca: Cornell University Press, 2016).
23. Ann L. Mullen, *Degrees of Inequality: Culture, Class, and Gender in American Higher Education* (Baltimore: John Hopkins University Press, 2010); Paul Tough, *The Years that Matter Most: How College Makes or Breaks Us* (Boston: Houghton Mifflin Harcourt, 2019).

24. Jessica S. Howell and Matea Pender, "The Costs and Benefits of Enrolling in an Academically Matched College," *Economics of Education Review* 51 (April 2016): 152–168, https://doi.org/10.1016/j.econedurev.2015.06.008.
25. Cliburn Allen and Alleman, "A Private Struggle"; Jack, *The Privileged Poor*.
26. Charles T. Clotfelter, *Unequal Colleges in the Age of Disparity* (Cambridge: Harvard University Press, 2017).
27. Wesley Ray Fugate, "Alike But Different: How Three Private Liberal Arts Colleges Communicate Prestige, Legitimacy, and Differentiation during the Student Recruitment Process" (PhD diss., The University of Georgia, 2012), https://getd.libs.uga.edu/pdfs/fugate_wesley_r_201205_phd.pdf.
28. Cliburn Allen and Alleman, "A Private Struggle."
29. Hearn and Rosinger, "Socioeconomic Diversity in Selective Private Colleges."
30. Rachelle Brooks, "Measuring University Quality," *The Review of Higher Education* 29, no. 1 (Fall 2005): 1–21, https://doi.org/10.1353/rhe.2005.0061.
31. Barron's College Division, *Profiles of American Colleges 2018*, 34th ed. (Barron's Educational Series, 2017).
32. Barron's College Division, *Profiles of American Colleges 2018*.
33. *College Navigator* (National Center for Education Statistics, n.d.), https://nces.ed.gov/collegenavigator/.
34. *College Navigator*; Barron's College Division, *Profiles of American Colleges 2018*.
35. Source withheld to protect institutional confidentiality.
36. Peter Kaufman and Kenneth A. Feldman, "Forming Identities in College: A Sociological Approach," *Research in Higher Education* 45, no. 5 (August 2004): 463–496, https://doi.org/10.1023/B:RIHE.0000032325.56126.29.
37. Barron's College Division, *Profiles of American Colleges 2018*.
38. Source withheld to protect institutional confidentiality.
39. Barron's College Division, *Profiles of American Colleges 2018*.
40. Dominic J. Brewer, Susan M. Gates, and Charles A. Goldman, *In Pursuit of Prestige: Strategy and Competition in U.S. Higher Education* (New Brunswick: Transaction Publishers, 2009).
41. Brewer, Gates, and Goldman, *In Pursuit of Prestige*.
42. John A. Davis and Mark A. Farrell, *The Market Oriented University: Transforming Higher Education* (Northampton: Edward Elgar Publishing, 2016); James Engell and Anthony Dangerfield, *Saving Higher Education in the Age of Money* (Charlottesville: University of Virginia Press, 2005).
43. Aries and Seider, "Class Identity and the College Experience"; Elizabeth A. Armstrong and Laura T. Hamilton, *Paying for the Party: How College Maintains Inequality* (Cambridge: Harvard University Press, 2013).
44. Hearn and Rosinger, "Socioeconomic Diversity in Selective Private Colleges."
45. Aries and Seider, "Class Identity and the College Experience."
46. Jack, *The Privileged Poor*.
47. Benjamin Ginsberg, "Administrators Ate My Tuition," *Washington Monthly*, August 28, 2011, https://washingtonmonthly.com/2011/08/28/administrators-ate-my-tuition/.

48. Hershey H. Friedman, "How the Creation of Too Many Academic Departments Stifles Creativity, Encourages a Silo Mentality, and Increases Administrative Bloat," *SSRN* (January 2, 2018): 1–27, https://papers.ssrn.com/sol3/papers.cfm?abstract_id=3095370#paper-citations-widget.
49. Benjamin Ginsberg, "Power Shift: How the Growth of Administrators Is Wrecking Our Campuses," *AFT on Campus* (Summer 2014): 5–6.
50. Pierre Bourdieu and Jean-Claude Passeron, *Education, Society, and Culture* (London: SAGE, 1977).
51. Davis and Farrell, *The Market Oriented University*.
52. Laura Hamilton, Josipa Roksa, and Kelly Nielsen, "Providing a 'Leg Up': Parental Involvement and Opportunity Hoarding in College," *Sociology of Education* 91, no. 2 (April 2018): 111–131, https://doi.org/10.1177/0038040718759557; Brian Jacob, Brian McCall, and Kevin M. Stange, "College as Country Club: Do Colleges Cater to Students' Preferences for Consumption" (NBER Working Paper 18745, National Bureau of Economic Research, Cambridge, MA, January 2013), https://www.nber.org/papers/w18745.
53. Kimberly Mass, "Lazy Rivers and Learning Commons: Observations on What Really Matters during the Initial College Visit," *Planning for Higher Education* 44, no. 4 (July–September 2016): 52–57, https://www.proquest.com/docview/1838982156?pqorigsite=gscholar&fromopenview=true&sourcetype=Scholarly%20Journals.
54. Jenny M. Stuber, *Inside the College Gates: How Class and Culture Matter in Higher Education* (Lanham: Lexington Books, 2011).
55. Mitchell L. Stevens, *Creating a Class: College Admissions and the Education of Elites* (Cambridge: Harvard University Press, 2007).
56. Daniel F. Chambliss and Christopher G. Takacs, *How College Works* (Cambridge: Harvard University Press, 2014).
57. Lee, *Class and Campus Life*; Tough, *The Years that Matter Most*.
58. Throughout the book we use the term "ideal/normal" to highlight the intersection of implicit student expectations about the experience they should have (in terms of ideals such as financial flexibility, campus engagement, food access without serious reflection, and so on) and the invisible normality of these expectations for all students.

Chapter 1. Selling the Dream

1. For a detailed accompaniment of individual high school seniors as they endure the high tension of college decision letters and navigate the decision process, see Paul Tough, *The Years that Matter Most: How College Makes or Breaks Us* (Boston: Houghton Mifflin Harcourt, 2019), particularly the first two chapters. As emphasized in Tough's work, the decision of where to attend college, even once acceptance and rejection letters are sent, is complicated for students of all backgrounds; entering college students consider family legacies, parental pressures, institutional reputations, financial aid packages, extracurricular programs, and subjective sense of fit in deciding where to ultimately enroll.

2. Mitchell L. Stevens, *Creating a Class: College Admissions and the Education of Elites* (Cambridge: Harvard University Press, 2007).
3. See Patricia M. McDonough, "Buying and Selling Higher Education: The Social Construction of the College Applicant," *The Journal of Higher Education* 65, no. 4 (July/August 1994): 427–446, https://doi.org/10.1080/00221546.1993.11778509; Tough, *The Years that Matter Most*.
4. "An elite degree," according to Mullen, "also serves as a kind of consecration, permanently marking its holders as worthy and entitled" (p. 211). However, the importance and influence of a particular degree is contested by scholars and journalists: whereas some conceptualize college degrees as meaningful markers of difference, others argue that too much is made of where one graduates. See Ann L. Mullen, *Degrees of Inequality: Culture, Class, and Gender in American Higher Education* (Baltimore: Johns Hopkins University Press, 2010); Frank Bruni, *Where You Go Is Not Who You'll Be: An Antidote to the College Admissions Mania* (New York: Grand Central Publishing, 2015); Charles T. Clotfelter, *Unequal Colleges in the Age of Disparity* (Cambridge: Harvard University Press, 2017).
5. Daniel F. Chambliss and Christopher G. Takacs, *How College Works* (Cambridge: Harvard University Press, 2014).
6. This chapter, and our larger employment of the campus tour focus, owes a great debt to Peter Magolda's work. See Peter Magolda, "The Campus Tour: Ritual and Community in Higher Education," *Anthropology and Education Quarterly* 31, no. 1 (March 2000): 24–46, https://doi.org/10.1525/aeq.2000.31.1.24.
7. All names, both persons and places, are pseudonyms.
8. Magolda, "The Campus Tour"; James A. Dearden, Suhui Li, Chad D. Meyerhoefer, and Muzhe Yang, "Demonstrated Interest: Signaling Behavior in College Admissions," *Contemporary Economic Policy* 35, no. 4 (October 2017): 630–657, https://doi.org/10.1111/coep.12216.
9. See Sarah C. Michalak, "This Changes Everything: Transforming the Academic Library," *Journal of Library Administration* 52, no. 5 (July 2012): 411–423, https://doi.org/10.1080/01930826.2012.700801.
10. Michalak, "This Changes Everything," 411.
11. Not until the late nineteenth century were college libraries even open to student access at all. Prior to that point, books were considered too valuable and potentially dangerous to simply loan out to students; access required permission granted on-site only. See John R. Thelin, *A History of American Higher Education*, 3rd ed. (Baltimore: Johns Hopkins University Press, 2019); Earl J. McGrath, "The Evolution of Administrative Offices in Institutions of Higher Education in the United States from 1860 to 1933" (PhD diss., The University of Chicago, 1936): 1–208, https://www.proquest.com/docview/301816391.
12. In fact, the lineage of the student union and gymnasium as common campus features in the United States find a shared and primary root in the initiative of students in the late nineteenth century, in the form of the collegiate version of the Young Men's Christian Association, or YMCA. The culmination of evangelical fervor and enthusiasm for meeting the needs of fellow students led to, among

other innovations, a nationwide but locally controlled campaign of fundraising efforts to establish much-needed meeting rooms and other facilities in an era when postbellum colleges were struggling financially, disinterested in student life, or both. Aspirations and buildings grew from the first modest structure, Murray Hall, constructed at Princeton in 1879 at a cost of $20,000. About a dozen years later future Nobel Prize winner John R. Mott would pen a widely distributed pamphlet, *How to Secure a College Association Building* (1892), based on his own experiences as student president of the "Y" at Cornell raising funds to erect Barnes Hall (circa 1889), named for its chief benefactor, publisher Alfred Smith Barnes, now most easily recognized by his connection to the Barnes & Noble bookstore chain. Yale, Dartmouth, Berkeley, Clemson, Texas A&M, Virginia, North Carolina, Johns Hopkins, and many other colleges both small and large benefited from this Y initiative. On many campuses the Y building became the de facto student union for the campus, providing such desirable resources as bowling alleys, movie theaters, barber shops, pools, gymnasiums, locker rooms, reading rooms, guest rooms, and of course, meeting rooms. In all, the Y students raised the funds to construct some fifty buildings in the fifty years that followed that first structure. See David P. Setran, *The College "Y": Student Religion in the Era of Secularization* (New York: Palgrave MacMillan, 2007); Dorothy E. Finnegan and Nathan F. Alleman, "Without Adult Supervision: Campus YMCAs" (Paper presentation, annual meeting for the Association for the Study of Higher Education, Philadelphia, PA, November 18, 2005).

13. For a brief history of the residential college movement, see Mark B. Ryan, "Residential Colleges: A Legacy of Living and Learning Together," *Change: The Magazine of Higher Learning* 24, no. 5 (September–October 1992): 26–35, https://www.jstor.org/stable/40165119. For an overview of the types of faculty-student interactions within residential colleges, see Bradley E. Cox and Elizabeth Orehovec, "Faculty-Student Interaction Outside the Classroom: A Typology from a Residential College," *The Review of Higher Education* 30, no. 4 (Summer 2007): 343–362, https://doi.org/10.1353/rhe.2007.0033.

14. See John C. Weidman, "Undergraduate Socialization: A Conceptual Approach," in *Higher Education: Handbook of Theory and Research* V, ed. John C. Smart (New York: Agathon, 1989), 289–322; Alexander Astin, *What Matters in College: Four Critical Years Revisited* (San Francisco: Jossey-Bass, 1993); Chambliss and Takacs, *How College Works*.

15. See Frederick George Bailey, *Stratagems and Spoils: A Social Anthropology of Politics* (New York: Routledge, 2001) for a fascinating—if not tangential—discussion of the ways that social systems create sanctioned outlets for social energy and behavior that violates social norms.

16. Sense of belonging, integration, and student fit have long been a concern for higher-education scholars and practitioners. Vincent Tinto's Theory of Student Departure posits that attrition and integration are linked, wherein students who assimilate to the campus environment through membership are most likely to persist. Vincent Tinto, *Leaving College: Rethinking the Causes and Cure of Student Attrition* (Chicago: University of Chicago Press, 1993).

17. Thelin, *A History of American Higher Education*.
18. William H. Cowley, "The History of Student Residential Housing," *School and Society* 40, no. 1040 (December 1934): 705–712.
19. Witness the Christopher Wren Building at the College of William & Mary in Virginia. Acclaimed to be the oldest continuously used academic building in the United States (circa 1699), it predates even the founding of the eventual colonial capital of Williamsburg in which it resides. The intervening 320 or so years have offered ample time for legend and myth to intertwine. Although the Wren Building did provide the space for Thomas Jefferson's education, it also burned to the ground three times, most recently when set fire to by Federal troops in 1862. Each time it was rebuilt using parts of preexisting walls, but with considerably different architectural details (witness the building's brief "Italianate" phase from 1859 to 1862). Further, despite its namesake, the Wren Building was unlikely to have been designed by (at best, "inspired by") noted English architect Sir Christopher Wren; no documentation exists that directly connects the two. Nevertheless, the Wren Building is the centerpiece of the "ancient" section of William & Mary's campus, figuring prominently in annual opening convocation and graduation ceremonies, as well as many alumni weddings. See the commanding two-volume tome: Susan H. Godson, Ludwell H. Johnson, and Richard B. Sherman, *The College of William & Mary: A History* (Williamsburg: King and Queen Press, 1993).
20. Indeed, two of our three case campuses had identical traditions. See Magolda, "The Campus Tour," for a description of the same practice in his institutional ethnography of the University of Miami (Ohio).
21. Magolda, "The Campus Tour," 40.

Chapter 2. Establishing the Ideal/Normal

1. Elliot Eisner, *The Educational Imagination: On the Design and Evaluation of School Programs* (New York: McGraw-Hill, 1985). Elliot Eisner defined the null, or hidden, curriculum as that which is not taught in a school curriculum but still transmits—often implicitly—educational values and perspectives. Bowles and Gintis further argued that the hidden curriculum of schooling is differentiated by economic class; Apple summarized, "lower-class students are taught punctuality, neatness, respect for authority," whereas students from higher socioeconomic classes "are taught open-mindedness, problem solving, and flexibility" (48). See also Samuel Bowles and Herbert Gintis, *Schooling in Capitalist America: Educational Reform and the Contradictions of Economic Life* (New York: Basic Books, 1976); Michael W. Apple, "The Other Side of the Hidden Curriculum: Correspondence Theories and the Labor Process," *The Journal of Education* 162, no. 1 (Winter 1980): 47–66, https://www.jstor.org/stable/42741975.
2. Eric Margolis, ed., *The Hidden Curriculum in Higher Education* (New York: Routledge, 2001); see also Rachel Gable, *The Hidden Curriculum: First Generation Students at Legacy Universities* (Princeton: Princeton University Press, 2021) for an excellent example of the use of "hidden curriculum" in the context of higher

education. The origins of the concept are largely in K–12 education, where scholars highlighted implicit messages about who "good" students are, and the norms and values embedded in educational systems. See Philip W. Jackson, *Life in Classrooms* (New York: Holt, Rinehart, and Winston, 1968).

3. Daniel Golden, *The Price of Admission: How America's Ruling Class Buys Its Way into Elite Colleges—And Who Gets Left Outside the Gate* (New York: Random House, 2016).

4. DiMaggio and Powell described three forms of institutional isomorphism—coercive, mimetic, and normative—to account for the striking homogeneity within a competitive environment, which they cited as the result of environmental uncertainty and constraint. Paul J. DiMaggio and Walter D. Powell, "The Iron Cage Revisited: Institutional Isomorphism and Collective Rationality in Organizational Fields," *American Sociological Review* 48, no. 2 (April 1983): 147–160, https://doi.org/10.2307/2095101.

5. See Lauren A. Rivera, *Pedigree: How Elite Students Get Elite Jobs* (Princeton: Princeton University Press, 2016).

6. Daniel F. Chambliss and Christopher G. Takacs, *How College Works* (Cambridge: Harvard University Press, 2014).

7. This assertion should not obscure the fact that these unequal pathways are not merely a matter of chances gained or lost, or opportunities seized or missed. Sociologists over the past half century have examined at length the ways that familial and educational precollege socialization prepare some students to navigate these spaces more advantageously than others. Preparation is often linked to parental education and wealth, employing Bourdieu's concepts of social and cultural capital and habitus, or the field of choices that seem obvious for one to make. Scholars like Bowles and Gintis or Giroux have also examined the ways that educational environments, imbued with cultural values and preferred behavior, reward or punish students based on their social class alignment, or alternatively, plant the seeds of resistance to and transformation of such values. Pierre Bourdieu and Jean-Claude Passeron, *Education, Society, and Culture* (London: SAGE, 1977); Elizabeth M. Lee and Rory Kramer, "Out with the Old, In with the New? Habitus and Social Mobility at Selective Colleges," *Sociology of Education* 86, no. 1 (January 2013): 18–35, https://doi.org/10.1177/0038040712445519; Bowles and Gintis, *Schooling in Capitalist America*; Henry A. Giroux, *Ideology, Culture, and the Process of Schooling* (Philadelphia: Temple University Press, 1981).

Recent scholarship has further explored ways that those from working-class and low-socioeconomic backgrounds might defy the expectations assigned to their upbringings, either by leveraging forms of capital uniquely available to them or by operationalizing the opportunities of advantageous high school socialization to navigate elite higher education. Tara J. Yosso, "Whose Culture Has Capital? A Critical Race Theory Discussion of Community Cultural Wealth," in *Critical Race Theory in Education: All God's Children Got a Song*, 2nd ed., eds. Adrienne D. Dixson, Celia K. Rousseau Anderson, and Jamel K. Donnor (Oxfordshire:

Routledge, 2016), 113–136; Anthony A. Jack, *The Privileged Poor: How Elite Colleges Are Failing Disadvantaged Students* (Cambridge: Harvard University Press, 2019).

8. Armstrong and Hamilton demonstrated this effect at a Midwestern university, observing how entering social class tends to result in women students collecting into similar social and academic pathways through college. Elizabeth A. Armstrong and Laura T. Hamilton, *Paying for the Party: How College Maintains Inequality* (Cambridge: Harvard University Press, 2013).

9. Julie J. Park, *Race on Campus: Debunking Myths with Data* (Cambridge: Harvard University Press, 2018), 3.

10. Mitchell Stevens, *Creating a Class: College Admissions and the Education of Elites* (Cambridge: Harvard University Press, 2007); Ann L. Mullen, *Degrees of Inequality: Culture, Class, and Gender in American Higher Education* (Baltimore: John Hopkins University Press, 2010); Elizabeth Lee, *Class and Campus Life: Managing and Experiencing Inequality at an Elite College* (Ithaca: Cornell University Press, 2016); Jack, *The Privileged Poor*.

11. Peter Magolda, "The Campus Tour: Ritual and Community in Higher Education," *Anthropology and Education Quarterly* 31, no. 1 (March 2000): 24–46, https://doi.org/10.1525/aeq.2000.31.1.24.

12. Magolda, "The Campus Tour," 38.

13. See chapter 8 in Stevens, *Creating a Class*.

14. Richard Pitt, Whitney N. Laster Pirtle, and Ashley N. Metzger, "Academic Specialization, Double Majoring, and the Threat to Breadth in Academic Knowledge," *The Journal of General Education* 66, no. 3 (2017): 166–191, https://doi.org/10.5325/jgeneeduc.66.3-4.0166.

15. Jean M. Twenge and W. Keith Campbell, *The Narcissism Epidemic: Living in the Age of Entitlement* (New York: Free Press, 2009).

16. See Paul Tough, *The Years that Matter Most: How College Makes or Breaks Us* (Boston: Houghton Mifflin Harcourt, 2019); Sara Goldrick-Rab, Deborah Faye Carter, and Rachelle Winkle Wagner, "What Higher Education Has to Say about the Transition to College," *Teachers College Record* 109, no. 10 (October 2007): 2444–2481, https://doi.org/10.1177/016146810710901007.

17. See chapter 8 in Stevens, *Creating a Class*.

18. Perhaps the point here is twofold: the gaming of the college entry system is a middle-class rite of passage that results in many intelligent and able test-takers who are not fully prepared for the rigors of college; second, that as Stevens argues, the middle-class social contract is that students will be taken care of, and services signal this commitment. See Golden, *Price of Admission*; Stevens, *Creating a Class*.

19. Chetty and colleagues, in analyzing data from 1999 to 2013, found that the earnings outcomes of students who attend the same university are similar, despite differences in social class. Raj Chetty, John Friedman, Emmanuel Saez, Nicholas Turner, and Danny Yagan, "Mobility Report Cards: The Role of Colleges in Intergenerational Mobility" (NBER Working Paper 23618, National Bureau of Economic Research, Cambridge, MA, July 2017), https://www.nber.org/papers/

w23618. See also chapter 2 in Christian Smith, *Lost in Transition: The Dark Side of Emerging Adulthood* (New York: Oxford University Press, 2011).

20. Kaufman and Feldman described the certification and gatekeeping functions of higher education, noting that "college certifies students for certain social and occupation positions in the world (usually of the middle and upper-middle classes), channels them in these directions, and to some extent ensures their entrance to such positions" (464). Peter Kaufman and Kenneth A. Feldman, "Forming Identities in College: A Sociological Approach," *Research in Higher Education* 45, no. 5 (August 2004): 463-496, https://doi.org/10.1023/B:RIHE.0000032325.56126.29. As a counterpoint emphasizing postcollege student agency, see Frank Bruni, *Where You'll Go Is Not Who You'll Be: An Antidote to the College Admissions Mania* (New York: Grand Central Publishing, 2016).

21. Stevens, *Creating a Class*.

22. See James B. Twitchell, *Living It Up: Our Love Affair with Luxury* (New York: Columbia University Press, 2002).

23. See Vincent Tinto, *Leaving College: Rethinking the Causes and Cure of Student Attrition* (Chicago: University of Chicago Press, 1993); Terrell L. Strayhorn, *College Students' Sense of Belonging: A Key to Educational Success for All Students* (New York: Routledge, 2012); Laurie A. Schriener, Michelle C. Louis, and Denise D. Nelson, eds., *Thriving in Transitions: A Research-Based Approach to College Student Success* (Columbia: National Resource Center for the First-Year Experience and Students in Transition, 2012); Chambliss and Takacs, *How College Works*.

24. For critiques of Tinto's emphasis on integration, see Sylvia Hurtado and Deborah F. Carter, "Effects of College Transition and Perceptions of the Campus Racial Climate on Latino College Students' Sense of Belonging," *Sociology of Education* 70, no. 4 (October 1997): 324-345, https://doi.org/10.2307/2673270; Louis C. Attinasi Jr., "Getting In: Mexican Americans' Perceptions of University Attendance and the Implications for Freshman Year Persistence," *Journal of Higher Education* 60, no. 3 (May-June 1989): 247-277, https://doi.org/10.2307/1982250; Samuel D. Museus, Varaxy Yi, and Natasha Saelua, "The Impact of Culturally Engaging Campus Environments on Sense of Belonging," *The Review of Higher Education* 40, no. 2 (Winter 2017): 187-215, https://doi.org/10.1353/rhe.2017.0001.

For an explanation of the connection between retention, rankings, and prestige, see Linda S. Hagedorn, "How to Define Retention: A New Look at an Old Problem," in *College Student Retention: Formula for Student Success*, ed. Alan Seidman (Lanham: Rowman & Littlefield, 2012), 81-99.

25. Here Chambliss and Takacs's *How College Works* is essential reading, invoking the work of Randall Collins and Mark Granovetter to illustrate how differently diverse networks result from involvement in different kinds of organizations.

26. Stevens, *Creating a Class*.

Chapter 3. Starving the Dream I

1. Alec's preferred pronouns are they/them/theirs reflective of their nonbinary gender identity.

2. Sendhil Mullainathan and Eldar Shafir, *Scarcity: Why Having Too Little Means So Much* (New York: Times Book, 2013).
3. Originally the "total institution" was conceptualized by Erving Goffman as the purposeful breakdown of barriers between "sleep, play [and] work" under the authority of a particular institution (p. 5). Scholars have since applied the concept to areas like university admissions and student socialization. See Erving Goffman, *Asylums: Essays on the Social Situation of Mental Patients and Other Inmates* (New York: Doubleday Anchor, 1961); Mitchell L. Stevens, *Creating a Class: College Admissions and the Education of Elites* (Cambridge: Harvard University Press, 2007); Heather M. Fitz Gibbon, Richard M. Canterbury, and Larry Litten, "Colleges as Total Institutions: Implications for Admission, Orientation, and Student Life," *College and University* 74, no. 2 (Winter 1999): 21–27, https://www.proquest.com/docview/225616470.
4. The growing use of technological, data-driven retention interventions and strategies, like early alert systems (EAS), enable institutions to monitor students based on backgrounds and behaviors and proactively support students at risk of not continuing their studies. See Renato Villano, Scott Harrison, Grace Lynch, and George Chen, "Linking Early Alert Systems and Student Retention: A Survival Analysis Approach," *Higher Education* 76, (2018): 903–920, https://doi.org/10.1007/s10734-018-0249-y.
5. Although it is well established within higher-education literature that living on campus relates positively to student retention, recent research highlights how students' socioeconomic backgrounds may constrain this effect: Schudde, drawing on the sociological concept of cultural mismatch, found that students from low-income backgrounds "see null effects of living on campus, while their more affluent peers experience enhanced retention" (p. 21). See Lauren Schudde, "The Interplay of Family Income, Campus Residency, and Student Retention (What Practitioners Should Know about Cultural Mismatch)," *Journal of College and University Student Housing* 43, no. 1 (September 2016): 10–27, https://files.eric.ed.gov/fulltext/EJ1149380.pdf. For foundational work on the connection between residency and retention, see Vincent Tinto, *Leaving College: Rethinking the Causes and Cures of Student Attrition* (Chicago: University of Chicago Press, 1993); John M. Braxton and Shederick A. McClendon, "The Fostering of Social Integration and Retention through Institutional Practice," *Journal of College Student Retention: Research, Theory & Practice* 3, no. 1 (May 2001): 57–71, https://doi.org/10.2190/RGXJ-U08C-06VB-JK7D.
6. DesJardins and McCall described "frontloading" as a new financial aid policy that "is typically defined as providing gift aid (scholarships and/or grants) in the first two years of college only," leaving upper-level students to pay for their education through "self-financing, work, and loans" (p. 530). According to the study authors, "The conceptual rationale for this policy is that upper-division students (juniors and seniors) are typically less price sensitive than their lower-division counterparts" (p. 530). See Stephen L. DesJardins and Brian P. McCall, "Simulating the Effects of Financial Aid Packages on College Student

Stopout, Reenrollment Spells, and Graduation Chances," *The Review of Higher Education* 33, no. 4 (Summer 2010): 513–541, https://doi.org/10.1353/rhe.0.0169.
7. Students from lower-income backgrounds are less likely to live on campus, due in large part to financial constraints; see Schudde, "The Interplay of Family Income, Campus Residency, and Student Retention." For students residing on campus, recent scholarship has uncovered the racialized and classed hierarchy of residence halls: Foste found "gross disparities in housing options" at three case institutions, where halls were segregated by both race and class (p. 183). Here, differences in pricing and quality informed students' perceptions of campus living options—as well as who belonged in such spaces. See Zak Foste, "'Oh, That's the White Dorm': The Racialization of University Housing and the Policing of Racial Boundaries," *Journal of College Student Development* 62, no. 2 (March–April 2021): 169-185, https://doi.org/10.1353/csd.2021.0015.
8. Darris R. Means and Kimberly B. Pyne, "Finding My Way: Perceptions of Institutional Support and Belonging in Low-Income, First-Generation, First-Year College Students," *Journal of College Student Development* 58, no. 6 (September 2017): 907-924, https://doi.org/10.1353/csd.2017.0071; Schudde, "The Interplay of Family Income, Campus Residency, and Student Retention"; Foste, "'Oh, That's the White Dorm'"; Braxton and McClendon "The Fostering of Social Integration."
9. For an overview of the positive effects of on-campus living, see Matthew J. Mayhew, Alyssa N. Rockenbach, Nicholas A. Bowman, Tricia Seifert, and Gregory C. Wolniak, *How College Affects Students: 21st Century Evidence That Higher Education Works*, vol. 3 (Hoboken: John Wiley & Sons, 2016).

Chapter 4. Starving the Dream II

1. The first appearance of the collegiate student union building is credited to the University of Pennsylvania, where a structure "part clubhouse and part country estate" was constructed in 1896, according to Brown and Taylor (p. 56). Patrick Brown and John Taylor, "Sustainability in the Union," *New Directions for Student Services* 2012, no. 137 (March 2012): 53–65, https://doi.org/10.1002/ss.20014. Far less widely recognized is the role of the Young Men's Christian Association (YMCA) student associations, which began constructing student union buildings to support the organization's evangelical mission as early as 1879, with the completion of Murray Hall at Princeton. By the early 1920s the Y men had constructed over 50 such unions, of various sizes and accouterments, across the country. In many cases, cash-strapped colleges that were overwhelmed by the influx of students relied on the Y buildings as the de facto student union until such time as the institution was able to construct its own. See Dorothy E. Finnegan and Nathan F. Alleman, "The YMCA and the Origins of American Freshman Orientation Programs," *Historical Studies in Education* 25, no. 1 (Spring 2013): 95-114, https://www.researchgate.net/profile/Dorothy-Finnegan/publication/236961685.
2. Petersen argues that the university functions "as a site of lifestyle," wherein institutions shape students' consumptive habits and aspirations through

marketing and branding, sports, and partnerships. See Anne Helen Petersen, "Welcome to the COVID Influencer," *Culture Study* (blog), August 30, 2020, https://annehelen.substack.com/p/welcome-the-covid-influencer. See also Tressie McMillan Cottom, *Lower Ed: The Troubling Rise of For-Profit Colleges in the New Economy* (New York: The New Press, 2017).

3. Ali Pourmotabbed, Sajjad Moradi, Atefeh Babaei, Abed Ghavami, Hamed Mohammadi, Cyrus Jalili, Michael E. Symonds, and Maryam Miraghajani, "Food Insecurity and Mental Health: A Systematic Review and Meta-Analysis," *Public Health Nutrition* 23, no. 10 (July 2020): 1778–1790, https://doi.org/10.1017/S136898001900435X; Monideepa B. Becerra and Benjamin J. Becerra, "Psychological Distress among College Students: Role of Food Insecurity and Other Social Determinants of Mental Health," *International Journal of Environmental Research and Public Health* 17, no. 11 (June 2020): 4118–4130, https://doi.org/10.3390/ijerph17114118.

4. A point made by a variety of authors, most recently and prominently Anthony A. Jack, in *The Privileged Poor: How Elite Colleges Are Failing Disadvantaged Students* (Cambridge: Harvard University Press, 2019).

5. Under a company store system, a local business—often one that dominates the employment market—provides employees with access to goods like food or clothing that they might not otherwise be able to secure, due to lack of transportation or access to other stores. The company store model was prevalent in raw material-gathering occupations that required remote on-site work such as mining and timber cutting in the nineteenth and early twentieth centuries in America but is still in operation in various forms around the world. Often the owners of production also own the housing, bars, or eating houses, as well as retail stores. Company stores accept cash payment and company vouchers, in addition to store debt lines, making them convenient and at times necessary options for employees, despite often higher prices on goods. The result is additional forms of income for the ownership company and an additional source of economic dependence for workers. See Price V. Fishback, "Did Coal Miners 'Owe Their Souls to the Company Store'? Theory and Evidence from the 1900s," *The Journal of Economic History* 46, no. 4 (December 1986): 1011–1029, https://www.jstor.org/stable/2121820.

Chapter 5. Starving the Dream III

1. Daniel F. Chambliss and Christopher G. Takacs, *How College Works* (Cambridge: Harvard University Press, 2014).
2. Sendhil Mullainathan and Eldar Shafir, *Scarcity: Why Having Too Little Means So Much* (New York: Times Book, 2013).
3. See Jennifer E. DeVoe, Alia Baez, Heather Angier, Lisa Krois, Christine Edlund, and Patricia A. Carney, "Insurance + Access ≠ Health Care: Typology of Barriers to Health Care Access for Low-Income Families," *The Annals of Family Medicine* 5, no. 6 (November 2007): 511–518, https://doi.org/10.1370/afm.748.
4. The Hope Center for Community, College, and Justice highlights the intersections of food insecurity, housing insecurity, and homelessness. In their 2016

survey, they found that 22% of students at two-year institutions experienced food and housing insecurity (8% of students also experienced homelessness). At four-year institutions, the rates were 16% and 6%, respectively (p. 15). Recent scholarship further explores the co-occurrence of these phenomena, including the application of a cumulative risk model to students experiencing food and housing insecurity, as well as their correlation to academic success (negative) and other marginalized identities (positive). See Sara Goldrick-Rab, Jed Richardson, Joel Schneider, Anthony Hernandez, and Clare Cady, *Still Hungry and Homeless in College* (Madison: Wisconsin HOPE Lab, 2018); Mary E. Haskett, Dana Kotter-Grühn, and Suman Majumder, "Prevalence and Correlates of Food Insecurity and Homelessness among University Students," *Journal of College Student Development* 61, no. 1 (January–February 2020): 109–114, https://doi.org/10.1353/csd.2020.0007.

5. See Sarah Ketchen Lipson, Emily G. Lattie, and Daniel Eisenberg, "Increased Rates of Mental Health Service Utilization by US College Students: 10-year Population-Level Trends (2007–2017)," *Psychiatric Services* 70, no. 1 (January 2019): 60–63, https://doi.org/10.1176/appi.ps.201800332; Patrick J. Michaels, Patrick W. Corrigan, Nupur Kanodia, Blythe Buchholz, and Sara Abelson, "Mental Health Priorities: Stigma Elimination and Community Advocacy in College Settings," *Journal of College Student Development* 56, no. 8 (November 2015): 872–875, https://doi.org/10.1353/csd.2015.0088.

6. *Loan aversion* describes this lack of borrowing among low-income students, who fear being unable to repay loans for college—a fear made more real by the looming student debt crisis. See Brent J. Evans and Angela Boatman, "Understanding How Information Affects Loan Aversion: A Randomized Control Trial of Providing Federal Loan Information to High School Seniors," *The Journal of Higher Education* 90, no. 5 (March 2019): 800–832, https://doi.org/10.1080/00221546.2019.1574542.

7. Cara Cliburn Allen and Nathan F. Alleman, "A Private Struggle at a Private Institution: Effects of Student Hunger on Social and Academic Experiences," *Journal of College Student Development* 60, no. 1 (January–February 2019): 52–69, https://doi.org/10.1353/csd.2019.0003. For a study that explores financial and additional barriers to food security for college students, see Nicole D. Peterson and Andrea Freidus, "More than Money: Barriers to Food Security on a College Campus," *Culture, Agriculture, Food and Environment* 42, no. 2 (December 2020): 125–137, https://doi.org/10.1111/cuag.12252.

8. Erin Velez, Melissa Cominole, and Alexander Bentz, "Debt Burden after College: The Effect of Student Loan Debt on Graduates' Employment, Additional Schooling, Family Formation, and Home Ownership," *Education Economics* 27, no. 2 (April 2019): 186–206, https://doi.org/10.1080/09645292.2018.1541167.

Chapter 6. Dreaming of More

1. Clare L. Cady, "Food Insecurity as a Student Issue," *Journal of College and Character* 15, no. 4 (November 2014): 265–272, https://doi.org/10.1515/jcc-2014-0031.

2. Charles Homer Haskins, *The Rise of Universities* (New York: Henry Holt and Company, 1923).
3. Perry L. Glanzer, Nathan F. Alleman, and Todd C. Ream, *Restoring the Soul of the University: Unifying Christian Higher Education in a Fragmented Age* (Westmont: InterVarsity Press, 2017); Barton Kunstler, "The Millennial University, Then and Now: From Late Medieval Origins to Radical Transformation," *On the Horizon* 14, no. 2 (April 2006): 62-69, https://doi.org/10.1108/10748120610674021.
4. Haskins, *The Rise of Universities*.
5. Kunstler, "The Millennial University, Then and Now."
6. Haskins, *The Rise of Universities*.
7. Xu Shanwei, "Study of the Tuition and Living Expenses of Medieval European University Students," *Chinese Studies in History* 50, no. 1 (January 2017): 4-13, https://doi.org/10.1080/00094633.2015.1189288.
8. Shanwei, "Study of the Tuition."
9. Ellen Perry Pride, "Student Life in the Medieval Universities," *The Social Studies* 32, no. 6 (October 1941): 267-271, https://doi.org/10.1080/00220973.1936.11016625; Shanwei, "Study of the Tuition"; Haskins, *The Rise of Universities*.
10. John R. Thelin, *A History of American Higher Education*, 3rd ed. (Baltimore: Johns Hopkins University Press, 2019).
11. Shanwei, "Study of the Tuition."
12. Pride, "Student Life in the Medieval Universities."
13. Charles Homer Haskins, *Studies in Mediaeval Culture* (Oxford: Clarendon Press, 1929) quoted in Pride, "Student Life in the Medieval Universities," p. 10.
14. Pride, "Student Life in the Medieval Universities."
15. Christina J. Hodge, "Consumerism and Control: Archaeological Perspectives on the Harvard College Buttery," *Northeast Historical Archaeology* 42, no. 1 (2013): 54-74, https://doi.org/10.22191/neha/vol42/iss1/5; Thelin, *A History of American Higher Education*. Emphasis added.
16. Harley P. Holden, "Student Records: The Harvard Experience," *The American Archivist* 39, no. 4 (October 1976): 461-467, https://www.jstor.org/stable/40291918.
17. Loomis Havemeyer, "Eating at Yale, 1701-1965," *Yale University* 12-1965 (December 1965): 1-42, https://elischolar.library.yale.edu/yale_history_pubs/9/.
18. Hodge, "Consumerism and Control"; Havemeyer, "Eating at Yale."
19. Hodge, "Consumerism and Control."
20. Such regulations included: the amount of wine students can be provided with at Commencement, no possession of drinks in the students' rooms, and restrictions on which foods can be purchased for students. See Hodge, "Consumerism and Control," pp. 66-68.
21. See Leon Jackson's masterful history of these events which spells out both the events and the fomenting social undercurrents that propelled them. Namely, Republican ideals of manhood and independence that were denied to students in the absence of a concept for young adulthood. This relegated students to the status of "children," justifying oppressive rules and punishments. Leon Jackson, "The Rights of Man and the Rites of Youth: Fraternity and Riot at

Eighteenth-Century Harvard," in *The American College in the Nineteenth Century*, ed. Roger L. Gieger (Nashville: Vanderbilt University Press, 2000), 46–79.
22. Jackson, "The Rights of Man and the Rites of Youth."
23. Kathryn McDaniel Moore, "Freedom and Constraint in Eighteenth Century Harvard," *The Journal of Higher Education* 47, no. 6 (November–December 1976): 649–659, https://doi.org/10.2307/1979120; Jackson, "The Rights of Man and the Rites of Youth."
24. Randall J. Peach, "Civil Rights—Law against Discrimination—Princeton Eating Clubs Must Admit Women Because Symbiotic Relationship with Princeton University Subjects Them to Law against Discrimination as Public Accommodations," *Seton Hall Law Review* 22, no.1 (1991): 235–255, https://heinonline.org/HOL/P?h=hein.journals/shlr22&i=253; Corinne Goudreault, "Men, Mansions, and Money: Inside the Gendered and Bounded Culture and Legacy of Princeton University's Eating Clubs" (honors undergraduate thesis, University of North Carolina at Chapel Hill, 2015), https://doi.org/10.17615/9r94-wz75.
25. Clifford W. Zink, *The Princeton Eating Clubs* (Princeton: Princeton Prospect Foundation, 2017).
26. Zink, *The Princeton Eating Clubs*.
27. Josephine F. Mitchell, "A Comparison of an A La Carte and a Contract Food Service at Oklahoma State University" (master's thesis, Oklahoma State University, 1960), https://shareok.org/bitstream/handle/11244/27982/Thesis-1962-M681c.pdf?sequence=1.
28. Frederick Rudolph, *The American College and University: A History* (Athens: University of Georgia Press, 1990).
29. Thelin, *A History of American Higher Education*; David P. Setran, *The College "Y": Student Religion in the Era of Secularization* (New York: Palgrave MacMillan, 2007); Dorothy E. Finnegan and Nathan F. Alleman, "Without Adult Supervision: Campus YMCAs" (Paper presentation, annual meeting for the Association for the Study of Higher Education, Philadelphia, PA, November 18, 2005); Rudolph, *The American College and University*.
30. Bessie Brooks West, Levelle Wood, and Virginia F. Harger, *Food Service in Institutions*, 4th ed. (New York: John Wiley & Sons, Inc., 1966).
31. Lee E. Krehbiel and David L. Meabon, "Gruel and Unusual Nourishment: The Evolving History of Collegiate Food Service," *American Educational History Journal* 33, no. 1 (2006): 117–125, https://www.proquest.com/docview/230048696/fulltextPDF/7C4D214F8E2C4459PQ.
32. Krehbiel and Meabon, "Gruel and Unusual Nourishment."
33. Gene Kellogg, "What Are the Trends in College Dining Services?" interview by Lionel Binnie, *M Source Ideas*, February 8, 2018, https://msourceideas.com/the-origins-and-history-of-college-dining-service-companies/; Ben Gose, "The Companies that Colleges Keep," *The Chronicle of Higher Education*, January 28, 2005, https://www.chronicle.com/article/the-companies-that-colleges-keep/.
34. Theodore S. Glickman, Jennifer Holm, Devlin Keating, Claudia Pannait, and Susan C. White, "Outsourcing on American Campuses: National Developments

and the Food Service Experience at GWU," *International Journal of Educational Management* 21, no. 5 (June 2007): 440–452, https://doi.org/10.1108/09513540710760219; Thomas F. Gaddis, "College and University Administrators' Attitudes Concerning Contract-Managed and Self-Operated Food Service" (master's thesis, University of Tennessee, 1992), https://trace.tennessee.edu/utk_gradthes/3733.

35. Hugh Hawkins, *Between Harvard and America: The Educational Leadership of Charles W. Eliot* (Oxford: Oxford University Press, 1972).
36. Havemeyer, "Eating at Yale."
37. Theresa M. Genovese, "Student Centers: Building Community with New Dining Experiences," *Planning for Higher Education* 46, no. 2 (January–March 2018): 42–50, https://link.gale.com/apps/doc/A538120549/AONE?u=txshracd2488&sid=bookmark-AONE&xid=f5d8520a; Nicholas A. Bowman, Lindsay Jarratt, Linnea A. Polgreen, Thomas Kruckeberg, and Alberto M. Segre, "Early Identification of Students' Social Networks: Predicting College Retention and Graduation Via Campus Dining," *Journal of College Student Development* 60, no. 5 (September–October 2019): 617–622, https://doi.org/10.1353/csd.2019.0052.
38. Kellogg, "What Are the Trends in College Dining Services?"
39. John R. Thelin and David H. Charlton, "Food for Thought: Dining Halls and the Collegiate Ideal," *Alumni Gazette: The College of William & Mary* 55, no. 1 (Summer 1987): 27–30, https://digital.libraries.wm.edu/william-mary-alumni-magazine-vol-55-no-01.
40. Krehbiel and Meabon, "Gruel and Unusual Nourishment."
41. Cobretti D. Williams, "The Future Is Served: The Evolution of Campus Dining," *HigherEd Jobs,* November 20, 2019, https://www.higheredjobs.com/Articles/articleDisplay.cfm?ID=2081.
42. Anthony A. Jack, *The Privileged Poor: How Elite Colleges Are Failing Disadvantaged Students* (Cambridge: Harvard University Press, 2019).
43. Thelin and Charlton, "Food for Thought."

Chapter 7. The Logics of Administrating Hunger

1. Clare L. Cady, "Food Insecurity as a Student Issue," *Journal of College and Character* 15, no. 4 (November 2014): 265–272, https://doi.org/10.1515/jcc-2014-0031.
2. See the College and University Food Bank Alliance (CUFBA), now under the direction of Swipe Out Hunger, a national organization committed to improving policies and pathways to end college hunger, https://www.swipehunger.org/cufba/.
3. John R. Thelin, *A History of American Higher Education*, 3rd ed. (Baltimore: Johns Hopkins University Press, 2019); Earl J. McGrath, "The Evolution of Administrative Offices in Institutions of Higher Education in the United States from 1860 to 1933" (PhD diss., The University of Chicago, 1936), https://www.proquest.com/docview/301816391; Sara Goldrick-Rab, *Paying the Price* (Chicago: University of Chicago Press, 2016).

4. Perry L. Glanzer, Nathan F. Alleman, and Todd C. Ream, *Restoring the Soul of the University: Unifying Christian Higher Education in a Fragmented Age* (Westmont: InterVarsity Press, 2017).
5. J. Patrick Biddix and Robert A. Schwartz, "Walter Dill Scott and the Student Personnel Movement," *Journal of Student Affairs Research and Practice* 49, no. 3 (August 2012): 285–298, https://doi.org/10.1515/jsarp-2012-6325.
6. Biddix and Schwartz, "Walter Dill Scott"; Esther Lloyd-Jones, *Student Personnel Work at Northwestern University* (New York: Harper & Brothers, 1929).
7. American Council on Education, "The Student Personnel Point of View," in *Student Affairs: A Profession's Heritage,* eds. Gerald L. Saddlemire and Audrey L. Rentz (Alexandria: American College Personnel Association, 1986), 123.
8. American Council on Education, "The Student Personnel Point of View."
9. Francis F. Bradshaw, "The Scope and Aim of a Personnel Program," in *Student Affairs: A Profession's Heritage,* eds. Gerald L. Saddlemire and Audrey L. Rentz (Alexandria: American College Personnel Association, 1986), 40.
10. Glanzer, Alleman, and Ream, *Restoring the Soul.*
11. For more on frameworks or paradigms in student affairs administration, see Simone H. Taylor, "What's Past Is Prologue: The Evolving Paradigms of Student Affairs," *Planning for Higher Education* 37, no. 1 (October–December 2008): 23–31, https://www.proquest.com/scholarly-journals/whats-past-is-prologue-evolving-paradigms-student/docview/212562541/se-2.
12. The first student-run food pantry opened at Michigan State University in the early 1990s by a retired university secretary and the graduate student government. See Colleen Callahan, "College Food Pantries Keep Students from Choosing between Food and Books," *Hunger Blog, Feeding America,* February 16, 2018, https://www.feedingamerica.org/hunger-blog/choosing-between-books-or.
13. Paul J. DiMaggio and Walter D. Powell, "The Iron Cage Revisited: Institutional Isomorphism and Collective Rationality in Organizational Fields," *American Sociological Review* 48, no. 2 (April 1983): 147–160, https://doi.org/10.2307/2095101.
14. Andy Kiersz, "US News Added a 'Social Mobility' Factor to Its College Rankings," *Business Insider,* September 11, 2018, https://www.businessinsider.com/us-news-adds-social-mobility-factor-to-college-rankings-2018-9.

Chapter 8. Administrating Hungry Students

1. John Field and Natalie Morgan-Klein, "Studenthood and Identification: Higher Education as a Liminal Transitional Space" (Paper presentation, annual meeting for the Standing Conference on University Teaching and Research in the Education of Adults, University of Warwick, United Kingdom, July 6–8, 2010), https://dspace.stir.ac.uk/bitstream/1893/3221/1/2010%20scutrea%20jf%20nmk%20storre.pdf.
2. Katharine M. Broton and Clare L. Cady, eds., *Food Insecurity on Campus: Action and Intervention* (Baltimore: Johns Hopkins University Press, 2020); Rashida M. Crutchfield and Jennifer Maguire, *Study of Student Basic Needs* (The California State University, January 2018): 1–53, https://www.calstate.edu/impact-of-the-csu

/student-success/basic-needs-initiative/Documents/BasicNeedsStudy_phaseII_withAccessibilityComments.pdf.

3. Nevitt Sanford, *Where Colleges Fail: A Study of the Student as a Person* (San Francisco: Jossey-Bass, 1967); American Council on Education, "The Student Personnel Point of View," in *Student Affairs: A Profession's Heritage*, eds. Gerald L. Saddlemire and Audrey L. Rentz (Alexandria: American College Personnel Association, 1986).

4. Sanford, *Where Colleges Fail*; Mary L. Roark, "Challenging and Supporting College Students," *NASPA Journal* 26, no. 4 (Summer 1989): 314–319, https://doi.org/10.1080/00220973.1989.11072122.

5. Arthur W. Chickering and Linda Reisser, *Education and Identity*, 2nd ed. (San Francisco: Jossey-Bass, 1993); William G. Perry Jr., *Forms of Intellectual and Ethical Development in the College Years: A Scheme* (San Francisco: Jossey-Bass, 1999); Lawrence Kohlberg, "Stage and Sequence: The Cognitive-Developmental Approach to Socialization," in *Handbook of Socialization Theory and Research*, ed. David A. Goslin (Chicago: Rand McNally, 1969), 347–480.

6. Katharine M. Broton, Graham N. S. Miller, and Sara Goldrick-Rab, "College on the Margins: Higher Education Professionals' Perspectives on Campus Basic Needs Insecurity," *Teachers College Record* 122, no. 3 (March 2020): 1–32, https://doi.org/10.1177/016146812012200307.

7. Anthony A. Jack, *The Privileged Poor: How Elite Colleges Are Failing Disadvantaged Students* (Cambridge: Harvard University Press, 2019). See also Norma González, Luis C. Moll, and Cathy Amanti, eds., *Funds of Knowledge: Theorizing Practices in Households, Communities, and Classrooms* (New York: Routledge, 2006).

8. Erving Goffman, "On Cooling the Mark Out: Some Aspects of Adaptation to Failure," *Psychiatry* 15, no. 4 (November 1952): 451–463, https://doi.org/10.1080/00332747.1952.11022896.

9. Donald Tomaskovic-Devey and Dustin Avent-Holt, *Relational Inequalities: An Organizational Approach* (New York: Oxford University Press, 2019).

10. Tomaskovic-Devey and Avent-Holt, *Relational Inequalities*.

11. Becca S. Bassett, "Better Positioned to Teach the Rules than to Change Them: University Actors in Two Low-Income, First-Generation Student Support Programs," *The Journal of Higher Education* 91, no. 3 (April 2020): 353–377, https://doi.org/10.1080/00221546.2019.1647581.

12. Andy Kiersz, "US News Added a 'Social Mobility' Factor to Its College Rankings," *Business Insider*, September 11, 2018, https://www.businessinsider.com/us-news-adds-social-mobility-factor-to-college-rankings-2018-9.

13. Sonja Ardoin and becky martinez, *Straddling Class in the Academy: 26 Stories of Students, Administrators, and Faculty from Poor and Working-Class Backgrounds and Their Compelling Lessons for Higher Education Policy and Practice* (Sterling: Stylus Publishing LLC, 2019); Carlos L. Dews and Carolyn Leste Law, eds., *This Fine Place So Far from Home: Voices of Academics from the Working Class* (Philadelphia: Temple University Press, 1995); Mary Blanchard Wallace, *First-Generation*

Professionals in Higher Education: Strategies for the World of Work (Washington, DC: National Association of Student Personnel Administrators, 2022).
14. Mary Dana Hinton, *Leading from the Margins: College Leadership from Unexpected Places* (Baltimore: Johns Hopkins University Press, 2024).
15. Broton, Miller, and Goldrick-Rab, "College on the Margins."
16. Cara Cliburn Allen and Nathan F. Alleman, "A Private Struggle at a Private Institution: Effects of Student Hunger on Social and Academic Experiences," *Journal of College Student Development* 60, no. 1 (January–February 2019): 52–69, https://doi.org/10.1353/csd.2019.0003.
17. See Christian Smith, *Moral, Believing Animals: Human Personhood and Culture* (New York: Oxford University Press, 2003); Theodore F. Cockle, Nathan F. Alleman, Sarah E. Madsen, and Cara Cliburn Allen, "The 'Goods' of the University: How Students from Low-SES Backgrounds Help Humanize Institutions" (Paper presentation, annual meeting for the American Educational Research Association, Chicago, IL, April 16, 2023).
18. Emily Hunt and João B. Chaves, "Imagining Structural Stewardship: Lessons in Resistance and Cultural Change from the Highlander Folk School," in *Christian Faith and University Life,* eds. T. Laine Scales and Jennifer L. Howell (London: Palgrave Macmillan, 2018), 205–220, https://doi.org/10.1007/978-3-319-61744-2_12.
19. bell hooks, "Choosing the Margin as a Space of Radical Openness," in *Women, Knowledge, and Reality: Explorations in Feminist Philosophy,* 2nd ed., eds. Ann Garry and Marilyn Pearsall (New York: Routledge, 1996), https://doi.org/10.4324/9780203760635.

Chapter 9. Navigating Pathways through College

1. Pierre Bourdieu and Jean-Claude Passeron, *Education, Society, and Culture* (London: SAGE, 1977); Daniel F. Chambliss and Christopher G. Takacs, *How College Works* (Cambridge: Harvard University Press, 2014); Patricia M. McDonough, "Buying and Selling Higher Education: The Social Construction of the College Applicant," *The Journal of Higher Education* 65, no. 4 (July–August 1994): 427–446, https://doi.org/10.1080/00221546.1993.11778509; Paul Tough, *The Years that Matter Most: How College Makes or Breaks Us* (Boston: Houghton Mifflin Harcourt, 2019).
2. Michael N. Bastedo and Ozan Jaquette, "Running in Place: Low-Income Students and the Dynamics of Higher Education Stratification," *Educational Evaluation and Policy Analysis* 33, no. 3 (September 2011): 318–339, https://doi.org/10.3102/0162373711406718; Pierre Bourdieu and Jean-Claude Passeron, *Reproduction in Education, Society, and Culture,* 2nd ed. (New York: Sage Publications, 1977); Anthony A. Jack, *The Privileged Poor: How Elite Colleges Are Failing Disadvantaged Students* (Cambridge: Harvard University Press, 2019); Mitchell L. Stevens, *Creating a Class: College Admissions and the Education of Elites* (Cambridge: Harvard University Press, 2007).
3. Chambliss and Takacs, *How College Works*; Tough, *The Years that Matter Most.*

4. Ernest T. Pascarella and Patrick T. Terenzini, *How College Affects Students: A Third Decade of Research*, vol. 2 (San Francisco: Jossey-Bass, 2005).
5. Nathan F. Alleman, Cara Cliburn Allen, and Sarah E. Madsen, "Constructed Pathways: How Multiply-Marginalized Students Navigate Food Insecurity at Selective Universities," *American Educational Research Journal* 61, no. 2 (April 2024): 328–365, https://doi.org/10.3102/00028312231217751.
6. Elizabeth A. Armstrong and Laura T. Hamilton, *Paying for the Party: How College Maintains Inequality* (Cambridge: Harvard University Press, 2015).
7. Alleman, Cliburn Allen, and Madsen, "Constructed Pathways."
8. Theodore F. Cockle, "The Importance of What Students Care About: A Grounded Theory Exploration of Student Pathways and Preferences" (PhD diss., Baylor University, 2021), https://www.proquest.com/docview/2564824816. See also Mitchell L. Stevens, Monique Harrison, Marissa E. Thompson, Arik Lifschitz, and Sorathan Chaturapruek, "Choices, Identities, Paths: Understanding College Students' Academic Decisions" (Paper presentation, annual meeting of the American Sociological Association, Philadelphia, Pennsylvania, August 2018), https://papers.ssrn.com/sol3/papers.cfm?abstract_id=3162429.
9. Chambliss and Takacs, *How College Works*.
10. Chambliss and Takacs, *How College Works*, 65.
11. Chambliss and Takacs, *How College Works*; Armstrong and Hamilton, *Paying for the Party*.
12. Cockle, "What Students Care About."
13. Cockle, "What Students Care About," 227.
14. Cockle, "What Students Care About."
15. Cockle, "What Students Care About."
16. Rebecca Covarrubias, Ibette Valle, Giselle Laiduc, and Margarita Azmitia, "'You Never Become Fully Independent': Family Roles and Independence in First-Generation College Students," *Journal of Adolescent Research* 34, no. 4 (July 2019): 381–410, https://doi.org/10.1177/0743558418788402.
17. Covarrubias, Valle, Laiduc, and Azmitia, "'You Never Become Fully Independent.'" Given the dearth of research on this topic, we can look to and glean from the literature of nonaffluent students to see how students across many class backgrounds experience this complicated relationship with communities of origin in college. For insight into the middle-class experience, see Caitlin Zaloom, *Indebted: How Families Make College Work at Any Cost* (Princeton: Princeton University Press, 2019).
18. Broton and Goldrick-Rab illuminate this lack of differentiation, noting that current research tends to aggregate data on food-insecure students across selective and nonselective intuitions and contexts. See Katharine M. Broton and Sara Goldrick-Rab, "Going Without: An Exploration of Food and Housing Insecurity among Undergraduates," *Educational Researcher* 47, no. 2 (March 2018): 121–133, https://doi.org/10.3102/0013189X17741303.
19. Sara Goldrick-Rab, Jed Richardson, Joel Schneider, Anthony Hernandez, and Clare Cady, *Still Hungry and Homeless in College* (Madison: Wisconsin HOPE Lab,

2018); Rashida M. Crutchfield and Jennifer Maguire, *Study of Student Basic Needs* (The California State University, January 2018): 1–53, https://www.calstate.edu/impact-of-the-csu/student-success/basic-needs-initiative/Documents/BasicNeedsStudy_phaseII_withAccessibilityComments.pdf; Kathryn Larin, *Food Insecurity: Better Information Could Help Eligible College Students Access Federal Food Assistance Benefits GAO-19-95* (US Government Accountability Office, December 2018): 1–62, https://files.eric.ed.gov/fulltext/ED594848.pdf.

20. In part, this is because studies tend to be either broad surveys focused on needs and resources or single-location case studies that are too small to identify patterns of this kind. See Goldrick-Rab, Richardson, Schneider, Hernandez, and Cady, *Still Hungry and Homeless in College*; Cara Cliburn Allen and Nathan F. Alleman, "A Private Struggle at a Private Institution: Effects of Student Hunger on Social and Academic Experiences," *Journal of College Student Development* 60, no. 1 (January–February 2019): 52–69, https://doi.org/10.1353/csd.2019.0003; Crutchfield and Maguire, *Study of Student Basic Needs*; Rositsa T. Ilieva, Tanzina Ahmed, and Anita Yan, "Hungry Minds: Investigating the Food Insecurity of Minority Community College Students," *Journal of Public Affairs* 19, no. 3 (August 2019): 1–13, https://doi.org/10.1002/pa.1891.

21. A note of caution: our strategic navigation typology was developed within the particular competitive, aspirational, and status-oriented context of our three case universities. As such, it should be applied with caution to other contexts generally and should be applied with care to similar environments.

22. Alleman, Cliburn Allen, and Madsen, "Constructed Pathways"; Eve Tuck, "Suspending Damage: A Letter to Communities," *Harvard Educational Review* 79, no. 3 (Fall 2009): 409–428, https://doi.org/10.17763/haer.79.3.n0016675661t3n15; Tara J. Yosso, "Whose Culture Has Capital? A Critical Race Theory Discussion of Community Cultural Wealth," in *Critical Race Theory in Education: All God's Children Got a Song*, 2nd ed., eds. Adrienne D. Dixson, Celia K. Rousseau Anderson, and Jamel K. Donnor (Oxfordshire: Routledge, 2016), 113–136.

Chapter 10. Navigating the Dream I

1. Anthony A. Jack, *The Privileged Poor: How Elite Colleges Are Failing Disadvantaged Students* (Cambridge: Harvard University Press, 2019).
2. Jack, *The Privileged Poor*.
3. The lesson these students learn is that the price of emerging adulthood is hunger. See Cara Cliburn Allen and Nathan F. Alleman, "A Private Struggle at a Private Institution: Effects of Student Hunger on Social and Academic Experiences," *Journal of College Student Development* 60, no. 1 (January–February 2019): 52–69, https://doi.org/10.1353/csd.2019.0003.
4. Sara Goldrick-Rab, *Paying the Price* (Chicago: University of Chicago Press, 2016).
5. Goldrick-Rab, *Paying the Price*.
6. William Elliott and Melinda Lewis, "Student Debt Effects on Financial Well-Being: Research and Policy Implications," *A Collection of Reviews on Savings and Wealth Accumulation* (March 2016): 33–57, https://doi.org/10.1002/9781119158424.

ch3; Erin Velez, Melissa Cominole, and Alexander Bentz, "Debt Burden after College: The Effect of Student Loan Debt on Graduates' Employment, Additional Schooling, Family Formation, and Home Ownership," *Education Economics* 27, no. 2 (April 2019): 186–206, https://doi.org/10.1080/09645292.2018.1541167.
7. John R. Thelin, *A History of American Higher Education*, 3rd ed. (Baltimore: Johns Hopkins University Press, 2019).
8. Casandra J. Nikolaus, Brenna Ellison, and Sharon M. Nickols-Richardson, "Are Estimates of Food Insecurity among College Students Accurate? Comparison of Assessment Protocols," *Plos One* 14 no. 4 (April 2019): 1–18, https://doi.org/10.1371/journal.pone.0215161; Kathryn Larin, *Food Insecurity: Better Information Could Help Eligible College Students Access Federal Food Assistance Benefits* GAO-19-95 (US Government Accountability Office, December 2018): 1–62, https://files.eric.ed.gov/fulltext/ED594848.pdf; Aseel El Zein, Karla P. Shelnutt, Sarah Colby, Melissa J. Vilaro, Wenjun Zhou, Geoffrey Greene, Melissa D. Olfert, Kristin Riggsbee, Jesse Stabile Morrell, and Anne E. Mathews, "Prevalence and Correlates of Food Insecurity among U.S. College Students: A Multi-Institutional Study," *BMC Public Health* 19, no. 660 (May 2019): 1–12, https://doi.org/10.1186/s12889-019-6943-6.

Chapter 11. Navigating the Dream II

1. Elizabeth Aries and Maynard Seider, "The Interactive Relationship between Class Identity and the College Experience: The Case of Lower Income Students," *Qualitative Sociology* 28, no. 4 (December 2005): 419–443, https://doi.org/10.1007/s11133-005-8366-1; MaryBeth Walpole, "Socioeconomic Status and College: How SES Affects College Experiences and Outcomes," *The Review of Higher Education* 27, no.1 (Fall 2003): 45–73, https://doi.org/10.1353/rhe.2003.0044.
2. Sonja Ardoin and becky martinez, *Straddling Class in the Academy: 26 Stories of Students, Administrators, and Faculty from Poor and Working-Class Backgrounds and Their Compelling Lessons for Higher Education Policy and Practice* (Sterling: Stylus Publishing, 2019).
3. Tara J. Yosso, "Whose Culture Has Capital? A Critical Race Theory Discussion of Community Cultural Wealth," in *Critical Race Theory in Education: All God's Children Got a Song,* 2nd ed., eds. Adrienne D. Dixson, Celia K. Rousseau Anderson, and Jamel K. Donnor (Oxfordshire: Routledge, 2016), 113–136.
4. For an application of these concepts to students experiencing food insecurity, see Nathan F. Alleman, Cara Cliburn Allen, and Sarah E. Madsen, "Constructed Pathways: How Multiply-Marginalized Students Navigate Food Insecurity at Selective Universities," *American Educational Research Journal* 61, no. 2 (April 2024): 328–365, https://doi.org/10.3102/00028312231217751.

Chapter 12. Navigating the Dream III

1. Peter Kaufman and Kenneth A. Feldman, "Forming Identities in College: A Sociological Approach," *Research in Higher Education* (August 2004): 463–496, https://doi.org/10.1023/B:RIHE.0000032325.56126.29; Laura T. Hamilton and Simon Cheng, "Going Greek: The Organization of Campus Life and Class-Based

Graduation Gaps," *Social Forces* 96, no. 3 (March 2018): 977–1008, https://doi.org/10.1093/sf/sox089.
2. Mitchell L. Stevens, *Creating a Class: College Admissions and the Education of Elites* (Cambridge: Harvard University Press, 2007).
3. Nationally, about 22.6% of students experience some level of food insecurity throughout their collegiate journey, which is almost double the rate among all US households at 12.8%, though as we noted in the introduction, COVID-era collection of this data raises questions about how well it represents current levels of need. See *National Postsecondary Student Aid Study: 2020 Undergraduate Students* (National Center for Education Statistics, 2023), https://nces.ed.gov/surveys/npsas/.

Chapter 13. Navigating the Dream IV

1. Information is often least apparent to those least informed; see Rachel Gable, *The Hidden Curriculum: First Generation Students at Legacy Universities* (Princeton: Princeton University Press, 2021); Eric Margolis, ed., *The Hidden Curriculum in Higher Education* (New York: Routledge, 2001).
2. "Hunger Free Campus Bill," Swipe Out Hunger, accessed April 4, 2023, https://www.swipehunger.org/hungerfree/.
3. Samuel D. Museus, "The Culturally Engaging Campus Environments (CECE) Model: A New Theory of Success among Racially Diverse College Student Populations," in *Higher Education: Handbook of Theory and Research*, vol. 29, ed. Michael B. Paulsen (New York: Springer, 2013), 189–227, https://doi.org/10.1007/978-94-017-8005-6_5; Daniel F. Chambliss and Christopher G. Takacs, *How College Works* (Cambridge: Harvard University Press, 2014); Becca S. Bassett, "Better Positioned to Teach the Rules than to Change Them: University Actors in Two Low-Income, First-Generation Student Support Programs," *The Journal of Higher Education* 91, no. 3 (April 2020): 353–377, https://doi.org/10.1080/00221546.2019.1647581.
4. Chambliss and Takacs, *How College Works*.
5. Peter Kaufman and Kenneth A. Feldman, "Forming Identities in College: A Sociological Approach," *Research in Higher Education* 45, no. 5 (August 2004): 463–496, https://doi.org/10.1023/B:RIHE.0000032325.56126.29.
6. Kenneth A. Feldman and Theodore M. Newcomb, *The Impact of College on Students*, 1st ed. (San Francisco: Jossey-Bass, 1969).
7. See "Amazon Partnered with Fuse to Drive Business with College Students," *Fuse*, accessed March 15, 2023, https://www.fusemarketing.com/project/amazon/.
8. "The Amazon Effect: No Longer a Phantom Menace," *Inbound Logistics*, November 2017, https://www.inboundlogistics.com/articles/the-amazon-effect-no-longer-a-phantom-menace/.
9. David K. Brown, "The Social Sources of Educational Credentialism: Status Cultures, Labor Markets, and Organizations," *Sociology of Education* 74 (2001): 19–34, https://doi.org/10.2307/2673251; John W. Meyer, Francisco O. Ramirez, David John Frank, and Evan Schofer, "Higher Education as an Institution," in

Sociology of Higher Education: Contributions and Their Contexts, ed. Patricia J. Gumport (Baltimore: Johns Hopkins University Press, 2007), 187.

10. Daniel K. Cairo and Victoria Cabal, "Neoliberalism in Student Affairs: A 'Both/And' Proposition," in *The Corporatization of Student Affairs: Serving Students in Neoliberal Times,* eds. Daniel K. Cairo and Victoria Cabal (New York: Springer, 2021): 85–131, https://doi.org/10.1007/978-3-030-88128-3_6.

11. See Steven Tolman and Christopher Trautman, "The Need for College Amenities and Their Benefit to the Student and Institution's Success," in *Colleges at the Crossroads: Taking Sides on Contested Issues,* eds. Joseph L. DeVitis and Pietro A. Sasso (New York: Peter Lang Publishing, 2018), 391–408, https://www.jstor.org/stable/45178186. These scholars make the bold argument for the virtues of campus amenities that reflect student consumerism based on professional values of serving the "whole student," providing broad-based developmental opportunities, and exposing students to new experiences that promote a more well-rounded individual.

12. Laura M. Harrison and Laura Risler, "The Role Consumerism Plays in Student Learning," *Active Learning in Higher Education* 16, no. 1 (March 2015): 67–76, https://doi.org/10.1177/1469787415573356; Rajani Naidoo and Ian Jamieson, "Empowering Participants or Corroding Learning? Towards a Research Agenda on the Impact of Student Consumerism in Higher Education," *Journal of Education Policy* 20, no. 3 (2005): 267–281, https://doi.org/10.1080/02680930500108585.

13. Anthony A. Jack, *The Privileged Poor: How Elite Colleges Are Failing Disadvantaged Students* (Cambridge: Harvard University Press, 2019).

14. Nathan F. Alleman, Cara Cliburn Allen, and Sarah E. Madsen, "Constructed Pathways: How Multiply-Marginalized Students Navigate Food Insecurity at Selective Universities," *American Educational Research Journal* 61, no. 2 (April 2024): 328–365, https://doi.org/10.3102/00028312231217751.

15. Dennis K. Orthner, Hinckley Jones-Sanpei, and Sabrina Williamson, "The Resilience and Strengths of Low-Income Families," *Family Relations* 53, no. 2 (March 2004): 159–167, https://doi.org/10.1111/j.0022-2445.2004.00006.x.

16. Angela Duckworth, *Grit: The Power of Passion and Perseverance* (New York: Scribner, 2016); Kelly T. Macdonald, "An Exploration of Protective Factors for First Generation College Students: Grit, Growth Mindset, Cultural Congruity, and Parental Encouragement" (master's thesis, American University, 2016), https://www.proquest.com/docview/1811614615; Michael Neenan, *Developing Resilience: A Cognitive-Behavioural Approach,* 2nd ed. (London: Routledge, 2018).

17. Duckworth, *Grit*; Neenan, *Developing Resilience*; see also Ann S. Masten, *Ordinary Magic: Resilience Processes in Development* (New York: The Guilford Press, 2014); Ingrid Schoon and John Bynner, "Risk and Resilience in Life Course: Implications for Interventions and Social Policies," *Journal of Youth Studies* 6, no. 1 (March 2003): 21–32, https://doi.org/10.1080/1367626032000068145.

18. Mae-Hyang Hwang and JeeEun Karin Nam, "Enhancing Grit: Possibility and Intervention Strategies," in *Multidisciplinary Perspectives on Grit,* eds. Llewellyn

Ellardus van Zyl, Chantal Olckers, and Leoni van der Vaart (New York: Springer, 2021), 77–93, https://doi.org/10.1007/978-3-030-57389-8_5; Ralph Brown, "Building Children and Young People's Resilience: Lessons from Psychology," *International Journal of Disaster Risk Reduction* 12, no. 2 (December 2015): 115–124, https://doi.org/10.1016/j.ijdrr.2015.06.007.
19. David Denby, "The Limits of 'Grit,'" *Culture Desk, The New Yorker*, June 21, 2016, https://www.newyorker.com/culture/culture-desk/the-limits-of-grit.
20. Tara J. Yosso, "Whose Culture Has Capital? A Critical Race Theory Discussion of Community Cultural Wealth," in *Critical Race Theory in Education: All God's Children Got a Song*, 2nd ed., eds. Adrienne D. Dixson, Celia K. Rousseau Anderson, and Jamel K. Donnor (Oxfordshire: Routledge, 2016), 113–136.

Chapter 14. Navigating the Dream V

1. To counter deficit perspectives in relation to Mexican American working-class and low-income families, funds of knowledge draw on the experiences, resources, and knowledge from home life and view them as a currency to exchange or to draw upon while navigating new sociocultural contexts, particularly educational contexts. In recent literature, the goal is to unearth students' funds of knowledge, honor these funds, and finally apply them to the students' current educational contexts. See Norma González, Luis C. Moll, and Cathy Amanti, eds., *Funds of Knowledge: Theorizing Practices in Households, Communities, and Classrooms* (New York: Routledge, 2006); Judy Marquez Kiyama, "College Aspirations and Limitations: The Role of Educational Ideologies and Funds of Knowledge in Mexican American Families," *American Educational Research Journal* 47, no. 2 (June 2010): 330–356, https://doi.org/10.3102/0002831209357468.
2. Sandy Baum, Kristin Blagg, and Rachel Fishman, "Reshaping Parent PLUS Loans: Recommendations for Reforming the Parent PLUS Program," *Urban Institute* (April 2019): 1–37, http://hdl.handle.net/10919/92646.
3. Anthony A. Jack, *The Privileged Poor: How Elite Colleges Are Failing Disadvantaged Students* (Cambridge: Harvard University Press, 2019).
4. Vincent Tinto, *Leaving College: Rethinking the Causes and Cure of Student Attrition* (Chicago: University of Chicago Press, 1993); Arnold Van Gennep, *The Rites of Passage* (Chicago: University of Chicago Press, 2019).
5. Sylvia Hurtado and Deborah Faye Carter, "Effects of College Transition and Perceptions of the Campus Racial Climate on Latino College Students' Sense of Belonging," *Sociology of Education* (October 1997): 324–345, https://doi.org/10.2307/2673270; Tara J. Yosso, "Whose Culture Has Capital? A Critical Race Theory Discussion of Community Cultural Wealth," in *Critical Race Theory in Education: All God's Children Got a Song*, 2nd ed., eds. Adrienne D. Dixson, Celia K. Rousseau Anderson, and Jamel K. Donnor (Oxfordshire: Routledge, 2016), 113–136.
6. Mitchell L. Stevens, *Creating a Class: College Admissions and the Education of Elites* (Cambridge: Harvard University Press, 2007); Elizabeth Lee, *Class and Campus Life: Managing and Experiencing Inequality at an Elite College* (Ithaca: Cornell University Press, 2016).

7. Peter Magolda, *The Lives of Campus Custodians: Insights into Corporatization and Civic Disengagement in the Academy* (Sterling: Stylus Publishing, 2016).
8. Ezra Marcus, "The War on Frats: Groups of Fraternity Brothers and Sorority Sisters Are Working to Kick Their Organizations Off Campus," *New York Times*, August 1, 2020, https://www.nytimes.com/2020/08/01/style/abolish-greek-life-college-frat-racism.html; Joey Lautrup, "Abolish Greek Life? See How a Campus Debate Reflects the Nationwide Racial Justice Reckoning," *TIME*, December 16, 2020, https://time.com/5921947/abolish-greek-life-debate/.
9. Charles A. Ibsen and Patricia Klobus, "Fictive Kin Term Use and Social Relationships: Alternative Interpretations," *Journal of Marriage and Family* 34, no. 4 (November 1972): 615–620, https://doi.org/10.2307/350312.
10. Cara Cliburn Allen and Nathan F. Alleman, "A Private Struggle at a Private Institution: Effects of Student Hunger on Social and Academic Experiences," *Journal of College Student Development* 60, no. 1 (January–February 2019): 52–69, https://doi.org/10.1353/csd.2019.0003.
11. Erving Goffman, *Stigma: Notes on the Management of Spoiled Identity* (New York: Simon & Schuster, 1963).

The Dream Revisited

1. Tracy L. Burrows, Megan C. Whatnall, Amanda J. Patterson, and Melinda J. Hutchesson, "Associations between Dietary Intake and Academic Achievement in College Students: A Systematic Review," *Healthcare* 5, no. 4 (September 2017): 60–83, https://doi.org/10.3390/healthcare5040060.
2. Pierre Bourdieu and Jean-Claude Passeron, *Education, Society, and Culture* (London: SAGE, 1977).
3. Anthony A. Jack, *The Privileged Poor: How Elite Colleges Are Failing Disadvantaged Students* (Cambridge: Harvard University Press, 2019).
4. Elizabeth A. Armstrong and Laura T. Hamilton, *Paying for the Party: How College Maintains Inequality* (Cambridge: Harvard University Press, 2015).
5. See Norma González, Luis C. Moll, and Cathy Amanti, eds., *Funds of Knowledge: Theorizing Practices in Households, Communities, and Classrooms* (New York: Routledge, 2006); Judy Marquez Kiyama, "College Aspirations and Limitations: The Role of Educational Ideologies and Funds of Knowledge in Mexican American Families," *American Educational Research Journal* 47, no. 2 (June 2010): 330–356, https://doi.org/10.3102/0002831209357468; Cecilia Rios-Aguilar, Judy Marquez Kiyama, Michael Gravitt, and Luis C. Moll, "Funds of Knowledge for the Poor and Forms of Capital for the Rich? A Capital Approach to Examining Funds of Knowledge," *Theory and Research in Education* 9, no. 2 (July 2011): 163–184, https://doi.org/10.1177/1477878511409776.
6. The gendered nature of educational access and expectation can be a function of local subcultures, related to acceptable adjacent employment and social roles, as Michael Corbett's exploration of schooling in Atlantic Canada aptly illustrates. See Michael Corbett, *Learning to Leave: The Irony of Schooling in a Coastal Community* (Morgantown: West Virginia University Press, 2020).

7. Sendhil Mullainathan and Eldar Shafir, *Scarcity: Why Having Too Little Means So Much* (New York: Macmillan, 2013).
8. Meg Prier, "UC Berkeley Basic Needs Today," *Berkeley Food Institute*, December 12, 2018, https://food.berkeley.edu/from-the-field/uc-berkeley-basic-needs-today/; Tyler D. Watson, Hannah Malan, Deborah Glik, and Suzanna M. Martinez, "College Students Identify University Support for Basic Needs and Life Skills as Key Ingredient in Addressing Food Insecurity on Campus," *California Agriculture* 71, no. 3 (July–September 2017): 130–138, https://doi.org/10.3733/ca.2017a0023.
9. Becca S. Bassett, "Better Positioned to Teach the Rules than to Change Them: University Actors in Two Low-Income, First-Generation Student Support Programs," *The Journal of Higher Education* 91, no. 3 (April 2020): 353–377, https://doi.org/10.1080/00221546.2019.1647581.
10. Sara Goldrick-Rab, *Paying the Price: College Costs, Financial Aid, and the Betrayal of the American Dream* (Chicago: University of Chicago Press, 2016). See Sara Goldrick-Rab, Jed Richardson, Joel Schneider, Anthony Hernandez, and Clare Cady, *Still Hungry and Homeless in College* (Madison: Wisconsin HOPE Lab, 2018).
11. Laura W. Perna, Elaine W. Leigh, and Stephanie Carroll, "'Free College': A New and Improved State Approach to Increasing Educational Attainment?" *American Behavioral Scientist* 61, no. 14 (December 2017): 1740–1756, https://doi.org/10.1177/0002764217744821.
12. Eve Tuck, "Suspending Damage: A Letter to Communities," *Harvard Educational Review* 79, no. 3 (Fall 2009): 409–428, https://doi.org/10.17763/haer.79.3.n0016675661t3n15.
13. Daniel F. Chambliss and Christopher G. Takacs, *How College Works* (Cambridge: Harvard University Press, 2014).
14. Donald Tomaskovic-Devey and Dustin Avent-Holt, *Relational Inequalities: An Organizational Approach* (New York: Oxford University Press, 2019).
15. Cara Cliburn Allen and Nathan F. Alleman, "A Private Struggle at a Private Institution: Effects of Student Hunger on Social and Academic Experiences," *Journal of College Student Development* 60, no. 1 (January–February 2019): 52–69, https://doi.org/10.1353/csd.2019.0003.
16. Mary Dana Hinton, *Leading from the Margins: College Leadership from Unexpected Places* (Baltimore: Johns Hopkins University Press, 2024).
17. Robert D. Putnam, *Bowling Alone: The Collapse and Revival of American Community* (New York: Simon & Schuster, 2000).
18. Sylvia Hurtado and Deborah Faye Carter, "Effects of College Transition and Perceptions of the Campus Racial Climate on Latino College Students' Sense of Belonging," *Sociology of Education* 70, no. 4 (October 1997): 324–345, https://doi.org/10.2307/2673270.
19. Sarah E. Madsen, Nathan F. Alleman, and Cara E. Cliburn Allen, "'I Know It to Be. I've Experienced It': Marginality and the Administration of Food Insecurity" (Paper presentation, annual meeting for the American Educational Research Association, Chicago, IL, April 14, 2023).

INDEX

administration: growth of, 148–151; response to student food insecurity, 19, 137, 148, 151, 164, 166, 193, 319. *See also* food insecurity: administration; student affairs administrators

administrative critical distance, 191–192, 195; definition of, 183

admissions, 6–8, 13, 15, 18, 25–32, 35, 44, 49, 59, 64, 67, 149, 221, 246, 295, 303, 312–313, 333

advisors, 65; academic, 18, 67, 324; career, 51; student, 13

advocacy, 173, 177, 193, 205, 234, 243, 300, 301, 314, 333; productive, 174, 179; self-, 171–172, 176, 315, 335; student, 122, 175

affluence, 209, 212–213, 268, 271, 276–277, 308, 314, 321; assumptions about students' level of, 161, 168, 193, 195, 205–206; and campus amenities, 85, 91, 102, 116; perception of institutional, 6–7, 9, 16, 19

agency, 123, 176–178, 181, 192, 202, 242, 279, 294, 319; student, 81, 147, 171, 173–174, 179, 194, 201, 295, 321, 335

alumni, 9–11, 20–21, 26, 55, 69, 144, 167, 179, 289

Armstrong, Elizabeth, 200

aspirations, 32, 47, 62, 181, 188, 276, 311; career, 260; college, 261; educational, 310; family, 70, 304; future, 243; graduate, 234; professional, 91, 246; student, 246

athletes/athletics, 9, 15, 18, 20, 37–39, 40, 73, 86, 88, 210, 219, 289, 296, 328; basketball, 89; football, 15, 38, 55, 68

basic needs, 3, 19, 70, 122, 126, 205, 207, 297, 312; administration, 148, 174; already met, 62; effects of, 121; family, 214; met at college, 42, 61, 214; resources, 72, 128; shelter, 77; struggles, 164, 190, 248, 313; students, 132, 139, 153, 163, 184, 192, 195, 318; support, 298, 318; unmet, 186

benefits, 2, 18, 105, 136, 269, 273, 317, 328; of convenience, 115; of employment, 125, 232; financial, 258; of internships, 260; off-campus, 282, 326; of a meal plan, 187

Bourdieu, Pierre, 306

campus life, 3, 7, 61, 79, 96, 106, 143, 161, 166, 168, 178, 186, 276, 321

campus navigation, 288, 309; strategy, 240, 302, 316–317; types, 209

Campus Navigation Strategies Typology, 205–206; Adapting, 206, 209–229, 250, 258, 262, 277, 281–283, 302, 338–339; Maximizing, 207, 258–278, 284, 302, 339; Prioritizing, 207, 241–257, 258, 263, 265, 282, 302, 326, 338–339; Sacrificing, 207, 230–240, 254, 258, 276, 277, 282, 326, 338–339; Surviving, 208, 279–305, 338–339

campus tours, ix, 30, 332, 50, 52, 59, 65, 73, 219, 244, 255, 333; alternative, 13, 17, 76, 85, 88, 90, 94, 99, 117, 132; as ritual, 65; official, 13, 17, 25, 60, 78

campus tour locations: academic buildings, 108, 117–124; administrative buildings, 124–136; campus convenience store, 42, 46, 62, 91, 99, 108, 110, 112–116; dining hall, 33, 42, 46, 56–58, 61–62, 72, 92, 99, 107–111; library, 33, 34–37, 61, 67, 70–71, 76, 78–85, 98, 143, 241, 268, 290; rec center, 33, 36, 37–39, 76, 86–91, 98; residence hall, 33, 41–44, 71, 76, 91–98, 108, 219–220, 224, 264, 289; student union, 44–50, 66, 72, 76, 79, 99–106, 143, 144, 146

371

Chambliss, Daniel, ix, 63, 201
choice: between food and other needs, 3, 91, 110–111, 115, 187–188, 189–190, 216–219, 224–227, 237, 240, 252, 281, 304, 311, 333; and customization of college experience, 49, 63, 64, 88, 201–202, 260; of food options, 17, 56–58, 62, 66, 145–146, 185, 190; forced, 121–122, 304; rational, 199; strategic, 15, 178, 179
classrooms, 17, 28, 30, 50, 52, 59, 66, 117, 120–121, 160, 162, 303, 308, 317
co-curriculum, 17
Cockle, Theodore, ix, 201–202
coffee shop, 35–36, 47, 84, 200, 219, 243, 307; The Grind, 61, 101–103, 105–106, 242
College and University Food Bank Alliance (CUFBA), 5, 156
college choice, 232
colonial universities, food in, 139, 141–143
Community Cultural Wealth, 239
consumption, 69, 85, 91, 114, 229, 334
convenience food, 67, 105–106, 124, 228, 251
cost-benefit, 94, 229, 245, 316
critical race perspective, 239, 288
culture, 7, 16, 20, 25, 172, 200, 295, 300; campus, 63, 88, 269, 288; elite, 16, 204; food, 300; institutional, 161; normative, 65, 335
curriculum, 59

debt, 16, 96, 142, 218–219, 229, 282, 285, 318
dining hall, 140, 144–145, 147, 209–210, 219–222, 225, 255–256, 291, 326, 329, 332. *See also* campus tour locations, dining hall

emergency funding, 154, 179, 300
employment, 8, 12, 47, 69, 70, 110, 150, 207, 231–232, 234, 305, 308; benefits of, 125, 238, 240, 282, 317; costs of, 235–237, 247, 271, 279, 317; off-campus, 66, 68, 88, 231, 316–317; on-campus, 265, 326; student, 334
engagement, 12, 19–20, 36–37, 66, 73, 106, 147, 162, 168, 193, 206, 207, 214, 220, 227, 230, 254, 255, 265, 310, 312, 322; academic, 118; campus, 64, 178, 207, 221, 299, 304; community, 264; creative, 259; full, 214, 233, 237, 248; intensive, 261; multicultural, 45; opportunities for, 48, 181, 271, 316; preprofessional, 230; social, 93, 144–145, 272; strategic, 239, 244, 302; student, 17, 20, 48, 83–84, 177

faculty, 2, 13, 20, 26–27, 64–65, 72, 139–141, 160, 183, 218, 232, 261–262, 265, 267, 276, 290, 313–315, 321, 327, 334–335; connections with, 201, 324; lessons for, 318–320; mentors, 71, 309; office hours, 68; in-residence, 29, 41, 72, 94; research, 14
FASFA. *See* Free Application for Federal Student Aid
familial capital, 239
family, 18, 26, 31, 38, 83, 170, 200, 209, 212, 218, 278, 279, 298, 302, 304; affluence, 6, 308; background, 16, 74, 186, 223, 308, 315, 338–339; connections, 239, 323; coping mechanisms learned from, 310; expectations, 224; extended, 1, 203; fictive kin, 298; financial status of, 67, 121, 215; grandparents, 26, 184, 218, 226, 279, 302–303; income, 9, 11, 16; obligation to, 204; perceptions, 66, 69, 305; separation, 311; siblings, 28, 76, 86, 111, 123, 203, 226, 241, 245, 264, 279, 287, 298, 315; strategies with food, 184–185, 220, 280, 287, 310; support from, 126, 203, 216, 229, 249, 264, 303; supporting, 207, 216, 240, 264. *See also* parents
fast food, 42, 62, 67, 91, 247, 255, 272, 315
Feldman, Kenneth, 270
fictive kin, 298
financial aid, 18, 96, 124, 128–132, 171, 179, 212, 214, 262, 284, 285, 325; administrator, 153, 159, 167, 170–171; advisor, 128–129, 131, 325, 51, 128, 130, 160; guidance, 67; office, 129, 173, 324; options, 29; packages, 180, 187, 225, 331; priorities, 318; situation, 213; structures, 3
first-generation, 182, 288, 338–339; administrators, 183; programs, 21, 220, 292, 316, 319; student anxiety, 281; students, 4, 18, 76, 92, 129, 163, 188, 206, 234, 280, 284, 287, 291, 294
food, aid initiatives, 1; from campus events, 100–101, 105, 236, 254–255, 263–267, 269, 277, 282, 284, 291; from employment, 238, 259–260, 283; from family, 216, 220,

222, 285; to friends, 267, 275, 301; from peers, 140, 211, 254, 271–272, 282, 301; rituals of, 85, 105–106; from romantic relationships, 255; from roommates, 126, 222–223, 225, 256, 259; from theft, 256–257; from university employees, 266, 291

foodstuffs, 143, 190

food insecure, 4, 12, 21, 91, 93, 122, 128, 173–174, 176, 191, 194, 205, 209, 217, 255, 259, 300, 321, 331; "cares," 202, 205

food insecurity, 2–6, 17, 139, 167–168, 170, 206–208, 209, 228, 262, 310; administration, 9, 144, 128, 148, 151–162, 173–175, 182–188, 190–195; affluent environment, 8, 13–15, 21, 131; coping strategies, 89, 216–217, 222, 252, 254, 259, 283; institutional and administrative responses, 8, 10, 123, 136, 166, 181, 328, 330; shame and stigma, 300–304

food pantries, 5, 11–13, 128, 132–136, 160, 162–165, 179, 181, 191, 193, 259, 289, 315, 326, 330–331; logistics, 66, 70, 83–85, 124, 148, 151–158, 290–292, 297; student-run, 10, 123, 256

food security, 3–4, 12, 215

food solutions, 158, 162, 252

food trucks, 58, 67, 267, 307, 312

Free Application for Federal Student Aid (FASFA), 281, 325, 332

Good Administrator, the, 15, 17, 19, 20, 22, 152, 164, 165, 195, 312

Good Student, the, 89, 91, 111, 121, 166–170, 172–178, 185, 191, 193, 205, 206, 209, 227, 233, 243, 257, 294, 303, 310, 311, 322

grades, 121, 136, 307

Greek Life, 12, 47, 73, 213, 214, 289, 296, 308, 334

GroupMe, 264, 317

Hamilton, Laura, 200

hidden curriculum, 59–61, 63, 65, 69, 73–74, 259

high school, 8, 26, 32, 35, 68, 107, 218, 222, 224, 241, 260, 261, 280, 287–288; counselors, 224, 261; involvement, 244–245; teachers, 223, 268

homelessness, 159, 278, 338–339, 355n4

housing, 12, 74, 112, 134, 140, 150, 182, 186, 206, 214, 218–219, 227, 260, 289, 293, 307, 325–326, 330, 334; affordable, 68, 95–96, 300; insecurity, 190; off-campus, 12, 68, 77, 232, 281, 299; on-campus, 12, 41, 57, 66, 94, 96–98, 173, 212, 213, 225, 228, 263, 275, 289; and unhoused students, 159, 278, 338–339; university-owned, 41

hunger, ix, 102, 115, 157, 160–161, 168, 181, 183, 186, 222, 304, 309; biographical experiences of, 159, 188, 190, 191–192, 195; burden of, 216; campus, 155, 159, 176; college, 147, 151–153, 154, 159, 184, 191; cost of, 120, 217, 227; effects of, 121; ignoring, 283; logics of, 162–165; student, 2, 19, 124, 147, 154, 156–157, 160–162

ideal/normal paradigm of college experience, 21, 60, 63, 74, 86, 88, 92, 98, 120, 167, 205–206, 213–214, 228, 234, 235, 237, 240, 243, 257, 259, 308, 334

identity, 21, 36, 55, 62, 88, 166, 184, 194, 202, 203, 235, 264, 268, 294, 301, 304, 308; cultural, 165, 280; ethnic, 243, 261; goods, 316; institutional, 27, 187; momentum, 202; social, 314; student, 270

individualization, 152, 158, 164, 193

institutional prestige, 8, 14, 15, 20, 50, 92, 163, 312

Institutional Prestige Seeking, 14–15, 21, 111, 136, 165

institutionalization, 152, 155, 157, 164, 191, 193

integration, 12, 65, 71, 84, 86, 200, 288; social, 50, 214

internships, 12, 20, 63, 64, 66, 73, 110, 173, 199, 237, 247, 253, 260, 276, 277, 309, 313, 314, 318, 326; food from, 226, 260, 267; paid, 231, 332; research, 215, 260, 265; unpaid, 126, 230, 231, 282, 326

Integrated Postsecondary Education Data Systems (IPEDS), 8, 9, 11, 150

isomorphism, 152, 157; mimetic, 156

Jack, Anthony Abraham, 276, 308

Kaufman, Peter, 270

LGBTQI+ students/groups, 4, 21, 47, 48, 214, 221, 234, 270–271, 338–339, 352n1

loans, 129, 131, 182, 218, 225, 229, 249, 281, 325
low-income, 183, 213; backgrounds, 10, 88, 181, 212, 296; communities, 73; families, 85, 118, 125, 263, 285; households, 11, 16; students, 3, 4, 6, 12, 76, 95, 163, 181, 186, 204, 234, 283, 320, 331, 332

Magolda, Peter, ix, 55, 65
marginalized, 161, 164, 208, 276, 314, 316, 334; administrators, 186, 195, 278; backgrounds, 4, 7, 16, 239; historically, 16, 18, 188, 288; status, 309; students, 83, 152, 164, 314; systemically, 95
margins, 315, 334; administration, 183, 194, 195; economic, 22, 72, 73, 309, 321; financial, 80, 98, 106, 111, 180, 264, 284, 304, 313; on the, 8, 65, 161, 178, 236, 287, 320; social, 298, 319
Maslow, hierarchy of needs, 32, 222
massification, 144, 150
McNair Scholars, 108, 234, 241, 243
meal plan, 57, 62, 93, 96, 101–102, 107, 110, 111, 159, 172, 173, 242, 258, 281, 300, 317, 320, 327, 331, 332; benefits of, 187; "big," 56, 172, 243, 250, 301; dining hall, 56; financial burden of, 97; flex dollars, 46, 47, 114, 145; gaps in, 103, 108–109, 210–217, 228, 254; independence and, 223–237; structures, 218–223; swipes, 5, 56; unlimited, 46, 57, 61, 66, 262; variable number of meals included in, 46, 56–57, 61, 66, 172, 243, 250, 262, 301
measurement and evaluation, 151
medieval universities, food in, 139–141, 144
mental health, 92, 218, 234, 236; issues, 127, 136, 170, 285, 302; resources, 127; services, 128, 150; students, 40; support, 48
mentors, 63, 71, 100, 265, 266, 276, 307, 309
mobility, 223, 334; social, 8, 16, 26, 274; upward, 10
motivations, 84, 202, 204
multicultural affairs office (MAO), 100, 264–267, 277

National Survey of Student Engagement (NSSE), 150
Needy Student, the, 166–170, 172–178, 186, 191, 193, 310, 311

noblesse oblige, 132
Northwestern University, 149–150

opportunity cost, 2, 73, 104, 109, 254, 310
Opportunity Paradigm, 14–15, 19–22, 63, 65–67, 71, 79, 82, 99, 165, 194, 230, 233, 243, 266, 277, 309, 318–319, 322, 334
organizations, 5, 45, 61, 63, 74, 105, 118–119, 149, 169, 179, 200, 226, 228, 230, 237, 240, 245–248, 253, 259, 261, 263, 265, 268, 293, 309, 314, 319, 323; campus, 258, 282, 291, 317; preprofessional, 64, 244, 313; spirit, 233; student, 7, 12, 15–17, 20, 27, 47–49, 64, 66, 71, 73, 243, 266, 289, 316
orientation, 2, 42, 95, 100, 162, 170, 176, 192, 207, 265, 330, 335; biographical, 183; first-year, 18, 331; justice, 312; organizational, 289; professional, 17; programs, 314, 334; student, 72; of university, 14
Oxford, 53, 140–141

Parent Plus loan, 285
parenting, 25, 289, 333
parents, 25, 47, 60, 65, 68–70, 92, 94, 145–146, 302–303; advice from, 129; citizenship, 131; desires, 202; education level, 64; employment, 280; financial situation, 189; lessons from, 216, 287; separation from, 284–285, 301, 304; support from, 140–141, 217, 264, 324; support to, 159, 190, 217, 253, 262
Park, Julie, 64
pathways, 64, 119, 194; college navigation, 199–207; "preferred," 63
Pell Grant, 3, 16
pre-med, 49, 76, 89, 227, 260, 261, 266
prestige, 50, 60, 71, 84, 90, 136, 139–147, 180–181, 194–195, 295–296, 313–314, 318, 320; environments, 333; hunger and, 162–165; institutional, 92; pursuit of, 135, 180; prestige-oriented, 2, 7–8, 13–22, 25–26, 33, 52, 60–61, 63, 70–74, 193
programs, 14–15, 150, 185, 244, 283, 289, 290, 297, 316, 335; academic, 28; effectiveness of, 312; extracurricular, 16; faculty-in-residence, 29; first-generation, 21, 319; governmental, 125; loyalty, 272; mentorship, 267; orientation, 314, 334;

374   Index

preprofessional, 117, 313; study abroad, 27, 29, 73; summer bridge, 21; transfer student, 319

race, 183, 188, 201, 210, 213, 214, 239, 261, 264–265, 266, 287–288, 293, 314, 316, 323, 352n24, 366n3
racialization, 94, 95–96, 287–288, 354n7
racism, 59
ranking, colleges and universities, 7–9, 11, 14, 16, 92, 161, 180–183, 267, 312
recommendations, for admin, 318–320; for students, 313–318
Relational Inequality Theory, 179
relationships, 43, 63–64, 65, 69, 71, 152, 163, 201, 236, 253, 266, 276–277, 304; with administrators, 2, 130, 151, 158, 161, 166, 170, 267, 314, 335; with faculty, 118, 120, 201, 243, 309, 314, 323; with financial aid administrators, 131; with mentors, 265; organizational, 159; social, 213, 275, 318; with students, 43, 160–161, 316, 323, 334
resilience, 186, 278
resource claims, 178–179, 181, 194
resource sharing, 213, 316
roommates, 126, 222–223, 225, 226, 256, 259, 282, 289, 298

Sanford, Nevitt, 169
scholarships, 73, 96, 129, 131, 210, 223, 225, 231, 262, 265, 307, 315, 317, 320, 324, 332
scientific management, 149, 151
Scott, Walter Dill, 149
services bubble, 210, 213–214, 228–229, 258, 281, 326
sexual orientation, 338–339
social capital, 188, 260
social class, 94
spring break, 6, 111, 211, 241, 291

Starbucks, 36, 42, 45–47, 62, 84–85, 90–91, 105, 231–232, 238, 251–252, 271–272, 316
stealing, 131, 140, 256–257, 274, 294
Stevens, Mitchell, ix, 25, 65, 333
stigma, faced by nonaffluent students, 123, 134, 140, 161, 302
student affairs administrators, 150, 158, 161, 188, 295; history, 149–151; logic of care, 151, 152, 158, 160–165, 193; logic of efficiency, 151–154, 157, 158, 162, 164, 165, 193
Student Personnel Point of View (SPPV), 149–151
studenthood, 166–167, 193, 195, 270
study, 34–37, 45, 66, 71, 79–83, 101, 106, 118, 121, 185, 236, 246, 316, 327, 332
study abroad, 6, 18, 20, 25–27, 29, 51, 64, 67, 73, 125, 243–244, 261, 277
Swipe Out Hunger, 5

Takacs, Christopher, 63, 201
Thelin, John, 53
time management, 101, 169
Tinto, Vincent, 71
total institution, 92, 93
total support, 92, 98, 326
twentieth century, food on campus, 143–146
transition, 65, 143, 262, 289, 296, 313; to college, 288, 322; to off-campus living, 224, 251, 262; to adulthood, 217; with food, 215

vending machines, 51, 82, 90, 111, 118–119, 122, 145, 252–253, 283

work-study, 76, 128, 132, 231, 237
working-class, 125, 183, 188

Yosso, Tara, 239

Explore other books from **HOPKINS PRESS**

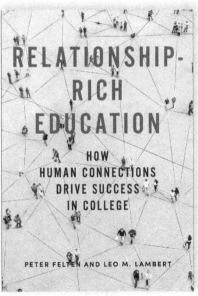

 | PRESS.JHU.EDU |